The Suffering of the Immigrant

The Suffering of the Immigrant

ABDELMALEK SAYAD

Preface by Pierre Bourdieu

Translated by David Macey

polity

First published in 2004 by Polity Press Ltd.

Published with the assistance of the French Ministry of Culture – National
Centre for the Book.

Polity Press
65 Bridge Street
Cambridge CB2 1UR, UK

Polity Press
350 Main Street
Malden, MA 02148, USA

A catalogue record for this book is available from the British Library.

Library of Congress Cataloging-in-Publication Data

Sayad, Abdelmalek.
    [Double absence. English]
    The suffering of the immigrant / Abdelmalek Sayad ; preface by Pierre
Bourdieu ; translated by David Macey.
        p. cm.
Includes bibliographical references and index.
    ISBN 0-7456-2642-4 (hb : alk. paper) – ISBN 0-7456-2643-2 (pb : alk. paper)
    1. Algerians–France–Social conditions. 2. Immigrants–France. 3. France–
Emigration and immigration. 4. Algeria–Emigration and immigration. I. Title.
    DC34.5.A42S2913 2004
    305.892′765044–dc21
                                                                    2003012711

Typeset in 10.5 on 12 pt Sabon
by Kolam Information Services Pvt. Ltd, Pondicherry, India
Printed and bound in Great Britain by TJ International, Padstow, Cornwall
For further information on Polity, visit our website: www.polity.co.uk

Contents

Acknowledgements

I would like to thank Pierre Bourdieu, without whom this work could not have appeared in its complete form.

For several years, Abdelmalek Sayad had been planning to collect and put into perspective his studies and reflections on the phenomenon of migration and, more specifically, on Algerian immigration in France. Exhaustion and illness did not leave him the time to bring his project to fruition. And yet, on the eve of an operation he was dreading, he handed Pierre Bourdieu a bundle of texts and an outline plan, a sort of 'table of contents' of the book he wished to publish.

After the death of my husband, Pierre Bourdieu, reassured by the trust he had always shown in him and by an intellectual closeness that had never been shaken over the years, saw it as his natural duty to construct this book, to make it coherent, to breathe life into it and to give it a title. Given the number of texts involved, this was a weighty undertaking that involved some delicate choices. Undertaking and completing this task required the sort of courage that comes from the heart.

I would like to express my deepest gratitude to Pierre Bourdieu for having brought this book into being.

With great generosity and skill, my husband's colleagues and friends at the Centre de Sociologie Européenne and in the Collège de France's Department of Sociology, as well as Monsieur Mohammed Boudoudou of the University of Rabat, also lent their cooperation to this publication; I am thinking in particular of the team made up of Eliane Dupuy, Salah Bouhedja and Patrick Champagne, to whom I owe particular thanks.

I would like to say a big thank you to all of them.

Rebecca Sayad

A Note on Terminology

The commonplace expression '*l'immigration algérienne*' has two inseparable meanings. It refers, that is, at once to the process of emigration from Algeria and to a population of Algerian immigrants resident in France. The journal *Actualités de l'immigration*, for instance, is about and addressed to that population. Standard English usage would of course speak of 'the Algerian community in France'. The term 'community' offends, however, the classic French notion of a secular and universalist republic which simply does not recognize the existence of 'communities' defined by ethnicity, culture, language or even gender. Although it departs from normal English usage, 'Algerian immigration', and sometimes even 'the Algerian immigration', has therefore been adopted here to reflect the double meaning of *immigration*.

David Macey

Preface

It was a long time ago that Abdelmalek Sayad conceived the project of bringing together in a synthetic work all the analyses he had presented, in lectures or scattered articles, of emigration and immigration – two words which, as he never ceased to recall, refer to two sets of things that are completely different but indissociable, and which must at all costs be considered together. He wished me to be associated with his project from the outset. In one of the most difficult moments of his difficult life – we had lost count of the number of days he had spent in hospital and of the operations he had undergone – and on the eve of a very dangerous surgical intervention, he reminded me of this project in a serious tone we rarely used between ourselves. A few months earlier, he had entrusted me with a set of texts, some already published and some unpublished, together with suggestions – a plan, outline questions and notes – so that I could, as I had already done so many times before, read and revise them with a view to publication. I should have set to work at once – and I often regretted that I did not do so when I found myself having to justify, alone, certain difficult choices. But Abdelmalek Sayad had survived so many ordeals in the past that it seemed to us that he would live for ever. I was, however, able to discuss with him certain basic courses of action, and especially the decision to produce a coherent book centred on the essential texts, rather than to publish everything as it stood. In the course of our last meetings (and nothing cheered him up more than our working conversations), I was also able to show him several of the texts I had reworked, and which I had sometimes changed considerably, mainly in order to cut the repetitions involved in bringing them together and integrating them into the logic of the whole, and also to rid them of those stylistic infelicities and complexities which, whilst necessary or tolerable in publications intended for the academic world, were no longer appropriate in a book that had to be made as accessible as possible, especially to those it talked about, for whom it was primarily intended and to whom it was in a sense dedicated.

As I pursued my reading of these texts, some of which I knew well and some of which I was discovering for the first time, I could see the emergence of the exemplary figure of the committed scientist who, although weakened and hindered by illness, could still find the courage and strength needed to meet, to the end and in such a difficult domain, all the demands of the sociologist's profession. He was able to do so only because of his absolute commitment to his mission (not that he would have liked that big word) to investigate and bear witness. His commitment was based upon his active solidarity with those he was taking as his object. What may have looked like an obsession with work – even during his stays in hospital, he never stopped investigating and writing – was in fact a humble and total commitment to a career in public service, which he saw as a privilege and a duty (so much so that, in putting the final touches to this book, I had the feeling that I was not only fulfilling a duty to a friend but also making a small contribution to a lifetime's work devoted to the understanding of a tragically difficult and urgent problem).

This commitment, which was much deeper than any profession of political faith, was, I think, rooted in both a personal and an affective involvement in the existence and experience of immigrants. Having himself experienced both emigration and immigration, in which he was still involved thanks to a thousand ties of kinship and friendship, Abdelmalek Sayad was inspired by an impassioned desire to know and to understand. This was no doubt primarily a wish to understand and know himself, to understand where he himself stood, because he was in the impossible position of a foreigner who was both perfectly integrated and often completely inassimilable. As a foreigner, or in other words a member of that privileged category to which real immigrants will never have access and which can, in the best of cases, enjoy all the advantages that come from having two nationalities, two languages, two homelands and two cultures, and being driven by both emotional and intellectual concerns, he constantly sought to draw closer to the true immigrants, and to find, in the explanations that science allowed him to discover, the principle of a solidarity of the heart that became ever more complete as the years went by.

This solidarity with the most disadvantaged, which explains his formidable epistemological lucidity, allowed him to demolish and destroy in passing, and without seeming to touch upon them, many discourses and representations – both commonplace and learned –

concerning immigrants. It allowed him to enter fully into the most complex of problems: that of the lies orchestrated by a collective bad faith, or that of the real illnesses of patients who have been cured in the medical sense, in the same way that he could enter a family or house he did not know as though he were a regular and considerate visitor who was immediately loved and respected. It allowed him to find the words, and the right tone, to speak of experiences that are as contradictory as the social conditions that produced them, and to analyse them by mobilizing both the theoretical resources of traditional Kabyle culture, as redefined by ethnological work (thanks to notions such as *elghorba*, or the opposition between *thaymats* and *thadjjaddith*), and the conceptual resources of an integrated research team from which he was able to obtain the most extraordinary findings about the most unexpected objects.

All these virtues, which the textbooks on methodology never discuss, his incomparable theoretical and technical sophistication, and his intimate knowledge of the Berber tradition and language, proved indispensable when it came to dealing with objects which, like the so-called problems of 'immigration', cannot be left to the first person who comes along. Epistemological principles and methodological precepts are, in this case, of little help unless they can be based upon more profound discourses that are, to some extent, bound up with both experience and a social trajectory. And it is clear that there were many reasons why Abdelmalek Sayad could see from the outset what had escaped all other observers before him. Because analysts approach 'immigration' – the word says it all – from the point of view of the host society, which looks at the 'immigrant' problem only insofar as 'immigrants' cause it problems, they in effect fail to ask themselves about the diversity of causes and reasons that may have determined the departures and oriented the diversity of the trajectories. As a first step towards breaking with this unconscious ethnocentrism, he restores to 'immigrants', who are also 'emigrants', their origin and all the particularities that are associated with it. It is those particularities that explain many of the differences that can be seen in their later destinies. In an article published in 1975, in other words long before 'immigration' became part of the public debate, he tore apart the veil of illusions that concealed the 'immigrant' condition and dispelled the reassuring myth of the imported worker who, once he has accumulated his nest egg, will go back to his own country to make way for another worker. But above all, by looking closely at the tiniest and most intimate details of the condition of 'immigrants', by taking us into the heart of the constituent contradictions of an impossible and inevitable life by evoking the innocent lies that help to reproduce illusions about the land of exile, he paints with small touches a striking portrait of these 'displaced persons' who have no appropriate place in social space and no set place in social classifications. In the hands of such an analyst, the immigrant functions as an extraordinary tool for analysing the most obscure regions of the unconscious.

Like Socrates as described by Plato, the immigrant is *atopos*, has no place, and is displaced and unclassifiable. The comparison is not simply intended to ennoble the immigrant by virtue of the reference. Neither citizen nor foreigner, not truly on the side of the Same nor really on the side of the Other, he exists within that 'bastard' place, of which Plato also speaks, on the frontier between being and social non-being. Displaced, in the sense of being incongruous and inopportune, he is a source of embarrassment. The difficulty we have in thinking about him – even in science, which often reproduces, without realizing it, the presuppositions and omissions of the official vision – simply recreates the embarrassment created by his burdensome non-existence. Always in the wrong place, and now as out of place in his society of origin as he is in the host society, the immigrant obliges us to rethink completely the question of the legitimate foundations of citizenship and of relations between citizen and state, nation or nationality. Being absent both from his place of origin and his place of arrival, he forces us to rethink not only the instinctive rejection which, because it regards the state as an expression of the nation, justifies itself by claiming to base citizenship on a linguistic and cultural community (if not a racial community), but also the false assimilationist 'generosity' which, convinced that the state, armed with education, can produce the nation, may conceal a chauvinism of the universal. The physical and moral sufferings he endures reveal to the attentive observer everything that native insertion into a nation and a state buries in the innermost depths of minds and bodies, in a quasi-natural state, or in other words far beyond the reach of consciousness. Thanks to experiences, which, for those who can observe, describe and decipher them, are like so many experiments, he forces us to discover what Thomas Bernard calls the 'state-controlled' thoughts and bodies that a very particular history has bequeathed us and which, despite all the humanist professions of faith, very often continue to prevent us from recognizing and respecting all the forms of the human condition.

Pierre Bourdieu

Salah Bouhedja, Eliane Dupuy and Rebecca Sayad helped to finalize the manuscript, and to compile the bibliography and index of names.

Sources

Unless otherwise stated, all texts are by Abdelmalek Sayad.

INTRODUCTION

Pierre Bourdieu, 'Célibat et condition paysanne', *Etudes rurales*, 5–6, April–September 1962: 32–136.

Homo academicus, Paris: Editions de Minuit, 1984 (English translation by Peter Collier, *Homo Academicus*, Cambridge: Polity, 1990).

CHAPTER 1

'El Ghorba: le mécanisme de reproduction de l'émigration', *Actes de la recherche en sciences sociales*, 2, March 1975: 50–66.

CHAPTER 2

'Les "Trois Ages" de l'émigration algérienne en France', *Actes de la recherche en sciences sociales*, 15, June 1977: 59–79.

CHAPTER 3

'L'Immigration algérienne, une immigration exemplaire', in J. Costa-Lascoux and E. Temime, eds, *Les Algériens en France, genèse et devenir d'une migration*. Actes du Colloque du GRECO (Grenoble, 26–27 January 1983), Paris: Publisud, 1985, pp. 19–49.

'Coûts et profits de l'immigration, les présupposés politiques d'un débat économique', *Actes de la recherche en sciences sociales*, 61, March 1986: 79–82.

CHAPTER 4

'Emigration et nationalisme: le cas algérien', in *Genèse de l'Etat moderne en Méditerranée. Approches historiques et anthropologiques des représentations*, Rome: Collection de l'Ecole française de Rome, 168, 1993, pp. 407–36.

CHAPTER 5

'Les Effets culturels de l'émigration, un enjeu de luttes sociales', *Annuaire de l'Afrique du Nord*, XXIII, Paris: CNRS, 1984, pp. 383–97.

CHAPTER 6

'Le Phénomène migratoire, une relation de domination', *Annuaire de l'Afrique du Nord*, XX, Paris: CNRS, 1981, pp. 365–406.

CHAPTER 7

'La "faute" de l'absence ou les effets de l'émigration', *Anthropologica medica* (Trieste), July 1988: 50–69.

CHAPTER 8

'OS et double condition', in R. Sainsaulieu and A. Zehraoui, eds, *Ouvriers spécialisés à Billancourt: les derniers témoins*, Paris: L'Harmattan, 1995, pp. 295–330.

CHAPTER 9

'Santé et équilibre social chez les immigrés', XXII colloque de la Société de psychologie médicale de langue française: Psychologie médicale et migrants (Marseille, 30–31 May 1980), *Psychologie médicale*, 13, 11, 1981: 1747–75.

CHAPTER 10

'Qu'est-ce que l'intégration?', Pour une éthique de l'intégration, *Hommes et migrations*, 1182, December 1994: 8–14.

CHAPTER 11

'Les Immigrés algériens et la nationalité française', in S. Laacher, ed., *Questions de nationalité. Histoire et enjeux d'un code*, Paris: L'Harmattan, 1987, pp. 127–97.

CHAPTER 12

'L'Immigration et la "pensée d'Etat". Réflexions sur la double peine', in *Délit d'immigration. La Construction sociale de la déviance et de la criminalité parmi les immigrés en Europe*, textes réunis par S. Palidda, rapport COST A2, Migrations. Brussels: Communauté européenne, 1996, pp. 11–19.

Introduction

One cannot write on the sociology of immigration without, at the same time and by that very fact, outlining a sociology of emigration. One country's immigration is another country's emigration. The two are indissociable aspects of a single reality, and one cannot be explained without reference to the other. The two dimensions of the phenomenon can be separated out and made autonomous only as a result of some arbitrary decision. The caesura is introduced by a division of competences, interests and political stakes between political partners who are situated, with respect to one another, in a fundamentally asymmetrical relationship. On the one hand, we have emigration, just as there are countries, societies and economies of emigration and just as there is, or should be, a (political) power, a state and an emigration policy (on the part of the state), and also – why not? – a science of emigration. On the other, we have immigration, just as there are societies and economies of immigration, very definite immigration policies and, bound up with all that, a science of immigration. As an object that has been divided between political powers rather than disciplines, and between divergent social and political interests on continents that have been separated by a frontier that divides emigration and immigration, the migratory phenomenon cannot be fully understood unless science mends the broken threads and puts together the shattered fragments. This must be done by science and not by politics. Science may even have to resist stubborn political attempts to maintain the division.

In this domain (perhaps more so than in any other) science is *objectively* subordinated to politics[1] because of the imposition of a problematic that belongs to the social order (in all its forms: demographic, economic, social, cultural and, above all, political). As a result we are obliged to investigate the social preconditions for the possibility of a comprehensive science (a science that can borrow from all the disciplines of social science) of the migratory phenomenon by looking at its twin components: emigration and immigration. To be more specific, we are obliged to investigate the social preconditions for the emergence of certain questions that exist as social problems only because they are constituted first as objects of discourse and only then as objects of science. One of the peculiar features of sociological thinking about emigration and immigration is that it must also, and necessarily, be self-reflexive. In no other social context is sociology so closely bound up with its own sociology as it is here. The sociology of emigration and immigration is inseparable from the reflexive attitude that consists in investigating, in connection with every aspect that is being studied, the social conditions that made it possible to study it, or in other words the constitution of the object under consideration as an object of study and the effects this has on the aspect of the study that is being made. The first conclusion to emerge from this reflexive attempt to truly construct the social object known as immigration (and/or emigration) as a true object of science is that any project undertaken on this basis is at once a social history of the double phenomenon of emigration and immigration, and a social history of the discourse on the phenomenon in question – here, as with many social objects, the discourse on the object is itself part of the object and must be integrated into the object of study or must itself become an object of study. The discourse on emigration or immigration can be pronounced in turn from the immigration point of view and in the society of immigration, and from the emigration point of view and in the society of emigration. Any attempt to construct immigration as a true object of science must, finally, be a social history of the reciprocal relations between these societies, of the society of emigration and the society of immigration, of relations between emigrants and immigrants, and of relations between each of those two societies.

Without going into details about the conditions that now make it possible to ask a number of new questions about, and to arrive at a new understanding of – which remains to be communicated – the migratory phenomenon, one can only note the emergence of previously repressed questions about emigration and immigration. The many new themes, discourses and studies include, for example, the problematic that goes by the name of the '*cost-benefit* theory of immigration'. This is the product of the extension to 'cultural' matters of a problematic that was originally constructed just for the study of the economic aspects of immigration (and, to a lesser degree, emigration). It may have the beneficial effect of contributing to the elaboration of a 'total economics' of the migratory phenomenon which would also include the economics of the non-economic and particularly those aspects that are conventionally described as 'cultural'.

Because in many ways it is so reassuring, one has to be deliberately myopic to accept and reproduce the reductive definition of the migratory phenomenon that implicitly describes it as being nothing more than the mere displacement of a labour force. It is as though we had, on the one hand, a (relatively) surplus labour force – with no questions asked as to the reasons for that surplus, or about the genesis of the process that made this surplus available (for emigration) – and, on the other hand, jobs that are available – with no questions asked about the mechanisms that make these jobs available to immigrants. No doubt we will have to wait for the removal of the determinations which, in practice, mean that all we can see of such a vast object is its immediate or phenomenal function, which is also an instrumental function, in order to bring out the many other functions and qualities the 'instrumentalist' vision helps to mask. This operation of dissimulation is the very precondition for the constitution and perpetuation of the phenomenon.

But once they outlive certain social conditions, emigration and immigration eventually betray their other dimensions, and especially their political and cultural dimensions, which were initially concealed. No doubt the initial function of immigration has to become blurred, or to cease to appear to be the only function that, in both practice and theory, devolves upon immigration, before its other implications – and there are all kinds of them – can be revealed. This appears to occur when immigration ceases to be exclusively about labour, or in other words something that affects workers alone – assuming that there can be such a thing as the exclusive immigration of labour – and is transformed into immigration of families (or of settlers). We thus establish an artificial divorce between, on the one hand, the immigration of labour, which appears to concern only workers (who represent no more than an input of labour power) and which poses only labour problems, and, on the other, an immigration of settlers, whose meaning and effects are of a different order, whose implications are much more far-reaching, and which creates multiple problems on such a scale as to affect all spheres of society, and especially what we might call the cultural and political spheres.

To that extent, to immigrate means to immigrate together with one's history (immigration itself being an integral part of that history), with one's traditions, ways of living, feeling, acting and thinking, with one's language, one's religion and all the other social, political and mental structures of one's society – structures characteristic of the individual and also of society, since the former is no more than the embodiment of the latter – or, in a word, with one's culture. This is what we are discovering today, and we are surprised (not to say scandalized) by it, even though it was predictable as soon as the first act of immigration took place – in other words as soon as the first immigrant arrived. But although we might in theory have predicted it, we refused to do so because, if we had, immigration would not have come into being and gone on existing in the form that we know it. This is, in part, the meaning of the contemporary discourse on the cultural contribution or cultural effects of immigration, whether or not we delight in them or deplore them, praise them or denounce them – which is another way of recognizing them, a form of admission as well as a way of including these contributions, sometimes as 'costs' and sometimes as 'benefits', in the great bookkeeping exercise inspired by the presence of immigrants, which now includes things that do not come within the remit of accountancy itself (i.e. of the economy in the strict sense).

Reaching this point requires, however, more than changes within the phenomenon of immigration, within the immigrant population, and the correlative transformations that have occurred in connection to immigration. There must also be a sort of general cultural disposition (in other words, a disposition that can be transposed by the individuals or groups of individuals who possess it, to all spheres of existence) that is broadly shared, at least as an assertion of principle from which there is no reason to draw any practical implications. This disposition goes by the name of cultural relativism. It is a cultivated attitude – on the part of people with a cultivated relationship with their own culture – towards the culture of the others whom they thus constitute as an object of culture which they can then appropriate and which can enrich their own culture. The relativist profession of faith states that 'one culture is as good as another', just as one language is as good as another or even just as one religion is as good as another (but with more reservations, except on the part of the odd sceptic or agnostic, who tends to view them all with the same indifference or to subject them to the same negation). It applies, however, only to some pure and ethereal realm of cultures (or languages or religions). Now that relativism has been generalized and vulgarized or, to a certain extent, secularized (or in other words now that it has left its own territory or the territory for which it was designed, namely the epistemological sphere), it has, sociological realism notwithstanding, been turned into a sort of *absolute* (or dogma) that tolerates no relativization.

One could write a whole social history of cultural relativism. One could write a history of the social conditions of its invention, its diffusion and the effects it produces, or in other words a history of stakes and struggles that were and are struggles over the legitimate definition of the notion of culture. Every social class that is also a cultural class claims to define culture by appeal to its own standard or to contest, at least in the case of culturally dominant classes, the definition that the hegemonic culture (i.e. those who are culturally dominant) imposes. But in this struggle between unequal cultural partners, is not the insistence with which a culture that claims to be 'popular' tries to negotiate on equal terms with the culture it objectively recognizes as the culture of reference a way of paying homage to that culture? That is the whole meaning of the quarrel, which is never entirely lost, between 'popular culture' and 'cultured culture' (i.e. academic, dominant culture), which is 'culture' *tout court*, without any further qualification. The implicit confrontation between endogenous 'French' culture and 'immigrant' culture – the 'cultures of origin' which are complacently redefined as 'cultural contributions', (Berque 1985) or the 'culture in creation', which grafts onto the imported substratum borrowings imposed by the context of immigration and already in part adopted prior to immigration – is turned into an issue not so much by the immigrants themselves as by the society of immigration as it asks itself about its own cultural components. The confrontation is, it would appear and subject to all the distinctions that characterize the *sui generis* situation that immigration creates in this respect, no more than a paradigmatic variant on the old and still ongoing conflict between competing cultures.

Nor is emigration what we want it to be, or what we believe or pretend it to be so that it can occur and continue in such a way that we can accept it without a bad conscience and, ultimately, in the mode of the obvious. Emigration is not simply the export of labour power. It is not the export of a sort of labour force that is available for use, and that is available for use because it is not being used at home. Yet that is how emigrants are defined, first as unemployed men, and then as unemployed men who emigrate so as to cease being unemployed: nothing more and nothing else. Emigration and immigration are social mechanisms that must fail to recognize themselves for what they are in order to become what they must be. But, with the passage of time, immigration finally admits, and admits to itself, what it really is, namely something more than and different from the mere emigration (or defection) of a certain quantity of labour power; it eventually reveals all its other dimensions, all the other aspects it had to conceal in order to perpetuate itself. Even though, *mutatis mutandis*, the same causes always produce the same effects, the unmasking that occurs with respect to immigration in the society of immigration helps to provoke or accelerate the correlative unmasking of emigration within the society of emigration. A copy of a discourse about the object and theme of immigration is thus gradually installed in all spheres of society and even in scientific discourse about the phenomenon of emigration.[2] The two discourses, which echo one another, are homologous because, ultimately, they are both products of the same schemata of thought and the same categories (applied to symmetrical objects) of perception, appreciation and evaluation of the social world and in this case, to be more specific, the respective worlds of emigration and immigration.

1

The Original Sin and the Collective Lie

The text we are about to read is a translation, which is as literal as possible, of the discourse of a Kabyle emigrant recorded in France in 1975 on two different occasions: before and after a holiday in Kabylia. The commentary that is offered on it is not there to attenuate, thanks to linguistic or ethnographic notes, the opacity of an authentic discourse that mobilizes all the resources of an original language and culture in order to express and explain experiences of which that culture and language know nothing, or which they reject. The opacity of a language that is not immediately comprehensible is perhaps the most important piece of information – or at least the rarest kind of information – we could hope for at a time when so many well-intentioned spokesmen are speaking on behalf of emigrants.

'I was orphaned at a very young age. In reality, I am the son of an old man – or, as the saying goes, a "son of a widow".[1] It was my mother who brought me up, that's nothing to be ashamed of. My father "left" me when I was eight – so I am the last of the brood – Even then, before my father died – he was very old – it was my mother who took care of everything; she was already "the man of the house"! In any case, an old man's wife is always an old woman! I don't know how old my mother is, but she is much younger than my father, she's younger even than my elder sisters [who are in fact his half-sisters]; my father was married three times, I think, or at least had children by two different women.'

'I am the son of a widow'

'As far back as I can remember, I've always seen my mother working both inside and outside the house – and that's the way it is to this very day: she never stops. I remember my father only as an old man who never went any further than the doorstep.

'My mother is difficult; that's what they say, that's the reputation she has, but I think she needed to gain that reputation to defend herself, so as not to be "eaten" alive by others. A widow who remains at the mercy of her brothers-in-law, who has to wait for her son to grow up for there to be a man entering and leaving the house, is definitely not in a good position. If she doesn't defend herself, they eat her, rob her. For her part, she didn't do anything to humour them. I can say it now: which of my uncles hasn't at the very least insulted her? How many times has she been beaten? And always by her closest relatives, not by strangers. If the man who is most closely related to you doesn't harm you, a perfect stranger is not going to harm you. Where would someone who isn't a close relative come from? As for a complete stranger, it's not worth talking about; he would be afraid, because she is still the Xs' woman. But what does a relative have to fear? He can always say: she's our woman; and it then becomes something between relatives: the closer he is, the more he can let himself go. A lad like El – and it has to be said that he's calmed down a lot – what's there to hold him back? Do you think that "shame would eat his face," that he would say to himself: "My uncle [the immigrant's father was still alive at this time] is old, he has nothing, he has nothing, he can do nothing, he's only got her and, fortunately for us, she's there, it's she who makes sure 'his house is full' "'? Not a bit of it...

'When I compare the earliest years of my childhood with a few years later, I can even say that perhaps they showed my mother greater respect after my father died than during his lifetime. It's true, you'd think that "hearts" have changed since then.... That's what the life of a "son of a widow" is like! At a very early age, I had my fair share of troubles, cares and worries. It's not age that makes men, it's what happens over their heads; a man makes himself through his actions, and not because he's received a name from his ancestors. He may well be so and so – and yet, what if there is nothing inside him, what if "his market is empty"?'

'You didn't get up early, so why are you going to the market?'

'... Do you think that in their day [the allusion is to events going back to the years 1942–4 and to people who died, one in 1954 and the other in 1958] my uncles M.E. and N.L., who robbed my father of the only bit of land he owned, and which he ceded to them as a security against his debts, during the hard years of *elboun* [i.e. the years during the Second World War, when the system of ration cards was in force], so as to be able to buy, according to what people say – it was before I was born – barley in order to survive; do you think that they would have done what their children are doing today? "You want to build a house?" "OK, here's half a plot of land, we'll give you it, go and dig the foundations." With them, such a thing would have been impossible. Is it because hatred has left their hearts, or because stomachs are fuller these days? First, now that you can find no one to quarrel with, there is no more reason to quarrel. The insults, the screams, the hatred, the blows of the past – what was it all about? Someone walked through someone else's field, broke down the fence around his neighbour's field or diverted water from the canal when it was his turn to irrigate his own field. That was what fuelled the quarrels "part already there, part added". All that, all the hatred, all the ill feeling, those rages, those ancestral enmities handed down from father to son, as they say – it was all about land. Now that there is no one left to take care of the land, there are no longer any pretexts for quarrels. Why hold anything against a woman these days? Especially when you then have to go and ask her to take care of land that no one wants any more. All those who, in the past, couldn't tolerate my mother going near their trees, the fences around their fields, now beg her to work their land even though she doesn't even own a chicken. Peace has returned to earth; even though there are still reasons for men to quarrel, the women are kept out of it.

'The mother of a "son of a widow" is forgotten only when he has proved himself to be a man; otherwise, he will always be the son of such and such a woman. Under those conditions, how do you expect him not to be in a hurry? But when you are in a hurry, you can't do anything: you don't know where you're going; it might be "light" [success, happiness], just as it might be "darkness" [failure, misfortune]. It takes courage. How do you put an end to this situation? how do you get out of it?

'All I could do was work. At the beginning, I worked a lot. I could see that my mother never stopped working, and I started work as soon as I could. I've worked everywhere, for everyone, done everything, for money, for charity [without being paid]; I've ploughed, I've harvested the fields for all my relatives; I didn't even wait for them to come and ask me, I offered my services myself. What could I lose? I was paid in one way or another. Better do that than twiddle your thumbs. And I really was paid for my trouble; I've been paid in money, in services rendered, in kind, and especially in food. I could bring in the harvest for all my relatives; they couldn't refuse me that because I didn't spare any effort. I was encouraged on all sides. On all sides, they used to say: "M. is a worker – he still takes care of the land."

'I was a sharecropper – I even had a pair of oxen, and that had never been seen before in the house; no one could remember ever seeing an ox cross the threshold, and I'm not talking about the door that is there now. I mean the door of our ancestors. So in the space of a few years, I became a real fellah. But that did not last long, only until I woke up and realized that even the condition of a fellah [*thafalahth*] was my lot only because it had been neglected by all the rest of them. As the saying goes: "You didn't get up early, so why are you going to the market?" So I said to myself: "Have a rest!" '

'I became a "casual fellah" '

'I was overcome by lassitude. Why should I make such an effort? I'm just like everyone else. Am I any better than all those people who own land, but who look at it only from afar, and entrust it to me to work it? Their arms aren't paralysed, after all. There are moments when I catch myself saying: "You're the biggest fool of all; while you are wearing yourself out, he [the owner of the field] is living a life of ease, a comfortable life, doesn't give a damn ('a hundred come in and a hundred go out'). And what do you get out of it?"

'I was surprised to find myself behaving like everyone else. I became a casual fellah, working just as a last resort, when I was forced to do so. Bit by bit [gradually], I found myself, in only a short time, in trouble because of all the habits I'd got into, all the past commitments, all the land I'd accepted. For her part, my mother started following me around too; she was furious with me, and never stopped complaining, day or night, to my face when we were together, behind my back when she could find a sympathetic ear. She thought she could put pressure on me by giving up a lot of the outside jobs she did. "If you don't want to do anything any more, I'm fed up with it too; it's no longer worthwhile working myself to death all by myself. When you were little I made you a house, but now that you are grown up, it's up to you; whether you want to have a full house or an empty house; it's up to you. I don't want to do it any more." She actually got rid of all the patches of land she was renting, keeping only the garden and a little patch of land close to the house. That became her domain, and she looked after it by herself.

'Our country is fine for anyone who asks only to live [feed himself], as long as they are willing to live "according to the state of the land": you work all the days without counting, all the days that God sends, you bring in what you need to live on and what you bring in is all you have to live on. Everything else is ruled out. If you are satisfied with that, so much the better; if not, you have to start running. It's not as if it was just a matter of a hungry belly. It's true that no one goes hungry these days; but hunger is not just about what you need to put in your belly; it is also a hungry back [which has to be clothed], hungry feet [which need shoes], a pain in the stomach [which has to be cured], a hungry roof [which has to be mended], a hungry head [children who have to go to school]. It's not just a matter of: if you have no salt you eat tasteless food, or if you have no kerosene you go to bed in the dark! So you mustn't want anything, and above all you mustn't need money. But it is money that everyone needs; even in the village, you have to buy everything, like in the city. It's become the *elfilaj* village.'

'France is the only door'

'It wasn't because I'd got rid of everything to do with agriculture, sold the oxen and the donkey and handed back the land to its owners, that it was all over and that I stopped work altogether. No, I went on working, but in a different way – different things, anything. If I have to work in someone else's fields, it's either because I want to do him a favour and work one, two or three days; or, it's as a day labourer and then, in the evening, he has to put down my day [day's wages] in front of me. It's obvious. Working on the land is like any other kind of work, so long as it brings in some money. It's no harder than working with the masons, or on a truck, and I've already done that... What haven't I done to earn money? I've even gone so far as to accept slaps[2] because it earned me 11,000 francs [he still reckons in old francs, even when he is talking about dinars].

'My mother also got involved; it's as though she wanted to follow me in everything I did; she got out her sewing machine again, even though she said she was sick of it; she went back to her prosperous trade with the women, and started selling anything: eggs, the material that her brother – another "real snake" – brought back for her from France, jewellery, sometimes real, sometimes fake, but usually "copper and lies".[3] We too began to "glean small change"; our only problem was how to pick it up.

'Despite all the effort my mother and I put into chasing after money, we were always short of it. I never stopped working, I had calluses on my back, but I still didn't have any money, I didn't even have enough to buy cigarettes. Why work when that's all you get out of it? My head was full of troubles, and not much money was coming in. I was smoking more and more, I needed more and more money, and I had less and less of it. In no time at all, and without knowing how, I found myself with debts of 450,000 francs. 450,000! Just 50,000 more, and it's half a million! That's a lot of money. At that point, I became frightened, I felt totally discouraged! What could I do? Where could I find a place to lay my head? Where could I find the money to repay my debts? There was no way out of this situation; no escape, the only "door" that was left was France – it was the only solution left. All those who have money, those who have done anything, bought anything, or built anything, it's because they had money from France.'

'France is all they talk about'

'That is how France gets under your skin. Once you've got that into your head, it's all over; you can't work in the fields any more, you have no desire to do anything else: leaving is the only solution you can think of. From that moment on, France is inside you, and it will never go away. It's always before your eyes. It's as though we were possessed. If someone said to you "If such and such a *cheikh* wrote something for you, you could leave",[4] of course you would go and see him. It's madness! That's the way it is with the young people who want to leave nowadays. As soon as one of them begins to "refuse" [to be disobedient], to cause a bit of trouble: he refuses to work, gangs up with the rest of them, and is always in "places that are not full" [outside the village]; you can be sure of it, he's plotting to go away. In the past, people used to do that so as to get married when their parents were a bit too slow about making the arrangements. Nowadays, if you are married and want to leave for France, you sulk to the point of repudiating your wife. It's madness, there's no other word for it, it's like drinking or gambling, it's a little worm that "burrows tunnels inside us, like in the mine". When I think now of all the running around I've done, all the things I expected, all the journeys I've made, all the people I've begged, you really have to be mad to put up with all that, just to be able to get to France.

'Like everyone else, I've said the same things about France, day in, day out, night after night, year after year: "Would that God would get me out of this country." The country of "narrowness", the country of poverty, the country of wretchedness, the "twisted", "inverted" country, the country of opposites, the country of decline, the country that inspires scorn for its people, the country that is incapable of keeping its own people, the country that has been abandoned by God. And we swear, we promise: "The day I get out of here [this country], I will never again speak your name; I will never look back at you; I will not come back to you." I've said it too, when I think about it, the number of times I've invoked, not good fortune and all the good omens you wish upon someone who has to take to the road, but the strength of demons. I was more likely to say: "Let me be taken away, kidnapped" than to use the expression used to invoke blessings: "May God open or 'ease' the way."

'In reality, all that is just a lie, as the saying goes: "one lie after another". How bitter you can be, my country, when one dreams of leaving you. And how desirable you are, oh France, before one knows you! All because our village is full of France and nothing but France – France is all people talk about.

'From our village, we have more people in France than in the village. Much as I try to count and "keep a tally" [check], I always find there are more men in France than in our village. When I was back there in the village, there were moments when we [the men of the village] were filled with "wild solitude" [fear]. I was on the point of leaving, and everyone would say to me: "You are the only one who has stayed, and now you are going to join them. You will leave us 'emptiness'." There aren't many of us at home; all our people are in France; we are "filling" France and emptying the village. But what is there in the village? All the "broken" men, "twisted" men who are good for nothing. That's all.

'The only men in the village are French veterans [who have come back from France]. They came back from France because they were tired of it, or perhaps because it was France that was tired of them, if it was up to them alone – they haven't expelled it [France] from their hearts. On the one hand, there are those men; on the other, there are those who are getting ready to leave one day or another. And a small number, there are a few – they are all young men of my age – would get no one's approval if they too began to get the idea of leaving "into their heads". And in their heart of hearts, perhaps they too would like to go: those are the ones who have jobs somewhere or other in Algeria. So that is all – these are our men at home. There are those they talk about, the way they talk about the guardian of the hearth, the "*cheikh* of the *kanoun*", "his name is there, but you never see him" [meaning that he is like a ghost]; there's a whole army of them, the army of men – and I am one of them – who never stop coming and going between here and France; going and coming, that's all they do. They are a category apart; when they get older, some of them really do end up renouncing France, but those who replace them, here in France, are in the majority; there are more who come to France than there are who go back home. Some will end up dying here in France, I don't know why, but in the village they are counted as village men: the villagers count on them, their "heads are counted" every time [they are enumerated whenever taxes have to be paid or reimbursed according to how many men there are in the family], they are not forgotten although they themselves have forgotten their village, their relatives. Some of them have been in France for at least twenty years. S. – he's a relative – did not know his son until he had become a man; he left when his son was born, his wife died in the meantime, and when he came home he found his son, married, "with his house" – he found a daughter-in-law. It's like being in a fairy tale.

'The men who do live in the village – you could say that almost all of them have already worked in France. If you had to count the men in the village who have never been to France in their lives, I don't think you would find a dozen – I am not counting the young men of today, those who are my age. Who in our house [kinship group] hasn't been to France? One man! Because the machine [the train] left him behind [he missed the bus]. All the others are men that France has beaten up; they came home all "shaken up", all shaken with a pole [like olive trees]. In any case, they can no longer work; they are no longer either workers inside the house [in other words, at home] or workers outside [meaning in France]; all they are good for is staying in the village and doing nothing else. You see them wandering about, coming and going in the streets of the village, it is they who are "filling" the village. You can't understand what they are, they are whatever you want them to be: if you like, they are the village's wise men, even though they are still young, they are the village's "idle men" in their *gandouras* and turbans [the costume of men who are generally out of work], they are in the village as though they were on holiday all the time; at home, in their own houses, they like to be [treated] like permanent guests. But they are also, if you like, the labourers the village counts upon.

'Fortunately, it's no longer the way it used to be, there is no reason to fear the big brawls of the past because, if you were attacked, there wouldn't be a man you could count on these days. They are good for neither work nor fighting, they've all settled down, all they are good for is sleeping until "the warmest part of the middle of the day". This country suits them, now that they have brought their carcasses back from France; that's all France has left them; a pile of bones they've preserved; that's all they have left, they've left the important, living part of themselves behind in France. Besides, they've all come back [from France] with something: some have a retirement pension, others an invalidity pension. They've brought back with them "their share of France". France continues to "help" them and what France gives them is enough. It's better than nothing, like "finding a piece of fat in the bean soup". It is said of them that [their affairs] are "settled": they have no more major worries.

'The only thing all these French veterans don't have now is the ability to leave when they like, when the path is clear; to leave just like that – from time to time, as tourists, for a month, two months.[5] Each of them has a son, a brother, and a son-in-law or even a daughter they would like to go and see, to spend some time with them, to have a change of air and then come home, bringing back money, things, presents. That's what a tourist does! That's what holidays are like. If it was always like that, there would never be an end to it; it would be a circus, a perpetual coming and going: those in France would go back on holiday, in the summer; those back there would go to France on holiday, in the winter. Even in conversations, what do all the men in the village talk about? France! The veterans of France keep going on about their memories. Those "on leave" talk about France, in the middle of their village; they believe they are still in France; the young men who are waiting to leave dream of France. France is all you hear them talk about: France is like this, France is like that; so and so in France said this or that, did this, did that; bought a taxi [meaning a car, the French term is used in contrast to *camion* or truck], a motorbike and so on. Our village is a village that has been "eaten" by France; no one escapes it.

'In reality, no one knows anything [about France]. People talk about it as though they were comfortable there, and France seems to everyone to be lit up. That's the way it is. Everyone loves France, and France is beautiful in everyone's eyes ... But what do you really expect them to say about France? They know nothing about it. They say – they say that it is "the land of happiness", that's all.

'Before I went there, I didn't think that France was foreign [a foreign country]. I thought it was like going to one of the villages in the area, except that it was further – as though you were going to a country you knew. . . . It wasn't me who invented France, so many went before me, since time immemorial, I'm not the first and I won't be the last. Starting with my brother, he's now spent more than forty years in France. In his day, my father had already been to France; he worked in the coal mines of the Nord [*département*] and even in Belgium; he could remember the days when there were horses down the mines, he always talked about them . . . . Me, I'd heard talk of France since the day I was born, every day, ten times a day. That's why I had a very different image of it. I didn't even think that it might be like Algiers. Even though there were a lot [of men] from the village in Algiers, I didn't think I'd be left [to my own devices]. Even less so, I thought, in France, because the whole village was there; all my relatives, my paternal uncles and maternal uncles were together there. So I thought all I had to do was to get out of Algiers. As for the rest, it was like going to your own house. Having so many men in France and being afraid [to the point of] taking one step forward and one step back, it wasn't worth it!

'I thought that, even though it wouldn't be quite like the village, I would find it a bit like being in a neighbourhood of Algiers, but a neighbourhood where I would find all my relatives. It was no more than going to a neighbouring village; anyone who goes there knows where to go, and what has taken him there; when they see him, everyone knows whose house he is going to; they expect him to turn up and, after that, anyone can invite him. He is not one of those men who expect to be brought something to eat, or to be given directions to the mosque because they have no one on the spot. I expected it to be the same for me in France. Of course, I would start by going to my destination, to the home of my closest relative, or in other words my brother, and then all my relatives would be there. In fact, it did not turn out like that.'

'To be able to leave without having to ask anything'

'. . . I had great difficulty in getting to France. The formalities you have to go through, the time you have to wait, is nothing;[6] the hardest thing of all is hearing everything that is said about you whenever you are seen to be doing something. "Who does he think he is? I hope he doesn't succeed. He would do better to stay here; we need him here. He does not lack for bread, what more does he want? In any case, he hasn't a hope. Look how many men before him have asked to leave and who are still waiting years later. He's not going to fly away all by himself; let him stay where he is." I knew all that, and I said to myself: "If you do want to leave, the last thing you should do is go through the 'people here' [the local authority]." They'd already treated me the same way over something else – the things I heard during all the time I was going through the formalities to leave. In the village, everyone had an opinion to offer: they swore I was rushing around for no purpose, that I was just throwing money away. "Stay calm", they advised me. I let them talk. Even my uncle, the one I could count on to some extent, never stopped saying: "He'll come a cropper, and to no avail. He's just rushing all over the place. I tell you, he really will wear himself out working L."[7] I wept so many times. It sickened my heart to hear the mockery; people who have nothing better to do with their time than poke their noses into other people's business. I'd have paid a lot to prove them wrong. I prayed that I would not be dishonoured. I was spared that shame, thank God. I waited a year before I could obtain all the permits I needed, and I needed a lot of support. My great joy, my revenge, was being able to leave without asking anything of the people in the village. Every "paper" I obtained was a real struggle in itself.

'Getting the passport was my first victory! When I had it in my hand, I didn't know whether to wave it or hide it and wait for what happened next. You never know what's going to happen later. Be patient! But the news got around, despite everything.

'I couldn't do things by halves.... The second victory was when I got my exit visa. Then I could hold my head up high. I said to myself: "Now I can leave." But, in my heart of hearts, I was not at peace, I was more worried than ever: being able to leave Algeria isn't everything by any means; you still have to get over there, and not be sent back. It a gamble; I took the risk. In my own mind, it was all settled: either I would cross the sea, if only for a few days, see my brother and my nephews, and I would be as satisfied as if that was the only reason I had come; or I would be sent back from Algiers or France, and then I would never set foot in the village again, come what may! Where would I find the nerve to face everyone if, no sooner gone, than I had to be back. They would say: "He's brought back the provisions he took with him for the journey"; and all I would hear would be the rumours: "It seems that...It seems..." The worst of exiles is better than that shameful spectacle. God protected me from such a scandal.

'My mother was already spreading the news that I was leaving wherever she went. I don't know whether she told everybody about it out of joy or sorrow, of if it was a challenge....In the meantime, my debts began to pile up, all the money I'd had to spend to get the papers, the cost of a return trip. In my haste, I bought my ticket the very day I got my [exit] permit. A week later, I was in France.'

'In our France, there is nothing but darkness'

'And what a France I discovered! It wasn't at all what I expected to find...to think I'd believed France wasn't exile [*elghorba*]. You really have to come here to France to know the truth. Here, you hear things being said that they never say to us back home; you hear everyone telling you: "This is no life for human beings, this is a life you cannot love; in our country, dogs have a better life than this." I will always remember this image of my arrival in France, it is the first thing I saw, the first thing I heard: you knock at a door, it opens on to a little room that smells of a mixture of things, the damp, the closed atmosphere, the sweat of sleeping men.[8] Such sadness! Such misery in their eyes, in their voices – they spoke softly – in their words. That gave me an insight into what loneliness is, what sadness is: the darkness of the room, the darkness in the room...the darkness in the streets – the darkness of the whole of France, because, in our France, there is nothing but darkness.

'...They were talking about me to my uncle, who had brought me here: "Why've you lured him into this trap, why've you deceived him like this, why've you set this trap for him?" What was I hearing? I didn't understand a thing. So where am I? Am I in France, or is this just an intermediate stage, one more ordeal before I arrive in France? And yet the *aéroplane* [*avion*] did bring me to France. And then there are these men, I know them all; I know that they're in France, I remember them well: I've seen them in the village, not long ago; they were back from France, they were happy. Are these the same men? At the time, they seemed to me to be big, very big, and now they are little, little, hiding in their beds. What is all this? Can you deceive yourself to this extent? Deep in my heart, I was clinging on to something else, I preferred to put it down to jealousy, to the selfishness of men. I said to myself: "It's the same old story, just like home; as soon as someone gets out of a tight spot, he wants to be the only winner." I'm not even in France yet, and here they are doing all they can to make me sick of it, to predict the very worst. Why did you come? I don't know what stopped me from replying: "And what about you, what are you doing here? Have you forgotten? Do you think you're going to be the only winners?" The reason why I said nothing is that my head was all in a muddle, I still didn't know where I was, I wasn't "stabilized" yet, not settled.

'Afterwards, it all went very quickly. When you have seen this one and that one, been to this house and that house, you realize that it's the same every time; what one man has said to you is repeated by the other; what you've seen in one man's home, you find in the next man's home, and finally you reconcile yourself to the obvious. That's the truth. I discovered what exile [*elghorba*] is. When they go back home, they might well joke about "their homeland that has become a foreign land [*elghorba*]", but exile is always exile. Of course they say, "Home has become exile [*elghorba*] to me", when they are "caught in the darkness", but basically no one believes them.'

'Every word we say is a lie'

'No, they never explained to us what France was really like before we got to know it. We see them coming home, they are well dressed, they bring back full suitcases, with money in their pockets, we see them spending that money without even thinking about it; they are handsome, they are fat. And when they talk, what do they say? They talk about their work. When they say "I do a difficult job", we admire them. If we suspect them of lying, it's because they boast of doing a difficult job, a hard job; work is always hard, you have to be strong to do it, and that means that they are making a lot of money. That is what you believe when you haven't seen with your own eyes. No one talks about all the rest of it.

'When they come back on holiday, it's summer, with big crowds in the village, joy everywhere, parties. Before I knew, I thought it was always like that in France too, that they were bringing all that joy back with them. No, what do you expect from desolate faces? I realized that it was not *their* joy – quite the opposite – that they came back home to find, no matter what they said. . . . When I go back to the village, I'm like them too, what do you expect me to say? Even if I did talk about my work and told them the truth: "I do a dirty job, the poison gets into my stomach; I'm working myself to death, between the French I work with and us, it's like cat and dog."[9] It is as though I told them nothing about all that. Telling them that I am working is all that matters to them, and that is all they will hear. So why plunge them into the "darkness"? In any case, nothing will shake their faith. In order to understand anything about France, you have to have been there first. . . a man who has seen nothing [of France] listens and remains convinced that his happiness is in the "future", that it is waiting there for him, and that all he has to do is to forge ahead. If you have to come here to France in order to know the truth, it's a bit late – too late.

'. . . I too will answer the questions I am asked. What else can I do? It's not lying. But what I mustn't do is exaggerate out of pride or boasting. So, I'd rather keep quiet than say just anything – that is lying! We are to blame, we emigrants, as they call us: when we come back from France, everything we do and every word we say is a lie; it's our fault. If we attached any value to our money, it wouldn't be like that. We are too free with our money, it's as though it jumped out of our pockets all by itself: we throw it away as though it was pouring in through the doors and windows. Everyone is free to imagine that we earned it effortlessly. And now, the story they told you before comes true: it seems that over there, you have only to bend down to pick up notes of 10,000 francs. In fact, if they saw how we earn that money, the squalor we live in order to save money, it's enough to make you hate that money, it's too bitter, it really is oleander.[10] We are here, we remember nothing. When you have eaten, you forget that you were hungry, you spend "like someone who has come back from France", as they so aptly put it. When you need something, it's as though the need made you forget everything you have been through. If it weren't for that, why return to France, when you already know what France is like? It really must be a question of need. We are all the same; it's as though God had "struck" us; no sooner do we find ourselves in one place than God immediately makes the other place softer for us. No sooner have we got off [disembarked, in the sense of arriving back home], than we forget it all. We start all over again and go back to France as though nothing had happened.

'After what I've seen, I swear that I will never deceive anyone again! This summer, for the first time I've been back to the village – it hasn't even been a year – I saw them all arriving, I was back there long before them, I was back there in August. They found me in the village, as in previous years, I was in working clothes, I'd been harvesting, as in the past. Nothing had changed; it was the village's old Mohand, that's all. When it so happens that you all meet up as a group like that, those who have come back and those who have not yet gone away: just listen to them! Boasts, lies: "I've done this, I've done that; I've got this, I've got that", and so it goes on. I let him talk and when he has nothing left to add, I nettle him and make him jump: "I've come back too." A lot of people still don't know I'm in France; here in Paris, there aren't many of them [immigrants from his village] and in Lyon [where most of the emigrant population from the village is concentrated] only those who are close to me know. In my own mind, I tell all the rest of them: "Right, I'll 'bring out' all your lies; it's no good dressing things up and using fancy words." And the more wretched they are, the more they exaggerate. "Look, you, I know what goes on, I know what you've been up to, and how you live – I've seen you over there." "You're joking, how could you see me, have you got binoculars that can see from here to there?" "Because I've been there too, and you know it. I've just come back, I've only been here for a few days, that's all. So, don't tell lies, lie to the others, but not to me because I've seen it. Or do you think I'm going to cover up for you and take your side? Now, since that's what you want, we're going to tell the truth to those who are listening to us, who haven't seen. You boast about how much you earn – the truth is that you don't even earn half that. You don't even manage to make "two shares" of what I earn. Your room, which isn't yours, but B.'s, he took you in, didn't he? Are you denying it? How many times have you not had enough to pay for it? Either he or D. had to pay for you, otherwise you'd have found your suitcase in the street; you eat on credit in the café, I'm sure that even today, now that you are here among us, you still have debts: you haven't paid for what you ate last month. I take you all as my witnesses, go and ask Ch. at Y. if he paid for the journey that brought him here with his own money. If he paid, I'm the liar, and not him." Because, both over there and back here, your hair's always all over the place. He lets his hair grow long, and he goes to the barber's when he gets to Algiers. Two days after he gets his wages, he still has a little money in his pocket; but after two days, you mustn't ask anything more of him. After that, when he wants anything, even a cigarette, unless he can beg it from someone, he won't get it. That's the "little man" we have in France, that man there who is deafening everyone with his din. Back there, when monsieur has money, off he goes, because I've seen him go off like that and people have told me about his exploits, he is here and there, going from café to café, and the first guy he meets can get him to go anywhere. And so it goes on until his pockets are empty. Shake them, turn them inside out, and not a centime will fall out. And then you see our man coming back to the neighbourhood where everyone lives, head down, not a word to say, hugging the walls; he goes back to his room and never comes out – because he hasn't a bean in his pockets. And now he's like an "ascetic believer". And now that he's at leisure, now that "the situation is easy for him" he begins to ramble on and on.'

A spontaneous theory of reproduction

Mohand A. is a young immigrant aged 21 who came to France little more than a year ago. Originally from a village which, as he himself says, has 'many more people in France than at home', he belongs to that generation of young countrymen who, in a region with a very old and very strong tradition of emigration (the mountains of Kabylia), have no other future prospects and, initially, no ambition but to leave. Indeed, because, on the one hand, he was not of the right age to benefit from the recent education campaigns in rural areas (to use his own words, he did little more than 'slip furtively' into 'the makeshift school' that was opened in the premises where the *djemaâ* or local assembly met), he could not, unlike those young men with a minimal level of education (a primary education certificate or a vocational training certificate), hope to find a stable job either in the city, in neighbouring villages or even at home, that might prevent him from having to emigrate. And because, on the other hand, he did not belong to any of the traditional great peasant families who owned fields, trees and livestock, he could not, quite apart from the general disaffection that has hit traditional agriculture, and which not even members of land-owning families escape, resign himself to his condition as a sharecropper, or in other words a *fellah* working someone else's land for their benefit.

Being acutely aware of the peculiar position he occupies amongst all the other men of the village, and because he refuses to do anything that could be seen as a challenge, or to make any response that might look like a challenge, Mohand A. will, in the space of a few years, experience in a surprisingly short space of time and very directly all the upheavals that have overtaken the old peasant social order. The rural community is completely disintegrating and, as a result of various factors (primarily emigration and all its implications, which are not solely economic), it is not only traditional agricultural tasks that are being neglected because their archaism and futility are becoming obvious. The entire peasant spirit has been seriously damaged and all the old values are being undermined. To go on believing (or pretending to believe), if only for a while, in the peasant condition, and to go on clinging (or pretending to cling) to the land with all the strength of the neophyte, can in the circumstances only be a defiant attitude.

Indeed, attempting the impossible by working what he himself recognizes to be 'fields that, not so long ago, he was forbidden to cross', acquiring a pair of oxen 'in a house which, for as long as anyone can remember, has never seen an ox cross the threshold' – these are not the result of some desire to make himself stand out. Still less do they constitute some archaic desire to rejoin the clan of the 'farmers of the past' – survivors from another era who struggle to work the land as though nothing had changed, the naive *bou-niya*, 'men of a different time' – and of all the old widows who are inconsolable as they see the lands of their house lying fallow or being farmed so carelessly.

For this 'son of a widow', as he likes to call himself, who is from a 'family which has never owned a field or an ox', who boasts of having 'become a man by himself, through his actions and not through his name' (which was handed down to him like the rest of his heritage), making an entry into adult life and making a name for himself in accordance with the traditional norms that define peasant excellence (*thafallahth*) is, in a certain manner, his way of taking revenge on the old landed 'aristocracy'. The aristocracy, whose own sons are turning away from the land, are now, just like all the other men in the village, either local wage-earners or emigrants, or quite simply 'idlers' (*marthah*) of a new kind. Unlike those men (usually heads of families) whose social position ensured them the status of 'men who have the leisure to be at rest' and who were liberated from working on the land (or at least from the most onerous tasks) and could therefore devote themselves to prestigious functions that might be said to be 'representative', today's 'idlers' in fact tend to regard themselves as 'unemployed', when, in order not to have to admit to what they are, they do their utmost to come up with all sorts of alibi: illness, or the ambiguous status of being a former or future emigrant.

If he is not to lapse too quickly and too readily into this widely shared disaffection with traditional activities, he must first convince himself, and then others, that he can and will conform to the old ideal of the man of honour and the accomplished peasant. Proving to himself and others that he can, even though he started out with nothing, build a 'full house' in the old sense of the term – meaning a house with land, animals and produce – is of course still an eminently praiseworthy accomplishment that just has to be admired; but he has to do so at an inopportune moment, and that inevitably leads to disillusionment, especially because he has invested too late in a market that has lost its value. Indeed, because of the demonstrative value that has been assigned it, it is in the very nature of the task he has undertaken that, as soon as it has been successful and because it has been successful, its very function should disappear. There then follows a whole process which, as one thing after another is abandoned, leads to an awareness of the futility of trying to perpetuate agriculture in its old form. It leads to the accumulation of debts and, in the same way that one challenge leads to another, to emigration being seen as the only resort, as the final solution that can break the infernal circle of rural proletarianization, and as the 'emancipatory' act *par excellence*. 'Let he who wants to be a man go to France.' There is now no point in proving that one can work the landowners' lands 'better than they could do it', or that 'you can live off it as well as they did in the past'; that, like them you can own your flock, when what matters if you want recognition is 'showing what you are made of' in a different domain, outside the village and, in accordance with a different logic, other than by working the land.

The village from which Mohand A., together with the entire group of his patrilineal relatives, originates has been strongly influenced by emigration. Like other emigrants, A. likes to count how many men from his village are in France and how many have remained in or returned to the village: he says that his village has seen 92 families and 197 men leave for France. As a result of this, only 146 men are now at home, 105 of whom are former emigrants. If we exclude those men who have, with their families, emigrated to towns in Algeria itself, the agnatic group to which A. belongs has 33 men in France (13 of whom have emigrated with their families), leaving only 18 in the village. Within the minority that guarantees the group's presence in the village, only 10 men have never lived in France, and if we exclude the youngest of them, there is only one, now in his fifties, who has, for health reasons, never emigrated. Of the others, who are all under 30, only two can be considered possible candidates for emigration because, unlike the others, they have been unable to find relatively stable waged jobs at home.

The village has a long tradition of emigration. Of the total of 51 men who now constitute the same kinship group (*adhrum*), 38 have a father who either emigrated to France (when he was still capable of working there) or who was, at some stage, a worker there (or even in

Belgium, as was the case with Mohand A.'s father), and 11 have a grandfather who emigrated. That this migratory movement has a long history emerges even more clearly if we attempt to reconstruct the evolution of the number of men who left successively from 1913 onwards – that, it seems, being the date of the first emigrant's departure from the village (it goes without saying that account is taken only of those emigrants who, for one reason or another, are remembered): between 1913 and 1920 (in other words during the whole of the First World War), 11 men emigrated to France; between 1921 and 1928, 10 more followed; there was no further emigration until 1936, when 7 men emigrated between then and 1939. The Second World War interrupted the process, but it is from 1946 onwards that we find the greatest number of departures: in the space of three years, 15 men, all under the age of 20, emigrated; and in 1952–62 and 1963–73, respectively, 15 and 10 cases of emigration are recorded.

It is not simply that the length of stay outside the home country increases as time goes by (in some cases they might last more than ten years) and that they are now almost continuous (there are many emigrants who, over a period of some twenty years, have returned to the village only once or twice, and only for the duration of their annual holidays). The emigrant condition itself is becoming permanent, and the status of the emigrants is in a sense becoming more stable. Indeed, taking only the category of the youngest emigrants who arrived in France from 1946 onwards (their average age when they first emigrated was very young, the oldest of them being under 24), of a total of 34 men (excluding those who had died in the meantime, all the deaths having occurred in France), only 5 returned to the village for good and 3 settled in towns after their return to Algeria.

Of the emigrants of long standing who are still in France – they are also the oldest – some have spent almost their entire active lives in France; some of them are even beyond retirement age (two brothers who emigrated in 1919 and 1937 and who are now 73 and 61 years old respectively; two other emigrants aged 67 and 59, who came to France in 1928 and 1938 respectively, etc.).

It is not surprising that the entire life of the village should eventually become closely dependent upon the life of the emigrants; the entire local community 'hangs on' its emigration, which it calls 'France'. The village is constantly on the alert and listening to that part of itself from which it has been separated. It is responsible for amplifying in its own way the gossip that gets home. It adopts the rhythms of emigration as they are forced upon it by the news – letters and postal orders – that comes from France, as well as by the return of its emigrants, which occurs periodically.

At a more basic level, it is the very position of each family or group of families within the structure of the village that is determined by the age and size of its emigration. The first families to have 'delegated' emigrants to France were also the first to have monetary capital at their disposal. Those families that are sufficiently rich in men to be present both in the village and abroad are now in a good position to combine the advantages and signs of both kinds of capital on which the social hierarchy is based: economic capital (which is increasingly supplied by emigration) and symbolic capital (which depends upon the 'good use' the men who have stayed at home can make of that economic capital).

Ultimately, each individual's status is defined only in relation to emigration. The village men stand out only when, in very rare cases, they can avoid having to emigrate (or can, at the very least, find a relatively stable waged job) or when, on the contrary and in the majority of cases, they are forced to emigrate or experience their repeated emigration as having been forced on them. The latter are further divided into those who, because they can meet the demands made of anyone entering and remaining in France, have the institutional possibility of emigrating at a date and for a time that suits them and, on the other hand, those who, because they cannot conform to the regulations, can only sustain the illusory hope of becoming possible emigrants one day. Both groups (with the exception of those who have deliberately excluded themselves from the pool of potential emigrants) in fact live in the village only on a 'temporary' basis, rather as though 'they only spent their holidays there', because their day-to-day practice is largely determined by the emigration project. They are called 'stop-gap men' or 'men of the moment', as opposed to the life force that has deserted the village; or 'men of the house', 'inside men', i.e., those who perform the thankless and lowly task of working the land, as opposed to the 'outside men' who are involved in public relations, relations with the outside world, the market and, of course, work outside – in other words, in France. As they count only because they are physically present in the village, they are 'emigrants at home'. Having been freed from the need to emigrate, the youngest of them are inclined to break with, or have already broken with, the traditional peasant condition, precisely because of the stable and sufficiently prestigious jobs they have. Even if they returned from France a very long time ago, the others continue to behave as 'emigrants', or in other words as 'guests in their own house' or as 'masters of the house who have returned home only in order to leave sooner or later', but who insist on perpetuating a situation and making it look as comfortable as they can for 'as long as the money from France lasts'.

When asked to describe his experience as an emigrant, and especially the contradiction he discovers between the reality of his emigrant condition and the enchanted image he previously had of France (because that was the picture his group painted for him), the informant reveals the social conditions that produce that contradiction. Because he is constantly moving between one world and the other, his whole vision of emigration – what he calls 'France' – and the discourse through which he communicates that vision are both condemned to borrowing from the two worlds in which all emigrants are involved. Being an expression of this awkward situation, language itself 'plays on' the possibility of having recourse to both the registers available to it. Quite apart from the many borrowings, some used in their original sense and others reinterpreted, it makes from French (which are emphasized in the text), the very structure of the language appears to be the result of 'strange' combinations of form and content that, apparently, do not seem to be in perfect harmony.

At times, it is by using new expressions, borrowed from the French and then reinterpreted, that the informant best succeeds in describing an experience which, even when it appears to be new, still relates to the traditional mode. Thus, *thajarnat* (day) refers to a day of waged work, or the day's wage, as opposed to a day of work performed as an act of charity or barter (*ass urattal*). At other times, and conversely, traditional forms of discourse – sayings, proverbs, ways of speaking and turns of phrase – are used to express a new content: *elghith* (help), which is part of the rain ritual in which one 'begs pity (from heaven) by sacrificing a victim', is used to refer to small incomes paid to former emigrants (they are homologous with the rain which, in peasant tradition, assured prosperity throughout the year).

The experience of emigration itself is both organized and described in accordance with traditional schemata: the informant describes 'France' by resorting to the vocabulary of the mythico-ritual system. Descriptions of emigrants' conditions of existence borrow from the great traditional oppositions: inside-outside, full-empty, light-dark, etc. No matter whether it is described as the direct opposite of the homeland (in which case it is credited with having qualities that are denied the homeland, or, conversely, it is blamed for many ills that are unknown at home) or, on the contrary, as its equivalent, at least in some respects (the presence of many relatives), France is always characterized by a series of attributes which constitute the series antithetical to that applied to the homeland, a set of homologous oppositions (see table 1). All that is needed to make the same series express the converse experience is a change of sign or, more directly, an invocation of the vocabulary of reversal which, as is well known,

Table 1

Kabylia	France	Kabylia	France
Narrow	Broad	Weak	Strong
Twisted	Straight	Evil	Good
Wrong	Right	Poor	Rich
Inverted	Upright	Dark	Light
Backward	Forward	Accursed	Blessed
Contrary	Favourable	Loneliness	Company
Difficult	Easy	Fear	Confidence
Fall	Rise	Sadness	Joy
Scorn	Value	Etc.	Etc.

plays its role in ritual practices of inversion (*aqlab*); hence the use of a whole vocabulary with mythical connotations (*abdel*, 'change'; *a'waj*, 'twisting', 'inversion'; *aqul*, 'turn inside out', etc.) and the inversions to which the opposition between the land of exile (*elghorba*) and the native land (*elghorba* becomes *le pays*) is subjected: 'the land of our birth has become *elghorba*'.

The entire discourse of the emigrant is organized around the triple truth of *elghorba*. In traditional logic, *elghorba* is associated with 'sunset' and 'darkness', with going away and isolation (amongst foreigners, and therefore exposed to their hostility and scorn), with exile and fear (the fear inspired by night and the fact of getting lost in a forest or a hostile natural environment), with being lost (because you have lost your sense of direction), or with misfortune, etc. In the idealized vision of emigration as a source of wealth and a decisive act of emancipation, *elghorba*, intentionally and violently denied in its traditional meaning, tends (without completely succeeding in doing so) to bear another truth which identifies it, rather, with happiness, light, joy, confidence, etc. The experience of the reality of emigration dispels the illusion and re-establishes *elghorba* in its original truth. It is the entire experience of the emigrant that oscillates between these two contradictory images of *elghorba*. Being unable to resolve the contradiction in which he is trapped, because he would have to abandon emigration, his only option is to mask it.

It is by using the resources of the mythical tradition that the informant produces an actual model of the mechanism by which emigration is reproduced, and in which the alienated and mystified experience of emigration fulfils an essential function. The collective misrecognition of the objective truth of emigration is the necessary mediation that allows economic necessity to exercise its power. And the misrecognition is sustained by the entire group, by emigrants who select the information they bring back when they spend time in their country, by former emigrants who 'enchant' the memories they retain of France, and by candidates for emigration who project their most unrealistic aspirations onto 'France'.

2

The Three Ages of Emigration

To stay or to go . . .
To go or to stay . . .

Refrain:
And yet my heart wonders
Whether it should stay or go,
Whether it should go or stay;
Or if it has gone or stayed
Or if it has stayed or gone.
Its illness took hold long ago
And its life, poor thing, hangs by a thread.

My heart asked me for advice. I told it to stay
Whereas it wanted to go;
So I told it to go,
Whereas it wanted to stay.
I told it to go, it wanted to stay;
I told it to stay, it wanted to go.
It if had a guide it would stay or would go.

I wait for it to change its mind
Whether to stay or to go.
So I told it to stay,
It replied that it was up to you to go.
When I tell it to go, it wants to stay;
When I tell it to stay, it wants to go.
When I give it advice, whether I speak or remain silent,
It doesn't know whether to stay or to go.

One day it went, but in its thoughts
It came back before it had gone
Our law has neither settled nor decided anything

Our luck is poor
If I go, it wants to stay
If I stay, it wants to go
While I remain perplexed
My heart bleeds from its wounds

Sliman Azzem, Kabyle singer and teller of stories of emigration

Any study of migratory phenomena that overlooks the emigrants' conditions of origin is bound only to give a view that is at once *partial* and *ethnocentric*. On the one hand, it is only the *immigrant* – and not the *emigrant* – who is taken into consideration, rather as though his life began the moment he came to France. On the other hand, the problematic, both explicit and implicit, is always that of adaptation to the 'host' society. As a result, and useful as they may be, analyses of the emigrants' world are in danger of trapping themselves into two equally abstract and reductive discourses.[1] When compared with the behavioural modes of the dominant society – the society of immigration – which are thus constituted as norms, the behaviour of emigrants inevitably seems deviant. All that remains to be done, in order to explain it, is to impute it either to their conditions of existence, which are thus regarded as being responsible for their 'dysfunctional' modes of behaviour, or to their socio-cultural conditions of origin, seen generically as a mere cultural heritage and described as 'brakes' on or 'obstacles' to the process of adaptation to the new social environment.

Rather than devoting our efforts to explaining the situation of emigrants (who are in fact immigrants) purely and simply in terms of the history of their stay in France,[2] we must take as our object the relationship between the emigrants' system of dispositions and the set of mechanisms to which they are subjected by the very fact of their emigration. That relationship can be fully understood only if we investigate the differential processes that have brought them to their present situation, and their origins must be found outside their emigration. It is only through the total reconstruction of emigrants' *trajectories* that we can understand the complete system of determinations which, having acted prior to their emigration and continuing to act, in a modified form, has brought emigrants, in the process of emigration, to their current point of arrival. If, in short, they are to be fully explained, differences noted at the point of arrival must be related both to living and working conditions in France, and to the differences that initially – i.e., prior to and independently of emigration – already distinguished the emigrant or group of emigrants. Broadly speaking, two interrelated systems of variables have been constructed in the course of each of these trajectories, of which the period of emigration is no more than one phase. On the one hand, we have variables that might be said to be *of origin* – in other words, precisely that set of social characteristics and socially determined dispositions and aptitudes the emigrants displayed prior to their entry into France (characteristics that make it possible to evaluate the position the emigrant occupied in his group of origin, such as his geographical and/or social origin, the economic and social characteristics of the group, the attitude of the group or the individual subject towards the migratory phenomenon, as established by the local tradition of emigration, etc.). On the other hand, we also have variables at the *point of arrival* – in other words, differences between immigrants in France itself (in terms of their working conditions, housing, etc.) By comparing the two series of variables, which we can do once we have reconstructed and analysed a certain number of emigrant biographies chosen because of the exemplary nature of their itinerary in immigration, we can establish how the one series is retranslated into the other, and break with the all too readily accepted representation of a homogenous and undifferentiated immigration that is always subject to the same actions and the same mechanisms.

Reintroducing complete trajectories is also a way of breaking with an 'eternalized' image of immigration which, at best, was in the past adequate for a different state of immigration. Thus, the stereotypical image of the '*noria*' continues to be applied to all immigrants.[3] Because the immigrant has been identified once and for all with the image of a man from a rural background (a peasant) who emigrated alone (i.e. without his family) and for what was, of necessity, a limited period of time, immigration is seen as a perpetual process of replenishment that brings into France – and removes from France – men who are always new (even if this is neither the first time they have emigrated nor their first stay in France) and always identical.

This representation was, at least in part, correct when Algerian emigration to France began (and probably remained accurate until the period 1949–50), provided that we overlook the differences that may have arisen between regions or between groups from the same region that had been driven apart by their recent history), but it no longer corresponds – with some exceptions – to contemporary immigration. The reason it survives even though reality gives it the lie is that it has the advantage of reassuring everyone: the host society, the country (or group) of origin and the emigrants themselves. It is in fact in everyone's interest to sustain the retrospective illusion of a relatively inoffensive immigration that does not disturb any order. It does not disturb the peasant order of the society of origin which, in order to guarantee its salvation and perpetuation, is forced to 'delegate' the function of emigration to certain of its members; it does not disturb the moral, political and social order of the host country, which can accept and use emigrants all the more easily and in greater numbers when it can allow itself to treat them as though they were simply 'in transit'; nor does it disturb the order of the emigrants themselves who, being torn between two countries, two social worlds and two conditions that differ in every respect, try to conceal – and to conceal from themselves – the contradictions of their situation by convincing themselves of its 'temporary' nature, even though it is very likely to be permanent or coextensive with their active lives. Because it conceals the indirect and undifferentiated effects of the migratory phenomenon (in other words its frequently negative aspects) and sees only the immediate benefits, the 'continual rotation' image of emigration continues to have a highly seductive appeal for all sides. The host society is convinced that it will always have at its disposal workers (single men who are of an age and in a physical condition to begin work at once) without having to pay the price (or too high a price) in terms of social problems. The society of origin thinks that it will always be able to obtain the monetary resources it needs without suffering the slightest change for the worse as a result. And the emigrants are convinced that they are fulfilling their obligations towards their group (even though they are separated from it), their land (even though they are working in factories) and their peasant status (even though they are becoming wage-earners) without necessarily feeling that they are being untrue to themselves.

Three generations, three modes of generation

A combined analysis of the differential conditions that have produced different 'generations' of emigrants (in the true sense of sets of emigrants produced in accordance with the same mode of generation), and of the diversified classes of trajectories (or itineraries) followed by different types of emigrant in the course of their emigration, reveals the extreme diversity of the immigrant population. Emigrants who belong in chronological terms to the same phase of emigration (i.e. who are of approximately the same age and the same period) but whose *mode of generation* was different, may differ in all their modes of behaviour. Conversely, those who emigrated at different times may be relatively similar, rather as though the oldest had been precursors in terms of both the genesis of their emigration and the trajectory of their immigration. Because the history of one retranslates the history of the other, phases of immigration basically correspond to phases that can be distinguished within processes of transformation internal to the rural communities that produce emigrants. Thus, each of the great periods of the recent history of rural Algerian society, each successive state of the most basic structures of the peasant economy and peasant thought, and the entire social structure of the rural world, corresponds to a distinct 'age' of emigration – in other words to a different mode of generation of emigration and a different 'generation' of emigrants. During the first age, or until (approximately) the period immediately after the Second World War, the history of Algerian emigration to France corresponded to the history of a peasant society that was fighting for survival and which expected emigration to provide it with the means to perpetuate itself as it was. In the second age, emigration offered a mass of peasants who had been not only impoverished but also totally proletarianized, a privileged opportunity – and perhaps the only opportunity they would ever have – to fulfil ambitions that their new condition both authorized and prohibited. More recently (and especially since Algerian independence), a process that began almost three-quarters of a century ago has at last been completed: emigration has finally determined the implantation in France of an Algerian community that is relatively autonomous from both the French society with which it coexists and the Algerian society in which it originated.

The first 'age': an orderly emigration

Being both an effect and an index of the collapse of the old equilibrium in which the traditional peasant society and economy persisted, the primary function of emigration to France was to provide peasant communities whose agricultural activities no longer made them self-sufficient with the means to perpetuate themselves in their existing state. So the emigrant of the day, who was divorced from his people, his land and his activities only in physical terms and on a temporary basis, was mandated by his family and, more generally, the peasant society to undertake a very specific *mission* that was of limited duration because it had limited objectives. There was no difference between the emigrant, who was an accomplished peasant, and other peasants; he may have been chosen from amongst the 'best' of them because of the seriousness of the responsibility with which he was being entrusted. Even before the sharing out of tasks between the various able-bodied men of the family or group had gradually led to a quasi-specialization, and before any distinction had been made between the 'worker inside the house' (i.e. the peasant who, being 'good' for nothing but for working on the land, did not emigrate) and the 'outside' worker (i.e. the man whose essential – and before long exclusive – function was to emigrate in order to provide hard cash), the worker or peasant who cultivated the land was also the worker or peasant who emigrated. Being good at working *on* the land and *in* the house (an accomplished peasant), he was also good at working *for* the land and the house (a good emigrant).[4] Those who were delegated to emigrate were therefore chosen on the basis of the criteria that defined peasant excellence: they enjoyed the trust of their group, but could be neither young (nor too young) nor single, even though the peasant tradition, which placed an extremely high value on working the land – to which it subordinated all other activities – insisted that tasks 'outside' agriculture (i.e. those accorded least respect by the peasant world) were, as a priority, reserved for the youngest. As the seasonal emigration of agricultural workers was the 'test bench', it was often an opportunity for emigrants to France to prove that they could maintain their ties with their group, and remain true to their peasant status and their peasant honour.

'Who do you send to market to buy or sell? You send the man you trust. You do not send a child who might be "had", who might be fooled into being cheated; you make sure that someone reliable goes with him. Nor do you send someone who might cheat you: he'd come back empty-handed...France is like the market, it's a different market, a bigger market that is further way than the [local] weekly market, a market that lasts longer, not for a day, but for months and years...The further away the market – and this is important – the more precautions you have to take. That was the way we went to France. Anyone "in whom there was no trust", either because he was too young or because he wasn't used to it, had to be entrusted to someone else, someone older and more experienced, someone who would teach him.' (Former emigrant, aged 73, who spent eleven years in France between 1934 and 1957)

Because emigration served the needs of the peasant world and was subordinate to the agricultural activity for which it provided extra income, it selected its agents in accordance with the principles of the peasant *habitus*. That was not all. Stays in France fitted in with the peasant tradition in terms of their duration (or, which comes to the same thing, the duration of absences from home), their frequency, the periodicity of departures and returns and so on. The rhythm of the latter followed the calendar of agricultural labour and the high points of the social life of the countryside rather than the demands of the industries that employed the emigrants. Departures usually took place after the ploughing had been done, or at the end of autumn and the beginning of winter. Returns coincided with harvest time and that period of the year

when social relations were at their most intense (the season for marriages and all the transactions that took place after the harvest). The
mission constituted by emigration had to be accomplished in as short a
time as possible: neither the emigrants nor their group liked their stays
in France to last too long. If, in exceptional circumstances, the emigrant
was away for longer than was permissible, he attracted the disapproval
that was directed against all those who were lacking in self-control and
who did not know how to conform to the peasant ethic: the emigrant,
because he seemed to be developing a taste for the city and his emigrant
status; his family, because it had proved itself incapable of 'recuper-
ating' him or because, being too 'greedy' (rather than too poor), it
forced him to remain absent for longer (i.e. to make more and more
money and never to be satisfied with what he had).

When the same emigrant had to return repeatedly to France (as few
times as possible), he and his group experienced those stays as so
many *single acts* that were unrelated to either the previous or the next
stay (an eventuality that became increasingly common as it became
more and more inevitable). The same experience of emigration was
perpetually repeated, with the same search for work and housing, the
same apprenticeship in the life of the immigrant: 'We are like fleas. As
soon as we have warmed up our place, we hop out of it.'

Now that he had to come to terms with urban life and to submit to all
its mechanisms (especially in terms of consumption and spending), the
'good' emigrant, or the emigrant who was praised because he had
succeeded in remaining the authentic peasant (*bou-niya*) he once was,
owed it to himself to prove that he could tolerate his new emigrant
condition and could, despite his exile, continue to live and think as an
authentic peasant. That was the precondition for being able, for
example, to adopt the behaviour of a hard and thrifty worker, which
was so highly praised (amongst peasants). Rather as though it was
feared that contact with the city would blunt their peasant virtues,
emigrants were advised above all to be careful not to imitate the city
dweller, not to eat, dress or spend like him, and not to work like
someone who is 'too fond of himself', 'who works only for his stomach'.
Anyone who imitated the city dweller inevitably 'put on greed', 'avid-
ity', 'insatiability' – that unquenchable thirst for money once one has
begun to earn some – and 'immoderation' – 'the pretensions of those
who want to take hold of the world in one hand and in a single day'.

As one demand leads to another (and, at bottom, they are perhaps
one and the same), the emigrant who owed it to himself to be attached
to peasant values also owed it to himself not to renounce the values of
the group. Because *le pays*, or *thamourth* (the family, the agnatic
group, the village and the community as a whole) occupied their

every thought and inspired all their preoccupations and modes of behaviour, emigrants found it especially comforting to be able, in France, to live together in accordance with the schema of social structures and of the network of social relations with which they were familiar. By living amongst his own people, the emigrant could derive from his group of companions the strength he needed to resist the temptations and debilitating effects of urban life.[5]

Confronted, thanks to his exile, with (urban) ways of being and acting, feeling, perceiving and spending, living and consuming that are all rejected as being incompatible with his peasant status, the emigrant takes refuge in this sort of little country that has been reconstructed in France as an extension of the great country of his birth, and thus demonstrates his generalized refusal to become part of a world (that of immigration) which he finds decidedly foreign.

> 'Emigration is a clan. He [the emigrant] only goes where those from home [*de son pays*] are.... They are all there together.... So you go there, because that's where the people you rely on, the children of your country, are to be found.... For us, our misfortune, our sickness is.... that we live together, that we are always living amongst ourselves. When you are all alone, there is fear in your life; not many are brave enough to expatriate themselves on their own. He cannot keep away, distance himself from the other, move away from people from home; this one emigrates to his brother's, and that one to his uncle's, his brother-in-law's, and they call that emigration: this is *elghorba* [exile] around the *kanoun* [the domestic hearth]. We always stay in familiar territory; like back there [*au pays*], like the way we came, the way we live here.' (S.B.)

Keeping their distance from what, objectively, they were kept distant from, making use of the psychological and cultural estrangement that kept them apart from French society and its practices (or at least those that were accessible to them): these were sacrifices they had to agree to make to an activity whose rationale was not always perceptible to them (a temporary 'lying' activity, a social status that was artificial because it was culturally and socially 'foreign' to peasant activity), and to a condition (wage-earning) that was still unfamiliar and often accompanied by a feeling of having broken the rules.

A hidden act

Being a peasant with a mandate to emigrate, and a peasant who tried to survive the ordeal of emigration without ever betraying himself as a peasant, the emigrant – now more of a peasant than ever – would go back to his community and his emigrant condition. As though nothing had happened, he would once more take up the position that was rightfully his, and which he should never have left, amongst his own people. Rather as though they wanted to eradicate every trace of emigration, the emigrant and his group agreed to join in a celebration of peasant virtues whenever they gathered together; when he went back to his village, the emigrant was the object of an almost ritual 'reintegration'. In order to 'exorcise' the urban temptations he might have brought back with him, he rejected the clothes he had worn in the city, watched his language and censored all borrowings from 'city talk' and from French; for its part, the group was attentive to the slightest perceptible indices of changes in the behaviour and intentions of the emigrant, and was not slow to note and appropriately sanction any breach of peasant decorum. As though that vigilance were not enough, the emigrant's actions were designed to pay tribute to the peasant order: his first attentions were for the land (which he visited and 'cultivated' by tracing a few symbolic furrows, even though it was the wrong season), the livestock (especially the pair of oxen, which had to be 'taken out' especially) and the village community (showing his face in the village assembly and in the mosque). In short, so long as emigration remained subordinate to the traditional order and continued to serve the peasant condition, so long as the group could control it and bend it to its own values and imperatives, emigrants (with a few rare exceptions) approached their departure as peasants and endured their stay in France as peasants; and it was as peasants that they went back to their old activities and existence.

Being designed to preserve the peasant order, the emigration '*to order*' of the first 'age' was therefore an *orderly* emigration. Multiple control mechanisms were implemented at every moment of the process (before departure, during the stay in France and on returning home) so as to neutralize its potentially harmful effects and to ensure that it led to no permanent or profound change for the worse either for the emigrants or, because of them, their society. The most successful of all the mediations used to implement these various controls was still loyalty to the group of origin and, one thing being the precondition for the other, one of the essential functions of emigrant communities was precisely to 'keep order' in emigration and, by keeping alive the memory of home [*le pays*] thanks to constant contacts with people from home [*les pays*], to perpetuate and support the peasant order.

A 'mission'

'...In the past, it was the healthiest of emigrations: they were peasants, and it was a peasants' France. The poor man left his plough and went to France; he left for France as though he were leaving for the grave. He didn't go with joy in his heart....In the past, they used to walk backwards as they left home. If it hadn't been for need snapping at their heels, they wouldn't have gone on....And the reason why these wretches lived so badly, lived on so little, was that there was one goal and only one goal: it was because they had got into their heads that they wanted their brother to marry, or to rebuild the old house. Those men had a goal to attain, and they sacrificed themselves to it: their cousin was going to sell the land back home, they couldn't let it go, it had to stay in the family, you get into debt and you send someone to France to pay your debts. That was how they came in the past. In the past, it was in order to buy a piece of land, to have a big house: a house with its land, its pair of oxen, its mule, its big men and its little men, a lot of people....It was a question of *nif* [honour]: staying big [big peasant houses], still having the oxen, the mule, even if they had to buy all the fodder for them....I know that there used to be houses that, at the beginning of summer, were already starting to buy straw, forage and barley...for their animals, for the oxen and the mule. And you need money to do that....That's why they left for France. But in France, it was double-quick time; all they wanted was to run away....It was temporary emigration; it was episodic: I came [to France] because I was forced to, I work, the constraints are removed, I go back home and if I do have to come back [to France], I come back three or four years later. Emigration was a commitment. When you devote yourself, you commit yourself for a definite time: for two years, for three years, as short a time as possible is best....'

'...The emigrant knows why [he has emigrated] and he tightens his belt. He says: "I'll sacrifice myself" – "I will get the money I need; to do so, I'll tighten my belt....It's a dog's life."...He says to himself: "I've come to work", and he would work day and night if he could. Hurry up, get on with it, that's so much put away, money set aside, less time to be spent in France. If you could see how they eat, the conditions they live in, the way they live...you have to understand them. All that to save money and to get back home quickly, to live like everyone else. There isn't anyone who doesn't love himself, but a man [of honour] is a man who forgets about himself, that's what they keep telling themselves. That is so that they can put up with all the privations...amongst us, it's more than thrift.... The poor men go without: boiled potatoes, so as to be able to save money.

'...*Thamourth! Thamourth*! ["country"] When they leave, they are still thinking about home. That is what allows him [the emigrant] to hold out, everyone thinks of home and of what he has come here to do.... The country, the house are always there before our eyes; they don't disappear even when we are asleep, in a waking state or in our dreams; their shadow is always there in front of us, that is what noble-hearted men [emigrants] with a heart never stop telling themselves.'[6]

The second 'age': loss of control

Despite all the efforts the peasant community put into controlling the emigration of its members, it could not always master all its implications, and nor could it protect itself forever against its disintegrative effects. Even if the peasant spirit on which emigration was based had not suffered other 'aggressions', starting with those resulting from contact with the colonial society and especially the generalization of monetary exchanges, emigration would have been enough to bring about its destruction. Indeed, being inseparable from attachment to the land and from the peasant community, and therefore being unable to survive a prolonged separation, the peasant attitude towards the world and towards others, which constitutes the traditional peasant, could not resist deracination for long. What is more, because emigration was the principal, if not exclusive, source of monetary revenue that was circulating in the rural milieu, it helped to spread more widely the spirit of calculation that is correlative with the use of money and, thanks to all its other economic and social effects, to transform peasant life. Emigration modified a whole lifestyle by modifying dispositions towards the economy in particular. As its own effects combined with those of other upheavals, including those that lay at its origin and which, because of its backlash effect, it tended to exacerbate, emigration finally destroyed the peasant spirit that inspired it and had sustained the first emigrants. It thus accelerated and exacerbated a process of 'depeasantification' (Bourdieu and Sayad 1996: 15–60) that was already under way (in varying degrees, depending on which regions, social groups and individuals were involved). 'Depeasantification' was the result of all the economic and social transformations that had occurred within peasant society (partly as a result of emigration itself), and its necessary effect was to modify totally the initial preconditions for emigration. To the extent that they reflected a generalized disillusionment with working on the land and with the old conditions of existence, and because they led to a systematic modification of patterns of behaviour and the peasant ethos, the new conditions experienced by the rural world were to generate a new form of emigration and a new type of emigrant. The emigrant of the first 'generation' was as different from the emigrant of the second 'generation' as the *bou-niya* or 'authentic' peasant (who was increasingly rare), or at least the 'still peasantified' peasant who, despite being impoverished, was striving to remain a peasant in the face of everything and everyone, was from the 'depeasantified' peasant. He only appeared to be a peasant, because everything about him negated traditional peasant values (aspirations towards non-agricultural, full-time waged labour, and economic individualism, but also social individualism, urbanization and its system of behaviour, especially in terms of consumption). Whereas the first-generation emigrant could go on thinking of himself as a peasant, even though there was no possibility of his really behaving as a peasant, the emigrant of the next generation had ceased to be a peasant in both his own mind and his intentions, independently of his emigration and often long before he had emigrated. Whilst the first emigrant exiled himself from the world he was familiar with only in order to perpetuate himself as a peasant, and made only minimal sacrifices (of time, interest and attention) to his emigration, the new emigrant seemed to expect his emigrant condition to give a meaning and a function to his existence and his activity.

Unlike 'first-age' emigration, 'second-age' emigration was to provide the break with the peasant community that was objectively inscribed in the social characteristics of the emigrants of the day with the opportunity to become a reality. Several factors could, no doubt, encourage emigrants to reject one thing after another, but a total reorientation of their practices towards a more pronounced individualism was possible – as one break leads to another – only if they refused, at the very least, to sustain a privileged relationship with the emigrant community.

'Hello, goodbye, I'm polite to everyone [other emigrants], but I prefer to live alone. Each to his own idea; they have their habits, but I'm different. I've drifted away from them, and that's all for the better, that way there is no trouble. . . . It's not that I reject them, but I prefer not to live with them, all on top of one another' (S.B.)

As it was no longer a mission entrusted by the group to one of its members, but the act of an individual acting on his own initiative and on his own behalf, emigration was becoming an individual undertaking that had lost its initial collective objective. Emigrating was no longer a way of helping the group, but a way of escaping its constraints. It was no longer a way of serving the communitarian objective – and still less was it a way of living in accordance with hallowed customs. There was only one objective, which was no longer to live, as in the past, amongst other emigrants and in the same way as them, but to have an original individual experience. This form of emigration proved to be a fundamentally individualist 'adventure'.

> 'Nowadays, there is also emigration as adventure; you have an adventure, you have the guy who goes on an adventure; that guy is all alone, even if "adventurer" is not quite the word. It means that he looks after himself, all alone, that he gets by on his own, without relying on anyone.... You are on your own, you have to do something because you no longer rely on anyone, you have to defend yourself, there is no longer anyone else to defend you; you are on your own, you have to do something, work and even work harder than you would have to do otherwise.... I've tried my luck all by myself: when you want to do that, you have to be able to take responsibility for your own actions.' (S.B.)

Provided that the old attachment to the group and to the values that founded the group had broken down, emigration also provided the opportunity for a long and laborious apprenticeship in new modes of behaviour, which were different in every respect to the communitarian attitudes that were de rigueur in the earlier state of rural society and emigration.

Being more deeply affected by the transformations of the rural world and by the new conditions of existence in the rural milieu, the young, who were also less attached to the land and the peasant community, were more likely to display dispositions that might further estrange them from traditional agriculture and the old ways, and would make them look for jobs in the modern sector on a permanent basis. It is therefore not surprising that they should have been the first to try to emigrate or that there should have been so many of them. This development emerges very clearly if we compare the social characteristics of the emigrants of these two 'generations'. There was very little of the peasant about the second generation emigrants – for lack of *habitus* rather than lack of land, as it happens – and they were, on average, younger when they came to France.[7] They were also more likely to be single – and that was not simply because they were young.[8]

> 'Most of these emigrants [those of the second "generation"] came when they were young.... Because they had other ideas in their heads, they didn't get married. Oh yes, if you're looking for adventure, when if you've decided to do what you like, to just do things

your own way, to work for yourself and not for others, for your stomach, for your head – and you are criticized for it – then you must not get married.' (S.B.)

Perhaps because they emigrated at an increasingly young age, but more probably because they were 'depeasantified', they were less likely to have been farmers or, a fortiori, shepherds before they emigrated.

As the process of 'depeasantification', which lies at the origin of second-generation emigration, continues, the bases of emigration expand until they affect (unevenly) the whole countryside and, more recently, a fraction of the urban population. All able-bodied men (and not only those in a determinate age cohort) in the rural groups on which it has already had a marked effect are equally affected by emigration, quite irrespective of their position within the family or their attitude towards the peasant condition (as a general rule, these are no longer *bou-niya* peasants, but peasants who sustain, as best they can, an outward semblance of 'peasantness'). Similarly, none of the families that were once reluctant to emigrate can avoid doing so now. Emigration now affects even *maraboutiques* families which pride themselves on their 'prestige' (even if it is a thing of the past) and their social 'vocation' (even if the real world has destroyed it) for producing 'clerics' (who might be *bou-niya*, but not manual labourers), and which therefore will not allow themselves to 'break the rules', and especially not by emigrating – i.e. giving themselves up to an activity that borders on the *illicit*, to the most profane of all profane activities. It also affects the old landed families, who were the last to be contaminated, and who made it a point of honour 'not to work on others' land, either on land belonging to others or in the service of others'. Now that it no longer spares anyone, emigration has become the common condition of the vast majority of men, if not all men.[9]

What is more, because a major exodus of rural populations (especially from those regions that were won over to emigration to France long ago) has transferred potential emigrants to France to towns within Algeria itself,[10] the earlier trend is being completely reversed. Urbanization of the future emigrant (in other cases, the family of an emigrant who is already in France is urbanized by going to an Algerian city) now tends to take place at one stage before actual emigration to France, whereas when emigration was almost exclusively a matter of movement between the Algerian countryside and France, it was quite exceptional for it to be converted into urban emigration within Algeria itself.

This new form of emigration, which might have been expected to provide the basis for a 'forced' urbanization that is both inscribed in the reality of the rural world and impossible for that world, contains within it the very mechanisms that perpetuate it. It is one way – and in some cases the easiest, or the only accessible way – of satisfying the new economic and social demands that have been forced upon peasant society. Emigration has to supply, in ever-increasing quantities, the monetary income that rural communities now require *as a matter of course. And it must do so on a continuous basis.* Some of the first emigrants saved money in France until they had the nest egg they needed and then brought it back with them (having borrowed from emigrant relatives on their arrival in France, they spent their time there repaying the debts they had contracted). Others, who left later or at a time when they were already forced to extend their stay or to make more than one stay, transferred the whole of their savings by sending relatively large sums home (usually in the form of postal orders), as the idea of keeping some of their wealth for themselves seemed scandalous to them. The second-phase emigrant, by contrast, is solely concerned with meeting current expenses – both his expenses in France and those of the family he has left behind at home – and devotes himself to providing the latter only with help with food: the postal orders become regular, usually monthly, and are calculated to cover identifiable and predictable needs.[11]

'My whole life is in there'

'My whole life is in there [he shows a fat wallet containing pay slips, attestations of employment, service record, correspondence from the social security and the pension fund; throughout the interview he constantly puts these papers into his wallet, only to take them out a moment later]. It's all together in there: there's my toil, my sweat, my blood – yes, my blood, because my blood flowed, I was injured. It took an effort to collect all that, I thought I was going to be robbed, that they were going to eat all my work.... There's twenty-three years of work in there; and even then they've stolen at least four years from me. In the early years there was none of all that, we didn't know all those things: you've done your work, here's your money, get on with it.... Fortunately, I was careful – ever since I've been [a man], I've always kept my papers – and so does the mine, because they keep everything too, they remember everything, you don't lose a single day [of work] if it's written down in the records. Otherwise, it would have vanished into thin air; that's how the first years [of work] vanished into thin air. My France would have been reduced to nothing, I'd have got nothing out of it! It would have been as though I'd never come, never worked, toiled. God has preserved my toil. He did not want it to be lost.... It's good to keep all these papers, good or bad; you never know, you don't know which to keep, so you keep them all.... It's a good idea to keep them, it's a precaution...; you don't know what might happen tomorrow. The paper you throw away today, that's the one you'll need tomorrow.' (Former emigrant, aged 63, temporarily resident in France waiting for his pension to be settled, staying in the hotel where he lived when he was a worker and where he has found, as he puts it, 'perhaps not exactly the same people as in the past, but the children of those people, because things have remained as they were: the walls, the owners, the clients')

As the meaning and function of emigration have changed, it has had to be reorganized from top to bottom. From one generation of emigrants to the next, the modalities of their stays in France and, therefore, their relations with emigration itself, with the emigrant condition and with their country of origin, have all been modified. Stays have become so long as to become almost permanent,[12] or interrupted only by short periods coinciding with annual holidays. Correlatively, it is increasingly the case that trips home, which are now subordinated to the calendar of industrial activity, occur at holiday times and for the full duration of the holiday.

'You come to France for a while, you act as though you were here for a while, but, year after year, then it's five years, then ten years, then twenty years, and then you retire! When you add it up, it's your whole life. If they stay here until they retire, how much of the thirty years, or the twenty-five years, have they spent what I call living – one month in twelve, working eleven months to live for one – I mean living amongst their families, with their own people, with their children, their wives? With an average of twelve months in twelve years, he [the emigrant] will have lived one month a year at home: the twelfth month! That's what you should be saying.' (S.B.)

By giving the emigrant, who is no longer a 'peasant' without necessarily being a 'worker', a stable and long-term job, emigration does, of course, provide him with monetary gains, but it also gives him a definite status. Quite apart from its economic significance, the ambition to learn a trade (which, in many cases, means emigration) is also a desire to have a status that can be named and that can wrest the 'depeasantified' peasant away from the indeterminate nature of his position. Being neither a full time traditional fellah nor a wage-earner defined by the activity he performs, and not even really unemployed, but combining something of all those things, he experiences with an immense feeling of unease the ambiguity of a status that has no legitimate definition. Not having (and knowing that they do not have) the aptitudes needed to make their mark in Algeria, where the labour market is extremely restricted and dominated by competition from urban workers (or the urban unemployed), second-generation rural emigrants in France know – not from direct experience, but from habit and almost a social sense of what is accessible to them – that their only chance of finding a real job is synonymous with their emigration to France.

Amongst 'depeasantified' peasants who are candidates for emigration, the conviction that they will not be able to find in Algeria the work they so badly want is so strong that it discourages them from looking for work there or, to be more accurate, prevents them from even thinking of looking for work at home before they emigrate. None of the emigrants interviewed had attempted or had been tempted to try to find work in an Algerian town. Even when they did go back to their own country both more regularly and more frequently (at most, every two years) only a few of them – 6 out of 280 – had, at least once, made a real job application either in person or by writing to a potential employer: only 19 other emigrants had tried to do so to set their minds at rest – in other words, they had made it known to those around them that they wished 'to be able to find a job so as to stay and not to have to leave for France again', or had turned to an intermediary, 'a relative, a friend, someone born and bred there who is in a good position to procure them a job'.

'Algeria, land of unemployment. Algeria, no work, no factories. Algeria, where there are lots of hands, so many hands that there is no work for them. When you have nothing in your hands, no trade and don't know how to do anything, you're not going to turn up in Algiers looking for work ... you come to France. ... There is work in France, everyone knows that; you never hear it said that so and so, this one or that one has left, and isn't working, is unemployed. It just doesn't happen. ... So you come to France: your brother, your cousin, all the men in your village, all the men of your age – you're just like them, and they're just like you – they all find work in France, so you come to France too and you are sure to find work. ... In Algiers, you are not sure to. How can you be sure, when no one [no one he knows] has found work there: [someone] like me, of course; if he is a 'son of the town', if he is educated, if he has a trade, of course, he will find ...' (Emigrant of rural origin, but educated at a French school for five consecutive years; came to France aged 21 in 1954, joined by his family – his wife and daughter – in 1957. Has been back to his own country on no more than four occasions, twice on his own, before and after his family emigrated, and twice with his family)

The increase in and the continuity of the time these emigrants spend in France, the periodicity of their trips back home and the quality of the time they spend in the *pays*, prove, if proof were needed, that the economic and social life of their rural communities of origin has been subordinated to the industrial activity of the country that uses the emigrants' services. The *economic* integration of emigrants into the host country's market is manifested in thousands of ways, the most significant being, on the one hand, the emigrants' attitude towards their work, their trade and everything to do with it and, on the other hand, the efforts by which they betray their awareness of having a new *social identity* – or at least of being in search of that new identity – defined, this time, more by their position as workers (and therefore immigrants) than by their position as peasants who have emigrated.

The identity of the emigrant

'Wage slips, wage slips, nothing but wage slips! No matter where you apply for a job, that's all they want! . . . You'd think they were afraid you were going to eat their bread, bread that you haven't earned. So much for trust. It's incredible how much trust there is in this society, how much trust there is in the workers! Let's say no more about it. But when it comes to us, to the immigrants, it's unbelievable: when it comes to us, they're immediately suspicious, and it's not just the regulations. It's not just regulations. When it comes to us, you have to prove that you've earned your money, otherwise you've stolen it, and you become suspect. You have to show them that you have enough to live on, otherwise you're a thief or a beggar, and it's the same in both cases; it's not allowed, especially when you're an immigrant. A foreigner, an immigrant is meant to be working; if an immigrant isn't working, why not? What use is he? What is he doing here? . . . You go to the post office to send your money home, you have to prove that you earned it, in other words that you haven't stolen it; at the social security, you have to prove that you're in work. I think that even before you can die in France, you have to prove that you worked, that you worked yourself to death . . . . If you don't die in an accident, they have to find your pay slips on you, otherwise you don't have the right to die. So what are you here? Nothing but a monthly pay slip. Without a pay slip, they don't accept you; they don't trust you; that's what wage slips are for; you have to prove to them that you're working, that you've worked for them, otherwise you're suspected of living off them.' (Emigrant aged 28; living in

France for only three years, relatively well educated (three years of secondary school); employed in the service sector, an insurance company, where he does both manual and intellectual labour: 'When I have to go down to the archives to sort the parcels, I'm doing a labourer's job...when I have to help in the office, I'm a pen-man, an intellectual! That's the way it is, you have to do everything')

Realizing that they must insert themselves more actively into the professional world to which they have dedicated themselves in France, today's emigrants have had to modify their attitude completely, especially where work is concerned. Unlike their elders, they adopt a narrower and more 'self-seeking' attitude, and that results in a greater stability in employment. They tend to remain with the same firm,[13] (or, failing that, the same branch of activity), and in the same place of residence;[14] Greater attention is paid to professional activity (in relative terms and within the strict limits authorized by their situation as emigrants), to having a 'career', to the advantages that accrue from length of service, to the mode of remuneration and how it is calculated, to the life of the company, to social or union activities, to the possibility of promotion, etc.

In terms of the acquisition of the calculating attitude that is encouraged by the experience of waged labour in France, working out overtime plays – as one can readily imagine – an important role. As it makes up a large proportion of their overall monthly income and is responsible for most variations in wages, overtime is the object of detailed and minute attention on the part of even illiterate – and, one is tempted to say, especially illiterate – emigrants.[15]

When overtime is reduced, or when there is no overtime, the monthly wage often loses one quarter of its value. The adoption of the calculating disposition that is part and parcel of wage-earning is therefore not an abstract (or intellectual) process, but something that is learned from harsh experience, from the repeated experience of going for days (or fortnights or months) with or without overtime. Some fortnights and some months are 'leaner' than others, and when that happens, the family's postal order is smaller or non-existent: 'that month, you have to tighten your belt by another notch'. Their ability to avoid having to resort to working overtime is conditional upon their having achieved a certain status and having certain skills, as the comments of this emigrant demonstrate:

'I hate overtime. The boss is the only one who benefits. You have to be stupid, as stupid as an animal, as stupid as a worker or an immigrant [laughter] to believe that that's the way to get rich. . . . Yes, our people do chase after overtime; that's all they have to live on, with the starvation wages they get on building sites or as labourers: 1,600, 1,800, never 2,000. They have to make a living, so they make up for it by working overtime so as to be able to send money home.... But it's no answer. Besides, overtime is for labourers and OS,[16] men like me don't work overtime.... As far as I'm concerned, they can keep their overtime, I have to make a living and work is not just about making money.' (Emigrant, aged 30, educated, although from a rural background, two years of vocational training in Algeria, adult vocational training in France, electromechanical engineer; skilled worker [*ouvrier qualifié*], monthly salary of 3,000–3,200 francs; single, sends almost no money back to Algeria; spends his annual holidays in European countries, has visited Italy, Spain, the Balearics and Austria; on the one occasion he did decide to spend a month's holiday in Algeria, he spent seventeen days in Morocco on his way back)

As emigrants' contact with the social organization of labour in the factory becomes more prolonged and intensified, and as all the determinisms inscribed in waged labour begin to have more effect, a new social identity is forced upon them. Their old identity, which, despite emigration, remained inseparable from their membership of the group of origin, the peasant condition and the system of values that went with it, is replaced by a new way of defining themselves, and a different self-representation. This has an effect on the old schemata of perception and evaluation, which are reinterpreted to fit the circumstances.[17] The mediation responsible for this conversion appears, at first sight, to be the 'effect' of the wage slips themselves, which, in the eyes of emigrants, embody and symbolize their new condition as workers or, to be more accurate, as emigrants who have 'settled into' the emigrant condition.

Quite aside from his relationship with work, it is the emigrant's whole relationship with French society (at least to the extent that it is accessible to him) that is transformed. Unlike his predecessor, who was confined or chose to confine himself within the 'refuge-world' constituted by emigrants and who excelled at cultivating an attitude of 'reserve' or self-segregation, the new emigrant, being more 'integrated' at least into the condition of the working class, is forced into a (relatively) closer encounter with French society. The difference between the two attitudes can be seen in the different perceptions that emigrants of the two 'ages' have of their position within emigration, and in the reactions that their modes of behaviour provoke on the part of French society Whilst the 'good behaviour' (or the social sense of limits which, in certain conditions, was a distinctive characteristic of the dominated of the first age) had the effect of protecting them against racism (at least in its most manifest form), the (social) audacity of the second-age emigrants predisposes them to a sharper and more frequent experience of racism.

Segregation and self-segregation

'Act stupid, act more stupid than you are, like everyone else: shut your eyes, see nothing; block your ears, hear nothing. There is a remedy for that sort of racism: you stay at home, within our own limits, stay on your guard, that's all; we're used to it. Time passes, nothing lasts, you're just passing through.... Remember that you are not at home, don't forget that, you are a foreigner in a foreign country.... That's the truth, and the truth is your salvation.... Don't be provocative; besides, that's what good behaviour means: watch yourself, take precautions, and whatever you do, never put yourself in a situation where you might feel you're being scorned. If you're not careful, that's your problem.... If anything happens to you, it's your own fault, you were asking for it!... Keep your distance, don't be hostile towards them – as if we were hostile when it's always us that's gets the hostility. So why mix with them [the French]? What reason do you have you to mix with them? As little as possible is best.... Stay amongst us, and you'll see: racism and racists don't exist! That's what you hear, that's what the old men used to tell you, when you complained about racism. There's a lot of talk of racism now, but it wasn't talked about in those days. Racism has always existed, but it does not exist when we are amongst ourselves. Stay in your room, amongst your brothers, they're all like you so there's nothing to be afraid of, no one knows you, you don't know anyone. Where is the racism going to come from, how can it get in? Through the door or the window? It won't jump on you from across the *kanoun* [hearth]. Your poverty, your hunger, your worries, that's your racism. That's enough, you don't need to go looking for the racism of others: that of the French, leave it to them, leave it where it is, keep away from it.... Come and live amongst us, with everyone you can see here, and can I promise you that you won't know what racism is.... Amongst us, the word does not exist, it's a word we never pronounce, and you will never hear it. Personally, I don't know what it is.... But if you go looking for it, you'll find it every day and you mustn't complain.... When you don't want to have any dealings with them [the French], you will never come up against racism: [nobody suffers from] racism if they don't want to.

'...We are careful. You see them [the French] dressed up on Sundays, and you say to yourself: after all, I'm like them too, I earn the same pay as them, I ought to be like them too.... The ones who think like that are the most disappointed. You notice that you are not dressed like them, you see that you are not fashionable; there's always a frontier, you're not the same as them.... He [the emigrant] begins to take an interest in girls: he goes to a dance, and that is where he discovers racism: you discover that there is always a barrier. The worst racism is the racism of the dance hall. Especially when you try to mix with French people that way ... it's not just at dances that you encounter racism. Even at work, you can't be anything but a labourer; they're not used to that. If they see you trying to get on a bit, they tell you: "You're not like the rest." Afterwards, it depends: if you don't get in their way, they think it's funny too; they laugh at you, and you become a general laughing stock ... now, if you do begin to get in their way, they imagine that you're treading on their toes, and then they turn against you. "Get back to your own country, get back to where you came from, you're just an Arab!" That means, go back to your brothers, go home; "home" might mean the *bled*, but it could also be Barbès ....[18] Of course you have to work, but there's always a certain racism, and there always will be. That's the way it is: either they don't give a damn about you, or they put you down. They've never seen a Kabyle foreman, an Algerian or an Arab boss. It's unheard of where they come from. So they do all they can to put a spoke in your wheel; they can go as far as to refuse to speak to you. It does happen.... Before I became a foreman, I used to be a team leader, and even that irked them: they don't like having an Arab giving them orders. The only thing is, when that's the way it is, it always gets sorted out; the boss, it's in his interest: that's because they need you, that's all, and because you cost them less. Otherwise, a foreigner is a foreigner; skilled or unskilled, you are always a foreigner.... There aren't many of us [*ouvriers qualifiés*: skilled workers], but there are still too many of us as it is: our place is in the immigrant jobs, as they put it, all the filthy jobs where you lose your health and perhaps even your life.' (S.B.)

Because he stands out from other emigrants of his era, even in his attitude towards French society, the 'marginal' emigrant who is described as (socially) *audacious* uses his own categories of perception (in the dance hall, at work, especially if he is an *ouvrier qualifié* [OQ]) to compare his experience of racism with the experience of the emigrants he has abandoned and who, as they remind him, prefer to exclude themselves rather than run the risk of segregation.

When he returns to his family, to his village, to his peasant community, the emigrant goes home as a 'holiday-maker'. He is virtually a 'foreigner' in a world that seems increasingly foreign to him.[19] Everything about the way he behaves – his use of time, the hours he keeps, his activities, his movements, his leisure activities, his spending habits, his eating habits (the number of meals he eats, the time he eats them, the things he eats), his clothes – is designed to remind everyone of his emigrant status (i.e. a city dweller), of his position as 'a guest in his own house'. In other words, his behaviour is designed to show how emigration has allowed him to distance himself with respect to his group and with respect to the common condition of the peasants. It is with some ostentation that he usually refuses to take part in agricultural labour, when it is still done with any conviction.

If by chance an emigrant 'on holiday' does agree to take part in agricultural labour and other acts of peasant piety (visiting the fields, agrarian rites), he does so on condition that he can behave 'in his own way', as an 'emigrant' – in other words as he sees fit (partly as a joke and partly out of exhibitionism) and in accordance with his 'French habits' ('the way we work in France', 'working French hours' and in 'French work clothes and turned out in French style'). If he does agree to take part in communitarian manifestations, acts of religious fervour (prayers, pilgrimages and alms-giving) or traditional sociability, it is often a matter of pure ostentation, and with a sort of 'hypercorrection'. He conforms to all these practices, which he knows are both in keeping with peasant tradition and out of date, only in a gratuitous and external way. He does so to prove that he can be an 'emigrant', and at the same time be willing and able to challenge even the best peasants when it comes to peasant excellence (working as well, eating just as frugally, honouring his obligations with as much dignity as the traditional peasant).

> 'We may well be emigrants, but we still know how to work [the land] when we have to.... Because we've been through it [the state of being peasants] we can go back to the land of our fathers and grandfathers if we have to...and perhaps more easily and better than the men of today, these youngsters who have never worked, either "in the house" [at home, on the land] or "outside the house" [i.e., in emigration]. We know how to be fellahs too; we've forgotten nothing...
>
> 'We don't like to talk about anything but our work in France! In reality, if we worked here [at cultivating the land] as much as we do in France, eight-hour days, ten-hour days, we would be "winners".... We like working in France, that's all. But basically, it is harder, more tiring, and longer; it never ends, summer or winter, day or night. A whole day spent ploughing or harvesting is much less tiring than getting through a day in the factory.' (Words of an emigrant who, half-seriously and half-jokingly, is justifying himself for spending a few days of his holiday harvesting the fields of his aunt, an old widow who lives alone. But he has left a sharecropper to work the best of his own land, and has left the rest fallow)

It is not only the 'behaviour of a holiday-maker' that the emigrant introduces into his group. He also introduces a great number of attitudes imbued with a calculating spirit and the economic and social individualism that goes with it, and these have more serious implications.

'The way we live now'

'To "find" your son these days, you have to flatter him, take precautions with him, pay him in kind words, speak softly; you mustn't upset him, and even then you can't be sure of the outcome; you do all that and hold in your stomach [be afraid]. Only lies are acceptable. I admire the courage of fathers who dare to say that their children are bad children; it isn't nice for anyone, unless it is whispered and under the seal of secrecy. They softly whisper the truth in your ear, and then it's all you hear: "By God, he [the emigrant son or brother] has abandoned me, there isn't even a letter from him, I let him know this and that, sent so and so to see him, he's aware of everything, knows everything [implying: "knows what we need"]. We just pretend..." And there are a lot of them who just pretend. What can I say? That my son has abandoned me, that he is a bad son! There are still some who cannot do that, they are ashamed of themselves. You ask them for news of their children: "Fine. Everything's fine. Couldn't be better." – Your son remembers you, thinks of you [sends you money]? – "Oh yes, thank God." Even though the truth is that the poor wretch hasn't a penny and has had no news from his son.... That's the way it is in the modern world we live in. Partly out of discretion, a sense of proportion, self-respect [honour]; partly self-interest and as a precaution, for the future – you never know, you mustn't rush things, perhaps God will bring him back to the straight and narrow one day, he will make amends – best not to say too loudly that your son has abandoned you. Why say it? They'll only laugh at you and despise you all the more.... On the contrary, if word gets around, you have to deny it: the letter came last week, even if it [actually] dates from last year. The last postal order hasn't been cashed, even if it is five years old.... No one will contradict you, even though it is easy to tell that it's a lie from the way you are behaving.... But if you start complaining in public to Kaddour and Chabane [anyone who comes along], it will become public knowledge and, very quickly, what could be seen as a youthful mistake, an *elghorba* mistake [exile, in this case the seductions of the town], will become a divorce between father and son.... Obviously, when the father behaves like that, fears the shame of having to admit that he has a bad son, the son certainly wouldn't like to look like a bad son either. They could at least agree about that. We have a lot of people in France, and it's the same there as it is here: there are things that you hide, and things that you cannot hide, and the thing you cannot hide is the way you behave.... I've been through it too in France: everyone knows everything, you can't hide anything: I suppose that when someone drinks or gambles, it's obvious and cannot go unnoticed; it is not worth asking him [asking the father of the emigrant if that is how he behaves] if his son is a "good son", if he works for his parents. But despite that, there are still things that you hide. "Did you send your father a postal order?" "Yes, last week." It's always last week. I suppose a lot of people lie like that. It's better that way: that's *baraka* [luck]: what we get from him [the emigrant] is more than we need, and may *baraka* be with him.' (Father of two emigrants, his only two sons: one, a bachelor who has been in France for more than fifteen years, is totally 'lost', has never written, has never sent money and has never 'set foot' in the village; the other, who is younger and married with three children and who has already spent more than ten years in emigration, does little more to help his family)

Undermined and amputated by emigration, thrown out of order, wounded deep inside, in other words in all its structures (morphological, economic, spatial and temporal), the peasant group loses faith in its own values. In addition to the material poverty that lay at the origin of emigration and its sequence of disruptive effects, there is now also a moral poverty that reveals the internal crisis that haunts the group, and it renders it particularly vulnerable to any borrowings and any transformations. As emigration progresses, the peasant community gradually loses its old ability to control and regulate it. The community is completely restructured around emigration, but is no longer able to integrate its effects. The changes affecting the structure of the peasant family provide an exemplary illustration of these disruptions, which can in part be imputed to the indirect effects of emigration.

The relationship that initially linked emigration to a system of joint ownership and responsibility (*indivision*), that ancient form of internal organization within the family and domestic production, is also inverted, just as relations between emigration and agricultural activity are inverted. Whereas joint ownership originally existed prior to emigration, and made it possible, a makeshift arrangement is now reconstituted on a temporary basis for the sole purpose of making emigration possible. The emigrant finds a substitute who 'can come in and go out for his people, in his stead and in his place'. The relative who stays at home simply manages the funds that are sent to him, and it cannot be said that the services rendered are totally devoid of self-interest on his part (in many cases the emigrant gives his correspondent 'something extra' whenever he sends him a postal order, not to mention the parcels and other gifts he sends). Being accustomed to calculating and doing all they can to valorize the product of their labour, emigrants tend increasingly to resent this system as an additional expense rather than as a guarantee of security. Even amongst close relations (brothers who are placed under the authority of a father who is still alive and who are therefore necessarily living under an arrangement of joint ownership, between father and son, etc.), calculations and the calculating spirit introduced by emigration, undermine the foundations of the solidarity of old and destroy the feeling of fraternity which once knit the family together.

'That's their due'

'I send them only what I see fit because they ask for hundreds of thousands [of old francs]. They don't ask for a little. . . . I send a postal order and I ask them to send me accounts, to tell me how they have spent the money: we bought this for so much, we spent so much on this and that. Until they do that, I wouldn't dream of sending them another postal order; if they don't send me their accounts, too bad, they get nothing. . . . . In any case, I know what they need; they can't fool me by saying the same thing over and over again: we need semolina, we have to pay the workers [waged labourers recruited on a daily basis to work on the land]. They always say the same thing. . . . 100,000 [old] francs every three months, that's their "due", that's enough, unless there are exceptional expenses. . . . I've become their "monthly supplier" [*achahar*, from *achhas*: 'month']. It's wrong for some to work and for others to fold their arms [literally, 'knot their limbs'] and to eat what others have worked for; it's not right for me to "starve" in France and for everything to reach them back there ready-cooked. . . . My money is better [invested] here: I need to have money at my side too; it keeps me warm, it keeps me company. Trust has vanished from the world; nowadays, there is no more trust between brothers, or between father and son. . . . It's for me, my stomach comes first. My stomach is apart from everything else; if it is satisfied, it is self-satisfied, if it is hungry, it is the only stomach to be hungry, and whether other stomachs are full or empty, it makes no difference to mine'. (Emigrant from a family that is relatively rich in land, with three emigrants in France – i.e. all the adult men in the family, with the exception of their father, an old man who was, in his day, also an emigrant in France)

Separation

'All this [the quarrel with his father] came about because he [his father] wanted us to stay the same for ever. . . . He'd already tricked me over my marriage, he tricked me at a time when I didn't want to get married; he tricked me when I was twenty-one. You have to get married. My mother was on his side too: get married, get married!

They did it to keep me quiet; they were frightened of I don't know what: that I would run off, that I would sleep around, that I would bring them back a French girl.... But once I was married, leaving the house was out of the question, we all had to live together on top of one another, even though the house was small.... I had to bring my pay home and leave it over there on the mantelpiece until monsieur saw fit to give me something.... It's no life, my wife suffered martyrdom for two years; going out was out of the question for her.... Then I found a two-roomed apartment; okay, it's expensive; it was in a filthy state when I found it, I had it done up, too bad if it cost me money, I borrowed it and repaid it.... We left with just the clothes we stood up in, with nothing, absolutely nothing, not even underwear, not a plate; we ran away. Fortunately, afterwards, gradually, my mother and sisters brought us something every day.... Fortunately, my mother and my wife have always got on, have always been on good terms; the quarrel is between my father and me. As he himself used to say, it used to be the daughter-in-law and the mother who quarrelled, it was the mother-in-law who drove out the daughter-in-law. Now, it's between father and son, it's the father who drives out the son. I think he's understood. He wanted to keep me at home by marrying me off, but it was marriage that made me leave home.' (30-year old emigrant who came to France in 1951 at the age of 11. Holds a CAP [certificat d'aptitude professionnelle] in accountancy, has followed courses in law (basic qualification in law) and other management disciplines at the Conservatoire national des arts et des métiers. Eldest boy in the family, married in France to a girl from his village (marriage arranged by mother), who also has a CAP and is an office worker. Both employed by the same employer, a small bonded forwarding agency)

The rejection of the community and solidarity of old that results from emigration is now becoming more widespread, and it is resented all the more strongly because everyone – and emigrants more so than anyone else because, ultimately, only their paid work is regarded as real work – is convinced that they are working on behalf of someone else. We thus find a total modification, within the family, of relations between different generations. Because emigration was in many cases an opportunity for young men to emancipate themselves from the authority of their families and to escape for ever from the servitude of devalorized agricultural work, it ensured their promotion and led to a reinterpretation of family roles and an inversion of the old hierarchies. Because they alone could supply the monetary needs of their families, emigrants tended, even though they were young and absent from home, to take on the functions and authority of the head of the family, which used to be the prerogative of its oldest members. They are no longer accountable[20] to the head of the family for their work or for how they make use of the product of their labour, as they were in the past. On the contrary, they now demand an explanation, based on the accounts they keep, of what has happened to their remittances, to the share of *their* money they send to their families.

And yet, no matter how great the emigrant's contribution to the domestic economy, no one – neither the emigrant himself nor his family – is easily reconciled to these totally disenchanted relationships:

> 'He sent me money, but not a single word to go with it . . . I know it's him because I know I have a son in France. . . . He hasn't "left" us when it comes to money, but as for anything else, nothing. . . . He's a complete miser: no letters, not a word, no greetings, no sign . . . we never have the joy of seeing him come home.' (Mother of an emigrant, speaking to someone who asked for news of her son)

> 'You tell him: "France is not just money. If the money is there, so much the better; if it's not there today, it will be there tomorrow. In any case, it will never be enough, work as you may, persevere, so you'd best come back like everyone else, and at the same time as everyone else." You tell him: "Your mother, your mother tells you to come back empty-handed, I'll take care of everything else [gifts for relatives, or in exchange for those that have been received]." All he has to do is come back, go out and come in [the door of the house]: everyone will see that we have a man too. The day he comes home means more to me than all he will earn in a month, more than the cost of the journey: a hundred thousand, two hundred thousand, that's all. Too bad for them [the sums of money].' (Mother using a go-between to insist that her son should make up his mind to come home at the same time as everyone else, i.e. during the holidays)

> 'Anyone who has a worker in France obviously expects more than just money from him. They also need a host of those little things we call *tsafakour*, remembrances; it's nothing, just little things, a greeting, a word.' (Father of an emigrant who says he has been 'abandoned' by his son in his heart but not in his pocket [money])

Just as relationships within the family have been transformed, so the entire system of economic (and symbolic) exchanges between the generations is being modified.

> 'In the past, the paths were clearly marked out: children worked for their parents, and that's all there was to it. They rose [grew up] in the house amongst those who worked, and they worked with them; the ones who did not work were the "grown ups" in the house. When the "grown ups" left, others came to take their place, and so on; perhaps their turn will come one day [the turn of today's youngsters],

and it will come. Why not? At least that is what they tell themselves. In the meantime, all they have to do is work, inside the house and outside, at home and abroad. In those days, everyone had their place, and everyone knew their place; everyone worked for all, for the house, and the house worked for all; there were no "little houses inside the house"... Everything was in order, because no one had anywhere to go. Where could they go? Where could they run to? The house wasn't going anywhere.'

This description by an old man of how it used to be has been replaced by a different state of relations between the generations in which the young have set themselves up as their parents' 'protectors'. Whilst we know what young men (emigrants) contribute to the new structure of the distribution of tasks when they still fulfil their obligations – to provide essentially monetary resources – one might wonder what the old give in return. In order to re-establish the equilibrium, they obviously have to 'pay' a high price in praise and symbolic gratifications – or at least to refrain from showering abuse on the emigrant when he fails in his duty – 'when you undress your own, you undress yourself' – but, increasingly, that is not enough. They are therefore often obliged to give in to the emigrant's demands because he is the family's primary support. Indeed, it is no longer sufficient merely to earmark some of the family heritage for him (a traditional, if exceptional, solution) or to reserve for him some of the purchases that have been made thanks to his subsidies. Increasingly, he must be recognized to have the right to dispose of some of his money as he sees fit, to save on the spot, even in France, and to build up a nest egg for his own use, as distinct from the domestic economy. Whereas 'good children' were traditionally praised for 'carrying their parents' or 'carrying the house', today's talk of 'good parents' is not merely mockery. The old formulae that enjoined children to 'work for their parents' are now replicated by symmetrical formulae that speak of parents' (i.e. welfare recipients) duties towards their children (their 'protectors'). Parents themselves recognize that 'new' duties are now incumbent on them, and promise and swear not to 'eat the work' of their emigrant sons: 'just as there are good sons, there are bad parents'; 'there is also a curse on parents who "eat" their children's toil'; 'parents too make their children's houses,' 'it is wrong for one person to work so that others can take advantage afterwards' (i.e. after the breakdown of joint ownership).

In a word, it is the dialectic between family structures and the structures of emigration, first in Algeria and then in France, that lies at the heart of the process of the transformation of emigrants' conditions and positions.

The third 'age': an Algerian 'colony' in France

Once the process of transformation gets under way, the characteristics of the second 'generation' of emigrants inevitably become more pronounced. Tendencies that were already present in the emigrés' previous state are now inevitably taken to the limit by the continuous extension of their stays in France, by the 'quasi-professionalization' of their emigrant status,[21] and above all by the increased volume of emigration and its spread to every region of Algeria, to all the men in the group – peasants and non-peasants, the young and the not so young, families and children etc.[22]

Now one of the basic properties of Algerian emigration is that it has always tended to establish itself as a *permanent* structure within France. Every new wave of emigrants that came to France found an established community made up of earlier emigrants into which it could incorporate itself. Because the tradition of emigration allowed it to weave an internal network of links of solidarity, without which it could have been impossible for it to perpetuate itself,[23] the emigrant community was in a sense guaranteed to be able to find within itself the preconditions for its own cohesion. All the mechanisms of solidarity – the search for work, welfare during periods of unemployment or illness, in the face of death or accidents, and in the face of not only material but above all moral difficulties – acted in their turn as powerfully cohesive factors. Like little societies of compatriots, even though they were no more than pale copies of the social structures of their communities of origin, the groups formed by emigrants therefore served as a constant reminder to 'first-generation' emigrants of their obligations to the land and the peasant condition, and of reminding those of the second 'generation' of their more limited duties towards their families. Being both pressure groups and intermediaries between the society of origin and those of its members who had left it, the groups acted as factors that regulated and controlled emigrants who, once they had banded together in this way, sustained the ties that bind them to their country in a less destructible and fragmentary way. Ultimately, the very nature of the emigrant's relationship with the society of immigration and his country of origin are closely determined by the form and intensity of the relations that bind him to the group of emigrants around him; his whole attitude towards both societies (the society in which the immigrant is living and the society from which he came) seems to be mediated by his relations with the community of his compatriots. Being a sort of projection on to France of the 'big country' from which the emigrant originates, the 'little country' that has been established in France fulfils ambivalent functions for emigrants. Whilst it ensures that they are permanently present in France, it also sustains *the feeling that their presence is temporary.* Amongst other things, it helps them to overcome the contradictions inscribed in the emigrant condition, but it does so by reduplicating them. It helps to confirm emigrants in the condition that has been imposed upon them and which is the result of two complementary facts: on the one hand, the exclusion from the host society which, in varying degrees, affects all immigrants and, on the other, a break with the land of their birth which is not merely spatial.

Even though every emigrant is convinced that he is objectively involved in a condition that can only last, he still continues to live that condition with the feeling that it will not and to behave in many domains as though his emigration were no more than temporary. This feeling of the 'the temporary that lasts', which determines a whole set of specific practices, also conditions the emigrant's perception of the social and political world. Being a basic characteristic of the emigrant condition, the temporal contradiction within him eventually imprints its mark on the whole of his experience and his awareness of temporality.

Torn between two 'times', between two countries and between two conditions, an entire community lives as though it were 'in transit'. Being condemned to refer simultaneously to two societies, emigrants dream, without noticing the contradiction, of combining the incompatible advantages of two conflicting choices. At times, they idealize France and would like it to have, in addition to the advantages it gives them (a stable job, a wage, etc.), that other quality of being a 'second' land of their birth – which would be enough to transfigure the relationship and to magically transform all the reasons for the dissatisfaction they experience in France. At other times, they idealize Algeria in their dreams or after spending time there during their annual holidays. They want it to correspond to an idealized France (i.e. an Algeria that offers them what they go to France to look for). We can thus understand how the ambiguity of their relations with both societies and the contradictions inherent in their condition – some of them generated by emigration, and others transformed and exacerbated by it – inevitably encourage emigrants to perpetuate, despite the refutations supplied by reality, the collective illusion of a temporary emigration. It was in fact by concealing, and concealing from itself, the truth of its condition that Algerian emigration eventually brought together in France a population of emigrants, which has, almost without realizing it, established itself as a relatively autonomous 'little society'.

The world of contradictions

'What kind of life is it when, in order to feed your children, you are forced to leave them; when, in order to "fill" your house, you start by deserting it, when you are the first to abandon your country in order to work it?... Their country is back there, their house is back there, their wives and children are back there, everything is back there, only their bodies are here [in France], and you call that "living"....Living for one month when they find themselves back there with everyone else.... The emigrant's existence is always back there – back there at home when he goes back – and not here [in France]. Tomorrow – he will go back tomorrow, but not today. That's the emigrant for you; it's always "later", "afterwards", "and then"....Men who have the right to be at home for one month, that's all, they are men for one month a year, that's all, they are men for one month a year throughout their lives; the rest of the time, you don't know what they are; men, but there's nothing manlike in their lives; the women aren't like that, the women they have left at home are better men than they are; they outdo them, they manage without their husbands, they're the real men. Who are these people? Men, but men without women: their wives are without men, but they're not widows because their husbands are alive; their children are without fathers, orphans even though their fathers are alive....I ask myself: who are the real widowers, the real orphans – is it them [the emigrant men], or is it their wives? Is it them, with their beards and moustaches, or is it their children?...The future is always uncertain. If you are sure of living, you build, you dig foundations. You say: this is my house, I'm going to build it bit by bit, and eventually I'll live in it; then you have a future, you have a goal. But here in France, they're not really alive, since they can't live like people here [the French]; so no one has a future here, no one has his future. There's no such thing as a real future in a foreign country. It's a watch: the hands go round and round, that's all: days, months, years....You are in a country, you spend your entire youth there, your health, when you are in the prime [of life], you work, but you are not at home....You act as though you were only here for a while. It's enough to drive you mad; it's made a lot of people ill, all of us [so long as] we are here. For us, nothing is certain: it's no life, whatever you try to do, you say that it can't be done given that, sooner or later, I don't know what might happen; you are on the alert. What's going to happen tomorrow? What if?...What if? And what will become of me if they send me back? That's what emigration is like, that's what it's like to live in a country as a foreigner....Our *elbhorga* [exile], it's like someone who always arrives late: you get here, you know nothing, you have to find out everything, learn everything – for those who don't want to stay the same way they came – you are behind the rest, behind the French, always catching up; later, when he goes back to his village, he [the emigrant] realizes that he has nothing, that he has wasted his time.

Someone like me, for example, I don't know anyone any more; you have to start from scratch, start all over again. You see them getting married at 55, at 60, like a young *isli* [a young man who is marrying for the first time]; they start having children when they are old, build a house, all the things you do when you are 20, 25, it's not natural. I now have a son who is three, at my age... our whole emigration, all emigrants are like that, that's the way it is.... The emigrant is a man who is in two places at once, in two countries; he has to have one foot here, and the other foot there. If he doesn't do that, it's as though he has done nothing, he is nothing. Everything within them [emigrants] is divided: their ideas, what they think, their projects. They are divided between here and back there [*le pays*]. As the saying goes, "They neither profit from this world [on earth] nor hold to [place their trust in] God", they lose in every way, all their calculations are false.... Their bodies are here, and their thoughts are here – they have to be because their sweat is here – but everything else, their spirit, their bodies, their gaze, is back there.... That is the situation of emigration: it is "tight" [oppressive] for them.'

The some 900,000 Algerians in France – 550,000 men and 71,000 adult women (over sixteen), or one woman for every seven adult male immigrants – form the largest foreign community.[24] This community, which initially consisted mainly of adult men, has evolved very quickly. Indeed, as the second stage of emigration came about, all the preconditions were in place for the migratory movement of families to begin and develop: although the first signs appeared as early as 1938, family emigration didn't really get going until after 1952. Here, as elsewhere, the struggle for independence provided rural society with the alibi it needed to admit to the existence of a process that had, in effect, already started, mainly because of the accelerated transformations and catastrophic chain reactions it determined. And today, with a total of almost 100,000 families with some 270,000 children under sixteen between them (30 per cent of the whole of the Algerian population in France), Algerian emigration has ceased to be the emigration of adult male labour. The morphological transformations experienced by the community reveal its tendency to compensate for the structural imbalances (more adults than children, more men than women, more single men than men living with their families, etc.) that resulted from the initial conditions of its formation. It can find within itself the resources needed to meet the expenses essential to its workings; similarly, it supplies the means required for its own reproduction. It has, that is, its own artisans and shopkeepers, and their function is to cater for certain needs: catering, hotels, hygiene, entertainment and leisure, food and clothing, and even funeral parlours. It has its notables, who are comparable to the wise men of traditional society – they have religious or '*maraboutiques*' responsibilities, and function as mediators and conciliators, and may even have magico-ritual powers (therapeutic or divinatory practices, etc.). It has its executives and its members of the liberal professions, such as doctors and lawyers (especially in Paris). Because it constitutes a far from negligible clientele and is therefore the object of certain attentions, the Algerian community has had to produce for itself the many intermediaries who are responsible for maintaining as best they can the few essential contacts that it has to have with French society. This is particularly true of the many canvassers whose role is to win over Algerian customers for insurance companies (car insurance, insurance for business – especially bars and cafés), haberdashers, dealers in domestic appliances, jewellers, second-hand car dealers, travel agencies, etc. Not even the female clientele of the temporary hostels and council flats of the Paris suburbs, especially when women are excluded from the market,[25] escapes the attentions of 'visitors' (other more 'urbanized' Algerian women who are more familiar with commercial circuits) who, without the knowledge of their husbands, come to their homes to sell them – often at very high prices – material and jewellery (which is sometimes said to have come from Mecca!). A mediating role is also played by the 'gangers' whose only qualification and function in certain industries (and especially the building industry) is to guarantee, as cheaply as possible, the discipline and control of gangs made up exclusively of Algerian workers.

As a result of these morphological transformations, the emigrant community developed a veritable marriage market that clearly demonstrates the relative autonomy it has acquired with respect to French society. Whatever type of marriage is envisaged – a traditional marriage within the context of kin or village endogamy, or a more 'modern' marriage – it is no longer necessary for a young emigrant to go home in order to be able to marry. In 1973, a total of 2,298 Algerian men and 1,172 Algerian women celebrated their marriages in France, and 827 of those marriages (36 per cent of men and 70.5 per cent of women) took place within the Algerian community; more than half the Algerian men (52.7 per cent) and 15 per cent of Algerian women married French partners.[26]

All these factors help to allow the community of Algerian emigrants to find the principles of its cohesion within itself, and not, as was the case in the past, in its relationship with its groups of origin. At the same time, and as a result of these new inputs, the community has a tendency to expand. The birth in France of almost 20,000 Algerian children per year; the arrival on the labour market of children who have been brought up and educated in France, as well as the arrival of recent immigrants who are, in relative terms, better educated and better equipped than their predecessors to take vocational courses or to improve their vocational training; the slight tendency on the part of young people of both sexes (of urban origin, and with more educational capital, or even professional qualifications, who come from Algeria for intellectual rather than directly productive activities), whose modes of behaviour are similar to those of the children of immigrant families, to leave, not for strictly 'work' reasons, but for reasons of a cultural order – all this will lead to a greater diversification of the social composition of the Algerian colony in France. Even though it is still scarcely perceptible (in statistical terms) and has no profound effect on the structure of the jobs they do, a process that involves some form of internal hierarchy and stratification does seem to be evolving within the Algerian immigrant population.

3
An Exemplary Immigration

In speaking of an 'exemplary immigration', I do not wish to suggest that Algerian immigration is, as it were, an 'example' for all other immigrations, past, present and future. On the contrary, the term has to be understood as meaning that we are speaking of an immigration without parallel. This is an immigration that is exceptional in every respect, both in the overall terms of its entire history and in terms of each of its detailed characteristics – and the two aspects are not unrelated. Because it is extraordinary, this immigration seems to contain the truth of all other immigrations and of immigration in general, and it appears to display, as clearly as possible and with the highest degree of 'exemplariness', attributes that we find dispersed and diffused in other emigrations.

Without wishing to analyse in detail the past and present characteristics of Algerian immigration in order to demonstrate the sense in which it is 'exemplary', we will take only a succinct and purely indicative inventory of what seem to be its most significant aspects. Given that the migratory itinerary – the individual itinerary of each of these emigrant-immigrants and the collective itinerary – that makes up the very history of the process of emigration and immigration is also an epistemological itinerary, it too reveals an order that is both logical and chronological. It has both a main theme and an overall framework or background for all the questions that can be asked about the migratory phenomenon in its totality (emigration and immigration). It proves to be an excellent mnemo-mechanical support or a means of raising and organizing the various questions that make up, broadly speaking, an analysis of the conditions that led the future emigrant first to break with his condition of origin, and with a whole world in which there was no distinction between the social, the economic and the cultural (his ways of living and working, his modes of social being) and, then, to *immerse* himself in a different social, economic, cultural and political world which also has an internal logic of its own – which is quite the opposite of that of the original order – a spirit and style of its own, and a fundamentally distinct intention.

A singular genesis

It is increasingly widely accepted that emigration-immigration is the product of underdevelopment, that it is underdevelopment's most obvious expression, that it can be explained only as one of the effects of the relationship of domination of 'rich' countries (countries of immigration) over 'poor' countries (countries of emigration). It is also widely accepted, thanks to its backlash effect, that emigration-immigration is a factor in underdevelopment that helps to perpetuate the relationship of domination of which it is a product. If, however, we go further back and beyond this first causality, the entire history of the colonization of Algeria, of the colonized Algerian peasantry and, correlatively, of Algerian emigration are exemplary illustrations of the fact that emigration-immigration is the direct 'child' of the very colonization that generated the underdevelopment in the first place. Being a veritable 'laboratory experiment', or a sort of 'social surgery', which was itself the result or the cumulative outcome of an infinite number of other interventions that were just as brutal and had equally catastrophic consequences, Algerian emigration was, in its genesis, just as 'exemplary' as the colonization of Algeria itself. Algeria was colonized first in the literal sense of the term (the land was occupied and appropriated by newcomers) and then in the historical sense that a new system of social relations and a new mode of production made a violent intrusion. And because this conflict between radically different orders was inscribed within an extremely unequal balance of power, it resulted in a total upheaval that the old order could survive only in a fragmented, exhausted and anachronistic form. Because the entire (social) history of emigration fuses completely with that of the Algerian peasantry, or in other words with the history of land seizures (and, more specifically, with the history of the property laws which, by allowing those seizures, destroyed the foundations of the traditional economy and shattered the whole armature of the original society[1]), it is not really until the fifth and sixth decades of colonization, and in the aftermath of the great insurrection of 1871, that we see the beginning of the era of emigration to France (which has yet to end) and into French factories (into industrial waged labour). Prior to this, emigration, both seasonal and permanent, had taken the form of a local movement to the farms of the colonists. Being interdependent, the 'exemplariness' of the cause and the 'exemplariness' of the effects reinforced one another. The 'exemplariness' of Algerian emigration, both old and 'young', results largely from the 'exemplariness' of the colonization experienced by Algeria. Correlatively, one of the inevitable and major effects of this 'exemplary' colonization (which outlived it) was an exemplary emigration. The colonization of Algeria was total, systematic and intensive. This was a colonization not only of property and wealth, but also of men and 'bodies and souls', as the saying went, and a colonization that was, above all, relatively early. One of its effects was an emigration that was exceptional or 'exemplary' both in terms of its numerical scale, its continuity and systematicity, and its particular organizational form, its particular mode of presence *here* (in immigration) and its mode of absence *there* (in emigration), etc., and, especially, in terms of its *precocity*. In retrospect, Algerian emigration proves to be the first (at least to France) to have originated in a country belonging to what we now call the Third World. This is the only way of understanding the contemporary nature of Algerian immigration in France or, above all, the fact that it is at once already an 'old' immigration (which has a long history behind it) and yet still a 'young' immigration (in the specific sense that it originates from a 'young' country in the sense that the countries of the Third World are said to be 'young' in terms of either their national existence and their cultural products, or in terms of the 'ground they have to make up'). If we overlook this major characteristic (and we will return later to both these points), we cannot understand the nature of the relations which use emigration on the one hand and immigration on the other to bind together the countries concerned.

Without wishing to subscribe at all costs to the schema that describes all immigration as the result of the conjunction of two forces, namely a 'repulsive' force which drives emigrants out of their own country (and which supposedly explains emigration) and an 'attractive' force (which supposedly explains immigration), there is one particular feature of Algerian immigration (and not simply emigration) in France that adds to the 'experimental' (as though deliberately provoked) character of the undertaking. When we begin to look for eyewitness accounts of the arrival in France of the first Algerian immigrants – who were not called 'Algerians' at the time – we find that their migration was, in a context which explains this innovation, something that was undertaken deliberately, knowingly and with almost full knowledge of the facts. If we also take into consideration the effects of conscription and incitements to enlist for service in the French army, or of the requisition of workers for the war industries or to dig trenches during the First World War (240,000 Algerians, more than one third of the male population aged between twenty and forty, were mobilized or requisitioned (Ageron 1962)), we can evaluate the extent to which the Algerian immigration was, from the outset, deliberately encouraged. In this case, and perhaps only in this case, history allows us to resolve the following dilemma: was it 'immigration' that created 'jobs for immigrants', or was it the reverse? Similarly, history allows us to break the circle, or the inter-action between objective discrimination and those who were or could be discriminated against. Algerian immigration was, from the very beginning, engineered. But before it could be engineered, Algerians had to have already been made available for emigration. They had to be transformed into either potential emigrants who were waiting to become actual emigrants (i.e. waiting to immigrate), or into virtual immigrants who were waiting for immigration to call them and turn them into real immigrants. Colonization achieved this, intentionally or otherwise, and it did so very quickly and even before immigration (in France) had need of a supplement of future emigrants and immigrants.

Once the preconditions for emigration had been created, the temp-tation to use these available immigrants made itself felt in both France and Algeria. Indeed, the temptation was all the greater in that this immigration had the advantage or the attraction of seeming 'innocent' of any experience (or any idea) of the social condition of the working class. This was an appreciable benefit, even if the employers chose not to mention it (which was fair enough) or tried to minimize it, and preferred to complain long and loud about this new or untried labour force's lack of technical experience. All that was needed for the movement of emigration-immigration of Algerians to France (and, to this very day, only to France) to begin and to expand of its own accord was proof that this additional work force was being put to good use.

'Labour immigration'

For the sake of convenience rather than any concern for scientific truth, it is thought necessary to make a distinction between 'labour immigration' (and nothing but labour), which supposedly affects only, or mainly, adult male workers, and 'settler immigration' (which is in addition to the former, because it is implicitly recognized that it also comprises labour immigration) in which the proportion of families (men and women, adults and children, active and inactive persons) is noticeably greater. Supported by a whole series of objective indices and morphological and behavioural observations, the distinction is built up into a systematic opposition which is assumed to produce two radically antithetical forms of immigration. The proportion of adults, of masculinity, of activity and, correlatively, the indices of nuptuality, natality, mortality and morbidity, in the length and, more important, the modalities of their stays in France and in their countries of origin, etc., are all different. What is open to challenge in this construction is not the differences that are noted, but the use that is made of them, as it borders on the nonsensical. The two immigrations that have been identified in this way become autonomous realities. They are divorced, as though they were different from the outset and for ever, as though they were by their very nature separable, or in other words existed outside all social or historical determinations and, above all, as though one could choose to have one without the other, or choose to have one without provoking the other. As neither is anything more than we wish to see in it, both are destined to be and remain what we would like them to be and to remain (at least in our mental categories, in our habits), namely *labour immigration* on the one hand and *settler immigration* on the other. 'Labour immigration' is and will always be labour immigration, and 'settler immigration' has always, from its beginnings and from the outset, been settler immigration. As the distinction is established a priori, there can be no suggestion that the forms that have been so identified might be united by some relation of continuity, or even descent, with one extending or deriving from the other. No matter how obvious it might look, any necessary evolution of one into the other can only be described as a scandal. The scandalous thing about Algerian immigration is that what was once a 'labour immigration' (we continue to think of it and take decisions about it as though it were still what it was in its beginnings) has, contrary to all expectations, become a 'settler immigration'. This is something that none of the parties concerned dares to fully recognize. They are therefore unable to draw the appropriate conclusions. Of course everyone knows how simplistic, how arbitrary and how false the distinction is; and if it continues despite that to find a certain audience, we also know the assumptions that underpin its popularity. The whole history of migrations bears witness to the fact that – except, truth to tell, in the case of the exodus of the population of one country to another (a case far removed from what we now call immigration, that is, the displacement, for essentially economic reasons, of a labour force that is available here, to job vacancies there) – there has never been a so-called settler immigration that did not begin as a 'labour immigration' that took place over a longer or shorter period of time.[2] Conversely, perhaps there is no such thing as a so-called labour immigration that does not sooner or later end up, provided that it continues, by becoming a 'settler immigration', even though everyone (the emigrant-immigrants themselves, their country of origin of course, and the country of immigration) would like it to remain what it once was. This is certainly the case with Algerian immigration, which proves to be exemplary in this respect too.

Being the first instance of immigration from the underdeveloped world, it has had to struggle hardest against the 'individualism' (and the morality that goes with it) which, in a certain way, lay at its origins and which, moreover, it continues to reinforce and to implant in every domain of life. The reason why we have to stress this characteristic of origin, which is a novel characteristic in the case of Algerian immigration, is that we are talking about the emigration-immigration of men who remain, or who for a long time remained, deep inside themselves 'communitarian' men. Strongly marked by the communitarian *habitus*, they were men who (ideally) existed only as members of the group. Peasant labour is, of course, the explanation for the mass identification of each individual with the group to which he belongs and for the high degree of their integration into the group itself. To be more specific, it is the peasant state, together with a whole art of living, a way of being, thinking and acting, a way of perceiving the world, or in short a whole *ethos*, which meant that belonging to one's community and one's land (which were one and the same thing) was the only way an individual had of being – and of being *excellently*.

Because it presumably does no more than put the finishing touches to the disruptive action of many factors (transformations of all kinds – demographic, economic, social and moral – which might all be said to lead, *grosso modo*, to *individuation*), emigration-immigration completes the break with the group, its spatio-temporal rhythms, its activities and, in a word, the system of values and the system of communitarian dispositions that are the group's foundations. We can therefore understand that emigrating cannot, as is believed so complacently, be an easy thing to do. In order to understand why the emigrant comes to – and tolerates – the 'hell' of immigration, we have assume that, when he emigrated, he believed he was running away to some 'heaven' created from fantasies and the series of 'social lies' concocted by immigrants to justify their condition.

We can thus understand why emigration is inconceivable, why it cannot take place, cannot be tolerated and cannot be perpetuated unless it goes hand in hand with a real effort to justify it or, in other words, to *legitimate* it in the eyes of the emigrant himself and in the eyes of his whole entourage. Given that it is, in itself, already and from the outset, the product of an initial upheaval within the group, emigration certainly constitutes a serious threat – once merely potential, but now very real – to the integrity and survival of both the group and the emigrant himself (in terms of his being true to himself, his position as a member of the group and his position as peasant, which are all one and the same thing). We can thus understand why emigrants still, in a very anachronistic way, insist on proving by their every act and their every word that emigration to them is not just a matter of 'defection', total 'bankruptcy' or a singular, individualist and egotistical act but, on the contrary, an 'altruistic' act, a collective way of demonstrating their devotion to the group, an act performed for the good of all, and a willing sacrifice to the cause and service of the group.

Towards 'family immigration'

It is not easy to emigrate, even for a single man. It is not easy for his group to allow him to emigrate. A fortiori, it is infinitely more diffi-cult for a woman or an entire family to emigrate. Above all, as one can imagine, this is especially difficult for the group which, as it is gradually sapped of its substance as it allows whole families to emigrate, witnesses its own decomposition without being able to stop it. It is when the group finds it most difficult to control or organize the emigration of its men that it allows itself to indulge in family emigration. Before emigration can reach the final phase of taking away whole families, the insidious process that destructures the group by destroying the bonds that once tied its members to one another and to the group itself has to be dangerously far advanced. The initial causes responsible for the first form of emigration – that of single men – must have been considerably (almost catastrophically) exacerbated, usually as a result of emigration itself, before the second movement – the emigration of families – could get under way. Whilst the first signs of the latter form of emigration were visible even before the Second World War, at least in those regions that were first and most strongly marked by the emigration of their men and by the effects imputable to that emigration, it took a further twenty years for family emigration to become established as a real trend.

Once again, the war years (1955–9 [the Algerian war]), because of their direct effect (insecurity) and indirect consequences (the regroup-ing of the rural population, especially from the mountain regions, in purpose-built centres under the control of the French army, which was a way of destroying the last bonds and the last forms of family or village solidarity), were to the emigration of women and, more generally, families what the years of the Great War were to the emigration of men. Now that all the essential conditions for the actualization of both forms of emigration had – each in their own time – been virtually met, the war and its constraints – an example of *force majeure* – provided the necessary alibi for the completion of something that was already ready to be completed, and served as a pretext for admitting what people could not even admit to themselves. For a long time, family emigration was undertaken, and above all experienced, as though it were a shameful act. It was an act that people were so anxious to conceal that they left their villages by night despite (or because of) the fact that it was a deliberate *individual* decision taken by the emigrant and his wife (by the couple instituted by emigration), who, by acting in this way, knew that they were infringing the communitarian rule and offending the morality of the group. The fragmentation of families had to become widespread and reach its extreme limits with the conjugal-type family (the family we find in immigration), and the rural exodus into the towns of Algeria (for which emigration to France was largely responsible) had to depopulate whole villages before the emigration of families to France could take place in broad daylight, openly and without any restraint.

Even though the emigration of families seems always to have been a sort of permanent temptation which no doubt haunted all emigrants and was always on the minds of emigrant men, it nevertheless took almost half a century of uninterrupted emigration on the part of single men before this 'labour emigration' was boosted by family emigration and became 'settler emigration'. Without wishing to underestimate possible opposition from the society of immigration, it does seem to be second (in chronological order) and secondary (in order of importance) compared to the resistances and taboos specific to the society of emigration. It is as though the work of censorship (which is also a work of prevention and preservation) had been done, and well done, in the realm of emigration, and that there was therefore no need for it to be done in the realm of immigration. We know that this task of control and regulation, i.e. the adaptation of emigration to the needs of immigration, was, whenever necessary, done during the emigration-immigration of the men. Even today, and quite independently of the technical difficulties raised by family reunification, many emigrants decide – unless there are exceptional circumstances, when excuses will be made for acting in this way – not to do what they regard as the extreme solution: to emigrate with their families. They sense, in varying degrees, that this would not be without its risks. Indeed, whilst it does seem to provide a remedy to the emigrant's absence vis-à-vis members of his (conjugal) family and does indeed guarantee that they are present 'for one another' (albeit in immigration), there is always the danger that family emigration will, first, complete the break inaugurated by the man's emigration and, second, further commit him to the society into which he is now 'immigrating' his wife and children (and he fears that this commitment will be irreversible. So does his group, which disapproves of family emigration, regarding it as superfluous and something that cannot be justified given the disastrous cost that has to be paid). There is also, finally, a danger that it will create more, and more serious, problems and will exacerbate or worsen, in quantitative and above all qualitative terms, a contradiction that had hitherto been experienced only by men (male emigrants). Although it is inscribed within the first emigration – i.e. in the conduct of the first emigrant – family emigration therefore introduces a difference of nature. The emigrant who once worked amongst others and for others (even though the migratory phenomenon's constituent illusion strives to establish a different equilibrium: by working for others, the emigrant-immigrant is also working for himself, for his family, for his group and for his *pays*) now becomes a *progenitor* living amongst others and (whether he wishes to or not) for others.

When we speak of the emigration of families, we are therefore dealing with *assimilation*, no matter what terms or euphemistic variants (adaptation, integration, insertion, etc.) are used to designate that social reality. No one has any illusions about this: neither those who fear the emigration of families because it concerns the dissolution of those families and their fusion into the society that absorbs them, and because they will, to a greater or lesser extent and over a longer or shorter space of time, identify with that society, nor those who disapprove of the immigration of families which are judged (pre-judged) to be difficult to 'assimilate'. And the classic distinction between 'labour immigration' and 'settler immigration' is, ultimately, no more than a disguised way of making, with a semblance of (ethical) neutrality and by using a supposedly objective vocabulary, a distinction between an 'assimilable' immigration (it can be assimilated because it initially concerns individuals who are almost *similar* to 'us', even though the fact is that this similarity is no more than relative) which will be rapidly (and if need be, with our help) transformed into a 'settler immigration', and an inassimilable immigration (which is characterized from the outset by its radical alterity and heterogeneity) that can only be and remain (and if need be, we will make sure that it is) a 'labour immigration'.[3]

To speak of 'settler immigration' is to give a name to the immigration of those who, in their family and social life, behave like 'us'. They have adopted the same social and family structures as 'us' and, along with those structures, the same family *habitus* as 'us', or in other words a set of shared representations and practices. These influence relations between different members of the family, as defined by the position they occupy, age, gender, the sexual division of labour, the education of children, budget management and leisure practices, or, in a word, a whole practice of living, a whole domestic atmosphere imbued with 'intimism' and marked by the family's withdrawal into itself (this, no doubt, is what is designated by the term 'culture'). These immigrants do not tolerate being separated for a long time, and certainly for no longer than is necessary, from their wives and children, and cannot wait for their families to join them (they have the same domestic morality as 'us', and that is a mark of civilization). All this demonstrates the trust they place in the people to whose country they are immigrating. They even go so far as to approach them without any reservations, and to entrust them with what they hold most dear and most important (their wives and children, or in other words their entire future). They are, in a word, *good* immigrants.

'Labour immigration', on the other hand, is another way of giving a name to those who, in their family and social lives, behave in a completely different way from 'us', and who have adopted completely different social and family structures, and a domestic morality in which 'we' cannot recognize ourselves. Witness the primacy of the group and of the communitarian spirit which, because it is opposed to the triumph of individualism, becomes a gregarious instinct. A family that lives in a system of joint ownership or an extended family becomes a sort of magma with indefinable limits. Its pertinent units – collectivities of men, women and children – merge to such a degree as to be unidentifiable. Its domestic practices are quite alien to our traditions. Kinship endogamy, for example, always looks suspiciously like incest to us, whilst polygamy is quite alien to our 'manners and customs'. (It offends against public order, in the sense in which civil or international private law understand that term; it offends our sensibilities and social morality. Because it is a factor that militates against assimilation, it is incompatible with naturalization – see article 69 of the Code de la nationalité.) Relations within the family are ruled by a different morality, governed by different principles and conform to other values such as, for example, the highly discriminatory hierarchy of genders and different age groups, and so on. These are all so many indices of a different 'culture' (to use contemporary language, or 'race', to use the vocabulary of the past). These immigrants readily tolerate being separated from their wife (or wives) and children, for whom they do not, besides, display the feelings we have for our wives and children (which is another way of saying that they have no feelings because, as everyone knows, one's own feelings – which are legitimate *or* worthy of being described as such – are the only real feelings, just as there is no culture but our culture). They insist on emigrating alone, and in order to do so, they mobilize every element that might prevent the emigration of their wives and children (patriotism, 'communitarianism', and everything that this national, patriotic fundamentalism feeds upon: language, religion, cultural traditions and the entire series of other signs whereby they recognize one another and distinguish themselves from 'us'). In these conditions, immigrating without one's family is, in our view, equivalent to an attitude of defiance.

When we speak of labour immigration, we are not talking about a purely demographic phenomenon, but about a broader set of considerations relating to different orders (social, cultural, political and ethnic). In that sense, the exemplariness of Algerian immigration is not only what it once was and what it still is – even today, now that we have to recognize that it has been ('illegitimately') transformed into settler immigration – namely, the prime example of labour immigration, but also, and above all, all the other aspects and all the other dimensions of all the other meanings that are concealed by the distinction between 'labour' and 'settlement'.

Shared illusions and dissimulations

If it is to be able to remain what it is, Algerian immigration, more so than any other, must sustain, and then dispel, the series of *illusions*, simulations and dissimulations that explain the generation and perpetuation of the migratory phenomenon. We in fact know that many sustained collective illusions are necessary, first, for emigration to be conceivable in the first place and, secondly, for it to be able to reproduce and perpetuate itself, initially through the rapid replacement of its numbers ('noria-immigration'), and then by counting on the same men as they spend more and more time in immigration ('stabilized' immigration). We have noted elsewhere the degree to which the 'temporary' illusion and, correlatively, the *alibi of work*, are integral to emigration and immigration. On the one hand – and this is the very definition of the immigrant – a foreigner resides *temporarily* (at least in theory) in a different country and exclusively for reasons of work. He is therefore excluded from the political sphere, which is the reserve of natives or nationals. His exclusion from the political is also a matter of *politeness*. On the other hand –

and this is the very definition of the emigrant – we have a native or national who is absent temporarily (at least in theory) and essentially (not to say exclusively) for work reasons. He therefore continues to enjoy (at least in theory) all the political attributes and competence of the nation to which he still belongs (to compensate for the political exclusion that affects him to the extent that he is resident in a foreign country). These are the dominant (or official) definitions that constitute the same individual as, respectively, an immigrant and an emigrant, and they are at once interdependent and complementary. This double definition cannot produce all its effects unless it remains masked. For that to happen, a whole collective effort must be made to conceal the truth of emigration and immigration – and all parties, in other words both the society of emigration and the society of immigration, collude in it. And, as though in accordance with a sort of historical necessity (a necessity that is constitutive of emigration itself, from the conditions of its genesis to its present form), Algerian immigration really does seem to have *cultivated* the illusions typical of all immigration, and to have truly perfected the work of dissimulation that is required to sustain them. This historical necessity weighs more heavily upon Algerian immigration than upon other immigrations, and more so than on contemporary immigrations, which are dissimilar because they are intra-European. Algerian immigration is also more deeply affected than equivalent immigrations that are similar in terms of their origins and social conditions, but which occurred later. This is, no doubt, because of the origins of Algerian immigration, its long-standing nature (which was, as it happens, possible only because this huge effort to deceive could be sustained) and, as a result of all that, its insistence on remaining, or pretending to remain, what it always had been. This work of dissimulation is not simply an *abstract* mechanism that analysis owes it to itself to reveal. Being lived and experienced in the most intense manner by the emigrant-immigrants themselves, it constitutes their attempt – and it is sometimes a desperate attempt – to overcome all the contradictions inherent in the emigrant-immigrant's condition. The basic contradiction of the 'temporary that lasts' (an emigration-immigration which is neither a temporary state nor a permanent state) is transposed from the temporal order to the spatial order and it becomes an impossible 'ubiquity'. The emigrant is fated to go on being present even when he is absent and, correlatively, to not be totally present where he is present. The paradox of the immigrant is that he is partly absent from the communitarian order from which he comes (there is a contradiction between, on the one hand, the communitarian order of origin and the *habitus* that goes with it and, on the other, the 'individualist' order the emigrant discovers, submits to and learns in immigration). Confronted with all the harsh contradictions that constitute his social world, the emigrant-immigrant is forced to exacerbate them because he cannot resolve them, and this is sometimes detrimental to his own social or psychical equilibrium.

It is not only at the individual level that each of the three partners involved in the migratory phenomenon – the country of emigration, the country of immigration and those who are most closely concerned, namely the emigrant-immigrants themselves – has to sustain the series of illusions needed for the perpetuation of the process. They must also collaborate in this indispensable exercise in dissimulation in a complicit, and *objectively complicit*, manner (which means that there is no need for any prior consultation). The complicity is all the greater that this deception is in everyone's interests. The stakes are all the higher in that both emigration and immigration are long-standing and contradict their theoretical definitions.

When it became independent, Algeria 'inherited' from its colonial past a tradition of emigration that was already more than half a century old – in those regions with a strong and very old tradition of emigration, almost all the men in any given village already had some experience, in either the long or the short term and on one or more occasions, of living and working in France. It also inherited an emigrant population numbering some 350,000 people (it already certainly included more than 5,000 families; by the end of 1954, some 6,000 families, with 15,000 children, had already emigrated to France). This no doubt made it necessary to enter into a 'contract' with the country of immigration (the former colonizing country) in order to determine the new status of this emigrant-immigrant population and, if need be, to regulate the emigration-immigration of new contingents. But in all logic, the fact that it was necessary did not give either of the partners, on either side, the authority to sign, so to speak, a contract for the definitive or quasi-definitive transfer (to the extent of being politically sanctioned by the granting of French nationality to the French-born children of the transferred families) of those Algeria saw as part of its population or its *emigrants*, whereas France saw them as part of its future population or as some of its immigrants. That cannot be done because it affects the national order of both the nation of emigration and the nation of immigration (and the latter had been established very recently, and at a very high cost). We can thus understand why it is that the two countries that have, in terms of emigration and immigration respectively, the most loaded history, have managed to sustain (and have the greatest interest in sustaining), despite all the evidence and even despite the laws of social change, all the illusions and all the dissimulations that ensure that emigration and immigration continue to be experienced, thought of and discussed as though they were still what they were in the beginning. To be more accurate, they are experienced, thought of and discussed as though they actually were what they are in *ideal and abstract* terms (outside all social determinations and outside history, i.e. eternally and universally). It is also true that this loaded history rebounds upon emigration/immigration, which is ultimately no more than the outcome of that history. This collective work of dissimulation is indispensable if we wish, on the one hand, the emigrant (i.e. another country's national) to remain an emigrant for ever even though, strictly speaking, he is not an emigrant from the country that claims him as its 'national', and has been born in France of emigrant parents. The same dissimulation is necessary if we wish the immigrant to remain an immigrant for ever, no matter how permanent and continuous his presence, no matter how great his involvement in the economic, social, cultural and even political life of the nation, and no matter how 'integrated' he may be. There is on both sides a sort of national 'fundamentalism' (sustained by many other distinctive characteristics: cultural, social, linguistic, religious, political and even ethnic), which ensures that emigration cannot correspond to the exclusion or even the self-exclusion from the nation of emigrants or, correlatively, to their full identification (i.e., even and especially their political identification) with the nation and especially the national population of people to whom they are foreign (in terms of their history and ethnic origins rather than the nationality they already have or acquire). Despite the *objectively* antithetical divergences and interests of the country of emigration and the country of immigration, and precisely because of those same divergences of all kinds and those very oppositions, an objective complicity therefore still necessarily binds together the two partners in the migratory phenomenon.

The costs and benefits of immigration

What do immigrants cost and what do they bring in? This question seems to run through all that can be said about the presence of immigrants, rather as though it were contained within the implicit definition of immigration. Immigration is meaningful, and intelligible to the political understanding, only if it is a source of 'benefits' or, at the very least, only if the 'costs' imputable to it do not outweigh the 'benefits' it may procure. This presupposition is the starting point for the constitution of a whole method of analysis that consists in calculating the effects, some positive ('benefits') and others negative ('costs'), of immigration.[4] But because it is not simply just an investigation into the effects of all kinds that immigration may have, the usual way in which economists and especially econometricians 'discuss the problems of migration in complimentary or antithetical terms of benefits and costs' (Scott 1966) is possible only if there is no investigation either into the way what are conventionally termed 'costs' and 'benefits' are defined respectively, or into the political meaning of what is presented as being, ultimately, no more than an 'accounting' technique, an administrative technique of the 'rationalization of budgetary choices' type or even preparatory material for planning commissions.

In this domain, economic practice and econometric calculation assume that their definition of 'costs' and 'benefits' has an *absolute* value – i.e. one that is invariable and universally applicable – and that the arbitrary dividing line between the two is *necessary* and immutable. As the distinction has been established once and for all, nothing remains to be done except to refine the investigation of the elements to be taken into consideration so as to establish a balance sheet for each column and, finally, an overall balance sheet for immigration and to specify the basis on which it has been drawn up. This is usually done by introducing a certain number of distinctions such as, for example, between short-term effects and long-term effects, or concealed effects that are slow to emerge, or even, in the best of cases, between *quantitative* effects (essentially economic effects, and even then those that are easiest to quantify) and *qualitative* effects. In other words, and broadly speaking, this implies the introduction of a whole series of social, political, cultural, etc. presuppositions (or prejudices) that the economy, in the strict sense of the term, cannot grasp, still less measure, and therefore simply mentions or suggests.[5] Each of the elements taken into consideration in order to draw up this accountant's balance sheet of the 'costs' and 'benefits' of immigration in fact constitutes something of a struggle. This not simply a struggle between theoreticians of the economics of immigration or even specialists in the social management of immigrants: it is also a matter of social struggle. The struggle to represent immigration and immigrants in economic terms of 'costs' and 'benefits' is in reality the classic example of political work being disguised as a purely economic measure. Using the language of economics to rationalize a problem that is not (or not only) economic is tantamount to converting ethical or political arguments into purely technical arguments.

We ask ourselves about and quarrel over what immigration 'costs' and what it 'brings in' as though these questions pertained to its very 'nature'. This problematic is so dominant as to appear to be self-evident, to be the only possible problematic. Not only does this remove the need for any other questions; it also means that the problematic itself is immune to any critical reflection. The exercise in accounting that retranslates it cannot be reduced to what it wants and believes itself to be, namely a mere technique designed to 'rationalize the choice' of the decisions to be taken. Because it is applied to a population enjoying a particular status, it has nothing in common with analogous exercises dealing with other groups. In discussions of children, the young or the elderly, the only question that arises is how to calculate and identify the resources required to treat the populations concerned in the way we wish to treat them. In the case of the immigrant population, it is a question of establishing the benefits and costs of the policy of having recourse to immigration, or in other words the costs and benefits of the *existence* or 'disappearance' of the immigrant population. Thanks to an apparently technical question, it is the whole problem of the *legitimacy* of immigration that is objectively being raised, and that problem haunts all discourses of this kind. Almost nothing else is said about immigrants, especially when, as in the case of the 'economic theory of the comparative costs and benefits of immigration' the discourse deals, knowingly and explicitly, with the function of immigration, and consists solely in either *legitimizing* it or denouncing its (basic) *illegitimacy*.[6]

The struggle around the 'immigration's social balance sheet' may well, like many struggles around political issues, be an endless struggle because of the many constructions and reconstructions generated by the multiple – countless – effects of immigration, and because they can all be counted either as 'costs' or 'benefits'. Because 'the economic theory of the comparative costs and benefits of immigration' has, to date, given rise only to disagreements as to which elements should be taken into account, we have to agree from the outset to accept what it is that the theory demands we accept without any prior discussion. We have to accept the principle that differentiates between 'costs' and 'benefits', or the principle that establishes a positive or negative balance for immigration. This masks a whole series of other questions which now become unthinkable. They include, for example, the question of who pays the 'cost' of immigration and who 'benefits' from it. At a more basic level, describing, exclusively, discernible and arbitrarily divorced elements of a whole as 'costs' or 'benefits' when they have no (economic and political) reality except as a totality is, however, tantamount to giving an a priori definition of the meaning that is to be given to each of those elements. We impose that meaning all the more imperatively in that we do not realize what is going on. The best examples of this attempt to 'technicalize' the political are provided by Anicet Le Pors's (1977) study of the monetary flows for which immigration is responsible, and the discrepancies between his findings and those reached by Fernand Icart on the basis of much the same data.[7]

If there are 'costs' that have to be imputed to immigration, the first that comes to mind is, of course, the monetary cost borne by any country that has recourse to immigration as a result of the transfers made, on the one hand, by immigrants themselves 'from their savings' and by social agencies on the other (family allowances, social security payments, retirement pensions, various other pensions, etc.). But what might be seen as an obvious and indisputable 'cost' is not without 'benefits' of other kinds:

> We might, in particular, raise the question of the incidence of the transferring abroad of savings.... Now, it transpires that a fall of one million francs in the amount transferred abroad means that the balance of payment falls by only some 38,000 francs. An *ex ante* fall in transfers abroad in fact leads to a rise in domestic consumption; much of that rise is accounted for not by a rise in domestic production, but by rising imports or falling exports. What is more, a fall in the transfer of savings to foreign countries restricts the purchasing power of those countries' currencies and therefore their imports, including imports from France. (Le Pors 1977: 185)

Conversely, if countries of immigration do enjoy one immediate and initial 'benefit' that appears to be net of any corresponding cost, it is that of 'importing' adult men who are still young and therefore 'useful' and productive on the first day that they arrive. This 'benefit', which consists in the savings made on what Alfred Sauvy calls 'breeding costs', is considerably underestimated in Fernand Icart's report, or even transformed into a 'cost'. The 'quality' of these men, who have been brought up in poor underdeveloped countries, and therefore at a 'cost' lower than the average French rate, means that they are more 'expensive' (or at least more 'expensive' than one thinks) because of the 'cost' of adapting them to the society and the labour that use them.

By these criteria, anything can be both a 'cost' and a 'benefit'. What one vision of the phenomenon of immigration sees as a 'cost' can be seen as a 'benefit' by another, and conversely. One could spend a long time enumerating 'contradictions' of this kind, as each of the criteria that is retained can be classed either as a 'cost' or a 'benefit', or at least as having a 'cost' element and a 'benefit' element. And the further we move away from those factors that are traditionally or primarily within the economic domain or, in other words, the closer we come to factors that are overlooked by economic techniques because they are resistant to (quantitative) 'measurement', the greater the indeterminacy. It becomes increasingly apparent that the facts we are analysing and interpreting as purely economic data are also, and perhaps primarily, political, social and cultural facts and realities. Take, for example, the birth rate of immigrant families in general, and of families originating from North African countries in particular. At times, there are official rejoicings over the demographic surplus that these families bring to a population that is in decline and ageing; at other times, we deplore (just as officially) the same rise in what we still call the 'immigrant population' (even though the younger generations born in France have not emigrated from anywhere) because it is 'expensive', because it demands too much of family welfare agencies – which is not to say that it is a burden. This is because 'economic' arguments, or the reformulation in economic terms of arguments of a different nature, are more easily or more innocently admissible. And what is said about the ambiguity of the immigrant population's birth rate or, in other words and basically, about family immigration and about the old immigrant's – a single isolated worker without his family – transition to being a progenitor, now applies, because of the difficult labour market, to another characteristic of the immigrant, even though it constitutes and defines him, namely his status as a worker. The 'benefit' represented by the labour-power he supplies – and for which he is compensated by the wage he is paid, and which he can transfer – tends to be redefined as a 'cost'.[8] It is redefined as a direct 'cost' when the immigrant is unemployed and thus no longer has any personal justification for his existence, and as an indirect 'cost' when the immigrant is employed, rather as though the job he holds represented a sort of loss of income, or a virtual wound inflicted on the national labour force.

Being the product of a constructive operation whose objectively political genesis and significance may escape its authors, the parallel established between what immigration 'costs' and 'what it brings in' inevitably contrasts different groups which, because they have an unequal or different 'interest' in immigration, are inclined to produce antagonistic definitions of it. Whilst it is easier and more agreeable to speak of these 'costs' and 'benefits' – and especially the 'costs' – in the technical and relatively neutral language of economics (or what is intended to be or is perceived as neutral language), it is still the case that this language cannot conceal the fact that it is in reality a matter of 'costs' and 'benefits' relating to value systems that have nothing to do with the economic sphere in the strict sense of that term. In order to be acceptable, this sort of 'economics of immigration' would have to be a total economics; it would, in other words, have to include all the other 'costs' and all the other 'benefits' that are overlooked or totally ignored by a strictly economic theory.[9]

Things become more complicated still when we recall that, because it too is a product of the same logic and is vulnerable to the same criticisms, 'the cost-benefit economic theory of immigration' can be transposed to the country of immigration and give rise to the constitution of a homologous theory. This 'cost-benefit economic theory of emigration' is, as it happens, beginning to produce its first findings. They are products of the same analytic schema, and of the same combination of simulations and dissimulations, of the partial disclosure and partial concealment of the real meaning of the criteria which it derives from struggles in which it is itself an issue. These accountancy descriptions of immigration on the one hand and emigration on the other finally produce a sort of accountancy description of the entire migratory phenomenon. That description is itself an issue in the struggle between the two partners – the country of immigration and the country of emigration – who meet and come into conflict over this issue. By making explicit the interests of each of the contracting parties, the treaties they sign, the 'bilateral agreements on labour and social security' and the negotiations they conduct to that end, establish the ground for the objectification of struggles over the simultaneously economic and political definition of the respective costs and benefits.

The truth of power relations

The problem of the 'theory of the comparative costs and benefits of immigration' (and emigration), which intrinsically haunts the entire migratory phenomenon (and emigration), is also present, implicitly and as a schema that generates forms of behaviour and discourses, within emigration and in the country of emigration. It affects its ways of thinking about emigration, its overall attitudes towards it (in other words the relationship between emigrants as a whole on the one hand, and the society of emigration on the other) and, in addition to all that, the system of relations that binds it to the country of immigration.

Relations between France and Algeria with regard to emigration are in that respect 'exemplary', and provide the best illustration one could hope to find of the relationship between dominant and dominated, which is objectively inscribed in the relationship between countries of emigration and countries of immigration. This lack of symmetry emerges all the more clearly, and is therefore all the greater and all the more conflict-ridden, in that both partners agree and strive to mask – to mask from themselves and to mask from one another – the truth of their relationship. Both partners pretend to believe – and this is an implicit precondition for any possible contract – in the bilateral and even reciprocal character of the contractual relationship they establish, even though that relationship is contractual only in form and only for the duration of the contract, and even though it is reciprocal only in theory (there is no way that the 'immigrant' will receive in the host country the treatment reserved for the 'cooperator' in his native country). The dominated country (the country of emigration) tries to the best of its political, economic and even technical and intellectual ability (its potential understanding of its emigration and of its partner's immigration) to reduce the gap or distortion of which it is the victim. The dominant country (the country of immigration) ignores the intrinsic advantages it derives from its dominant position, and can agree to concessions, either out of condescension or because they procure for it advantages of a different kind (economic, political or diplomatic) – and usually both at the same time – designed, apparently, to reduce the gap, or even to deny the inequality of the relationship and, by that very fact, its inherent violence.

At this level, the exchange is intrinsically and incontestably in favour of the country that supplies the surplus jobs and, no less incontestably, to the disadvantage of the country that exports a labour force that becomes available for emigration once it has discovered and realized that it is not being used (see Sayad 1979b). The thesis, which is frequently and all too readily accepted, that emigration constitutes, for countries of emigration, a 'safety valve' on the social or even the political level, or that it allows them to get rid of a surplus of unemployed men, which is always dangerous, etc., influences all negotiations relating to the transfer of labour. Should any difficulties arise (periods of crisis in the labour market, crises in relations between the two countries), the same thesis comes close to providing the opportunity and the means to blackmail the country of emigration. Both partners know this, even when one or both of them pretends (which is a reasonable strategy) that the bilateral confrontation takes place on equal terms.

Both the inherent advantage that accrues to the country of immigration and its corollary – the intrinsic weakness of the country of emigration – can also (provided we leave the strictly economic sphere) be expressed in terms of *presence* and *absence*. The country of immigration has the 'advantage' of having present in its territory, under its sovereignty and under its authority (the authority of its law, its institutions, its courts, its police, its rules, etc.) immigrants, i.e. nationals (emigrants), from some other country. This can also, and *a contrario*, be described in terms of the 'weakness' of the country of emigration, or the original 'tare' of emigration. Its emigrant nationals (who are immigrants in another country, or the other country's immigrants) are *absent*, outside its territory, its sovereignty, its authority and, more generally, beyond the action of the integrating mechanisms and identificatory processes typical of any society. They are, in short, outside its common culture (and, correlatively, in the territory and under the sovereignty and authority and, more generally, subject to the integrating action and culture of some other nation).

The combined history of colonization and emigration-immigration also means, and will do so for a long time to come, that part of that community, namely the young people born in France after 1 January 1963 (or, paradoxically, after Algerians in France became real immigrants in the juridico-political sense of the term), is divided and will remain divided. These young people have a twofold status (that of the emigrant and that of the immigrant), but they are also divided between two countries, two societies and two nations. They are also divided by their dual *nationalities*. They are of Algerian nationality by descent (they are children born of Algerian fathers) but they were automatically granted French nationality. That fact cannot be challenged by either the French government, should it wish to deny them that nationality (unless it infringes its own law and the provisions of the French code of nationality), themselves (should they wish to avoid this obligation and the effects of their possession of that nationality, and especially military service), or, a fortiori, Algeria – because of what French nationality law terms the fact of 'dual birth'. One of the effects of this 'division' is that if they are still 'emigrants' (i.e. Algerians, or in possession of Algerian nationality), even though they have never actually emigrated from Algeria, they disappear as 'immigrants' (at least in legal terms). The French nationality they have been granted denies their existence: they are but foreign immigrants in France. They are now 'divided' between the nation of their immigration (and its nationality) and the nation of their emigration or their parents' emigration, just as the whole of Algeria was 'divided' between the conquering nation (and its imposed nationality) and the conquered 'nation' (and its negated or forbidden nationality). Both products and victims of this double history, they are also a living reminder of it. They are its anachronistic actualization. The conflict of nationalities they generate is all the more acute in that it relates basically to the definition that is given of the territorial competence of French sovereignty (articles 6 and 8 of the Code de la nationalité). France refuses (for the moment) to 'infringe' (or revise) its own legislation, and refuses to discuss, even implicitly and retrospectively, the state of affairs that prevailed until the independence of Algeria (i.e. under colonization). Algeria, for its part and leaving aside considerations of pride or what might be called purely symbolic interests, refuses to recognize the automatic and unilateral 'naturalization' (by the will of French legislation) of its 'children' (its 'natural' children or those it regards as such). It therefore resists the infringement of its national integrity in the name of the integrity of *its* population (even though, having been born abroad, it resides outside the national territory) and its national integrity, and refuses to surrender to the old colonial order it fought and from which it liberated itself. As a result, both parties demand, in all objectivity (and as though independently of the will of the agents concerned) an exclusive allegiance to the nationality of one or the other state on the part of the children over whom they are in dispute.

Another bizarre feature of these state-to-state relations is that those who are regarded as emigrants by one state, and as immigrants by the other, are ultimately no more than 'raw material' for a phenomenon that these states have to come to terms with. They are *immigrants* in the fullest of senses (that is to say, they are totally 'immersed' in and deeply involved in French society and all its manifestations in a way that no other foreigner could ever be) but, despite that, they are *emigrants* almost from the very first day of their emigration (that is to say, they are still strongly attached to Algeria, the country of their emigration or their origins, even if they know very little, or nothing at all, about it). This *paradoxical* position, which is one of the *exemplary* characteristics of Algerian emigrant-immigrants in France, actually makes them marginal to the inter-state interests recognized by the two parties that enter into contracts over emigration and immigration. Whilst the interests of the emigrants do originally coincide with those of their country – or, more specifically, with the closer interests of their families, their kinship groups and their communities rather than with the more distant, indirect and abstract interest of their state (its political interests) – these systems of interests inevitably tend to diverge as their emigration lasts longer and longer and as, in the long term, relations between the country of emigration and its emigrants become more distended. The one exception is, it seems, the symbolic domain, where the interests of the state and of individuals (pride) merge totally and are both inseparable and mutually reinforcing. Honour is a capital that can never be shared. In every other domain, the interests of the emigrant-immigrants tend to become autonomous, distinct from or even opposed to (at least partly) the interest of both the country of emigration and the country of immigration, and certainly to the common interests of both those countries. All the negotiations to which emigration and immigration give rise involve a real attempt to make *official* interests prevail, as they are the only interests worthy of consideration in the eyes of politicians. This is another reason for the objectification of the intrinsic basic 'complicity' that must bind to-gether the two countries if both emigration and immigration are to exist. Ultimately, it is easy, or easier, to accept that the interests of emigrant-immigrants and, correlatively, their country of emigration may come into conflict with the official or state interests of the country of immigration (and may be thwarted by those interests), given its experience of immigration and of the super-profits it creates for its users (this opposition is, like the broader opposition between the immigrant population and the country of immigration, a paradigmatic variation on the more basic opposition between a wage-earning labour force and its employers, between the proletariat and the bourgeoisie, etc). But whilst the interests of those same emigrant-immigrants can diverge from, or even come into conflict with, the interests of the country of emigration – interests which that country often likes to present and impose on all as 'higher' interests or as 'the overriding interests of the nation' – it requires the degree of complexity (and exceptionality) reached by Algerian immigration to create a situation that borders on the scandalous. The indispensable duplicity (which is automatic) inherent in the migratory phenomenon determines the illusion that, although contradictory, the interests of the three parties involved (the countries of emigration and of immigration and the emigrant-immigrants on whose behalf and in whose name the first two partners take decisions whilst pretending to ignore the fact that they may have specific interests of their own) can be reconciled and regarded as complementary and almost mutually interdependent, but this involves an agreement between only two of the parties involved. The country of immigration is thus implicitly obliged to recognize that the interests of immigrants (to the extent that they are 'emigrants') and the interests of the country from which they have emigrated, are one and the same, and that to further the interests of the country of emigration (or origin) is also to further the interests of both emigrants and immigrants; the interests of the two parties, which are presumed to be interdependent, are identified to such an extent that, having as-sumed (not without reason) that the interests of the immigrants are also and necessarily the interests of their country, it quite naturally comes to accept that the interests of the country of emigration – when they are (in the best of cases) really discussed – inevitably coincide with the 'real' interests of the immigrants and that, ultimately, the immi-grants' only 'real' interests are those which both countries recognize as also being the interests of the country of emigration.[10] It is all the easier for the country of immigration to succumb to this illusion when it helps to 'moralize' its recourse to immigration and, especially, in these circumstances, its relationship with the country (or countries) of emigration – especially now that immigration, which has become the result of a contractual arrangement between states, is seen as having the additional virtue of being a new aspect of a policy of cooperation or of the provision of development aid. Such, in any case, is the 'exemplary' role the 'training-return' policy agreed upon by both countries is being asked to play. Quite independently of the way it is applied and the results that will, or will not, be achieved, it therefore already appears to be 'exemplary' in terms of both its genesis, its functions and its overall meaning. Either there will be neither 'training' nor 'return' (no training because there is no return), or the 'training' will be divorced from the 'return' (which is not to say that there will be 'no return' in the sense that the fact that there is no obligation to return provides a guarantee that training will be given). That is how the country of emigration understands it; the country of immigration tends to understand it as meaning primarily 'return', as the 'training' is, in this case, no more than an extra, not to say an alibi (at least in terms of the spirit in which training was defined, and in which annual quotas for trainees and returnees were established). Such a formula is without doubt a wonderful illustration of this interplay of faith and bad faith – or faith defined as bad faith – that is inherent in anything to do with emigration-immigration.

We cannot conclude without at least evoking one further aspect of Algerian immigration, as it too is *exemplary* in more than one sense: the type of relationship which exists between Algerian immigrants in France and Algeria as both representation (political, cultural and symbolic) and will, or as self-representation (insofar as they 'will' themselves to be Algerian) and reality (social, economic, cultural, etc.). I refer to the history of that relationship, which has not always been serene, even though it is basically the history of their relationship with themselves. In order even to introduce this topic, which it is not possible to discuss here, we would have to analyse the whole of the discourse about its emigration (and, in a sense, itself) that Algeria addresses, first, to the emigrants themselves and even more so to the country to which they have 'emigrated', and then to itself. More specifically, we would have to analyse the genesis and functions (and especially the symbolic functions) of the discourse on 'reinsertion', as it sheds a particular light on the relationship Algerian society has with itself thanks to its emigration. Algeria sees in its emigration an image that is a variant (envied or detested) on itself and a variation on its history (which might have been possible). We would have to determine the exact role that Algeria, or the policy it adopted with respect to emigration, played, against all expectations and even though it contradicts the desired goal and the expected results (a policy of maintaining contact and reintegration from a distance, or despite the distance), in the gradual constitution of the (relative) *autonomy* that the Algerian immigrant community has, on the one hand, acquired, and that it has, on the other, had thrust upon it. We would have to determine the role of an entire discourse that denounces emigration as 'an accident of history', praising (officially) the emigrant population as an 'integral part of the nation', making the 'reinsertion' of emigrants a national 'obligation' (and this discourse inevitably provokes jealousy and helps to propagate the view that the emigrant is a 'profiteer' and, therefore, to create around him and about him a climate of suspicion and a feeling that he is guilty, if not a traitor, because he has withdrawn from the 'national game').[11] We would have to look at the effects of seminars and national conferences on emigration, of 'national emigration day'. We would have to examine the role of the organization and 'moralization' of emigrants in France itself, which is entrusted to a quasi-'official' organization with considerable technical and financial resources at its disposal, and a large staff paid out of the Algerian state's budget. The association is defined by French law (and governed by the 1901 law), but in the eyes of all (its own eyes, the eyes of Algeria, the eyes of the emigrant-immigrants, of course, but also, with a certain bad faith and when it suits its interests, in the eyes of France itself) it seems to be an official Algerian organization and the FLN's [Front de libération nationale] official representative in France. Indeed, it is almost officially treated as such (by France). We would also have to consider the existence in France of the 'official' press of the country of emigration (a weekly in French and a magazine in Arabic), etc.

I would like to hope that, even though it says nothing new about its object, this picture, although crudely painted in broad brushstrokes, goes some little way to explaining the particular and particularly significant position that this particular immigration occupies in the overall panorama of immigrations past and present, no matter whether they originate from European countries or Third World countries and, in the case of the latter, from the former French colonial empire or from countries that were not formerly colonized by France, etc. I would like to hope that it contributes to an understanding of the *symbolic* value of this immigration, as much for the country of immigration in its relations with the immigrant population as for the immigrants themselves and for all immigrants.

4

Nationalism and Emigration

Does it have to be recalled that all emigration is a *break*, a break with a territory and, by that very fact, with a population, a social order, an economic order, a political order, and a cultural and moral order? But although it is the cause of breaks, emigration is itself the product of a fundamental break. If emigration is to commence and then perpetuate itself, all the structures that once ensured the coherence of society must have broken down. And we know that the initial break is, in the case of Algerian emigration to France (and, surely, in the case of many other emigrations), the direct product of colonization. The entire history of this break, and therefore of emigration subsequent to that break, merges with the history of the peasantry, which was and still is the major supplier of emigrants. It supplies slightly fewer emigrants today than it did in the past, and it does so less directly because candidates for emigration to France who, in the past, would have left their rural home villages without any intermediary stage now (when they can emigrate) spend a transitional period of variable duration with their families in some Algerian city before emigrating to France.

An objectively political act

To emigrate objectively (that is, without the knowledge of partners and independently of their will) constitutes an act that is, without any doubt, basically political, even if it is in the very nature of the migratory phenomenon, in the form in which we know it in France, for example, to mask and deny that fact. This is even truer in cases where emigration is inscribed in a colonial context: it is political despite the fact that its destination is the metropolis or, to be more accurate, because it moves in the direction of the metropolis. It was totally bound up with its genesis but also, albeit in a less direct and visible way, with another emigration, which was completely and immediately in the service of and for the benefit of the colonists (the emigration of permanent or seasonal agricultural workers attached to colonial estates). The colonial establishment therefore inevitably saw emigration to the metropolis as a rival emigration. It was, that is, 'unfairly' competing for a labour force that was already available in abundance and, what is more, for a potential labour force that the colonists regarded was rightfully theirs as having been definitively or structurally created for its exclusive benefit. Under these conditions, providing any other work for that work force was, even though it was superabundant, inevitably seen as a sort of embezzlement. Emigration was necessarily a political act in this sense too. Even though they denied it, the emigrants themselves experienced their emigration to France in that way because it exempted them from the other emigration to which they knew themselves to be destined: to the farms of the colonizers. No matter whether they were or were not agricultural workers (either permanent or seasonal) – that being the initial form taken by rural emigration and the proletarianization of the *fellahs* – those who emigrated to France were more or less consciously aware that, by acting in this way, they were escaping the most direct and most visible form of colonial exploitation and *objectively* freeing themselves from the allegiance they were required to show with respect to the colonial order. This was an expression of a necessarily political 'nationalism' on the part of the first emigrants, even though it could not be expressed in truly political terms. No immigrant from the colony, and no native who emigrates to the metropolis, can forget that he is first and foremost someone who has been colonized (and not just an immigrant in the sense that any foreigner can be an immigrant). Because he was a man who had been colonized, or a man whose political and historical national existence had been denied, emigration provided the Algerian emigrant with the opportunity to discover politics and nationalism – because in the last analysis and for a colonized man, politics inevitably means nationalism.[1] We can say that exile necessarily takes on a political significance in all these senses. More so than any other circumstances that are likely to create or strengthen bonds of solidarity, the exile into which the emigrant is forced – in other words the minority existence that is forced upon him and which must be endured when he has to live *amongst others* (who are, as it happens, also the colonizers[2]) – inevitably forges new and collective thoughts and hopes, if not militant demands and actions or even truly political aspirations. And even if this is its only effect, the detour via emigration does have positive features: because of the alienation effect it has on every emigrant, it forces them all to relativize their original condition. This is an imperative necessity, not only in intellectual terms but also in very practical terms. Having already been forced upon even those of the colonized who were least exposed to the new order of colonization, this necessity becomes imperative for all immigrants, and particularly for colonized immigrants in metropolitan society. Both are committed to a course of action they cannot escape or even, in the case of the latter, avoid by marginalizing themselves in the way that they still could in the colony thanks to those pockets of 'traditionalism' that had survived and perpetuated themselves, but which emigration was now beginning to penetrate. This situation is no more than an example of or a paradigmatic variation on what can, in the circumstances, be regarded as a generic law: whenever there is contact between cultures, it is the culture that is in the dominated position that is required to make the greater and more immediate attempt to reinvent itself and to arrive at a relatively truer and better understanding of the dominant culture. Ethnocentrism is primarily a characteristic of the dominant, and it is part of the culture of the dominant (a culture which aspires to being universal, absolute and the only culture that is a culture). Given that they have every confidence in themselves and in their culture, there is nothing for the dominant to 'reinvent', and nothing to understand in a practical mode. And when, exceptionally, they do acquire the means to understand these 'others', who are culturally foreign to them, their understanding remains at the level of intellection, of theoretical reflection. Even when they understand it best, or even when they try to avoid ethnocentrism, their understanding still remains a product of their own culture. The first reaction of the first emigrants was no doubt one of *astonishment* in the strongest sense of the word. The 'relativization' experienced by the emigrant and by the colonized before him – and the experience was more intense for the former than the latter – was equivalent to the discovery of not only cultural 'arbitrariness' – almost in the sense in which academic anthropology understands that term – but also of *history*. The discovery is all the greater and more profound because, as immigration becomes more prolonged – i.e. expands and intensifies – the emigrant's investigation into, and the knowledge he acquires of, the other world into which he has been thrown become more profound. He lives in a cosmos that is very different from his own, a world which consists of a mode of relations, a mode of existence, a system of exchanges, an economy, a way of being, etc. – in short, a culture, and the comparisons to which the investigation gives rise provide an effective introduction to two differentiated social existences and to the differences between them. Simply because it helps him to break with his initial colonized condition (being colonized in the colony), emigration authorizes a new social, and therefore political, world-view, a new representation of his relationship with the world, and of the position he occupies within it. Whereas the old attitude, which was historically and culturally determined, made him seem deeply attached to the colonized condition, which was perceived – and how could it be otherwise? – not as a product of history, but as a sort of natural 'given', he now discovers the historicity of that condition; in other words, he ascribes to it an origin, a social genesis and, therefore, a historical meaning. Emigration provides an experience of a social, economic, cultural and, in a word, political world that is different from the familiar world. It supplies a minimal guarantee for the time being and, thanks to a supply of relatively stable and organized jobs, it provides for the future. The emigrant condition is therefore superior to the colonized condition and has, so to speak, the virtue of containing the seeds of the principle that differentiates between the *status of proletarians* (and emigrants who have come to France tend to become proletarians) capable of elaborating potentially revolutionary projects, and the *status of sub-proletarians* (and peasants who have been deracinated and 'depeasantified' at home tend to become sub-proletarians) who inevitably have eschatological expectations. And although the condition of the wage earner does have differential effects in this respect, that is not the effect of some magical metamorphosis it induces in those who enter the wage-system but, rather, the effect of the way it inculcates a certain type of disposition. These are expressed both in the daily practices of existence and in the projection of a future which, in the circumstances, can only be revolutionary. Such are the political 'virtues' of immigration, which is to be understood here as meaning the experience of waged labour, and of anything to do with waged labour that is capable of structuring a new *temporal consciousness* and a new *social consciousness* (even if this 'lesson' does not always have the effects one might expect it to have, or produces them unevenly, mainly because of the differential dispositions of emigrants or groups of emigrants).

When the same experience is undergone in Algeria, assuming that it is possible in Algeria, it is just as powerful as its equivalent in emigration. It is just as productive, if not more so, because the social origins and the social and cultural capital of this initial kernel of the Algerian working class (and they are very different in every respect to those of the marginal population that provided both the local agricultural labour force and emigrants to France) appear to be such as to encourage – at home rather than in emigration – a more rapid, more confident and more real integration into the world of labour and its modes of organization (unionization after the extension of the 1884 law to Algeria, involvement in working-class struggles, an understanding of the bargaining power of strikes etc.). The very structure of the colonial economy, which never created many industrial jobs, combined with the essentially discriminatory nature of the colonial regime (the few non-agricultural waged job opportunities that were available were reserved as a matter of priority for the European population, which had its own proletariat) obviously left little room for the formation of an Algerian working class. But, even though it was in the minority, it was beginning, against all the odds and very timidly, to constitute itself. And it is significant to note that, throughout the entire interwar period from 1920 to 1937, it was those sectors that employed an Algerian work force, even in restricted numbers (the abattoirs, docks, mines, etc.), that were most active at the forefront of social demands and strikes (for example, the miners' strike in Beni-Saf, the workers' strike at the Bastos cigarette factory in Oran, the strike organized by the municipal workers' union in Oran in 1919, the railwaymen's strike in 1920, the strike in the abattoirs of Algiers in 1921, the municipal strikes, and especially those of 1924 and 1929, in the docks of Mostaganem, Arzew and Oran, the Algiers refuse collectors' strike of 1927, etc.). Algerian workers were obviously involved in the joint strikes called by the unions or organized by the European fraction of the proletariat and the objective meaning of this involvement was the most elementary degree of solidarity.[3] More significantly, more autonomous strikes were led by Algerians (and here, there is a parallel with what is happening today within immigration in France).

But just who were the immigrants of the day who provided the backbone of support for the Etoile nord-africaine (ENA)[4]? In order to arrive at a real understanding of this generation of Algerian emigrants, we would have to construct, within a single perspective and from a single viewpoint, several parallel histories, and demonstrate how they helped to establish a truly political formation amongst Algerian emigrants. First would be the history of the colonization of Algeria and, more specifically, of the viticulture introduced after 1880 – a speculative venture which, after so many pipe dreams, sealed the colonial destiny of Algeria. Next would be the history of the (waged) labour provided by the 'reserve army' constituted by the dispossession and, worse still, the 'depeasantification' of the *fellahs*. We would then have to look at the outcome of all this, at the history of emigration in the true sense of the word and, finally, we would have to construct the history of both the political movements and the whole socio-political complex (in Algeria, obviously, but also in France), to which emigration necessarily bears witness.

Reconstructing all these conditions also allows us to outline a possible profile of the emigrants of the interwar period (1920–38) who were to be, at the same time, actors and spectators, militants, sympathizers or merely witnesses of the formation and action of the ENA. Having said that, we must be wary of believing, as a certain hagiography would have us believe, that the ENA was created *ex nihilo*, or that it was the novel creation of a few individuals or a group of pioneers whose only assets were their 'revolutionary' virtues or faith. Similarly we must, at least until such time as more information becomes available, be suspicious of the official thesis that a 'revolutionary' continuity leads successively from the Etoile nord-africaine (first version) to the (new style) Glorieuse Etoile nord-africaine, then to the PPA-MTLD (Parti du peuple algérien / Mouvement pour le triomphe des libertés démocratiques) and finally to the FLN, which was the liberation front of the war of independence and then the only party in independent Algeria. The political bias and ideological character of this thesis are too obvious for it not to come under suspicion of being a partisan reading of history, and its incorporation, along with that of many other readings, into the history of the Etoile itself, is a precondition for historically objective work.

The field of associations

Because they are no more than elements of a broader structure, associations have to be analysed in terms of a *field*, whether or not they are of a political order (parties or modelled on political parties) or associations of a different nature – as the ENA was in its day, and as are the community associations to be found amongst today's immigrants. Taken in isolation, each part (i.e. each formation) derives its function and significance only from the position of the other parts, and from its relationship with each of them and with the whole they constitute. In order to be able to understand the position occupied within that field by one of the elements that constitute it, namely the ENA, we therefore have to reconstruct the totality of the field – in other words, the set of positions that is socially possible at a given moment and in the context of the day. Although it may have had specific characteristics of its own, the ENA was, truth to tell, neither the first nor the only association to have come into its own through the channels of emigration or thanks to the emigration of Algerian workers to France. Even when the stated and self-proclaimed function of these associations was no more than that of mutual aid, relief or assistance, the colonial context imprinted upon even the most 'apolitical' of them an overdetermination that objectively gave them a political significance and function, no matter whether they were solidarity associations, associations to defend material and moral interests (or what we would now call social and cultural interests) or charitable associations. No matter whether they were associations inspired by or based upon openly political bases – assimilationism, reformism or, a fortiori, revolutionary nationalism – 'forming associations' was in itself, in the case of emigrants from the colony, necessarily a political act, as was the very act of emigrating from the colony. The colonial administration in both the metropolis and the colony clearly understood this. It rigorously pursued these associations (even those that were effectively established at its suggestion) and subjected them to vigilant controls and repression. It was as though any kind of self-proclaimed association that aspired to a public existence and visible activity was, so to speak, an embryonic form of nationalism even before nationalism found an explicit voice and a truly political expression. But, with the exception of the ENA, the twofold isolation that affected such associations condemned them to an inevitable death because they could not put down roots. *Actual forms of interdependence* which espoused the traditional framework of the relations specific to emigrants (kinship, as defined by various hierarchical relations, villages, regions of origin, etc.) made it unnecessary to have recourse to the formulae preferred by explicitly organized associations such as local groups, political parties, trade unions, etc., which were, in institutional terms, more bureaucratic, or at least less personalized, at both the constitutional and functional level.

These associations, or the more or less ephemeral attempts to create them, all had to be based on structures of a different nature (political parties of the right or the left, trade-union associations and other currents of opinion, etc.) with which they felt some sympathy or kinship, and of which they were sometimes mere emanations. They had to try to transpose to France political tendencies that were emerging in both colonial and Muslim opinion inside Algeria (the Jeune Algérien [young Algerian] movement, the Fédération des élus [Federation of elected representatives], the reformist Muslim current, etc.). Amongst the associations that aspired to fame or a national dimension, one could cite the Comité d'action pour la défense des indigènes nord-africains, the Ligue de défense des musulmans nord-africains, the Comité d'action et de solidarité en faveur des victimes de la répression de Constantine, the Comité d'organisation des Nord-Africains de Paris, the Comité d'action pour le retour de l'émir Khaled,[5] the *Nâdî al-ta'dib* ('circle' or 'educational circles'), etc. and, finally, the ENA. Others, which had links with the Confédération générale du travail unitaire (CGTU),[6] included the *amicales de protection* ('protection associations') established to mobilize Algerian workers for demonstrations and meetings (8 November 1924, or the anniversary of the Bolshevik Revolution; 23 November of that same year, which was the day on which the ashes of Jaurès were transferred to the Panthéon).

The same phenomenon can be observed at the local level, either because these organizations tried to migrate to towns and regions with a strong Algerian presence, or because ad hoc associations were created at the local level. These included the Association des travailleurs algériens in Lyon, the Amicale protectrice des Nord-Africains in Marseille; Solidarité algérienne, the Comité de défense des droits et des intérêts des Algériens, the Cercle de l'éducation de Marseille, the Association franco-musulane and the Comité provisoire de la mosquée de Marseille.[7] One could certainly find just as many examples in every region of France (especially in the north and the east) where the population of Algerian emigrants was concentrated.

The ENA was undoubtedly the organization that was to become best known. It was the most explicitly political of all these associations. It was the most active and, of course, the most subject to repression. And, despite the repression, it was also the most long-lived (some of its supporters and founder members ended up in the PPA, which was a truly political formation, then in the PPA-MTLD, which was the PPA in electoralist and legalist guise, as well – why not? – as in the FLN). Some historians like to trace the very origins of the nationalist movement back to the ENA. Insofar as it is a historical reconstruction, that genealogy is a real focus of social and political struggles, as everyone hopes that the history they are reconstructing in this way will give them a particular kind of advantage, such as the symbolic advantage of being able to *legitimize* subsequent history and, therefore, the position they currently occupy or lay claim to.

However that may be, the necessarily 'nationalist' history of the organization known as the ENA, which was a national and nationalist organization despite the communist or internationalist veneer it was able to acquire or had to acquire, is based upon two errors of judgement. On the one hand, it reads the history of that formation solely in terms of the contributions made by an external formation, namely the Parti communiste français (PCF), and Algerian political formations. On the other hand, it fails to distinguish between the positions of all the partners involved in this encounter: the Etoile itself, the Parti communiste algérien (PCA) and all the other political formations contemporary with or subsequent to the ENA that came into being in Algeria and in Algerian society.

On the one hand, the way in which relations between the ENA and the PCA were seen already prefigures the supposedly irreducible distinction, which has now become classic, between nationalism and communism. It would have been more prudent to have adopted the working hypothesis that the two movements and the formations inspired and created by them complemented one another, not only in ideological terms (where we now have a complete theoretical incompatibility), but also at the practical level. Given the way the immigration of the colonized resulted in a combination of the colonial phenomenon (and the nationalism which is both its product and a response to it) and the social dimension of the working-class condition, in which immigrant workers were a new component, it would take a very clever man to make a clear distinction between the respective roles played by the two movements in their common struggle against the colonial yoke. Such an approach has never been in favour with historians, and it has also to overcome a whole series of other objections, which are paradigmatic variants on the major distinction that is conventionally made between nationalism and communism, both of which are usually regarded as pure abstractions. One of these variants, and it is both the most subtle and the most pernicious of all because it seems self-evident simply because we are dealing with colonized labourers and workers in the metropolis, concerns the definition of the Algerian proletariat's localization. For some, Algeria is a society which has its proletariat in France (cf. Ageron 1962: 'The Algerian proletariat was, for the most part, formed in France before its return to Algeria'), whilst, for others, Algerian emigrants living in France were no more than a 'component part of the French proletariat' (R. Gallissot).

On the other hand and quite apart from the fact that it shares a complacent vision of the history it is trying to perpetuate or enhance, the view that the ENA has a 'revolutionary' pre-eminence helps to blunt our awareness of the need to undertake real historical work, and in doing so slows down the work itself. It is, in other words, an obstacle to any real re-evaluation of the history of nationalism – in other words, of the entire history of colonization and its structural effects on Algerian society, which had been radically transformed when it emerged from the colonial ordeal, and ultimately of the entire

history of Algeria. The partisan views that have always been expressed about it on both sides (these views are obviously diametrically
opposed, but the outcome is the same) mean that this history is
doomed to be permanently mutilated.

Emigrants and politics

How does the political (in this case, nationalism) come to immigrants
and how do certain immigrants (which ones?) come to politics and a
political apprenticeship? More specifically, should we not be asking
how it is that they come to a politically constituted and formulated
nationalism given that, in the circumstances, the only possible politics
is a nationalist politics? This type of question has to be answered as a
matter of priority.

Immediately after the Great War, or at a time when emigration
concerned a permanent total of about one hundred thousand workers
(the actual figure was no doubt higher, mainly because of the rapidity
with which emigrants replaced one another at this time), a very
different kind of emigration was also beginning to take shape. We
can describe it as 'political emigration', as opposed to so-called
'labour emigration', even though it did not consist exclusively of
'politicals', or of men who were known to be political before and
independently of their emigration, and who went into exile so as to be
in a better position to act politically. Any emigration-immigration,
especially when it is of colonial origin, eventually attracts, generates
or produces an exclusively *political* component of its own. This may
be because a community of colonized men who have emigrated to the
metropolis for work reasons proves to be a favourable terrain which
sometimes produces truly political exiles and sometimes individuals
who later reveal themselves as political militants. It may also be
because certain members of the emigrant community eventually
become transformed into political agents because they have a number
of distinctive characteristics and a social and cultural capital of a
particular kind. At the same time, these 'political' emigrants are, of
course, also 'labour emigrants' just like all the rest. But strictly speaking, their identical status does not mean that they can be totally
identified with one another.

There are in fact two different and relatively distinct forms (or two
modalities) of emigration and, correlatively, two different categories
of emigrant, but, despite everything that might divide them and make
their emigration different, their common condition as colonized men
makes them interdependent. And because there are two forms of

emigration, there are also two different forms of the same national-ism. Indeed, given the colonial context of the Algeria of the day, which denied the colonized any possibility of expression and a fortiori any possibility of political action, especially when, because of the social origins of its supporters and spokesmen, that expression became tinged with a nationalism that was slightly more radical than the nationalism of the 'elites' (or, as was said at the time, of 'evolved' native politicians), how could they not be tempted to emi-grate to the metropolis, which they discovered to be different because they wanted it to be different? How could they not be tempted by emigration when, quite aside from its strictly economic function, it provided them with an opportunity to escape the repression incurred by anyone who saw fit to transgress an order planned and established by colonization? Indeed, if we wish to understand the appeal emigra-tion had for this new category of political militants, for whom there was no room in the Algeria of the day (even in the field conceded to 'natives'), it has to be recalled that the only voices that could make themselves heard, and even then within restricted spheres, were the voices of those who were able to come to terms with the limitations imposed by colonial domination. Such men were able to conform to institutional mechanisms specific to the colony and to the rules of the political game characteristic of the colonial situation. These were the voices of those who could observe the form and content of the demands that any dominated political discourse had to respect on pain of being banned. In order to speak of their dominated position, they were, that is, able to adopt the very language of the dominant, which was the only language that could be heard, at least in formal terms (the dominant language as spoken by the dominated who designate the dominated position of the colonized), and adopt forms of representation institutionally designed for that purpose, as they were the only ones tolerated.

The attractions of emigration – but not necessarily the need to emigrate – appeared all the greater in that emigrants discovered, in retrospect, that a period spent in France allowed them to enjoy infin-itely more liberal conditions for political activity (in other words, nationalist activity) than those experienced in the colony. Indeed, all emigrants – militants and non-militants alike – encountered in France political living conditions that were new to them: some while doing their military service in the metropolis of the day (as was the case with Messali in particular), others – a minority – while they were studying there (the first generation of North African students in Paris), as well as those, which was less unusual, who experienced the common lot of the emigrant in the course of their working lives (social struggles, strikes, unionization, etc.). They enjoyed greater latitude for move-ment and speech, and greater freedom of expression and action. They found it possible to reach an understanding with a variety of political currents, including political and trade-union formations and, more generally, a huge anti-colonialist movement from which many expres-sions of solidarity could be expected. They could become involved in various kinds of active struggle and they could attend 'international' meetings, first between nationalists from the various French colonies (who had all sought refuge in Paris for the same reasons) and, later, between those nationalists and their counterparts in other European capitals, etc. All this prefigured the possibility or eventuality of a unitary anti-colonialist or anti-imperialist movement that could bring together all nationalists living under French colonization. Even in this early period, when colonial society was *one*, when no distinction was made between metropolis and colony, when the colo-nial regime and the imperialist system were *one*, and centred on the metropolis, we therefore find the colonized constructing the myth of a 'liberal', 'generous' or 'good' France (or at least a France that was better than its colony), of the France of the 'real' French, as opposed to the 'repressive', 'wicked', 'unjust', 'racist' France incarnated by the 'French' of Algeria, the false French, the neo-French and the neophyte French. The latter had been 'made French' for circumstantial reasons and in order to meet the needs of colonization, partly because of their direct experience – that is, their experience of relations with metro-politan French that were objectively different from those they had with the 'colons' (the 'French' in the colony) – and partly because they were less directly or less immediately involved with the colony. This myth, which was constantly maintained by the very history of colon-ization and sometimes complacently maintained by the 'good' French (who also had an interest in this myth), was to have a long political life, as it was perpetuated beyond the colonial era in the strict sense of the term.

But who were these emigrants that convention describes as 'polit-ical' emigrants? In other words, what social capital and what social dispositions had been acquired by these emigrants who were not like the rest? What was it that distinguished them from run-of-the-mill emigrants? What social determinations led them to imprint a distinct-ive or even exceptional trajectory on their emigration? The vast majority of emigrants were, as we have seen, pauperized peasants who, although they were not unaware of the threats it posed to both their own equilibrium and the shaky equilibrium of their society (the communitarian order and the economic order of traditional society), resorted to the extreme, or even desperate, solution of emigration because they were convinced that by doing so they were helping to safeguard their peasant status. The 'political' emigrants who were their contemporaries were, in contrast, usually from the towns. If they were not from the towns, they already belonged to that section of the rural population that had discovered certain forms of urbanization in Algeria. A good proportion of them had attended school, some having enjoyed a good primary education – a characteristic that was not common at this time, even amongst the urban population – whilst others had reached a higher level (secondary education) and, in some cases, a very high level (higher education). That was a quite exceptional characteristic, especially if we compare their level of education with the overall standard of education of Algerians and with the social origins, which were always modest, of these relatively privileged emigrants. A large number of them had also done their military service in the ranks of the French army. As immigrant workers, they had jobs which, whilst they were not high-ranking, were not, strictly speaking, the labouring jobs of other emigrants and which left them 'leisure' time that they could devote to other activities and that brought them into contact with the public – French and emigrant. They tended to extend their network of social relations far beyond the very restricted and relatively closed world of work (that is, work amongst compatriots, if not members of the same tribe), to say nothing of domestic life. They tended to undertake stays in France that were much longer and therefore more intense, or at least much longer than those effected by other emigrants who regulated their absences from their country in accordance with the needs of the calendar of agricultural labour. They were interested in understanding their new environment – and it was in their interests to invest in it and understand it: witness their cultural good will, their thirst for education and the great effort they put into auto-didacticism. Their political commitment was itself to a large extent no more than a further manifestation of those same intellectual dispositions. They eventually established solid relationships and even friendships (through their political work or their involvement with the unions, etc.) within French society, often married or lived with French women and, in some cases, took French nationality.

The ordinary structures of the family – in other words the distribution of functions and the sharing of responsibilities established between all the men of the same undivided unit – nominated certain types of men for emigration. They were of necessity married men, that is, men bound by ties of marriage. They were reliable men who had proved their worth and who were neither too young, and therefore in danger of failing to meet their obligations, nor too old and therefore freed from the servitude of the most material, and therefore the least noble, of tasks. Those who became political militants in emigration – as a result of their emigration – were single, although this was not the reason they had emigrated. To be single was to be available, especially for political action, which was not without its dangers. Because the very structures of their society denied single people (even men) any legitimate status, these ageing bachelors met with general disapproval. Militants in revolutionary movements are often single. The same is, a fortiori, true of nationalist movements in a colonial situation, and still more so of Algerian nationalist parties, and especially of those most exposed to colonial repression (the ENA, the PPA-MTLD and, to a lesser extent, the UDMA[8]). Their failure to observe the conventions of social morality still exposed them to criticisms that usually remained unspoken, or to discreet reproaches that were voiced only in the form of regrets. A sort of agreement was reached as to the political meaning of being single and, as one thing led to another, celibacy became acceptable. Everyone – the families and family groups of the single militants, the political organizations and their companions in struggle, and the forces of repression (in other words, all forms of police) – concurred that the marriage of the most active militants, the *enfants terribles* of a certain social and political order who put the militant ideal before their private interests, was an index or at least proof of their willingness to 'get back in line', of their acceptance of what can, depending on one's point of view, be described as either their demobilization or their embourgeoisement.

Such, in all likelihood, were the emigrants who were to figure amongst the pioneers of political action in France. They became the pioneers of militant nationalism, and they became the sons, the founders or, in the majority of cases, the backbone of the ENA, especially in its early days (1926–9). In the space of less than a decade, certain of the distinctive social characteristics of the pioneers (such as, for example, elementary education and familiarity with the urban order or even urban origins) would become generalized and extended to relatively larger groups of men. Several illustrative examples will be found in the excellent biographical dictionary that Benjamin Stora (1985) has devoted, after much patient research, to 'Algerian nationalist militants (1926–1954)'.

The militant emigrant

Whilst the above characteristics are clearly important, we have to define emigrants of this type other than in the way they define themselves and other than in the way they are defined by a certain historical tradition. We must, that, is avoid both the hagiography (of the heroes or martyrs of nationalism) and the ethnocentrism that can do no more than bring to life unique, singular or collective individuals – which everyday language tends to write with a capital letter: 'Proletariat', 'Revolution', 'Nation', etc. We can do so only by reconstructing the relationship between states of the social: the history that is objectified in institutions or in structures that are at once social, economic and political (colonization, the Communist Party, but also religion, language, education, etc.) and the history that is incorporated and embodied in individuals in the form of systems of socially determined and durable dispositions. These are structured structures to the extent that they are the product of history, but they also act as structuring structures to the extent that they determine the particular form of presence in the world presupposed by acting on that world. In the absence of that relationship between history and the *habitus* of agents and, in this case, the *habitus* shared globally by all emigrants of the period and, within that *habitus*, the more specific *habitus* of militant emigrants, we inevitably subscribe to that vision of history which insists that the principle of historical action – that of politicians, intellectuals, militants and workers – resides in a subject who comes into conflict with society (colonization or colonialism, the administration, capitalism, the bourgeoisie, imperialism, etc.) as though it were an external object. All that then remains to be done is to assume that the principle of history resides either in consciousness or in things, or in consciousness of things. All these intellectual habits are associated with the polemics of politics or ideology, which must at all cost establish who was responsible, and who was responsible for both best and worst.

Militants who have acquired this *habitus* are, in short, very close to the extreme case of those emigrants described by their own communities as *jayhin* (the plural of *jayah* or *imjahen*, which is the plural of *amjah* in Kabyle). It is, in this case, legitimate to adopt the language of the morality that the society of the day (and especially the peasant society of the day) shared and reinvested in its emigration. What is a *jayah* emigrant? Literally, one who has become lost, who has been destroyed or annihilated – by an accident or a catastrophe. He is someone who has gone a different way, who has lost his way in the course of his journey, who has been led astray or has strayed from his path, who has not succeeded, who has become a bad subject, a wastrel, a coward, a poltroon, etc. The term is applied to an animal that is not docile, that is always on the edge of the flock and ready to take flight – a sort of 'black sheep'. The *jayah* emigrant is therefore one of whom it can be said as an approximation that he is 'deviant', 'marginal' or 'individualist': he does not conform to the dominant or ambient norm. 'Lost' to both his group and himself, and lost to himself because he is 'lost' to his group, he has 'deserted' his community. He is no longer worth anything – material or symbolic – either to himself or to his people (being worth nothing to his people means that he is worth nothing to himself either). He has 'gone astray', in both the literal and the figurative sense, in both the physical and the moral sense. He is 'lost' in an unknown world – physical or human – in which he cannot find his direction, tell where he is or find his bearings because he does not have the categories he needs to do so ('he has lost sight of the east and gets lost at sunset') and, as one thing leads to another, he has 'gone astray'. He is 'lost' to his community, or is regarded as such by his community. He is, in other words, lost with respect to the social norm that is the truth of the group at any given moment in its history. (This interpretation of the term is in fact consonant in every respect with the meaning of the radical *jhy*, whose derivatives are applied to decaying fruit, to a harvest that has gone rotten, to a field, a tree or a female animal that has not lived up to its promise, that has failed or that has disappointed the hopes placed in it).[9]

In many respects, *jayah* emigrants are out of step with the usual order of emigration. This is no doubt because they were, even before their emigration, out of step with the social order that fuelled emigration and with the ethics shared by that order. Emigrants who conformed to the *doxa* of the period, or who were in other words so socially conformist that they met the needs of the moment and thereby contributed to the maintenance of the status quo, emigrated only in order to conform to what was expected of them. In contrast, those emigrants who were described as *jayhin* emigrated only because they contravened, or were inclined to contravene, the morality of their group, which was projected on to emigration and regulated its course. Being anomic, their emigration ultimately did no more than confirm the more or less explicit break that lay at its origins.

It is when they are compared with the figure of the *jayah* emigrant that the differential social characteristics, which historians and other observers read into the very personality of certain emigrants and groups of emigrants, take on their full meaning. To take one example amongst many: in 1938 (and, a fortiori, before that time, when the ENA still had only a narrow base in the Paris region and the Lyon metropolis and when – and the two things are linked – the Algerian emigrant population, being smaller and above all less socially differentiated, did not yet contain any component likely to be receptive to militant ideology), the city of Paris was home to 76 per cent of all *étoilistes* militants, whereas the Parisian region as a whole, which had the greatest concentration of migrant Algerian workers, was home, in 1937, to only 38 per cent of all emigrant Algerian workers. It has to be remembered that Paris had (and still has, in the eyes of a fraction of the emigrants who are more comfortably settled in the provinces, which is both a cause and an effect of the great concentrations of emigrants of the *jayah* type in the capital), the reputation of being a den of vice, or at least a 'trap of a city', a city of temptations. Paris was a city that was not especially recommended to workers who were 'honest', or in other words careful with their money, obviously enough, but also, and even more so, with their time, their preoccupations and their aspirations, or to workers who did not allow themselves to be seduced by urban hedonism (as seen by austere and stern peasants), or by the various attractions offered by the city (and especially Paris). Political involvement, or even union involvement, was the most subversive of those attractions. The vast majority of emigrants were workers even though (or because) almost all of them came from peasant backgrounds. Emigration distanced them from both agricultural labour and from the work that had freed them from, or could free them from, the proletarian condition (shopkeepers, merchants etc.). Emigrants were suspicious of – or had reservations about – all those activities, no doubt because each in its own way demanded an investment of time, expectations and interests that is incompatible with what is expected of the ordinary or traditional emigrant. His attention cannot at any moment or under any pretext be distracted from the one objective that gives his emigration a meaning, namely sacrificing everything to the family (in the wide sense), the group and the social order from which he has emigrated. These are some of the historically defined characteristics of any emigration of poor peasants who have been impoverished by their encounter with the economic, social and cultural effects of the urban order.

Whilst the ENA did encourage its militants and sympathizers to acquire businesses (especially hotel-restaurants), even though it was somewhat suspicious of their owners or of this new category of bosses who were emigrants like any others but who had 'risen above' the condition common to all emigrants, it did not do so simply in order to acquire mediators and good recruiting agents or propagandists. Nor did it do so to increase its influence over the emigrant masses who had no choice but to use those same hotels and restaurants, which were in fact real social centres offering a host of services (guaranteed lodgings and food for new arrivals, places for the exchange of news, networks for job-seeking, credit extended to the unemployed, money lending, not always at extortionate rates, moral guidance, etc.). Much more significantly, what might be described as the structural affinities between the system of dispositions characteristic of a small trading aristocracy that had emerged in emigration and as a result of emigration, and the system of objective expectations inscribed within the militant function, meant that a single social category could play two roles, either simultaneously or alternately. Such men could be both shopkeepers (workers 'with white hands' or workers who had leisure-time) and militants. Becoming a shopkeeper or a militant was already a way of becoming a 'notable'.

The first Algerian emigrants who took it upon themselves to throw themselves into the social struggles of the time in order to attain an emancipation that was at once social and national could not, in a word, have been notables exactly. But nor were they necessarily labourers or even 'real' workers. Their emancipation was initially bound up with the emancipation of the social class they came into contact with and whose support they enjoyed in the same struggles. They then acquired a greater autonomy in terms of both the very finality of those struggles and of the way they were waged (a programme, demands, means of action and organization, etc.). The earliest stages of emigration coincided exactly with the transition from one era to the next – in other words with the transition from the era of land-owning 'patriotism' to the era of political nationalism or of political and politically institutionalized opposition to colonialism. For the first time, or for the first time since the beginning of the colonial conquest and certainly since the end of the peasant and popular tribal insurrections led by the aristocracy of the sword (the great insurrection of 1871 appears to mark the end of both that period and that first form of resistance to colonial intrusion), emigration had the effect, even before it could be done in Algeria, of bringing about an encounter, or at the very least the possibility of an encounter, between, on the one hand, the mass of ordinary emigrants (peasants who had expatriated themselves in the direction of France and the working-class condition; peasants who had been converted into workers for the duration of their emigration) and, on the other hand, 'political' emigrants, or individuals whose migratory trajectory, social trajectory – both prior to and during their emigration – modes of behaviour and accumulated experience were different in every respect. This historic encounter, for which there was no precedent in the entire history of colonized Algeria, was a truly *political* event, and it already signalled and prefigured the subsequent evolution of Algerian nationalism. That this crucial encounter took place.

(paradoxically) in France and not in Algeria, and that it took so long for it to be reproduced in Algeria – that would not happen until immediately after the Second World War – is, it seems, one of the specific effects of emigration. This is, so to speak, the vital contribution emigrants made to the advancement and radicalization of the nationalist idea. We are now discovering the particular role played by emigration in the formation of nationalism and expressing surprise at the enormous time-lag that exists between the political discourse (which is both social, not to say socialist, and national) which, in France and in immigration, was addressed to emigrants, and the discourse that was *de rigueur* in Algeria. The latter was a discourse of compromise (a compromise which, after the event, may have seemed to some to have been a shameful compromise), of half-tones, simulation and dissimulation. It would quite simply be naive to explain the time-lag solely in terms of emigration itself, or to see in it only one of the intrinsic virtues of emigration, or, in other words, one of those miraculous conversions brought about, as though by some social alchemy, by the very fact of emigration. Indeed, without wishing to deny completely either the political and pedagogical importance of the experience of emigration or the positive role it played in that sense, we should not allow ourselves to overstate its importance simply for the sake of it. We must not succumb to the effects of some romantic illusion or exaggerate the outcome of an experience when we still do not understand its ins and outs. The social (and political) metamorphosis that is believed to have come about because of the educational function of emigration in fact affected only a few individual cases, about which many questions remain to be answered. Before we universalize the miraculous conversion that emigration supposedly brought about for all emigrants, we must never lose sight of the exceptional nature of that conversion. And even when that conversion can be proved to have taken place, it was basically no more than a change of attitude that was, in most cases, conditioned by the context of the day. It was usually no more than a very transient change of attitude that could be reversed or which was, at the very least, liable to regress. This relatively ephemeral conditioning, which is the very opposite of what might be regarded as a permanent disposition that has been profoundly internalized, that is interchangeable and that can be transferred to all spheres of existence, proves *a contrario* that the emigrants of this period remained, with some exceptions, 'men of tradition' and usually men who wanted to appear as such. They wanted to seem like men who were being true to themselves, or men who had not been 'changed' (i.e. changed for the worst) by their emigration.

An exceptional situation if ever there was one, emigration appears to have acted as a catalyst precipitating a development that was inevitable. In Algeria, on the other hand, the situation was so different that it would take a long time to produce the results that emigration produced experimentally (that is, in the mode of a laboratory experiment and as a scaled-down model, but also as preparation for a real experience that would take place on the ground, on a grand scale and in accordance with a natural model) but also, it has to be said, somewhat artificially and, basically, superficially. It is not until just before the outbreak of the war of independence that we find – and even then it was episodic and bound up with only a few great revolutionary moments – the combination of a very syncretic popular nationalism (or spontaneous patriotism) and a politically elaborated nationalism endowed with a truly political theory, programme and line of action. The links that were, thanks to emigration, established between these two forms of nationalism and, therefore, between the two categories of emigrants attached to those forms, could not, of course, be totally different from the usual (ordinary) relations that traditional solidarity and customary mutual aid established between all emigrants and which, as we can well understand, they reproduced still more actively and more intensely. What is more important still, those links were the very condition of possibility for what is explicitly described as 'political emigration'. Destined from the outset to help and mutually support one another, emigrants in these two categories could unite only on the basis of the sort of complicity and collusion, which was basically quite natural, that everyone could experience, or hope to experience, in the friendly terrain or second homeland constituted by the emigrant community. The very existence of a reputedly 'political' emigration is in fact inconceivable without the simultaneous presence of 'ordinary' emigrants (labour emigrants). This whole process can take on the real meaning of 'political' emigration in the eyes of those concerned – whose 'political' alibi is homologous with the 'work' alibi of other emigrants, or at least a supplementary alibi in addition to the work alibi – thanks only to this other emigration and those other emigrants: labour emigration and labour emigrants. If 'political' emigration is to exist there must be labour emigration to provide it with a new 'homeland' (an 'expatriate' homeland). It was only because it had the support of a community of labour emigrants, which was necessarily larger and older, that a community of 'political' emigrants, which was necessarily more restricted – not, as might be believed, because it was only just emerging but, more basically, because in its very nature it had to be a very minority community involving only a few individuals or individualities – could find a

rationale for its existence and, more importantly, establish the preconditions for its efficacy. This conjunction, which began to appear as
early as the 1920s, continued and became more pronounced as the
history of emigration progressed. The post-Second World War generation, which played, but on a much greater scale, the same role with
respect to the PPA that the post-First World War generation had
played with respect to the ENA – the same historical continuity exists
from one generation to the next, and from one political generation to
the next – was to become the great propagator (and propagandist) of
a truly political nationalism amongst the rural populations.

Basically, had it not been for the almost experimental and provi-
dential – in other words, fully anticipated – encounter that emigration brought about between the two categories of emigrants and,
ultimately, between two socially differentiated categories within the
Algerian population, the 'political' emigration of the colonized would
have been obliged to adopt the stop-gap solution of putting itself
completely in the service of those political forces in France that
were favourable to it. It would have been recuperated by all those
who were in a position to help it (for either ideological, sentimental,
charitable or condescending reasons) and in whom its cause could
find *objective* allies. Those forces certainly expected political profits in
return for the aid they had given. Political emigrants would have been
reduced to being no more than a new clientele for a certain number of
political parties, a sort of ethico-political support for the whole anti-
colonialist movement, a back-up force for the unions – and a force
that was all the more appreciable in that it had discovered the very
logic of trade-union action (union action and its efficacy are, as we
know, based upon numbers, the demonstration as a means of struggle
being, of course, a demonstration of numbers and of the greatest
number). Whilst 'political' Algerian emigrants (and, more generally,
'political' emigrants from the colonies) did succeed, as best they
could, in escaping their total subordination to the political formations
(in the broadest sense of the term) whose militant support they had
already won, they owed their relative autonomy to the fact that they
could, even in France, count upon a clientele that was 'genetically' (in
the social sense of the term, i.e. a clientele produced by the same
conditions of genesis: it was both colonized and emigrant) and 'nationally' similar to them. Because the alliance was not a vassalage, but
an assertion of the 'nationalist' objective, or a prioritizing of that
objective over the other imperatives characteristic of the social and
political struggles specific to the French political field, we have here
the beginnings of the entire history of the disputes between Algerian
nationalism and the political and social forces of the French left. This,

no doubt, is the way in which we should understand the difficult relationship between the PCF in particular and the ENA (the first version, and even more so the second), and, more generally, communism (first French and then Algerian) and Algerian nationalism from the beginnings of its constitution until the final phase represented by the stormy rivalry between the PCA and the FLN during the war of independence – attempts to establish an autonomous 'communist' *maquis*. This also explains why relations between the PCA and the older PCF deteriorated, especially when the latter voted for 'special powers'. It explains why most of its *'pied noir'* clientele abandoned the PCA. It explains the FLN's hegemonic will and its struggle to have an undivided monopoly on militant nationalism. It also explains, finally, the sabotaging of the PCA immediately after independence on the pretext that both formations believed in the virtues of the single party.

5

The Backlash on the Society of Origin

The effects of emigration have, since the 1970s, become the object of a polemic against what is known in Algeria (thanks to a highly significant change of vocabulary) as 'immigration'. The polemic takes the form of a discourse on the 'reinsertion of emigrants' and it is in part dictated by the discourse on the 'reinsertion' of immigrants into 'their' society, 'their' economy and 'their' culture which prevailed in France after immigration was halted in 1974. Thanks to this official and nationalist discourse, and thanks to the measures that had been taken or were about to be taken to promote the reinsertion of emigrants, the subterranean and repressed conflict between an Algerian society that was becoming introverted – this was the time of 'exit visas' – and was cut off from the consumer goods with which it was familiar and to which it had become accustomed (foodstuffs, but also work, education and health, etc.), and 'emigrants' burst into the open. Treacherous and sated, these bad Algerians enjoyed both the advantages of the benefits they derived from the society of emigration, and those promised them in exchange for their reinsertion: exemption from customs duties, education in French, reserved quotas for jobs and housing, etc.

Before turning to emigration's effects (real or perceived) on Algerian society, it seems appropriate to retrace the history of the process whereby the Algerian population resident in France (regardless of whether it emigrated from Algeria or has reproduced itself in France) has achieved a (relative) degree of autonomy from Algerian society. Family emigration, which marked a radical break with the long tradition of emigration on the part of single men, began this process of autonomization, which was then accelerated by new conditions relating to Algeria's accession to national independence (a change of a

political nature that had an immediate effect on the Algerian population that had emigrated to France because it changed its juridical
status: a population of *colonisés* or of 'Muslim-French' working in
France, and who were so to speak, the successors to the 'colonial
workers' who had preceded them, became – legally – a 'foreign'
population that had emigrated to France). Algeria made a stubborn
political effort to integrate that part of itself that was outside it by
using a ritual discourse that attempted to reassert both the emigrant
population's unshakeable loyalty to the mother-nation and the
mother-nation's attachment to its emigrant population. Paradoxically,
it was this that did most to establish the 'emigrant' population as an
autonomous reality.[1] Here too, the very different reactions of the
society of immigration and the society of emigration to their immigrants and emigrants are structurally identical. The 'pile of sand'
metaphor used to explain the formation of a population of immigrants – immigrants are seen as individual units who arrive separately,
but it is never foreseen that they will combine to create a totality –
finds its equivalent in emigration. As they accumulate, isolated absences eventually, and without anyone realizing it, create a gulf.
Hence the paradox of 'the abyss' and of 'an abyss made up of small
voids'. The old dust of individuals who have emigrated, or in other
words who are simply 'absent' from here and 'present' there, is
replaced by another reality, another representation and another definition of the emigrant (as an abstract character, a purely nominal
category or a pure stereotype) and, as a result, another mode of
relating to emigration (as both a process and a social category) and
sometimes to concretely defined emigrants.[2] There is probably not
a single family in Algeria that does not have 'its' emigrant in France (a
member of the family, a kinsman or a relative by marriage, or simply
a very close friend), but this does not prevent anyone from speaking
of emigrants (i.e. of emigration in general) in terms of denunciation,
accusation, stigmatization, etc. No one sees the slightest contradiction
between the overall judgement they have just passed, which is a
generic condemnation, and the direct experience they have of emigration thanks to the immediate, concrete, actual and affective (and
affectionate) relationship they have with their emigrant.

There is now no generic discourse about the emigrant, who has
become a sort of social or historical figure. People speak of the
emigrant in just the same way that, in other circumstances, they
speak of the peasantry, the proletariat or the bourgeoisie, etc. Conversely, the emigrant's discourse about his 'country' [*pays*] – the
abstract country, the country as entity (written with a capital:
Algeria), rather than the 'little' country (*petit pays*), the local country,

which remains the country with which he is familiar, the country where he knows everyone and everyone knows him, the effective and affective country (*el balad* or, in Kabyle, *thamourth*) – inevitably tends to take the form of a polemic in which each party blames the other. The terms of this mutual polemic are, in its early stages, often borrowed from economics. First, this is because competition for things economic (for all consumer goods) is the first form of competition to appear, especially in a poor economy in which there are shortages. Second, because of the 'technical' effect it has, the recourse to the language of economics makes it possible to state and denounce things that could not otherwise be said without risk, or without leading to the (relative) disqualification of what is being said and who is saying it. To that extent, borrowing from the vocabulary of economics has a euphemistic effect. For a long time people praised the sacrifices these men made and the abnegation they displayed when they were forced to go into exile in order to work and satisfy the needs of their families, and therefore made their contribution to the country's economy, or in other words had to face the ordeals, hostility and adversity to which exile exposed them (this is the lot of any immigrant and, more specifically, of the colonized immigrant or former *colonisé* who originates from a third world country). Emigrants are now publicly, and in the most official terms, criticized for no longer being able, or being less able, to restore the balance of payments in hard currency.[3] These 'currency exchanges', which have become common between non-emigrant Algerians (who supply dinars in Algeria) and Algerian emigrants (who supply francs in France), are the object of bitter reproaches on both sides, as the emigrants look like modern-day 'filthy usurers', whilst Algerian visitors to France look like vulgar 'profiteers', or greedy and pretentious consumers of the 'luxury' produced in France even though there is nothing to authorize or legitimize such a mode of consumption.

The Algerian visitor and his 'emigrant banker'

At this point, we must cite an Algerian in his fifties who lives in an old lodging house in Saint-Denis and who has worked in France since 1949:

'They have no money, so they should stay at home . . . you can't play the tourist when you don't have a penny . . . they turn up here [i.e. in France] and they think that here [France] is like where they come from [Algeria]. . . . They do not see how we earn our money here, and how we save; we do without, because I never buy my wife and children the things they come here to buy.... And whose money do they buy all that with?... Our money.... *Their* money? It's not worth the paper it's printed on: if it were worth anything, they'd bring it out here, they would show it here.... They give them dinars back there [in Algeria] and tell them to "sort things out", to buy whatever it is that they want.... And then they criticize us for bankrupting the Algerian treasury... but they are the ones who waste money; they are the ones who throw money around. And they make us pay dearly for it; they pay us back in our own coin: 1,500 francs, and back there they give you 815 dinars! But when they come here, they want French money at any price: they give you 2,400, 2,500 dinars for 1,000 francs, because they need the money.... All we ask is for them to stop accusing us of robbing them, ruining them and betraying them; everything else is their business, their government's business, not ours. I don't go to Algeria to beg for dinars; they come to France to beg for francs.'

In response to the criticisms the emigrant makes of his Algerian partner, we often hear another form of accusation: the Algerian has 'his' emigrant-banker (in France, and in francs):

'They're sucking our blood, ruining us.... They're moneygrubbers: they imagine that we, here [in Algeria], have only to bend down and pick up dinars [this is a reworking, adapted to a different context, of the anecdote about how the immigrants, to whom it was initially attributed, saw the mirage of emigration]. When I get there and see the poverty, the hovels they live in, the work they do, the racism they suffer and accept... If I were them, I'd never accept that, I'd rather live in material poverty at home, it's healthy, I'd rather keep my dignity... than all the gold in the world. I feel ashamed for them, I suffer on their behalf. And then they rub their money in our faces, they flash it in front of us ... the way all upstarts do, or the way they fail to; to try to impress you, they make an effort, they go out with you to show you they know their way around Paris... it makes me laugh, the way they go on. They make a show of taking you to places they think are smart... but they know nothing about them. It's obvious, they're not at ease, they're not at home there. They are all embarrassed. They don't know how to sit at a table, they don't know how to order [a drink].... Ultimately, I can forgive them all that; I don't ask that much of them. They might be being kind, I can accept that.... But there's also the unpleasant impression that they want to show you that they are successful, that they have money... that they can do you a favour, put you in their debt, that's it. You're in their debt. But that isn't the real problem at all, that's not how I see it. All that I ask is that, here, I can give you that... and when you come to Algiers, you give that... here's the address. That's all, I've made a deal, that's all. No need to get emotional. And often, having dragged it out for hours and hours, when you get down to brass tacks, he tells you: "Oh, I don't have the money, I'll try to get it for you somewhere else, come back tomorrow ..." I remember the first time I came to Saint-Denis, I had no idea what it was like. I'd never set foot there; it was just an address someone had given me in Algiers. I took a taxi, the taxi driver had already warned me: "Monsieur, I'll drop you some way off, because it's a dangerous neighbourhood and I don't venture into it..." It's enough to give you the shivers when a taxi driver talks like that. I got there...and it really was a dark labyrinth, mud...my pair of shoes...I was ashamed of them when I got back to the hotel....So much for relations with our "brother" emigrants in France.' (Doctor from Algiers, son of a former railway employee at the time of the SNCFA, originally from a region with a very strong and very old tradition of emigration to France)

When one knows the real social condition of the two partners who are the interlocutors in this 'dialogue', the truth of their relationship and its profound meaning appear in a different light:

'He is a doctor from home...one of the family; we all know his father...a good man. He was no upstart; he remained a *fellah* like us. He "educated" his children – we know that – he did without a lot of things to do so, he put himself to a lot of trouble, you have to congratulate him for that, he was a man [of honour]. When his son turned up here one day and knocked on our door, it was a surprise, a joy, immense happiness. Because we had never seen him before, we knew of his existence, that's all. We knew that so and so's son was a doctor in Algiers, that's all. He'd gone to school of course, he'd lived in the city, got married there and didn't go back to the village any more. All that is natural. When he got here, we all rallied around and gave him a good welcome. We were very flattered. We had a doctor in the family. Everyone wanted to see him, talk with him, an intelligent man, and one of the family....We know...when someone comes from Algiers to see you, you know why: he needs money. It was certainly not the first time he had been to Paris, he studied in Paris, but this time he came to us, to our home. We found him some money. As much as he wanted, and at a rate that was very much to his advantage....We gave him part of it at a rate of 1,000 here, 1,000 back there, and part at the 'normal' rate, which was better than anyone else got. That's all right. And then it became a habit, he came regularly; he used to write to us before coming. That's the trouble: that's the way they are. They've forgotten the way their fathers and grandfathers used to behave. When he needs money, he comes, and only for the money, but when we try to get the money back in Algiers, we have to chase...after our money. He leaves you a business card, with his address, with his telephone number, "Doctor" and all the rest of it...You arrive in Algiers – you know what it's like, we get off the plane, through customs and there are always taxis outside, two or three of us to a taxi, and straight to the village. You leave Paris in the morning, and you're eating at home in the evening, two hundred kilometres from Algiers. We have no time to waste, and Algiers is of no interest to us, we're not tourists in Algiers....You have a telephone number, you call, you get a Frenchwoman, like here...no, his wife is Algerian, a Kabyle, but on the phone, and not just on the phone, at home I suppose, she's French, like a French-woman, there's no difference. And so you hear: "Who are you, monsieur. My husband isn't here, monsieur, what do you want with him? If you want an appointment, go to the hospital....Monsieur, I don't know you, call back this evening." What are you going to say to this woman? Even here in France, we live amongst French people, and I can't talk on the phone, you have to be able to speak good French to speak well on the phone. And a woman, what can I say to her on the phone? Here in France, the factory secretary is the only one I can talk to on the phone, and she knows me in any case. As soon as she recognizes my voice, she says: "Ah! It's Belaïd, what's happened to you? Are you ill?" She talks for me. But back there in Algiers, what can you say to this woman you've never seen?...How many times have I said to myself: "I'll speak to her in Kabyle, I'm sure she'll understand me"...but I also know that she will pretend not to be able to speak Kabyle, and I'm also sure that she does know me – her husband must have told her everything – but she pretends not to know who I am....I can't say to her "I gave your husband some money; he should give it back"....After that, I hang up....Go and knock on the door? As I told you, I'm not going to play the tourist in Algiers. And what difference would it make? I'd find myself outside the door of a block of flats, down there, at the top of what used to be the rue Michelet...I knock on the door, and it's the same dialogue as on the phone....So I let it drop, and I wait for my money to arrive of its own accord....It comes in the end. Yes. I have to admit that there have never been any arguments about that. But I know why it always comes in the end...so that they can come back here to look for more money....That's the way it is....It also means that, even though we are related, we do not live in the same world. They live back there, and we live here. When we go back, either we find ourselves at home, in the village, with the family, or we find ourselves amongst other from France. But with the rest of them, with Algerian society, it's each to his own. I think it's definitive.'

These divergences appear to centre on modes of consumption, objects of consumption and the price to be paid for them – the price that some have to pay for them, and the price that the other 'makes' them pay – and on legitimate and illegitimate ways of consuming them, etc. But they are really about social relations and competitive relations between groups or class fractions that are beginning to be divided or thrown into conflict by their specific trajectories or history. That is what is really at stake in the struggles which are developing within social groups (which are still identified in terms of modes of perception and a principle of unification that still owes a lot to the earlier social order: a unit based on kinship unity, or which uses it as the archetypal model for all social relations, as a model that can be extended to encompass the entire nation: all Algerians are 'brothers' or 'like brothers', and so on).[4]

We cannot understand the spiteful way they talk about each other – and it is in fact non-emigrants rather than emigrants who speak in this way – if we do not bear in mind the 'disruptive' effect of emigration in general and of the emigration of families in particular. The most unexpected effect of emigration seems to have been a blurring of the boundaries between social groups and of the boundaries of the social hierarchy. This is because it gives emigrants the opportunity and the social means to achieve a promotion that inevitably seems 'illegitimate' because it has been acquired outside the socially accepted norms, and outside the orthodoxy that governs even the most accelerated and total (i.e. revolutionary) social transformations. The (relative) social promotion (or, to be more accurate, the illusion of promotion) that emigration guarantees is all the more annoying in that it is basically suspect. It occurs in a different social, economic, political and linguistic order, or in other words a different cultural order, and with the means supplied by that *allogenic* order. The weak point, the indelible defect of this kind of promotion (which is more apparent than real), is that it does not, it would seem, directly result from internal struggles, or from conflicts that can be resolved within the national order and in accordance with a truly internal historical logic. Whilst it does have something to do with that order (at least at the two extremes of the emigrant's itinerary), the promotion that emigration brings is achieved almost by proxy. It is, no doubt, this objective 'cheating' ('objective' in the sense that it is not knowingly or deliberately intended), which might be called 'the ruse of emigration', that is being denounced both spontaneously and unanimously. What their counterparts who have not emigrated, or who have emigrated differently, are retrospectively criticizing today's emigrants for in a thousand different ways (both implicit and explicit) is having left the homeland, or having left it almost out of cowardice or treachery, so as come back better armed, and with weapons other than those that society has socially authorized.[5] We can thus understand why all the criticisms addressed to emigrants, and the denunciations or stigmatization of which they are the object, should take the form of a 'nationalist' discourse subject to categories that contrast 'national' with 'non-national', and why the second term of the opposition (non-national) can be (and is) expressed by its structural equivalent: 'denationalized' or 'denaturalized', 'national', by what is 'not national', 'outside the nation', etc. We can understand that, in many respects, the emigrant looks in a way like someone who was colonized at the last moment, like a *colonisé* who has outlived a colonization from which he cannot liberate himself, like a postcolonial *colonisé* and therefore someone who wants to be colonized (because he wants to remain an emigrant).[6]

Just like the language of economics, the language of culture constitutes a form of euphemization through 'technicalization'. It allows all these denunciations to be made openly, without any restraint, and often with a condescension authorized by 'good intentions'. Emigration decultures because it acculturates one to a foreign culture; emigration 'depersonalizes', etc. And it is significant that the criticisms made of emigration, and, by that very fact, of emigrants, are directed mainly and most violently against the female emigrant population and, more specifically, women's bodies. Criticisms are made of the way they dress, of their corporeal *hexis*, their ways of holding themselves, speaking and behaving, especially in public – in other words, their physical deportment and comportment. It is pointless – and it would take too long – to dwell upon the symbolic significance accorded to the female body, which is the object of an intense and dramatic cathexis, and to the 'body' of women (in the sense that women form a body), which is dedicated to a tradition, to the point of celebrating fidelity to that tradition and the female values that respect it. Innovation is possible for men alone, and only on the part of men. Outside the male world, all innovation is forbidden without further discussion.

6

A Relationship of Domination

Just as there is a superabundance of literature on immigration in countries of immigration (and it is produced for the needs of the society of immigration), so there is a shortage, or even a complete dearth, of the literature on *emigration* that we are entitled to expect from countries of emigration. Just as the former is diversified, ranging from journalism to scientific literature and including essays, militant literature, legislative and political texts and even novels, so the latter, when it does exist, describes emigrants only to the extent that they are immigrants living amongst others, or in other words, and broadly speaking, in the same way that those others, who are preoccupied with immigration, speak of them. This is indicative of the extent to which the discourse applied to emigrants in countries of emigration is quite devoid of any autonomy. Being subordinate to the discourse on immigration, whose essential themes it reproduces and from which it often borrows its intellectual structures and the material it analyses because it has not succeeded in making emigration and the emigrant an object of science, the discourse on emigration is doomed, despite or perhaps because of the polemical intention that inspires it, to be no more than a pale reflection of what is being said about immigration. Because it brings about a strange inversion of at least the chronological and genetic order of the migratory phenomenon, the emigration it discusses seems to be the product of immigration. This inverted discourse usually simply replaces the terms 'emigration' and 'emigrant' with the terms 'immigration' and 'immigrant'. This is not simply a matter of word play or linguistic niceties; the meaning, to say nothing of the effects, of these changes of name is not as anodyne as it might seem.

Dependency in discourse

The colloquium held in Algiers on 28, 29 and 30 March 1981 under the aegis of the CREA (Centre de recherches en economie appliquée, University of Algiers) on the theme 'Maghrebin Emigration to Europe: Exploitation or Cooperation?' provides all the proof we need of this subordination to the dominant language. How are we to understand this title? We are so accustomed to hearing and understanding 'immigration' and 'immigrants' when we say and write, when we hear and write, 'emigration' and 'emigrants', that everyone (speakers, listeners, authors and readers) quite 'naturally' immediately effects the work of the correction and rectification of meaning that is required to give this discourse its true meaning. Significantly, the fact that the words can actually be taken literally is a cause of general surprise. It is rather as though it were accepted on all sides that 'emigration' and 'immigration' on the one hand, and 'immigrant' and 'immigration' on the other, were interchangeable and could be used by the same discourses. It is as though the differential use that is made of them actually depended upon the position from which one is speaking and the intentions with which one speaks.

This colloquium, held in a country of emigration and supposedly about emigration, was in reality a colloquium on immigration for the benefit of countries of immigration and especially for the benefit of the science of immigration. It was all the more to their advantage in that this colloquium on immigration (which dared not speak its name) was held in a country of emigration.[1] Do discourse and science always have to be about immigration? Given that the power relations, or the very relations that have generated emigration-immigration, also affect science, and especially the science of the migratory phenomenon, does immigration have to make emigration subordinate to the point of concealing it, even though it is no more than the other aspect of the same reality? This is a real question for the sociology of science, and the social history of the social sciences provides many examples of this kind of question. Just as the science of immigration has its conditions of possibility, which it has realized, so the science of emigration has its social conditions of possibility, which it has not realized (assuming that they can be realized). The first of those conditions is presumably a refusal to identify the two sciences, or a refusal to identify one with the other. The 'sociology of development' and the cultural anthropology of 'underdevelopment' – in other words the sociology and anthropology of 'precapitalist societies' – and economic thinking about the economies of those same societies at the moment when they came under the overall (economic and social) control of the developed countries, with all the effects that had, have contributed greatly to the advance of the sociological, anthropological and economic sciences themselves. They have convinced themselves that they have to think about their own assumptions (the assumptions of 'rationality' and *homo economicus*, etc.) so as to escape their own ethnocentrism, and thus advance the self-understanding of those societies and their capitalist economies. Similarly, a consideration of emigration can, even when it lags behind the science of immigration, serve only to advance the science of immigration by leading us to ask ourselves about the science of immigration, its conditions of possibility, and the intentions that lie at the origins of that science (and, correlatively, about the science of emigration and its absence). Is the disproportion, which we experience every day, between the language used about immigration and the language (or non-language) used about emigration no more than an effect of the lack of symmetry that characterizes the migratory phenomenon? Can it be seen as an index that we can use to assess the peculiarly unequal relations of force that exist between countries of emigration and countries of immigration?

A science of immigration and immigrants (i.e. the science of the society of immigration) is obviously easier to elaborate than a science of emigration and emigrants (i.e. the science of the society of emigration). There are several reasons for this. Some, being technical and social, are of a practical nature, whilst others, being ideological, are of a political nature. But both stem from one major fact: immigration results in a *presence*, and emigration finds expression in an *absence*. A presence makes itself felt; an absence is noted, and that is all. A presence can be adjusted, regulated, controlled and managed. An absence is masked, compensated for and denied. These differences in status determine the differences in the discourses that can be applied to both presence (immigration), which is amenable to discourse, and absence (emigration), of which there is nothing to be said except that it has to be supplemented. Immigration, or the presence of immigrants as foreign bodies (foreign to society or the nation), is the object of a problematic that might be said to be totally *imposed*, or external to the object it discusses. In order to meet the demand for *order* to which they must conform, explicit, and especially scientific, discourse on immigration has become accustomed to 'linking' immigrants with the various institutions with which they necessarily come into contact by the very fact of being immigrants. We therefore have studies of 'immigrants and work' (or unemployment), 'immigrants and housing', etc., and the questions asked of 'immigrants' concern, in the final analysis, *public order*, and are dictated by considerations of public order. This entire discourse, which is believed to have been produced on immigrants and for immigrants, is in reality nothing more than the discourse of a (national) society that is forced to deal with the immigrants it needs, with whom it has to reckon and who, if it is not careful, might disturb public order.[2] When confronted with immigration (i.e. the presence within the nation of non-nationals, and the presence of the non-national and the non-political within the national that has a monopoly on politics), public order must necessarily 'discourse' (politically, legislatively, statutorily, socially, economically, sociologically, culturally, etc.) on immigration in such a way as to neutralize the threat of disturbance and subversion. Scientific language about immigration is no exception to the rule.

Even though this language is a response to an enforced problematic, even though it is *objectively* (unwittingly) the product of a concern with order, and even though it does consist in an attempt to warn against immigration and to ward it off and in an attempt to introduce order, the fact remains that the living and working conditions of immigrants, their mode of presence within the society of immigration, and their mode of relating to that society and to themselves are explained only insofar as they are immigrants immersed in a social, economic, political and cultural order that is not theirs. The cumulative effect is the eventual production of a sum of knowledge that is of capital importance in two senses. It is important both from the practical point of view (i.e. for the control, adaptation, domestication and insertion of immigrants – in other words the neutralization or reduction of the alterity and the heterogeneity they bring with them), and from the heuristic point of view (i.e. for understanding the social, demographic, economic and cultural mechanisms that preside over immigration, from the initial act of immigrating to the final act of total fusion with or absorption or *assimilation*, in the sense of the digestive metaphor, into the society into which the immigrants are finally absorbed, and with which they identify). Ultimately, observation and quantification (through, for example, a census) appear to be possible only when applied to immigration and immigrants – i.e. to a *presence*, and to numbers and qualities that are *present*. The 'privilege' enjoyed by countries that take in (as immigrants) emigrants from other countries is very quickly translated into a political and economic advantage, and this is particularly advantageous when they come to negotiate with the country of emigration. Countries of immigration enjoy the 'privilege' of being able to control, quantify and enumerate how many of the other country's emigrants are present. They are able to acquire the desired knowledge of their immigrants (a knowledge of their emigrants that countries of emigration do not and cannot have for a number of reasons), and the power conferred by that knowledge (a power that countries of emigration do not have). They are able to gather a whole body of useful information about them, as well as the whole array of statistical data required to establish a 'good' dossier that is complete and well argued (or 'scientifically' established, as the saying goes).

A country that wishes to understand its emigration and its emigrants, in contrast, has no option but to study immigration and immigrants. It can refer only to what is being said elsewhere. It must accept the knowledge that the country of immigration has produced about immigration and immigrants, and adapt it to its own point of view, its own needs and its own interests.[3] How can a country escape its necessary dependence on the country of immigration, achieve full autonomy in this domain, and acquire an understanding of emigration and emigrants that owes nothing to the reflected knowledge that the country of immigration has acquired of its immigration and immigrants? For reasons which do not relate solely to immigration or solely to the history of Algerian immigration to France, and which have a broader relevance to all relations between the two countries and their shared history (the history of an intense and systematic colonization that is almost without parallel), Algeria proves to be one of the most 'dependent' of all countries of emigration. But it is also the country that is the most impatient to shake off that dependence. The intense negotiating activity it has entered into with the country of immigration, which in this case is also the former colonial power, inevitably makes Algeria aware, perhaps more acutely than other countries, of its dependency in this respect (which could in normal times be concealed). It inevitably makes Algeria all the more eager to try to shake off that dependence. This, no doubt, is how we should understand all the efforts that have been made in Algeria itself to 'count' its emigrants, and the efforts Algeria has made in France to assist in the taking of a census of Algerian immigrants (that is, of Algerians who have emigrated to France) and into making surveys of the Algerian community in France. The two general censuses of the population carried out in Algeria in 1966 and 1976 certainly attempted to ensure the inclusion of those who were 'absent from Algeria' (i.e. 'emigrants', which is a roundabout and elegant way of referring to Algerians who have emigrated to France and who constitute the overwhelming authority of those 'absent from Algeria'). But, although quite praiseworthy, this attempt both comes up against an even greater stumbling block, and raises an important epistemological question about the art of statistics and census techniques: what does counting the 'absent' mean? Any attempt to count them ignores the fact that, rather than giving a true picture of the total number of individuals who are absent, it merely records the degree of their integration into their groups of origin and, therefore, the integration of the groups themselves or, if we like, the memory that the groups interviewed retain of their emigrants. And we know that such memories are selective and differential, being socially determined by gender, age and a whole series of other social indicators specific to the absent individual (social origin, social position, how much property and how many descendants the individual has, social prestige, etc.).[4]

Social preconditions for a science of emigration

Does this mean that there can be no real discourse about emigration and emigrants, or that an autonomous science of emigration and emigrants is impossible? It seems not. There are, however, social preconditions for the constitution of such a discourse and such a science. There must, first of all and especially in the case of emigrations-immigrations in a colonial situation, be a politically and technically guaranteed (and therefore state-guaranteed) will to understand emigration, to institute it as an object of study. The indispensable condition for doing that is, as we have seen in relation to immigration and the science of immigration, the existence of a partner with an interest in emigration and the science of emigration (an economic interest, a political interest, an interest in negotiating, and interest in power, etc.). Emigration must cease to be that shameful 'thing' that can be talked about (in the comparative 'cost-benefit' mode) only, on the one hand, in order to thank emigrants (i.e. emigrant *nationals*) for their sacrifice, for the contribution they are making to the life and work of the nation, or in other words for the 'benefits' the country derives from them and, on the other hand, to praise the work they are doing in immigration and for the country of immigration, or in other words the 'benefits' they bring to that country (which is also a way of describing in negative terms the 'costs' the country of emigration has to bear because it has emigrants). To that extent, we are simply repeating what is being said about them in the country of immigration. We have to establish a way of perceiving and understanding emigration, both in itself and for itself, as an autonomous reality, or as a reality that has *arbitrarily* been made independent of immigration, or its other aspect. An autonomous discourse on emigration must be instituted and, before that can be done, the reasons constituting that discourse must be established.

Like the two sides of a coin or the complementary aspects and interdependent dimensions of a single phenomenon, emigration and immigration are mutually determined, and an understanding of one necessarily leads to a better understanding of the other. A complete investigation into immigration necessarily leads, upstream, to an investigation into the conditions of the production and reproduction of emigrants and, downstream, to an investigation into the social mechanisms that preside over their transformation from allogenous to indigenous. Similarly, a complete investigation into emigration also leads, of necessity, to an investigation into the effects emigration and emigrants have on the society of emigration and on what they become when living amongst others.

In addition to the contradiction in the temporal order – something 'temporary' that becomes permanent and something 'permanent' that is experienced as though it were temporary – that might be said to be constitutive of the nature of emigration (and immigration) and the emigrant (and immigrant) condition, there are further corresponding contradictions in all the other domains of existence. There are contradictions in the spatial order, in the communitarian order and in the cultural order. To complete and finally consecrate all these partial or regional contradictions, there is also a growing contradiction in the political (or national) order: absence *abroad* (and a foreign presence when abroad). The absence is, of necessity, a *temporary* absence which must be justified by some reason external to itself. It can be justified as an absence for work reasons, and as an absence that is totally subordinate to work. This presupposes an absence of work within the country, and for the duration of that absence of work. At the same time, or to put the same thing in different words, it also presupposes a presence abroad. This is a temporary presence and it is not a presence for the sake of being present. It has to be justified for some reason external to itself. It is a presence for work reasons, and a presence that is totally subordinated to work (for the duration of the job). Such are the three characteristics of, respectively, the absence of the emigrant and the presence of the immigrant, and they are both correlative and mutually dependent – each contains all the others. But of all these contradictions, there is one that determines more fundamentally the meaning of emigration. It has a specific impact on the meaning of emigration and the emigrant condition, and therefore cannot be overlooked by the society of emigration (and, therefore, the science of emigration) on which it is imposed. There is a symmetry between the presence realized, in a particular modality, by the immigrant in his land of immigration, and the absence realized, again in a particular modality, by the emigrant in his land of emigration. Immigration – in other words the particular *presence* that affects the society of emigration – has, as we have seen, determined a particular 'science' or at least a body of knowledge relating to immigration and immigrants and dictated by the fact of immigration. Similarly, emigration – in other words a particular *absence* affecting the society of emigration – should also determine a homologous 'science', or at least a body of knowledge relating to emigration and emigrants that is likewise dictated by the fact of emigration. Once again, the paradox of the science of emigration is that it appears to be a 'science of absence' and of absentees.

A 'science of absence'

If it is not to be a pure 'absence', emigration requires a sort of impossible 'ubiquity', or a way of being that affects the modalities of absence it generates (just as it affects the modalities of the presence through which immigration materializes). The condition or paradox of the emigrant is that he goes on 'being present despite his absence'. He goes on 'being present even when absent and even where he is absent' – which is tantamount to saying that he is no more than 'partially absent where he is absent'. Correlatively, he is 'not totally present where he is', which comes down to 'being absent despite being present,' and is '(partially) absent even where and when he is present'. The danger to the emigrant (who is also an immigrant) is that these incomplete forms of absence and presence will eventually, or sooner or later, become complete. The physical, and merely physical, presence of the immigrant will eventually become a moral presence too (he is present in body and soul, now and in the future, present because of work and parenthood – i.e. through blood ties, *de facto* and *de jure*). Correlatively, the material, and merely material, absence of the emigrant will eventually become a 'moral' (and 'spiritual') absence, a consummated absence and a complete break with his community.

Emigration represents a serious threat to both the integrity and survival of the emigrant insofar as he is a member of his community or his nation, and to the integrity and survival of those communities themselves. Emigration deprives them, first, of their men and then, and increasingly, of whole families. Now that the 'modern' mode of existence of the communities that supply emigrants takes the form of a *national* existence, or the form of the nation (one is an *Algerian* who has emigrated and, on the other hand, an *Algerian immigrant*) and now that emigration has become a *national* problem everywhere (and no longer a problem for communities faced with the emigration of their members), the whole nation is threatened with being mutilated by emigration. It is in danger of losing 'bits' of itself as it loses bits of its contemporary and future population (the reproduction of emigrant families outside the nation). Its sovereignty is at risk because part of the nation (part of the sum total of its nationals) exists outside it and outside its sovereignty. We can thus understand the double relationship of attraction and repulsion, of attachment and detachment, that is established between, on the one hand, emigrants who are always suspected of having brought about their own damnation (and at the same time that of their families), and their communities and society (or nation) of origin on the other. They are suspected of 'having lost their souls' or, in contemporary terms, of having been decultured or depersonalized – in the sense of alterity and cultural adulteration – and therefore of making their communities, their society or their nation lose their souls. They are suspected of sedition or even subversion, if only because of the example they set and the examples they import ('cultural models imported from abroad', as it is being said more and more often). We therefore have a mutual attempt to achieve integration or greater integration, as emigrant-immigrants and their communities of origin insist that they belong to one another. The former, who are immigrants living in some other society, claim that they are 'emigrants', or in other words that they still belong to *their* society, *their* country, *their* nation. Conversely, the latter, which have immigrants living in other countries, claim them because they are still *their* emigrants, and therefore still part of them. This is a reciprocal attempt at reintegration and reappropriation on the part of immigrants who reintegrate into and reappropriate *their* society, *their* territory, *their* country, *their* nation (and nationality) and repatriate themselves there, and conversely their countries, which try to reintegrate, reappropriate and repatriate their 'emigrants'. (If it has no more than this symbolic meaning, the Algerian discourse on the 'reinsertion' of emigrants will have more than served its purpose.)[5]

The *presence* of the immigrant lies at the origin of a series of studies which, whilst they ultimately prove to be of limited value, are not devoid of interest. The absence of the emigrant should likewise give rise to a series of studies analogous to those produced on immigration and inspired by the same concern for order – the order of the society of emigration, which needs to control these repeated absences and to regulate the effect of those absences. Faced with the threat of fragmentation, how can any society of emigration try, on pain of bringing about its own decomposition, to control the movement that is undermining it? How does it make up for these absences? How does it succeed in neutralizing the threat of contamination, adulteration or subversion posed by the emigration of its members, especially when emigration – which is undeniably an effect of a certain number of disturbances that inevitably exacerbate the causes that produced it – affects more people and affects, first and foremost, its most active elements, in other words men who are, in the majority of cases, young and, at a more fundamental level, the cornerstone of society? These questions can now be reformulated as a single question that can be posed in eminently *political* terms: how can one be Algerian or an *Algerian* emigrant (an Algerian who has emigrated) when one was not born in Algeria, was not raised and did not grow up within Algerian society in Algeria? How can one be Algerian when one has not been subjected to the process of socialization to which any society subjects its actual members in order to make them conform to it, and ultimately, as one thing results from the other, when one is 'called upon' to live and spend one's entire working life outside Algeria and outside Algerian society? To put it another way, how can one be a national of a nation when, from cradle to grave, one lives outside that nation? And conversely, how can a nation have 'nationals' who spend their entire lives outside the nation? We know how, during the first 'age' of emigration, communities succeeded in unfailingly binding their emigrants to them, and in neutralizing the risk, which any emigrant runs, of becoming a *jayah* (or *amjah*). They succeeded in subordinating emigration, and even its most perverse, disturbing and demoralizing effects, to their own objectives (communitarian objectives), and, in selecting its emigrants for those ends, they continued to 'inhabit' them in the true sense of the word throughout their emigration, because the individual was no more than the group *incarnate*. They continued to act upon every one of them, often through the intermediary of the group they constituted, which was itself no more than a constrained, reduced and mutilated reconstruction of the community of origin. It is, on the other hand, difficult to see how the nation – and this new 'age' of emigration, which is, so to speak, the ultimate phase of the process, concerns the nation – can now be so effective and so successful at perfectly integrating all its migrant nationals.

If we investigate emigration as an *absence* and then ask ourselves about the effects of that absence, we have to re-evaluate in different terms the way the economic theory of the 'comparative costs and benefits of emigration' allocates those costs and benefits to the country of immigration and the country of emigration. Both derive 'benefits' and incur 'costs' from, respectively, immigration and emigration. Whatever reservations we may have about this theory, which is, ultimately, no more than an exercise in *accountancy*, we can only deplore the fact that emigration has not produced, of and for itself, an equivalent theory of 'the comparative *benefits* and *costs* of emigration'.

What is more, the transposition of the theory of the 'comparative costs and benefits of immigration' automatically produces, here as elsewhere and as has been and is done for immigration, a sort of legitimation of emigration. Being correlative, the legitimation of immigration and the legitimation of emigration rebound on one another. An economic theory of immigration which reduces it to a set of 'costs' and 'benefits' helps to legitimate it. Immigration is a presence which, if it lasts too long and manifests itself everywhere and in every domain of public life, will eventually become illegitimate. When applied in the same reductive manner to emigration, this theory will help to legitimate that too. Emigration is an absence which, if it lasts so long as to become complete, will eventually become illegitimate. The discovery that emigration requires an autonomous process of legitimation that owes nothing to the analogous process that goes on elsewhere with respect to immigration means that the truth that the country of immigration has established about immigration can no longer be seen as a universal truth or taken at face value. We can no longer accept the way it divides the benefits and costs of immigration and emigration between itself and, correlatively, the country of emigration. We discover that a different balance sheet can be drawn up for both emigration and its 'costs' and 'benefits'. It does not have to be symmetrical, with the balance sheet drawn up by the country of immigration which, from its own point of view, has every interest in minimizing its 'benefits' and maximizing its 'costs' (and therefore maximizing the 'benefits' and minimizing the 'costs' of immigration to the country of emigration), and in attributing them to emigration and its authors. We discover that emigration may involve unexpected 'costs'. These are never taken into account by the balance sheet drawn up by the country of immigration. They include excess 'costs' for which there is no compensatory 'profit', and also costs *specific* to emigration (i.e. 'costs' for which there are no equivalent 'benefits' for the country of immigration), just as immigration also has *specific* 'benefits' (for which the country of emigration incurs no corresponding costs). We thus arrive at a very different evaluation of the phenomenon of emigration and immigration as a totality, and discover that, in addition to all this, absence is, in itself, enormously prejudicial. It involves 'costs' that are literally incommensurable, or which are out of all proportion to the 'benefits' they may bring (lower unemployment, an inflow of foreign currency). That being the case, we also begin to list and unmask all those effects of absence that are normally masked, denied or disguised (costs disguised as benefits). Although it is inseparable from a complete re-evaluation of everything to do with emigration, this complete re-evaluation of the effects of emigration is only possible within certain economic conditions. Emigration must have ceased to fulfil either its specific economic function or the function it is expected to fulfil – in which case it is a complete 'failure' and all that remains are the costs, the disadvantages and the losses. Alternatively, economic conditions (which lay at the origins of emigration) must have been transformed to such an extent that the contribution made by emigration becomes negligible or even superfluous. In the case of Algerian emigration, both these conditions appear to have been met, or to be on the point of being met now that, as a result of various factors, emigration seems to have lost sight of its original function, significance and importance. Regardless of whether they are a cause or an effect, these two conditions prefigure, on the part of Algeria and the whole of Algerian society, a total revision of attitudes towards the phenomenon of emigration itself and towards emigrants, and a total re-evaluation of the entire system of relations between Algeria and Algerian society, and emigration and the emigrant population. Emigration was for a long time the main, if not the only, source of disposable monetary income, especially in rural areas. At the national level, it was for a long time the main source of Algerian budgetary resources (equal to and sometimes greater than the income from petroleum products). It has now lost that function completely – indeed it lost it very quickly. It became much less important and therefore lost the sort of legitimacy it derived from that function. In order to reach the point where emigration can be denounced for the absence that it is (and, increasingly, it is denounced in political terms), or where the illegitimacy of such a total and prolonged absence can be denounced, all the good reasons that could once be invoked to justify and legitimize it, for one reason or another, must have disappeared. Once the 'good' reasons have disappeared, the illegitimacy of emigration becomes quite obvious. In other words all the reasons why it is suspect become obvious, as do its shameful nature and the desertion or treason it represents. In recent years, a whole series of factors has helped to strip emigration of both its most positive aspects[6] and the compensatory effects it claimed to have so as to redeem itself for the absence it caused, even to the extent of taking its revenge on the absent whilst at the same time accepting that this unbearable absence had been forced upon them.[7] Some of these factors are not directly linked to emigration – such as the rapid increase in the mass of income from petroleum products, which has considerably reduced the relative importance of resources due to emigration, and therefore emigration itself. Other factors, in contrast, do derive more directly from emigration, its evolution and the effects it has. Some are of a structural nature and relate to the transformations which, in the long term, have inevitably modified both the structure of the emigrant population and the very nature of the phenomenon of emigration. Others are conjunctural and can be understood only if we relate them to Algeria's monetary policy (a non-convertible currency, very strict exchange controls, etc.) or even to the Algerian economy as a whole (the nationalization of trade, and the establishment of a state monopoly on all imported goods) and, more specifically, Algerian society's system of consumption (a level of consumption that is relatively high and disproportionate, given the country's level of and potential for production; a demand for both material and symbolic consumer goods at a level typical of the developed countries; a habit of consuming French products and of 'French-style' consumerism). These factors are retranslated by emigrants – but now they are immigrants – into a whole series of strategies that make them more likely to settle in France rather than to keep close links with Algeria, although they do not actually cut them off from Algeria. These strategies include investment and savings schemes, or even in some cases simply hoarding, implemented in France itself.[8]

Of all the strategies that are responsible for reducing or even doing away with the remittances emigrants used to make from the money they had saved for that purpose, it is, moreover, the 'compensatory' operations which, for reasons that do not always stem from exclusively economic considerations, give rise to the greatest disapproval and the most accusatory and stigmatizing discourse about emigrants. A veritable parallel market for the exchange of Algerian dinars and French francs (and, more generally, of dinars and any other convertible currency that can replace the franc) has been established through the intermediary of emigration and emigrants. The result of all this is that the remittance of money through the post, which was practised by emigrants until not so long ago, has now dried up almost completely (see table 2). Whereas in 1971, the 697,000 Algerian emigrants (no distinction is made here between active and inactive, gender or age groups) who represented 20.5 per cent of the foreign population resident in France, were sending home 16.4 per cent of all moneys transferred by all foreigners resident in France, in 1978 that proportion was no more than 4.2 per cent (of an estimated total of 10,102 million francs). In 1979, it represented only 1.9 per cent (of the 11,119 million francs sent abroad by all emigrants living in France), even though the Algerian population had grown constantly (and in absolute terms) throughout that period, rising to 819,000 (or 19.6 per cent of the total foreign population resident in France). To use a famous saying,[9] every (non-emigrant) Algerian had his banker in France (for francs) and, conversely, every Algerian emigrant had his banker (for dinars) in

Table 2 Remittances from immigrants' own savings; share of remittances by nationality, 1971, 1978, 1979 (millions of francs)

Immigrants	1971 Population		Remittances		1978[1] Remittances		1979 Population		Remittances	
	Number	%	Amount	%	Amount	%	Number	%	Amount	%
Algerian	697,316	20.5	778	16.4	426	4.2	819,053	19.6	212	1.9
Moroccan	170,835	5.0	363	7.6	1,644	16.3	385,991	9.3	1,686	15.2
Tunisian	96,821	2.9	135	2.8	400	4.0	180,429	4.3	440	3.9
Italian	592,787	17.5	222	4.7	237	2.3	496,079	11.9	290	2.6
Spanish	601,095	17.7	929	19.5	1,901	18.8	457,134	11.0	1,962	17.6
Portuguese	607,069	17.9	1,711	36.0	4,346	43.0	873,736	21.0	5,308	47.7
Other	–	–	620	13.0	138	1.4	–	–	1,221	11.0
Total	–	100	4,748	100	10,102	100	–	100	11,119	100

[1] Population figures for 1978 not supplied in original
Source: *Migrations-Informations*, 38, September 1981, Ministère de la Solidarité nationale-DPM

Algeria. The almost total disappearance of remittances from the savings of Algerian emigrants emerges even more clearly if we compare their behaviour in this respect with that of emigrants from other countries close to Algeria and which, like Algeria, also have non-convertible currencies (Morocco, Tunisia) or from European countries (Italy, Spain and Portugal). Although it has not been continuous, that a drop in remittances from savings was taking place had been apparent for some years, but it was only in 1976–7 (a year that can be regarded as a watershed) that they accelerated and fell to such an extent that in 1977, 1978 and 1979 they were equivalent only to 54.4 per cent, 42.5 per cent and 21.2 per cent, respectively, of the 1976 figures. Such an extraordinarily rapid fall cannot, given the proportions it has reached, be explained by the changes, major and rapid as they may be, that may have occurred within the structure of the Algerian population resident in France. Which proves, *a contrario*, that the explanation is of a very different order. Whereas remittances made by the immigrant workers themselves fell, there was no proportional fall, in either absolute or relative terms, in other amounts sent to Algeria deriving from the work of Algerian emigrants in France (wages transferred directly by employers acting in the name of their employees, renumerations relating to work and other social benefits, especially family allowances, annuities and retirement pensions, etc.). It could even be argued that, in overall terms, the proportion of all remittances to Algeria in this category remained relatively constant throughout the period concerned (as can be seen from table 3 in the years 1971, 1978 and 1979 it represented, respectively, 20.9 per cent, 19.4 per cent and 18.4 per cent of all social transfers).

Table 3 Social transfers resulting from work of immigrants of six nationalities: 1971, 1978, 1979 (millions of francs)

	1971		1978		1979	
Immigrants	Total	%	Total	%	Total	%
Algerian	358	20.9	1,240	19.4	1,367	18.4
Moroccan	77	4.5	400	6.2		
Tunisian	25	1.4	152	2.4	616	8.3
Italian	157	9.2	594	9.3	637	8.5
Spanish	61	3.6	249	3.9	329	4.4
Portuguese	53	3.1	242	3.8	288	3.9
Other	980	57.3	3,523	55.0	4,207	56.5
Total	1,711	100	6,400	100	7,444	100

Source: *Migrations-Informations*, 38, September 1981, Ministère de la Solidarité nationale-DPM

That the level of remittances remained constant is, by contrast, all the more significant in that the number of Algerian families resident in France, and therefore in receipt of family allowances (and to a lesser extent of other social benefits), rose considerably (hence, no doubt, the slight fall of 2.5 points recorded between 1971 and 1979, 1 point between 1971 and 1978, and of 1.5 points between 1978 and 1979). What is more, and probably because Algerian immigration in France was so long-established, on such a large scale and of such complexity, in 1979 Algeria was in a good position with respect to all transfers other than the voluntary remittances made by the emigrants themselves (936 million francs: 26.5 per cent of all transfers in this category), and even ahead of all those EU countries that are not countries of emigration (Italy is, of course, the exception to the rule). This was primarily the result of transfers made in the form of family allowances (241 million francs, or over 41 per cent of transfers were made in this form). The fall in the share of remittances attributable to remittances from the savings of Algerian immigrants was not simply proportional to all transfers from France; it also fell in proportion to all social transfers to Algeria.

It is at the moment when it is most controversial, at the moment when it is revealed to be the site of a conflict between emigrants and their society of origin, that emigration reveals most clearly its truth and the truth about the emigrant condition. Neither is conceivable or tolerable unless it 'brings in' more than it 'costs'. Definitions of both benefits and costs are also the objects of incessant struggles (just as they are in immigration). This no doubt is how we have to understand the evolution of the financial measures that are adopted at the beginning of every year (see, in this connection, the series of annual finance acts). They take into account the effects of immigration, and regard financial contributions made by immigrants as receipts (without ever indicating the financial 'costs' or the loss of earnings, or the cost of even the nominal parity between the franc and the dinar, the loss of earnings resulting from tax exemptions, etc.). As the value of monetary income from emigration falls in both absolute and relative terms, and as the amount held in emigrants' foreign currency accounts decreases, as though to restore the original balance and in doing so to restore emigration to its original purpose and initial legitimacy, the 'privileges' granted to emigrants – in other words what a superficial 'cost-benefit' accountancy records as the 'cost' to be paid for emigration – also fall. A high point seems to have been reached when the law (the decrees implementing the finance law of 1982, which came into effect in May 1982) was introduced that required Algerian emigrants (wage-earners – unemployed or not – family members, etc.) to change the equivalent of a minimum of 700 Algerian dinars (1,070 francs) during their stays in Algeria. Emigrant businessmen and members of the liberal professions seem to have been 'taxed' at a higher rate. In 1979, emigrants sent home no more than 27 per cent of what they had transferred in 1971 by the most visible means (postal orders), and the amount transferred now is certainly much lower. Quite apart from the somewhat shameful character of the measure, and its effects on emigrants who are described as 'parasites' who have to pay for the time they spend in their own country, Algeria in fact encroached upon its own internal sovereignty by acting in this way. One of the inalienable attributes of a national is the unconditional right to enter his or her country unconditionally (subject to the requirement to prove his or her nationality; that is the function of identity papers), and especially without having to meet any financial conditions. This was not the only way in which Algeria damaged its own credit, or the image it should present to the emigrant, that hybrid being who is both a national and a non-national (and this, presumably, is something he cannot be forgiven for). The emigrant who cannot meet the requirement to change a minimum of 1,070 francs and, in addition, to be in possession of a return ticket or its equivalent in foreign currency (a requirement that normally applies to foreigners, but not nationals), is stripped not of his passport, but of his French 'certificate of residence', which is a document issued by a foreign authority and stamped with the seal (the sovereignty) of a foreign state. This means in effect that the latter document is regarded as more valuable than the former (which is objectively true) and that its confiscation is more repressive or more dissuasive. The document is objectively credited with bestowing freedom of movement (it is not uncommon to see emigrants who have gone through this ordeal kissing their 'certificates of residence' – the very same certificates they spat upon and cursed in France because of all the trouble they had caused them). Neither the document nor the freedom it brings are restored until the emigrant 'tourist' who is on holiday in his own country has proved, receipt in hand, that he has handed over the amount of foreign currency required for his 'liberation'. Despite all this, which is extremely wounding to the national pride – and Algerians are known to be very sensitive in this respect – these measures raised no objections and no indignation even at the level of public opinion. Indeed, they even enjoyed a certain popularity, as everyone found it 'natural' that emigrants should 'pay' (as though any emigrant who did not acquit himself of the obligations he had incurred by emigrating – to send money home – were a bad emigrant, a *jayah*, and also a bad national), that those who had money (meaning foreign currency) and shared in the opulence of the rich (meaning that they did not suffer the restrictions and shortages that were the lot of nationals) should pay a tax (a punitive tax, now that they no longer paid it voluntarily or of their own accord) that contributed to the country's prosperity (i.e. the prosperity of those nationals who lived there, and not of those nationals who had committed the sin – or had the good fortune – of being away from it). The only protests came from emigrants or, strictly speaking, the 'victims' of the measure, some of whom went so far as to swear that 'they would never again set foot in their country so long as it demanded a tribute (*maks*) or a fiscal tax before they could go home.

Once the 'benefits' – real or imaginary – of emigration have actually vanished or have vanished from the way they are represented (and here, reality consists entirely in its representation: it exists in and thanks to that representation), all that remains are its liabilities, or the social 'evils' that are attributed to it. The cost of living goes up during the period of the year (July–August) that sees the greatest influx of people coming back on holiday because of the high demand created by emigrants. Emigrants are seen as illegitimate 'tourists' (tourists in their 'own' country and, worse still, tourists who do not have the social qualities and cultural capital of real tourists). They are always assumed to have a lot of purchasing power (the prestige of foreign currency, exceptional or even conspicuous consumption for an exceptional period, excessive spending to make up for their absence from home, etc.). The number of road accidents rises during this holiday period, as emigrants have the reputation of being 'bad' drivers (they buy cars only for the holiday period and only to show off; they do not know the roads because they have been away; they buy only second-hand cars that are in poor condition). They are held responsible for every imaginable 'traffic' (there is a traffic in all kinds of consumer goods, not to mention gold and jewels, hunting rifles, spirits and so on) and for undermining the stability of the national currency. Even what are traditionally seen as the 'benefits' of emigration (which is the primary, if not the only, source of monetary resources in the countryside) come, in retrospect, to be seen as negative or even harmful. It is discovered after the event that the massive injection of currency was the cause of social, economic and cultural upheaval, and that as monetary exchanges become more widespread and more intense, especially in the countryside and amongst peasant populations, they lead to what is known as 'de-peasantification'.[10] As a result of a second backlash, what was initially an effect of emigration (i.e. the discovery of waged labour) becomes the cause of the expansion and precipitation of emigration (which is now being perpetuated) and, more generally, of the entire rural exodus.[11]

Do we have to wait for all emigration's component illusions to be dispelled, and for all the dissimulations or all the enchantments that are the very precondition for emigration (its advent, its diffusion, its reproduction and therefore its perpetuation) to be dispelled in broad daylight, before the conditions of possibility of a science of emigration can be established? Does emigration have to cease to be an absence that can be expressed only in affective terms (the absence of loved ones, who become all the more loved because they are 'absent', and the absence of loved ones who are all the more loved because one is absent)? Is that the indispensable precondition for an objective understanding of the problem? Must the object therefore cease to exist, or must it be on the point of dissolving completely, before, thanks to a strange inversion, a science of emigration can at last be a possibility?

7

The Wrongs of the Absentee

There are many indications that the immigrant's relationship with his work can be an 'unhappy' one. Some take the form of modes of behaviour that border on the pathological (unpredictable absences for which there is no explanation, 'nostalgic' forms of behaviour, 'stress' – although that term is habitually reserved for a different social category: management). They have as much to do with what creates the immigrant condition as with working conditions in the strict sense of the term. And this inevitably leads one to investigate not only the mode of presence that is attached to the immigrant in immigration but also, and more significantly, the effects of absence. No matter how justified it may be, emigration is always suspect. Unless emigration can be 'moralized' – in other words 'proved innocent' – which automatically proves innocent both those who are about to absent themselves (emigrants) and those who allow them to 'absent themselves' by colluding in their absence (the whole of the society of emigration), there is always the lingering suspicion of 'betrayal', 'running away' and, ultimately, repudiation. An accident along the way or a slight departure from behavioural norms are all it takes to give rise to the feeling of being at fault, of having committed the 'original sin' that is consubstantial with the act of emigrating. Culpability, culpabilization and self-culpabilization; accusations and self-accusations: these are the indissociably constituent elements of the emigrant condition and the immigrant condition.

The case related here illustrates in extreme terms the social cost of emigration. The Algerian immigrant who is the author of the narrative presented here was 51 years old when he agreed to be interviewed (in June 1985). Like many of his contemporaries who are of the same age and the same social condition, he first emigrated to France when he was only 19 (in 1953). In retrospect, his immigration looks like a particularly striking condensation of the entire history of Algerian emigration to France in the years following the Second World War. Having emigrated young and when he was still single, he returned to his village only for the duration of his annual holidays, 'and even then, only every other year' (he did so in the second half of his emigration, or in other words in 1963 and after having married at the relatively late age of 30). The only relatively prolonged break in his immigration was in 1958–9 when, because of the prevailing state of war, he had to spend more than fifteen months in his own country (arrest, temporary house arrest, refusal of the authorization required to leave Algeria, and so on).

In France, he experienced the various important moments that constitute Algeria immigration – i.e. the different ways in which the immigrant was set to work and the various jobs that corresponded to each of those moments. He was young and, as a new immigrant, he experienced many doubts and difficulties as he wandered around the country. The first job of which he has any good memories, no doubt because of the high level of integration that went with it (integration into the group of immigrants, who were either relatives or from the same village as him and who worked in the same place), was that of a coal miner (in Valenciennes) during a period when the production of coal was still greatly encouraged and even a cause for celebration. This was, he admits with a hint of regret, the best period of his immigration because 'everything was clear' (or seemed clear to him), even though, he adds with a play on words, he 'was working *in the darkness of the earth*' (i.e. underground) and at '*dark times*' (i.e. at night), in other words in the darkness of both the sky and the earth. Even today, and perhaps more so than ever, he cannot dispel his lingering nostalgia for a period when everything seemed to him to be well organized. This was probably the only moment when the meaning he gave to his immigration and to his life in immigration corresponded with what everyone on both sides of the line that divides emigration from immigration (i.e. the point of view of the society of emigration and the point of view of the society of immigration) expected it to be and with what he himself saw it as, namely a complete dedication to work that precluded any questions as to the real meaning of the act of working and, therefore, the act of emigrating and immigrating.

Then came a whole series of disenchantments – namely, the shattering of all the illusions that had helped to give a meaning to a situation which, when reduced to its naked truth, was neither intelligible nor tolerable. It was intolerable because it could not be given a meaning and therefore could not be intellectually tolerable. Unless the immigrant constantly reinvests with meaning (and not all immigrants can do this) an experience which, because it lasts too long, eventually gets out of control – or at least escapes the control of those immigrants who are the least socially capable of continuously mastering either a phenomenon that is beyond them or its multiple transformations (each more constrictive than the last) – the 'absurdity' of the immigrant condition suddenly becomes blindingly obvious to all, sometimes to the point of damaging the psychical integrity of the most vulnerable of them.

How are we to explain this particular vulnerability? We cannot do so unless we retrace the course of immigration in its entirety, even beyond or prior to emigration. We cannot do so unless we investigate the whole itinerary of the immigrant, both professional and social. By doing this, we can accompany him on his way and attempt to reconstruct, in retrospect and with his help, the social trajectory that has made him the representative of a certain mode of emigration and, as one prolongs and confirms the other, of a certain mode of immigration. The first lesson to be learned from this first attempt at an explanation is that we have to challenge the divorce that has been established between work and non-work – in other words, everything that exists outside the place and closed time of work. (This is what studies of 'health at work' are beginning to discover. Taking their inspiration from a synthetic approach, such studies attempt to reconstruct the unity of an object that has been divided between spheres that are assumed to be autonomous and between the disciplines specific to those spheres.) In the case of X, for example, some factors relating to the experience of immigration in the strict sense may provide a partial explanation for his conflict-ridden relationship with work (which may go so far as to become self-culpabilization or self-harming). These factors are easy to identify, and are easily located in time and space. They include the many changes of job that appear to suggest a professional 'instability', the many periods of sick leave for which there is no obviously pathological cause, or which are not the result of any organic pathology, and which may result in psychiatric hospitalization. They cannot, however, provide a total explanation. For, in order for them to be fully explanatory, they themselves would have to be explained and related to their possible genesis. Now that genesis lies elsewhere. It lies in what the immigrant will never admit, or will never admit to anyone who does not already know it from direct experience because he has been part of it. It lies in what he will not admit to himself as being the cause of his illness [*mal*] and the cause of the guilt-ridden relationship he has with himself to the extent that he is an emigrant (to the extent that he is absent from home) and therefore with his immigration and, in the last analysis, with his work, which is the explanation for both his emigration and his immigration, just as it is their ultimate purpose, and by that very fact the explanation for what is regarded as his 'original sin'. What is the point of admitting to something that is known to anyone who is interested in knowing it, to men who are so deeply involved in it that they cannot be unaware of anything (even though they pretend to know nothing), and that no one can hide anything from them? To whom can it be admitted and why should it be admitted? The 'ill' ('illness', *la maladie*; 'ill-being', *le mal-être*) lies in the publicly 'clandestine' or the secretly 'public' nature of the 'infamy' – that is how they speak of the 'thing' that is present in the mind of all the members of the group, but which no one wants to talk about, and for which immigration is ultimately held responsible. This is what gnaws away at the immigrant when he finds himself incapable of giving a credible meaning to his immigration or, worse still, reaches the point of denouncing his immigration, blaming it and 'putting it on trial'. It is a clandestine 'thing' in the sense that the affront to the honour and morale of the individual is a very private matter, and that it touches the very heart of the domestic sphere and the most intimate aspects of private life. But it is also a 'public' thing because it is inevitably known to everyone, at least within the limits of the circle of men he knows and who know him. That is the only world that counts or matters to anyone who identifies totally with the group of which he is a member, and who has no real social existence except because of the group, for the group and within the group.

What 'infamy' are we talking about? The interviewee describes it in these terms:

> 'One day, I received an envelope posted in Algiers and containing an extract from a birth certificate, but not a word of explanation. I can now guess who might have warned me in this way, I'm almost sure of who he is; he has nothing against me, he must have suffered as much as me, he couldn't hide this thing from me, he was right. . . . If I could, I would hug him, I would kiss his feet and his head. . . . At the time, it took me a while to understand, and yet the father mentioned in the certificate was me, it really was me, it was my name and my forename . . . so I was the father of a little girl I knew nothing about. How did I get her? I haven't been back to my house in Algeria, I haven't seen my wife for two years . . . I suffered a heavy blow to the head.'

Coming back to this 'trauma', he said: 'What do you expect? I no longer believe in the "sleeper" [i.e. 'in the theory of the sleeping child']. Perhaps that's a pity. But only those who want to believe it can believe it.'[1]

Having been taken off production after ten or so years of activity, X, who had worked in the same factory for fifteen years, was transferred to the cleaning department because of his medical history, even though he had hoped that he would have been assigned to what he calls 'door duty'. The astonishing thing about X is his solitary behaviour. Even when he is in a group he says nothing The rare occasions when he comes to life, when he seems to 'acquire a new taste for life' and engages with the thing we are talking about and with his own modes of behaviour, or the rare occasions when he 'comes back to earth', as he himself often puts it, occur when he is with a small group of good friends who are very loyal to him and who he has been able to turn into his accomplices. These are the men he knows to be so aware of everything that they can understand him and share all his troubles and misfortunes, without him having to say anything about himself and without them having to say anything about it to him. He knows that they all know, and he also knows that they know that he knows that they know. Outside this small group of close friends, X finds all environments hostile; and the work environment no less so than any other.

There is no denying that X is a melancholic who wallows in his melancholia. This is the *nostalgic* reaction of someone who is *attached to an order* that has been definitively and irremediably broken. Although immigration is itself a rupture, or an initial rupture that will be followed by many others, it does finally become 'ordered' and allows an order to be imposed on it. For *disorder* to appear, and for it suddenly to reappear as something irreducible, a second rupture must occur, either within or as a result of this first rupture, which was collectively organized and ordered. The second rupture is individual, as it represents *disorder* for an individual consciousness. An effective illusion, or in other words an illusion that fails to recognize itself for what it is (and this is the common condition of all immigrants), cannot exist unless it is collectively sustained. The illusion and the collusion go hand in hand. The order in question here implies a relationship with the world and with others. The relationship with the world is one of meticulousness, and X provides many examples of a meticulousness that can become a mania. It can be seen in the meticulous gestures which, when working on machines, can become extremely dangerous. It can be seen in the meticulous way he arranges his papers, and the way he looks at both the details of his life and his relations and, more generally, the 'spectacle' of the world. When he is with others, it takes the form of a desire to shut himself up within the limits of a social world organized around clear and solid references. Meticulousness and a hypertrophied conception of duty are symptomatic of the 'non-division of opposites' characteristic of anxiety. If one tendency becomes dominant, the result is a loss of equilibrium. Even, or especially, the most tightly knit groups of close friends and relations (the group made up of a spouse, children, parents, brothers and sisters) are not enough to protect him from loneliness. Loneliness is a total mortification of the being, and we can grasp only its symptoms, namely the transformations of all rhythms, and even of the most ordinary and day-to-day rhythms that structure social life (meals, sleeping and waking, work and leisure, or annual holidays, stays in France, trips home, etc.). Because they are experienced in *internal* time, these transformations encourage introversion, a specific *tempo*, and then result in a meticulous and suspicious introspection and a preoccupation with finding fault everywhere and with every living act and, above all, to detecting the original sin of immigration itself. That is the essential sin that has given rise to all the others he revels in listing. These minor, punctual sins are no more than so many re-enactments of the original sin. An exclusion that is both self-imposed and sought after, which is both painful and greatly appreciated because of the comfort it brings, can give rise to the most fearful monotony, to a hell covered by a shroud or what seems to be an immobile blanket of sadness, anxiety and suffering. The decisive factor lies in the *feeling of guilt*, in the obsession with a return to the past. Paradoxically, it is in the particular case where work is objectively called into question because it is immigration's *raison d'être* and, in the last analysis, the ultimate reason for the *mal* and the *mal-être* experienced in immigration and for which immigration is held responsible, that it tends to constitute itself as the central pivot of an existence that has been torn asunder and undermined from within (struggling with an internal contradiction) to such an extent that life loses all meaning. In this case work tends to be identifiable and to be totally identified with life because, in the restricted social situation into which the 'melancholic' retreats, work forces him to live, rather than simply allowing him to live. It therefore has a literally vital function, a saving function or even a therapeutic function. Because he has to go on living and must therefore go on struggling with all his resources against the block, this stupefying stagnation becomes synonymous with work because work is, in immigration, the only reason for living. The *feeling of guilt* constantly endangers the entire order. It is a threat to the *doxic* order he has established with himself and others, and it can destabilize it. The break with this internal and external order may reach such a level that it becomes intolerable. The surrounding world – the physical world, and even more so the social world (that is to say, others) – is then constituted from the point of view of, and in accordance with, the situation in which the person who sees it in that way finds himself. The apparent detachment affected by someone who appears to have seen it all before, the 'spectator' position he likes to adopt as he brackets out the world in which he must evolve and live, the way he distances himself from the 'century' in which he is, like it or not, involved (and one cannot not want to be involved) seem to represent the last stage or final stretch of a journey at whose end there is no longer any possible 'personal choice'. There is no more credible alternative that might provide a solution, and no way out of the impasse in which he is trapped. The despair or, to be more accurate, the loss of hope that is cruelly experienced at every moment, is a sort of 'internal' coming and going that no one can resolve, a coming and going between what was possible yesterday and is no longer possible today, between what was once no more than possible and what has now become irrevocable.

So what is left? Only the breakdown of the 'life perspective', being torn asunder, and self-destruction. Only the paradoxical situation of the living dead or the already-dead living, as immigrants themselves put it when they come close to a extreme situation that leads them to the discovery of their 'in-existence' and their (social) inability to situate themselves within a 'perspective' that might give a meaning to their existence.[2] It is the desperate attempt to reconnect the threads that existed before the rupture, to put the broken pieces back together that supports life, sustains life and fills all of one's life, in such a way that this effort finally comes to be totally identified with life and to constitute life to such an extent that the author of this attempt eventually forgets that there is another way to live, and forgets that life means living other than by striving to live. Necessity and freedom!

The interview as analysis and self-analysis

'How did I find myself in this job? You mustn't think I was taken on especially to do this job, to sweep and clean up the rubbish.... You tell me you're looking for shirkers [*planqués*], trying to understand how someone becomes a shirker – and even if this is a cushy number [*planque*] – and I wish it was – you need to know how much I paid for it. I paid for it in blood, with my flesh [he prods himself to show how thin he is, how much "flesh" he has lost at work], with my white hair.... A lot of people say: "Ah, there's a shirker."[3] If only they knew. You think the same thing. Is there really such a thing as a "cushy number" in this workplace, is there such a thing as a "cushy number" at work? No one asks that question.... Yes, when you're working, you do try to grab a minute here, a minute there, you try to cheat, to get something for nothing, as they say. But personally I still prefer to do like everyone else, like I did in the days when I was working on the assembly line, rather than now that I'm alone, walking the streets of the factory with my broom ...

'This job, I got it on doctor's orders, after lots of examinations, after consultations with the social security, with the company doctors. I was on sick leave for a long time, I was classified by the disability commission. I had to say no; I had to fight a big battle with the social security, the management, the company doctors to get them to agree to reclassify me.... If it was up to me, I'd have liked to be on the door, I asked to be. But it seems you have to be able to pull more strings than I can to get that ...

'Why did I like that? Because you could sit down all day, because you could be in the warm, because you had no one [implying: no boss] above or alongside you to keep an eye on you.... But ultimately I'm not unhappy being here, having been given a broom rather than being on the door, as I put it. In my job, I have the good luck to have my broom for my only companion; the two of us are inseparable: me and my broom. We know each other well now, we talk to each other, my broom witnesses everything that happens to me, everything I do, everything I think. It's another me. I prefer its company to that of anyone here; the broom has the great virtue of saying nothing, and yet I do talk to it, I tell it everything. There's nothing it doesn't know about me; it's another me. It is the most faithful man I know, it has never betrayed me, never given away a secret, never moves from the spot. I leave it there, and I'm sure of finding it in the same place whenever I need it, it doesn't move an inch, even if it has to wait for a year. No one could be more reliable, more faithful, more grateful than my broom; we are great friends, my broom and me, we are brothers [he kisses the handle of his broom, hugs it tenderly to him; on several occasions X will speak of how he loves his tool and the complicity he has established with it: this seems to be known to all those who know him, and they never fail to express their surprise, never fail to laugh at the quite extraordinary, or at the very least unexpected, relationship that exists between the worker and his tool. His investment in it is much greater than is traditional or conventional in the purely instrumental relationship a worker has with his tools], we get on wonderfully.

'Ultimately, I don't regret not having been put on the door. I can see that now; I'd have had lots of trouble, there's lots of trouble there. Whereas, here, with my broom – and a territory – I'm left in peace. So much the better. Peace! Good riddance. What trouble, you ask me? I'm not too sure, but I am sure that I'd have had trouble.

'... I like being alone, I like working alone, alone as God is alone. That's the reason why I ended up liking this job. And yet there's nothing enviable about it. What can I say? Filth, working in filth, sweeping and picking up other people's filth. A piece of filth like any other, that's what you are! Besides, that's how they threw me here, like a piece of rubbish!...But I'm not complaining, all the same. I work at my own pace, alone, one step at a time. As soon as I've got my overalls on, as soon as I have my broom in my hands, all my other cares vanish, I leave them in the changing room. I don't talk to anyone, and no one talks to me, hello, goodbye from time to time, hello to this one or that one as they pass me. It's not often that I fall in with one or two people I like. Like the person who is listening to me now, like you I'm talking to now [this is a polite formula], and who I enjoy chatting to for a minute or two. Apart from little things like that, I take no notice of anyone, and no one takes any notice of me. I work at my own pace. If someone is nice to me, I'm friendly towards him, I look up at him, when it's someone I don't want to see, I look at my broom when he comes near me. It's true, I get more pleasure out of looking at my broom than out of directing my gaze towards him.... I work with my eyes on the ground, and no one is any the wiser. Too bad. They say of me "He's unsociable"; yes, I'd rather be unsociable than force myself to smile: "How are you, my friend, how are you, brother, how are you, uncle!" Only an imbecile [*elbassal*[4]] would act like that. Having brothers and uncles all over the place; turning the first man who comes along into your brother, your father, your uncle; you really have to be no one, and have no self-respect to make a spectacle of yourself like that. I don't like that, I'm not made that way. God preserve me from that, and from everyone who behaves like that. They have no sense of their own honour and dignity.... They might think that I carry all the dishonour of the world on my shoulders, all the infamies, all the villainy, because I am a sweeper, but I prefer my broom to the lot of them, they're worth less than my broom. In reality, they are the ones who bow down, who crawl on their bellies, yes sir, no sir, it's a wonder they don't say "*Sidi*" because they see *Sidis* everywhere, they need *Sidis*. The dishonour and the humiliation are not in the broom I carry in my hands, but in their souls. If I've reached the point of preferring my broom to their work, to preferring this broom, which I dare not name in front of anyone respectable, it's because I know they are despicable, that they are not even worth looking at ...

'There are days when I spend the whole day walking. It's very good for me. When I'm walking, I see nothing and hear nothing. I am alone with myself, with what I have in my heart [meaning in his head]; I am alone with my thoughts...I go through everything in my thoughts, go through my whole life in my thoughts. I look at it closely, I try to remember everything, and it all comes back to me at certain moments, in the slightest detail. The first day I left – I was only eighteen, a kid, but a kid who had already lived through a lot because he had suffered a lot, [a kid] older than his years – I can still see it, the [first] day of my greatest misfortune. It is only afterwards, a long times afterwards, when it is already too late, that you realize these things. Everything stemmed from that; that first day was the cause of everything that happened afterwards. All that comes back to me, everything, in the slightest detail. There are things that can never be forgotten, all the things you would like to forget. So when I am alone, I think about it all, I think everything over, I examine it from every point of view. I try to understand; I try to understand how things happen. Do the things that happen really depend on me, or do they happen by themselves? They are written. It's enough to make you spend your whole life trying to work out who's responsible.... I know there's nothing that can be done about it, that we cannot undo what has already been done, but despite what they say, what has happened is not dead; it is still there inside us, in our memory, in our present and what we are living through now is no more than the sequel to what has happened. So I prefer to stay with my thoughts, that keeps me busy enough, I don't need to look all around me so as to add things. On the contrary, looking all around me dissolves everything inside my head...in any case I see nothing and hear nothing. The only real things are those I have inside me ...

'Yes, of course, we all need someone, someone we can tell things to, but it is rare to find that someone, that someone does not exist. So why waste your time looking for them?...Yes, it is nice when you have someone. As we say at home: the unique [solitary] man is forbidden by law to have a house [i.e. a family]. No one can exist in solitude. But we are never alone, there is always someone inside us. And besides, me, I've always got my broom, my constant companion. If you can't find a companion you can say everything to, you may as well stay at home; rather than meeting other people and, you never know, experiencing the hostility and scorn of those others, it is better to retreat into yourself, to look within yourself. That's where the real remedy lies: in your own strength, in what you have in your heart [that is, in one's courage].

'... Rather than doing the same as everyone else, pretending to forget until you do forget everything, personally, I prefer to remember everything, to keep everything in my mind.... That is the only way I can reassure myself, that I can see clearly into myself, because I try to find light where everyone else tries to find darkness.

'If only I could read my life the way you read a book! And yet, I can't read. But, with a few brains [points with his index finger to his temple], you can always connect the threads if you think about it properly. That is why, ultimately, I am fine where I am, I have no regrets, rather than being on the door and watching everyone pass in front of me, people I like and people I don't like. It's as though you were in the middle of the fair, it's a *souk*, a shop window, a spectacle. You watch the spectacle, the spectacle of them coming in and the spectacle of them going out. It's nothing to write home about.... And me in that hut, I make a spectacle of myself too, in my uniform and my cap. I get to see everything [literally: everything comes to my attention] like a guard, except that I have nothing to guard; there's nothing to guard, apart for being there in order to be seen...and to see who goes in and who comes out. I don't know if you've seen the guards, they never stop talking to each other – I ask myself what they talk about – and as soon as someone goes by, they never fail to call out to them, as though they were happy to have someone to talk to.... There's no difference between them and the concierge of a block of flats.... I don't want to be a concierge. So I prefer my broom to the bunches of keys they have in their hands.

'... Oh yes. A lot of people would like to have that job [as doorman], and as it happens you have to have someone big pulling strings for you to get it. They say you have to look good in the files down there, in the offices. They even say that they have spies there; they trust them, they ask them to keep an eye on everything, though you wouldn't think, they ask them to make reports. Besides, no one trusts them.

'Let me tell you: France is a loose woman, like a whore. Without you realizing it, she hangs around you, tries to seduce you until you fall into her clutches, and then she sucks you, drains you of your blood, gets you to do everything she wants and when she's had enough of you, she casts you aside like a worn-out old slipper, like something that has no importance [literally: 'no meaning']. She's an enchantress. How many men has she carried off? She has thousands of ways of keeping you prisoner. Yes, it is a prison, a prison you can't get out of, prison for life; it's a curse. Once you touch her, she grabs you and carries you off completely, squeezes you, crushes you until you can no longer stand up. She's had us all, she's cunning. It's a lucky man who does not know her, or who has been able to resist temptation! Even if you have to accept her [initial] poverty, because it's poverty that forced us into the arms of this worthless woman! We didn't really choose to come to France of our own accord.... True, no one put us in chains to bring us here of necessity [under duress].... Yes, it's true, I remember that: I waited impatiently for that day [the day of his departure for France]; when you are eighteen, you have your whole life ahead of you. You can see only one thing: the poverty you are living in; what comes next doesn't matter much, and in any case it can't be any worse than what you have. It can only get better, and for that you are ready to put up with any kind of poverty that might get us out of the poverty we are in here. France or somewhere else, I think I'd have gone with anyone who told me: "I'll take you with me, right to the other side of the world".... To be honest, I think that deep inside me, I was never completely fooled; I knew it was no paradise, and I knew it couldn't be paradise. We are not [socially] made for paradise, there is no paradise for us, but we imagine it, we just convince ourselves. Or we fool ourselves – I don't think I'm the only one in that position, no one is any different to me, but we just pretend.... No illusions, yes, I had no illusions. The reason why we were fascinated by France was to do with money; when you haven't a penny, that's all you see: how to get money, what you have to go through doesn't matter much, the price you have to pay for it doesn't matter much. In any case, you've no idea. As to the rest of it, you've no idea. You've just got to look at all the other immigrants, even if they say nothing. They only let you see the best side of things, and then, because everyone has their eyes on them, everyone wants to spoil them, flatter them, their families make a fuss of them, everyone around them, that's what you envy them for; they themselves fall for it. They're flattered by it; that's what gives them most pleasure when they come back home and they have the impression that that brief moment of happiness makes up for everything they have endured for the rest of the year. So, this is not the time for them to tell others exactly what it's like, and it's best to keep quiet. But when they're among friends, a small group will say sometimes something different. . . . A story that we tell at home. This was before emigration to France when people still went only to the Algiers region, to work on the farms, potatoes, tomatoes. There was a father and his son. One year, the father took his son with him to teach him a lesson. To show him what it was like working for the *colons*. When they got there, they bought a loaf of bread and shared it, and they took a melon. Struck with wonder, the son asked his father if that was what they were going to live on all the time. The father nodded, but was careful not to tell him that they had got hold of the melon in secret, without being authorized to pick it, and that they would probably never be authorized to do so. So the young son takes off his cap, throws it to the ground and cries out in joy: "Let the *pays* never return. Let me never see it again, provided I can go on living on white bread, melon and grapes." The story has become proverbial at home. That's how it is with all emigrants: so long as they have enough to buy their bread [*pain*], they don't even think about their sufferings [*peine*], their distress . . .

'Perhaps it's because I can't stop myself thinking about all that that I can never laugh like the rest of them, that I can never be as cheerful as they are, pretend like they do. . . . But times change, and the situation has changed too, both back there and here in France. I realize that myself. When I try to think back to the first years when I came to France, when I compare those times with the situation today, there have been a lot of changes. In what? Everything. Work, the way you live, the money you earn and the money you spend . . .

'I came to Valenciennes in the month of October 1953. I came with a group of relatives who were already in France. They'd go back home in the traditional way, in summer and autumn, during the good weather and at ploughing time, a bit earlier or a bit later, and then they'd all go back to France. They were all miners. And one year, when I'd got together enough money to pay the boat fare, I went with my maternal uncle. . . . I knew nothing, I'd never seen a town in my life, I'd never been on a train. It was one surprise after another. In Valenciennes, I went out only if there was someone with me. In the neighbourhood where we all lived, it was all right, I wasn't too lost. But my great fear was the idea of going to work, of going to work alone and of coming back and of being able to work, all by myself, without understanding what people were saying to me, what they were asking me. How could I work? All I wanted was to be lucky enough to meet, to work with someone from home, or just an Arab, so that we could understand one another. Working the same hours alongside a relative would have been ideal.... Unfortunately for me, there was none of that. No work at all. They said that times were hard, that there was a crisis, unemployment everywhere. No luck: wherever I went when I came to France: you are too weak [too young], we're not taking you on, you aren't strong. And of course I was very skinny.

'Once while we were doing the rounds of the building sites or going from factory to factory – I was never alone, there were always two or three of us, all unemployed like me, but they already knew the country – that's how we went looking for someone to take us on, as we used to say, I came across a coal merchant. It was winter, a very cold winter; I started work very early, at six in the morning, it was still dark, I was cold, I didn't have many things to put on my back, I humped sacks of coal: load the truck, unload it, carry the sacks down into the cellar. It was exhausting, dirty, the marks of the coal were still incrusted in my skin months and months after I left that job. And finally, after working for three weeks, I asked him for an advance because I didn't have a penny, not even enough to buy a coffee, and when the customer we delivered the coal to did give us a coin, the driver kept it all for himself and I didn't have the right to anything. No advance, and no wages or almost nothing at the end of the month, on the pretext that they gave me a meal at lunchtime. I found out later that they hadn't declared me to the social security. In the meantime, I wanted to act like a grown up, like everyone else: I had borrowed 3,000 [old] francs – it was an enormous sum at the time – and immediately sent it to my parents. It was a way of saying: your son is already in France and he's sending you a postal order already! It was the custom: as soon as you reached France, you borrowed money; in any case, everyone offered you money to do that. Everyone, that is to say those who had to do so. It's an obligation. Someone had obviously done the same for them when they came to France. It's always like that, the situation is the same for all of us: everyone knows... nothing is hidden.

'So, after that winter of 1954, a relative who had come from the East, from Longwy – we called it Germany, just as people say of us that we are in Belgium – came to see us. He found me in this state – unhappy, unemployed, living with this one and that one – everyone was looking for work for me, but no one could find anything. I even worked for some peasants. So, he offered to take me with him. He boasted so much that he would find me work, that it was easy over there, that no one was unemployed, that they made lots of money over there, the earthly paradise in short, that I allowed myself to be seduced; I was delighted and everyone was delighted for me. I felt that I was beginning to be too much of a burden for everyone, feeding me, housing me, trying to find work for me. That's fine for a month, two months, three months, but after a reasonable length of time it begins to grate. I was hearing people mutter that perhaps I should go home; there was talk of clubbing together for me, of collecting a bit of money to pay for the journey, to pay my debts – the 3,000 francs and a bit more on top of that – and to take home a little money. The shame of it! Anything you like, but not that. Going home at someone else's expense, you only behave like that if a girl is involved. A bad start to "my" life in France. What would people say? When even the lowest of the low, hunchbacks, the lame, the club foots, the idiots have come to France, worked, sent back money, succeeded, how could I think I was any better than them, how could I contemplate going back home with my tail between my legs, with my head hanging low? What face would I have to put on before I could show myself in public? Never! So, I had nothing to lose, let's go to "Germany". All the more for me, and so much less for the people in Valenciennes.

'When we got there, there was nothing of what he had promised. It was disastrous. Worse housing, worse food, no one I knew, no one from home. Total darkness. He was in reality unemployed himself and lived by sponging off others, but he was used to that. I lasted three weeks, I said goodbye to him at the end of that short stay. He didn't try to stop me. So it was back to Valenciennes again. It was like going back home, almost the same. All the more so in that, whilst I'd been taken to Longwy, there was no one to take me to Valenciennes, to take me back there, or to invite me to go back to Valenciennes. Should I warn them, let them know I was going back to Valenciennes? Who? I'd already been living in France for five or six months, I was beginning to get by a bit, to be less frightened, to be able to venture out. So I said to myself: you'd better move to another area, go and try somewhere else. One fine day, I left Longwy and found myself in the Haute-Marne, in Saint-Dizier, to be precise. When I got to Saint-Dizier, I eventually found some people from home, or from nearby. Fortunately, they were well disposed towards me, one of them was kind enough to take care of me: he got me taken on. To do what? Unloading trucks of coal, like railway trucks; two a day and get on with it: one in the morning and one in the afternoon, and you had to finish them. In all weathers and at all hours. I lasted from '54 to '56. Two trucks each, until they were empty, with a shovel. It's a steel plant, it was in a forge, *Les Forges de Haute-Marne*. And wire, wheels for barrows and lots of other things came out of that forge. There was also a furnace, what they call an open-hearth furnace; its hot breath pushes you back there, back over there [points with his hand]. It runs on coal and, so, coal was needed, two whole trucks, one after the other; two people here, two people there; two here, two there, and so on down the line. It was too hard.

'In this coal business, the first job I had in my life – that was "my" France and I began just as I had to. I began on my first day, 16 August 1954, I remember it as though it were yesterday. I lasted from '54 to '56, I'd had enough of that job. But those that followed were no better. In terms of work, I've always moved from one hell to the next. Do I have less luck, or is it the same for everyone? For me, work has always meant moving from one hell to another.

'. . . I changed and got a different job in a foundry: I was working with acid, that acid used for cleaning metals and other things. A drop of acid spills on to your trousers or some other piece of clothing, and it tears immediately. And we were breathing in that smell. . . . It's the same thing, all jobs are the same, none of them is better than any other. Always hard work. Not only hard, but dangerous too; nothing but poison. Ever since I came to France, never a job in which I've found a little pity, from first to last, nothing but hard jobs; and not only hard, they can cost you your life. "They hover over your head," until they get your head: an accident, or a drop of poison that gently seeps into you every day and, without you realizing it, digs your tomb. Hard, dangerous jobs, that's all there is.

'After that second job – I didn't stay in that job for very long – it was the same thing all over again. A curse on the devil! I've never had any luck with work. Some people, when they've finished their day's work, you'd think they'd just woken up to look at them; but me, I've always moved from one hell to the next. Again, I had a distant relative, there in Saint-Dizier, or a friend, rather: he was working in a different factory. He saw fit to take me away from there and get me into that other factory where he worked. That was to get me lighter work, because I was still too young, I didn't have the strength of a grown man. He was sorry for me. But in reality, it was just the same, the same martyrdom: like the first job, like the second, like the third, and like the others that followed. We did galvanization, we worked on wire, barbed wire. Me, my job, I was a galvanizer. I put the reels on to the drum (*dévidoir*: *dividouar*) and reeled it out (*dévidais*: *dividigh*) like this: I pulled the end of the reel; this is the lead bath, the wire goes through it, and this is the bath of acid. When the wire comes out of the bath of lead, it goes into the acid to be cleaned. Then the bath again, then the drier and finally the zinc bath. The wire goes all shiny . . . the wire becomes completely white. Here, you have the drums that turn. Drums weighing 120 kilos, 100 kilos, 80 kilos, it all depends on the order book: the lightest are 70 or 60 kilos. That's what you do the turning with. So by the time you've dipped the end of the wire into the bath of lead, the vapour gets you, first the lead, than you move on to the acid and then there's smoke, then it gets all hot – It's incredible! and the salt bath, then the dryer, the bath of zinc and, finally the whole reel. And we were competing with other workers, most of them French. We compete to see who can produce the most tonnage, because we work in shifts. We are paid by the month, but there's a bonus on the tonnage. There are three shifts. When we get here, the first thing we do is look at chart 1, shift 1, the first shift that works from 4 am to 12, that makes so many tons. Competition! Our shift starts at 12 and finishes at 8 in the evening. There are six of us; everyone has his own job; one keeps an eye on the reel, another on the baths, the third man is here; two men bring the raw materials. That makes five workers in all, and there is often one more; he's the sweeper, and he picks up the waste. I've seen an accident. God preserve us.

'In the end, I stayed in Saint-Dizier until the month of July '56, almost until July '56 died . . . I was tired of the Haute-Marne. I knew that it would always be the same so long as I stayed in the area: hard work and poor wages. What else is there there? Iron and nothing but iron, steel-making, that's all there is: you leave one factory for another, one foundry for another. . . . I was an OS1; it was only when I was working on the coal, in my first job, that I was a general labourer . . .

'I left the Haute-Marne and went "home" to Roubaix. I could go back to Valenciennes now, because I was a worker like any other, I was already an old hand. And like everyone else, I went down the pit, to work at the coalface. I found it was true, what they said about the pit at the time, what I had always heard people say: "as much money comes out of the pit as coal" . . . Yes, it has to be said that in our village, in our region, the pit went back a long way: men from my village began to work in the pit as early as 1930 or before. I knew about it even before I came to France. In our village, amongst ourselves, we talked about nothing else. Even those who have never been to France, who know nothing about either France or the pit never stop talking about the pit, they have all the time in the world for that. . . . What did they say? This was the time when miners were practically on piecework. It was a question of who could cut the most coal. And they would say: "You know, they say that so and so does so much a day, and earns so much a day." And someone would reply: "No, no. There's better than him, so and so gets more than him." And then there were three or four men everyone talked about. Young, strong, hard workers, very thrifty, they sent back lots of money. They were the stars. Everyone wanted to be like them.

'I stayed at the pit for two years, just over two years. . . . And in the Nord in 1958, with the Algerian war, there was too much trouble. The police, the "brothers".[5] I had to get away. . . . And yet, there was more to it than the nasty moments of the Algerian war; this was the best period of my life in France. We were amongst relatives, we stuck together, work was going very well, and we were amongst relatives, amongst friends. It was like when we all worked together in the village: the same jobs at the same period for everyone. I worked a lot there, and so did everyone else. Work was the only thing that mattered . . . We worked like slaves, we'd have worked day and night; we would count and recount our money. I worked till I was sick of it, till I'd had my fill of it; I flung myself into my work. Till that's all there was, me and my work, I worked till I was blind, until work was all I could see. I plunged into my work – work and me, it was all one; when I could, I would work Sundays too. Work was like a drug, and when I did stop, I realized that I was drugged, drunk on work. . . . What can I say? I had come to work, that's why I was there, so I drowned in work . . . it has to be said that we were young in those days; I was strong: thirsty for work and money, it was a question of who could do most work and send most money home . . .

'I was at peace – despite the war, despite everything we heard about our country, despite the fact that we could not go home, or not as often as we would have liked. At the time, things were clear, everything was clear. Home was back there; we were here only because we had to work, to make money for home, apart from that concern, nothing existed and nothing could destroy the concern we felt for our country. It was much greater than now – and yet we were in the middle of a war, we saw people being arrested every day, every evening, each of us was waiting for his turn, for the moment when he would be arrested.... Yes, it was clear, luminous; even the mine, the darkness of the mine was light compared with the disorder, the fog, the darkness [which also means error] of the present situation.... Light, even though it was dark in two senses, three senses: the night of exile [*elghorba*]; the "underground" night, the night of the bowels of the earth; and often working by night, as there was the night shift too. That's the way it is: "the dark" is found in hearts, they say that's where it takes shape; when the heart is limpid, "clean" [meaning serene], when it shines with light, then the darkness "outside" is light too.

'Despite all the difficulties, the best period of my stay in France was, perhaps, the time I spent in the Nord. Morale was still good at that time. We were like the fingers of one hand; it was thanks to that that we could last out, we held out, we supported each other. There were up to sixteen of us living in one room.... Meat...meat, we ate it once a week. We didn't have steak every day, like we do now. It was only once a week that we knew what meat was, if we were lucky! Wednesday was market day: one of us would go to get some meat, and it wasn't as though someone and others didn't get some meat in, because two, three, sometimes four comrades agreed to share their food and eat together to share the cost. In any case, no one cooked just for himself: everyone had an arrangement with someone else, and they reached an agreement about when to eat. We were well organized in that respect, and we all got on well together.... And yet we weren't all from the same village, or even the same *pays*: two of us were [originally] from what was then called Affreville – it's a long way, you know – two from Michelet, and I'm from Sétif. That was the best period I spent in France, and yet, how much were we earning in those days? 8,000, 9,000 a fortnight, the best of them made up to 30, 28 per month. That's all.

'But for other reasons, the problems with the war, I had to leave it all behind, leave the mine, leave the Nord, and I went to Paris. And I've been in Paris ever since, all the time I've been [in France], during all the troubles, and I've never been home. So, between '58 and '60, I started again, here in Paris. When I came to Paris, I was unemployed for nine months, nine months of unemployment.

'Then I got a job making mattresses. No, it was a real job and not just a cover.[6]...in a mattress-maker's. I was a quilter. It was a very small place, but we worked very hard in those days. Oh yes. We were on piecework, and we did make a living, that's true. At that time, we were making up to 70 or 80,000 – that was with overtime of course: 70–80,000 was a lot of money in those days, but we were working up to sixty-four hours a week. The press alone, when you have to put a mattress in the press and pull down on it, you have up to 200 kilos, the press and the frame, to get the mattress in position. And on top of that you have to work fast at stitching the buttons on. It was hard, but there was no comparison with the work I'd been doing in Haute-Marne. I don't think there is anything more unpleasant than working in front of fire. Compared with that, the pit is a complete rest. But being in front of fire, a fire burning at 1,700 degrees, or even fire that runs – acid – that's hellish.

'... There are often accidents in steel-making, with acid. And, God preserve us, they are not minor accidents; you lose your life, or part of you, a limb. A falling tool is enormous, like a mastodon. And it's always molten: the pig iron, it looks like a river of fire. As for the acid, take care, you have to approach it with caution, and you mustn't stumble. I've seen terrible accidents happen like that. When I was working with barbed wire, there was a worker, poor guy, who got caught by the spool. He was screaming like an eagle. Fortunately for him, as the spool revolved, it only caught his apron, and it tore it off him and carried it away. If it hadn't been the apron, it would have taken his head off. His apron was torn and carried away by the spool, and he was thrown out on the other side.

'Another workman – we were on the same shift – climbed up on top of the bath to push the wire in with a descaling lance. He lost his balance and fell into the zinc, he was plunged into that bath there. His whole foot went in. Fourteen months in hospital before his foot got better, poor guy. The bone was all that was left, he'd been so badly burned – best not talk about it.

'Someone else – he worked with me too – five fingers, three on the left hand and two on the right hand. All his fingers went into the spool. While it was revolving, he tried to adjust the spool by hand, to make sure that it would revolve smoothly, that it didn't become tangled, that it was properly wound. He tried to tap like that, with his hand. The spool trapped his fingers, he tried to pull them away with his other hand, and it sliced off two more fingers; in all, he lost five fingers. He didn't understand the machinery, he tried to adjust it with his hand while it was moving. You don't touch machinery with your fingers. That worker is from where I come from, he's in Algiers now. He told me he'd never come back [to France]; he told me "I'm going to try at all cost not to come back to France." So, he has a pension too. ... He went back to work here in France, his fingers had healed in the meantime, no, they cut them off. He's disabled. There were lots of accidents on that job. Anyone who worked there [in Saint-Dizier] and came back safe and sound is a happy man before the Eternal, because accidents were common enough. Not a week went by without someone carried out; you never know when an accident might happen.

'... Yes, we really ought to get back to my present job. Between all these jobs and the job I'm doing today, there was a long gap. In 1960, the inevitable happened. I was arrested, and they found a list of people at my place, of all the people who paid dues. Luckily, I'd just handed over the money I had; a few hours earlier, and they'd have found millions on me. They took me away. I don't talk about that. A few weeks in prison, in the forest at Noisy-le-Sec – a camp. Just over a year. They transferred me to Algeria, to Bône; and while I was there the ceasefire came, and I was released in Algeria. I stayed in Algeria for a while, in my village, like everyone else at that time, tried my luck in Algiers. I could get by as well as anyone else, find housing like anyone else; finding a place was still easy in those days, with all the apartments that had been left empty. But when you've got used to something steady, you can't adjust to a situation like that ...

'Obviously, I got married, and that may have been the most stupid thing I did in my life. But what do you expect? When you go back home, get back to the house, what else do you expect me to do? And then, I was already 30, and I was old to be getting married. It's true that I left the village young and before I was married, lots of young men of my age, 18, 19, had been married off before they were allowed to go to France.... Yes, it was a way of keeping them at home. It's true. In any case, none of them spent ten years in France without going back home, as I did. For me, France was ten years at a stretch, from beginning to end. And that leaves its mark, you're not like the rest. So I married, hung around for a while longer and, finally set off for France again. And in November 1963, there I was in France. This time, I went straight to Paris. I worked here and there, doing this and that, in a metal polisher's in the eleventh *arrondissement*, and even in a hospital, the Pitié-Salpêtrière hospital.

'During all this time, I was married, I began to have children, so I had to go back home regularly, but I went back only for the duration of my annual holidays ... one month a year, no more than that, or an extra week at most. Even so, I can't say I went back every year, it would be truer to say every other year.... I have no reason to go back now, there's no longer anything for me to do there. It doesn't interest me. Everything has changed, here and back there. Things no longer have the same meaning. You no longer know why you are here in France, what purpose you serve. There is no more order, the order that used to exist when things may have been difficult, but when they had a meaning. All that has changed now, I've lost my taste for it, I get no pleasure out of going back, even for the holidays, or out of staying here – but I'm here and I have to stay here. I didn't have a choice.... My children are with my mother, I have a girl and two boys.... Because their mother left, I got a divorce.... Better to divorce. When your wife is over there and you are over here, there is no man and wife, so it's better to give her back her freedom. What does it mean to have a wife when you are always away, a wife whose husband is never there? I've been through it, I know what it's like, and that's enough for me. It's what we call, in our country, a man who is forbidden to have a house, whom the law forbids from having a house. So it's best not to try to have a house, a wife. She is a widow even though her husband is still alive. You have to be mad, crazy to accept such a thing. I wish I'd never done it.

'Bring my wife? Never. Never! Impossible! I don't envy the situation of men who are here with their families one little bit.... Yes, so it would seem; as you say, it's the only way – if you don't want to separate, to divide the family; on the one hand, the husband who is in France, all by himself; and the wife and children on the other side. But when you think about it properly, it means getting your wife and children into the same mess as you, and that's even more serious for them than for the men who left to work on their behalf. No man in my family has ever done that. But, to tell you the truth, if you have to look at all the cousins, there's no shortage of men who have done it. On my mother's side, there are three families in Paris alone. What's their situation like? I can't tell you anything about that, we don't see each other often. One of them wasn't well for a while: they were seven or eight of then, what with his wife and all their children, and they were living in a one-roomed flat with a kitchen – they've not been in France for very long; they came in 1971 or 1972. Besides, all three of them work in the hospital and all three of them have children here. One has bought an apartment in Ivry: two rooms and a kitchen, with his three kids; the other is in a council flat in Champigny . . .

'And they are all people who still cling to our old habits, who still live in accordance with the traditions. The women, for instance, never go out except with them [their husbands]; never, unless they are accompanied, and only then to go to the doctor or for something that is worth it that is necessary. Not for fun [*ablagui*, from *blaguer*: 'to joke']. At home, there's no doubt about it, it's Arabic that is spoken as a matter of course; of course they speak Arabic amongst themselves [the adults, parents] and even when they are talking to the children, to the kids, they can't stop themselves . . . especially when they are talking to each other, they can't stop themselves, so it's French that loses out.

'Yes, the idea [of bringing his wife and children to France] did cross my mind, of course it did. Like everyone else, come to that, there's no one who hasn't dreamed of doing that at one time or another. But there are those who resist, who refuse to accept that, and those who give in. The idea did cross my mind at one point, it's true; there's no denying it. I thought of bringing them for one good reason: at that time, there was no school in the village for the children, so it was to send them to school. I had a son, who was older, and a younger girl. And I did bring the older boy with me, he went to school here in France. . . . He's finished his military service, and I think he's working for a national company, works in trade. . . . I'm counting on him a bit more to look after his grandparents; he's taken my place. It's fine for us men, and for him it started a long time ago now: that's our lot. But your wife, our unhappy wives here; if you bring your wife here, what are you bringing her to? A house that's worth it? Happiness here? Where is it? Whilst she might gain something by coming here – better food, better clothes, better health care – she'd pay a high price for it, very high, she would lose her freedom. It would only make her unhappy, lonely; she would be imprisoned in one room, dirty, dark, damp. That's all there is for her. She would long for the sun, the sky; she would miss the sky. I really have no regrets. God knows what he is doing, he acted for the best . . .

' . . . I'd rather they [his children] were backward, if they have to be, but they should stay at home. I know: a man who has no education is a dead man. And that is increasingly the case; the higher up you go, the truer it is. A man who has no education is a poor wretch who cannot do anything. He's a statue, a figurehead [or an image]. You can see that everywhere; you can still see it today, in anything and everything, at every moment, even here at Renault. Between you and me, all those people like me who are OS will remain OS. And the others who have an education, diplomas, who have learned a trade, they're immediately promoted over your head, he becomes your boss. That's education for you . . .

'The idea did cross my mind at one point, but I very quickly put it out of my mind. Besides, events didn't leave me the time. I only brought the eldest, the big lad with me, and I stayed in Paris. I kept him with me. He stayed here for two years. That was in the twentieth *arrondissement*. Finally, he ended up in a school for accountants, in the commercial branch, he studied accountancy. . . . Only the eldest, and what's more, he went back in good time. When I see all the children [of immigrant Algerian families] here, when I see what's become of them, they're always hanging around, they're good for nothing, you don't know what they are – they're not French, even the lowest of the French are head and shoulders above them, they don't have the means; they're not Algerian, so they have nothing in common with their parents; you don't know who to blame: is it the fault of the children? Is it the fault of the parents? But it definitely was a mistake to bring those families over here, rather than leaving them back there. . . . And then there's a lot of other things too. Frankly, we have to take a lot of the blame; we all have our faults too. What do you expect? All those who come back from over there, it's a complete disaster. They've not a good word to say about the country; they complain about everything. They make heaven fall to earth. What do young people from here think about it? They don't know anything about it. It's not their fault. If the country wants to please them it has to be better than here. So right from the start, they leave with a bad impression. And someone who is not used to being back there can't enjoy themselves, that's true enough. The parents don't do anything, they explain nothing to them, they don't prepare them, don't talk to them about their country. I know so many children of emigrants who are ashamed of their country. When they go there once every ten years, what do they have to say about it? "We don't like eating Algerian food – it's hot – you fall ill there." That's when they are young; as for the older ones: "there are no cinemas, no cafés, no dances, you can't have any fun." The outcome of all that is that it's scarcely good enough for a holiday. And if they could, they would stay behind in France and let their parents go to Algeria on their own. And that is what happens in most cases; when they are little, they choose summer camp; when they're older, they stay alone in France. Girls and boys alike. . . . If you listen to them, you notice that they talk about their country in the same way that the French do: "I eat Algerian food..." – they don't know the word for cous-cous, and *galette* has become "Algerian bread". They say: "I can't speak Algerian", which means that they can't speak Arabic. From that point of view, I think we can write off the children who were born here. We don't know what they are. You can't understand anything of it. You can't regard them as either *Roumis* [French] or Algerian. That's the impasse, the uncertainty. If you take all that into consideration, we'd do better to leave them at home, where they're like everyone else around them.

'Is that the real reason, you ask me? Yes and no!... It is and it isn't. I said all that because it does relate to the question you asked me. It's our conversation that led me to say all that [literally: it was the words that brought that]. But there is something of that in my decision; there is that, but there's also something else, lots of other things.... In any case, there's no point because I'm on my own now, I no longer have a wife; I've had a divorce. So the problem doesn't arise. We couldn't go on together; that's something that should be known, that everyone should know; she was back there in Algeria, in our village, and I was here in France; the woman stays at home and the man lives here in France. That can't go on forever. One day, you have to choose. Here or there? And the question has to be answered. Here and there in turn, a lot of time here and a little time back there, that's no answer.'

It was not until much later, and only after many conversations, some with the interviewee at his place of work and, more significantly away from work, and others, through his intermediary, with the very close group of his closest relations and, above all, the two or three people who were most attached to him, who take great care of him and show him every consideration because of his extremely fragile state of health – his mental rather than his physical health – that the admission finally came. His confidants who, with great delicacy and discretion, had warned me of the 'misfortune' that had befallen him and which was certainly at the origins of the mental problems for which he was being treated.

Some of the interviewee's silences, some of his disillusioned remarks, which were fairly elliptic or rather allusive but always very suggestive, could obviously not be understood, or could not become meaningful unless one was aware of the 'inadmissible', unspeakable dimension of the interviewee's life: his marital relations.

Listening to the most intimate confidences of an interviewee is always an emotional business, here more so than in other circumstances. They are a mark of the extreme trust he eventually places in the interviewer, who is always asking questions, who is interested in everything, who is always poking into everyone's past and present, into both their manifest and obvious modes of behaviour, and the explanations for those modes of behaviour and their ultimate finality, which are all secret or latent. This 'intruder' claims to know more about the truth of his subjects than the subjects who bear it within them, act upon it and implement it. When his work of observation and external analysis has been done, he always intervenes after the event, and claims to be telling the truth to the very authors of that truth. One cannot but surrender to the sort of fascination and seduction that seeing the interviewee making such a constant effort has for any lucid observer. One can see it in the way he behaves and in every word he says; he is constantly, tragically, trying to keep his self-control, and displays an astonishing lucidity for someone who simply needs, in the most banal and commonplace of senses, to sustain all the illusions that help to justify his present situation, or in other words all the illusions needed to conceal the truth about his situation.

Anyone who has long been familiar with or, to be more accurate, who has had much practical experience of what one might call 'cultural contacts', especially when they occupy the dominant position within those contacts, tends to take an astonishingly critical look at both their own behaviour and the behaviour of others (from whom they are separated in every respect and by everything), and therefore to adopt a deeply reflexive attitude. The type of experience of the social world that is born of astonishment and 'disconcertment' seems to reproduce in its own way the very attitude that lay at the origin of the ethnological tradition and that seems to have taught professional ethnologists the essential value of their discipline: cultural relativism. This socially constituted mental disposition inevitably leads to a practical understanding (an understanding that implies practice) of the intentions that lie behind the sociologist's questions and which are also objectively contained within the object under discussion. Because it is also, in part, a socio-analysis, any real sociological undertaking implies an element of 'self-analysis'. Although it is not always under proper control, is a 'wild' analysis and a totally personal undertaking, this self-analysis, which is also a response to the constraints imposed by certain particular situations, is very similar to the socio-analysis that sociology undertakes in order to understand those particular situations. The product of the sociological analysis thus becomes the instrument of a socio-analysis, provided that we restore the interviewee's ability to reappropriate the schemata used to perceive and evaluate the social and political world – and it is precisely the lack of that ability that explains the truly social and moral poverty of a whole social class. Provided that it also fulfils its liberating function, sociology has not failed in its duty because, in doing so, it does not just rob the interviewee of his discourse, or in other words of part of himself.

It is impossible to say who is in debt to whom. Is it the person who confides in some confidant a secret that is too burdensome, too deeply rooted in the social and psychic structure of the personality, a secret that is literally incorporated, made flesh, but which still has, despite that, a relative autonomy that allows it be objectified? Or is it the person who receives the confidence? As the interviewee himself put it, 'the first stranger in whom he (unfortunately) confided his misfortune; – a *misfortune* he cannot name or make public' – could not but be frightened at having to bear the weight of the secret with which he had been entrusted and at having to take on the obligations that result from it, starting with the most important of all: the obligation not to betray anything of the *sacred* message. It is 'sacred' in the strongest sense of the term; first, in the sense in which speech is something 'sacred', especially when it tells a secret, or 'speaks of what should not be talked about' but also in the sense that we are dealing here with the world of the sacred par excellence, with the world of the *haram* which, as the logic of honour has it, belongs to the realm of the 'forbidden' and the cherished, of the precious, of what is forbidden because it is precious, and precious because it is forbidden.[7]

If there is one thing that can permit and encourage one to use a discourse that has been recorded – obviously, in complete confidence (in other words, forgetting the interviewer–interviewee relationship, which is no doubt a precondition for trust, but also, and quite definitely, an effect of the trust that has been established) – it is the sort of relief, the highly visible but ephemeral joy, that follows the decisive moment when the most painful words – the words that are the most difficult to say – have been spoken. It was, as the interviewee and one of his witnesses admitted, 'like a veil being removed'. The confession – and it is a confession rather than a confidence – seems to provide greater freedom, to bring about a liberation, like a fragment snatched out of 'non-existence', and therefore a new piece of freedom: a small space, a brief encounter, an intermittent relationship, a few moments of chat during which and thanks to which one can exist. This is, of course, a partial existence, but it is also an existence that is socially sanctioned. The discourse that has been recorded was not only spoken in compete confidence, or even with great affection (or, as one would like to say, and as the interviewee and those close to him – without whom it would have been impossible to get him to say anything more than he usually said – did say to me, 'fraternally'). It is also imbued with a profound sincerity and an undeniable authenticity. It is all the more sincere and authentic in that everyone concerned – the interviewee and his friends, and the interviewer – more than once forgot the ultimate purpose of the operation, which is, on the one hand, to produce upon demand a certain discourse about themselves, and, on the other, to record that discourse for analytic purposes. This shared 'forgetting', which can be seen as the precondition for the authenticity of the discourse, can also be rightly regarded as the product of the trust without which there can be no fruitful relationship between interviewer and interviewee. Produced for its own sake and being an end in itself, the language of truth that one can speak about oneself is also, of necessity, a language in which one can communicate with oneself, and provide information about oneself, as well as (or rather than) a language for communicating with the other and providing information for others.

8

The Immigrant: 'OS for Life'

A consideration of 'the twofold condition of the immigrant worker and the OS',[1] or in other words of the relationship between the two and the mutual effects of one upon the other is, in my view, an indispensable preliminary to any understanding of both the function of immigration, the situation of the immigrant worker (his social status, his relationship with his work) and the description of the OS (which is social rather than technical). The Renault factory in Billancourt provides the best opportunity and the most appropriate terrain, in more senses than one, for grasping the almost systematic conjunction of the immigrant condition and the OS condition.[2]

A system of determinate relations

Like colonization, which, as Sartre once remarked, formed a system, immigration constitutes a system of 'determinate relations that are necessary and independent of the will of individuals'. That system organizes all the relations and all the representations of the social world in which the individual is obliged to live (as a result of, respectively, colonization and immigration). If we ignore this, that is, the system-effect, we surreptitiously erase that which creates the objective truth of the immigrant's situation.

The characteristics that establish immigration as a system include, first and foremost, the relations of domination that prevail at the international level. The sort of bipolarity characteristic of the contemporary world, which is divided into two unequal geopolitical ensembles – a rich, developed world, or a world of immigration, and a poor 'underdeveloped' world, or a world of emigration (either real, or merely potential) – can be regarded as the precondition that generates the migratory phenomenon. What is more important, it generates the form currently taken by immigration – which is the only true immigration (socially speaking) – i.e. immigration from all the countries or even continents that are grouped together under the rubric 'the third world'. The balance of power that lies at the origin of immigration is retranslated into effects that are projected on to the modalities of the immigrants' presence, on to the place they are assigned, on to the status that is conferred upon them, and on to the position (or, to be more accurate, the different positions) they occupy in the society that counts them as its *de facto* (if not *de jure*) inhabitants. Being the product of a twofold evolution that is simultaneously at work in international relations and in their effects in those areas where immigration occurs, immigration has finally acquired an intrinsic logic, secreted its working and reproductive principles and, ultimately, realized the preconditions for its relative autonomy, or at least the autonomy granted it within the space and the limits assigned to it. For all these reasons and assuming that we refuse to adopt a purely historical stance, the best way to characterize immigration is to regard it as a social form that has finally been imposed upon all. It has been forced, first, imperatively and practically on all those who are subjected to it and above all on those immigrants who rely, for everything they do and for all their representations in the social world, upon the system-effect characteristic of their present situation. Second, it has also been forced upon the society of immigration, but this time theoretically and in quite a speculative manner, and upon all those who are in a position to observe it or who wish to begin to study it.

The most visible manifestation of the systematic nature of immigration, or the manifestation that has the most implications and that is richest in meaning is, of course, the almost total identification of the immigrant condition with the position of the OS (which is supposedly a purely technical description). The relationship between the terms or, more accurately, categorizations 'immigrant OS' and 'OS immigrant' seems to extend beyond the present conjuncture, in which the vast majority of OS in the industry are recruited from amongst immigrants workers and, more significantly still, in which the vast majority of wage-earning immigrants are OS. The similarity that exists between the two conditions – the immigrant condition and the condition of the OS – certainly does not require any empirical confirmation. It is, in a way, independent of any experience we may have of it and extends beyond that experience, rather as though 'any wage-earning immigrant worker were by definition an OS', regardless of whether he is or is not technically an OS, and as though, correlatively, 'any OS were necessarily an immigrant worker'. To put it another way and, perhaps, in more sociological terms, the immigrant condition provides a description of the work that is done by the immigrant worker or which, truth to tell, devolves upon him. The definition of the OS is now no longer the strictly technical definition that it appears to be, and that is used within the taxonomy of technical qualifications; it is, rather and at bottom, a social definition.

The immigrant worker constitutes the ideal figure of the OS, much more so than other categories that can still supply OS (or their equivalents): the latest migrants from the rural world to the industrial world, or the newest recruits (who as a general rule are women) from the unskilled labour market. Objectively inseparable, the descriptions 'immigrant' and 'OS' merge completely – not only, to some extent, in material reality, but also in the individual consciousness of both immigrants, who are those most closely concerned, and observers.[3] Indeed, the way that the immigrant category and the OS category tend to be so confused is no more than the product of pure subjectivity or, more accurately, intersubjectivity, because it provides the basis for an objective agreement and because that agreement is not the result of some prior agreement but of shared social conditions. Its nature is such that it can transform a widely shared subjective relationship into an objective given.

Current developments in the social division of labour between a 'national' work force and an immigrant work force, combined with the technological developments which help to further concentrate immigrant workers into certain activities (working on the assembly lines, or what remains of them, in the car industry; public buildings and works, etc.) and into the least skilled categories (such as OS or production agents, to use the new terminology and, more generally, all those who used to be described as labourers),[4] appear to mean that the immigrant condition and the OS condition tend to overlap, to reinforce one another, and to take the specific characteristics of both to extremes. That a combination of the two conditions can actually come about, at a given moment, in a given place or a given type of society and, within that society, in a given type of activity, can only confirm in the practical mode and in an almost experimental manner, the identification that our analysis allows us to establish between immigrant workers and the OS. At the same time, it ensures that this identification is experienced more intensely and in more concrete ways. This conjunction appears to have been realized in the motor construction industry, which is one of the biggest employers of OS (and immigrants), and especially at the Régie Renault's plant at Boulogne-Billancourt. The Renault factory has characteristics of its own that distinguish it from other factories. It is located in the middle of the Greater Paris area (and therefore in the centre of a relatively limited pool of working-class jobs). It is old and plays a central role compared to the Régie's other plants. It is relatively large, exerts a specific influence and, most important, has acquired enormous symbolic capital and prestige over the years.

The car industry uses immigrant labour on a large scale (immigrant workers make up 59 per cent and 45 per cent of the workers employed at the Boulogne and Flins factories respectively) and seems to be intent upon concentrating almost all its immigrant workers in the least skilled jobs – i.e. in OS jobs – and, in contrast, to reserve skilled jobs almost exclusively for French workers. If we agree to regard as truly skilled workers [*ouvriers qualifiés*: OQ] all those described as technical production operatives, setters and higher-ranking skilled operatives – the P2 and P3, but not P1,who are similar to the OS – the proportion of the immigrant work force employed in this sector at the Boulogne-Billancourt plant, for instance, does not exceed 8 per cent.

In theory, the immigrant and the OS form two distinct groups, but, because they are actually made up of the same people, they have merged to the point of being interchangeable. There is of course nothing new about this. The history of migrations, starting with the history of internal migrations, teaches us that, *mutatis mutandis*, it has always been like this: in urban and industrial civilization, the lowest position in the social hierarchy and therefore in the professional hierarchy almost systematically devolves upon the last to arrive at the proletarian condition. The only thing that has changed, and it is this that gives the illusion that some progress has been made, appears to relate mainly to the fact that immigration has led to changes in the recruitment and the national origins of that fraction of the working class that is condemned to having OS jobs. But whilst this appears to be no more than a morphological change – a change in the recruitment and therefore the composition of the OS category and in the social status given to the OS at work and outside the workplace – it results in the transformation of the content and the very nature of the socio-professional classification and the social significance that is attached to its various divisions.

The way immigrant workers (OS or not) and non-immigrant workers perceive the position in the skills hierarchy that almost invariably devolves upon immigrant workers – the OS position – and therefore the social mechanisms that preside over recruitment and the progress of careers (which in most cases means an indefinite period of time stagnating in an OS job or, in the best of cases, a slight and exceptional promotion), means that any OS position is seen as a job for an immigrant worker and, conversely, that any immigrant worker is seen as a potential OS.

The OS category is being transformed, and its meaning is changing completely. It proves to be the product of a real 'discrimination' against immigrant workers in the workplace. It is a position within the internal hierarchy of work, but its ultimate rationale has nothing to do with the order of work. That is what everyone understands by the expression 'immigrant OS' and 'OS immigrant'. Immigrant workers themselves speak, in all seriousness, with no intention of joking, in all innocence and without seeing the internal contradictions of their remarks, of 'OS foremen', 'OS team leaders', 'OS setters' and so on when they describe immigrants who are foremen – as do non-immigrants who, both in the workplace (workmates, their immediate bosses, etc.) and outside it, stigmatize as 'immigrants' work' all jobs that do not require a high level of skills, that are technically and socially despised, or that are, in a word, OS jobs.[5]

Immigrant = OS

No matter whether it is true or false, objective or purely subjective, the immigrant = OS equation is obvious to all. It is a fact that belongs to that class of givens that are constitutive of our experience of the world – a posteriori givens that result from experience but which very quickly become a priori forms through which we apprehend reality. Rather as though the social indignity suffered by the worker has an impact on the work that is allotted him (the work of an OS), so it is precisely at that moment when the technical and strictly professional reality of the OS is established as the central pivot of the immigrant's entire existence that it is most discredited and most devalued. The social reality of the immigrant, which is not the same thing as his professional status (one is at once juridical and political, social and economic, ethnic and cultural, whilst the other appears to be no more than technical), begins to contaminate the strictly professional meaning of his job and to bring it into the same disrepute. This is the moment when the major preoccupations of the immigrant (and no doubt, to be more accurate, the emigrant) are completely reorganized and invert the order of priorities which had until then made emigration (that is to say, the emigrant's point of view) more important than immigration (that is to say, the point of view of immigration). At the same time, immigrants become more fully involved in the life of their country of immigration and, therefore, less involved in the social life of their country of emigration as a result of the recent developments that have led from the immigration of single workers to the immigration of families. From this point onwards, the immigrant worker's relationship with his work is not determined by his work alone. The effects of the whole environment in which he lives – social and political and, above all, cultural – are projected on to it. When redefined in this way and replaced within the general framework of life in immigration, the OS's whole job, and the very description 'OS' along with it, are no longer reducible to their technical dimension. This supposedly technical definition in fact reflects multiple determinations, the most important being of a political nature. The supreme criterion is that of nationality and, in the last analysis, the discrimination that is the very basis of immigration and which is now experienced even within the territory of work.

Politically based discrimination (i.e. discrimination based upon the criterion of membership of the nation) is justified by the social differences that can, for example, divide a labour force that has been technically trained, or is capable of being trained (and of undergoing further training) because it has already been educated, from an unskilled labour force that has not been trained and is unlikely to be trained because it has not been educated, because it has no industrial tradition, etc. The criterion of nationality appears to be irrelevant here, except insofar as we have, on the one hand, an essentially national labour force that has every positive attribute and, on the other, an almost exclusively immigrant labour force that lacks all qualities. Conversely, the social differentiation that works to the detriment of the immigrant workers is related, in order to explain (if not justify) it, to a whole series of factors that all relate to their national origin, which is tantamount to making a fundamentally political distinction. A sort of circular relationship is thus established between what is political and what is social in this domain. Should either of the two functions disappear, the other will reactivate it. The political dimension, for instance, ceases to be distinctive after the acquisition of French nationality (many immigrants and sometimes even immigrant OS have French nationality), but it is not therefore forgotten. The social dimension – in other words, membership of the working class and of the lowest category within it (OS) – is a constant reminder of the political dimension because it emphasizes the national origin of the immigrant, or simply reminds us that he is an immigrant. The same is true, again within the social dimension, when an immigrant who is much higher up the social hierarchy than most ordinary immigrants is described in terms of his status as a foreigner – to the extent that the juridical definition, and only the juridical definition, of that term applies to him – rather than in terms of the stigma of being an 'immigrant' (in the social sense of the term). Because political discrimination, which works on the basis of membership of a nationality, can be proclaimed quite legitimately, it helps to mask a social discrimination that would inevitably seem scandalous in technical, ethical and intellectual terms. The immigrant is the perfect embodiment of otherness: he always belongs to a different 'ethnic group' and a different 'culture' (in the broadest, vaguest and most ethnocentric sense of both words). He is also someone of poor social and economic condition, essentially because he originates from a country that is socially and economically poor. He is part of a different history, and the mode of his absorption into this society has nothing to do with its history. He belongs to or originates from a country, a nation, a continent that occupies a dominated position on the international chessboard, especially when compared with countries of immigration, and which is dominated in every respect (economically, culturally, militarily, politically, etc.). By moving from one differentiation to another, we thus come to the one difference that explains all the others and which contains them all: the political difference between the worker (who may or may not be an OS) who has to be described as a 'national' (because he regards himself as such and is regarded as such) and the worker (who may or may not be an OS) who cannot really be regarded as a 'national' (even though he regards himself as such, at least in juridical terms). The immigrant worker is obviously a worker like any other. Yet, despite the will to autonomy and even the independence he claims with respect to the political, the order of work and employment law do not necessarily escape the effects of the overdetermination that the political exercises over everything to do with immigration.

Nothing, it would seem, can destroy the identification of the immigrant condition with the status of the OS, and this applies in general terms to all immigrant workers. It cannot be destroyed by vocational training, which cannot *not* be talked about but which, because of the invaluable literacy schemes, just looks like an end in itself (it rarely leads to the acquisition of a recognized vocational qualification that is rewarded by promotion at work). No one, and especially not those who are most directly concerned, namely the immigrants themselves, seems to have any great expectations of such training. Nor can identification be destroyed by attempts at '*re*training', which is on offer only because of the economic climate and under pressure from the necessities of the moment – in other words in response to the sacking of many OS.[6] It cannot be destroyed by the continuous progress of a career that should, logically, lead to some 'promotion',

or by the possibility of changing jobs, or exchanging a highly structured and rigid job (an OS job), like those offered by big industrial
companies, for a more 'supple' job in which the distribution of tasks is
less rigid (smaller businesses, the service sector, etc.). The present state
of the job market rules out any such hope. So what is left? Either
resignation or the prospect of going back home – in other words, the
end of immigration and therefore almost magical negation of the
social destiny that the crisis is helping to objectify.

The immigrant and the OS are both subjected to the same codifica-
tion which establishes the minimum they are to be given in every
domain: a living minimum wage, minimal gain for minimal consumption, minimal consideration, minimal autonomy, minimal freedom of
movement and disposable time, etc. The immigrant, who is today's
OS, is probably the only worker who is now called upon to realize, in
all its truth, the condition of his past counterpart or his predecessor in
this double genealogy of the immigrant and the worker at the bottom
of the social and technical hierarchy of trades that once resulted from
a different form of immigration, namely the rural exodus internal to
the country. His condition is that of a man who has been reduced to
labour, to being a pure productive force that has only to be fed, first,
by maintaining and restoring it, by repairing it, letting it rest and
recuperate, and whose perpetuation has to be ensured by a constant
renewal as a wave of new immigrants replaces the last wave. These
are the true topoi of working-class discourse: the theme of food and
the corollary and symmetrical theme of poverty may seem somewhat
dated (although they have never completely disappeared) and may
appear anachronistic, given the present state of the national labour
force. And yet they find a new topicality in the words of all immigrant
workers: 'earning a crust', 'chasing after bread', 'bread gives the
orders', 'what wouldn't we do and what wouldn't we put up with
for our bread', 'you have to leave you country to earn bread for your
children', or 'my country is my bread, my bread is my country', 'all
we are asking for is bread', and so on. And, symmetrically, the themes
of getting out of poverty, putting an end to the misery: 'misery (*el
miziirya*) drove us from our homes', 'we are paying the price for our
misery', 'this is a wretched situation', 'emigration leads to misery',
'starvation wages', 'a life of misery that forced us to come here', 'a
state of misery', 'wretched jobs' (OS jobs). All these expressions not
only revive, in accordance with a particular modality, the language
specific to the condition of the working class; when used by immigrant workers, they also take on the meaning of an alibi. They become
what everyone sees as the indispensable alibi for thinking and talking
about the twofold condition of the emigrant-immigrant.

The theme of 'earning one's bread' where it is impossible to earn it, and therefore the related theme of the poverty (or hunger) that one has to flee (by emigrating), and the themes that haunt all conversations, thus help to ground in experience the permanent division between, on the one hand, 'countries of bread' (work) – i.e. countries of immigration – and, on the other, 'countries of hunger' (unemployment) – i.e. countries of emigration. More so than for any other category of workers, these appear to be the 'facts' that objectively constitute the condition of the immigrant and the OS. Everyone – employers, unions and immigrants themselves – agree that the OS is nothing more than a 'machine' that has to be fed, that has to feed itself, that asks only to be fed and that works only in order to be able to feed itself and its family.

As a general rule, the immigrant worker has, in addition to the characteristics that derive from the immigrant condition and from working in immigration, a certain number of other characteristics that he brings with him and which, for want of a more accurate term, we can call 'characteristics of origin' or 'capital of origin'. All these characteristics, which are inherited from a social history and a cultural tradition in which the very notion of work has a different meaning to that normally given it in an industrial society, inevitably undergo a transformation when they are transplanted. We therefore have to be careful not to see them as something that can be divorced from their social conditions of production and reproduction and from their social mechanisms, or to ignore completely the system of determinations that immigrant workers still bear within them and that they bring with them. Both these contrasting attitudes involve the possibility of error. On the one hand, the over-facile tendency to reify the system of original dispositions prevents us from seeing that the system has been destructured by expatriation and by the decontextualization brought about by emigration – and which in fact began long before their emigration – and is therefore doomed to become totally inoperative. On the other hand, the complacent denial – in the name of clever talk of 'modernity' – of the heritage imported into immigration leads us to conceal one of its major effects: the way it *informs* the perception that immigrant workers have of their work in the context of immigration and, more generally, of their position within the society of immigration.

Being and work

A worker like any other worker, the immigrant is, without any exception, both identical with his non-immigrant workmates and different from them. The explanation for this specificity lies not so much in how they are set to work or in how they actually do their work, as in their relationship with work, and that relationship itself is no more than a particular realization of the broader relationship they have with the economic system that they discover thanks to their immigration. The immigrant OS, who is usually an immigrant originating from a non-industrialized country and who therefore does not have the advantages that only a long tradition of a modern economy can give, is plunged by his immigration into an economic cosmos of which he has not even an immediate intuition. Nothing in his economic and cultural tradition has given him the long-term preparation that might allow him to acquire the type of dispositions (economic, social and cultural dispositions, and especially temporal dispositions: looking to the future and calculation) required by the economic situation to which immigration introduces him. Nothing has enabled him to acquire a 'native' familiarity with that system, because such familiarity is the result of a whole education, both explicit and implicit, that has been undergone, individually, since early childhood and collectively over several generations.

As a result, he can no more invest the meaning of the economic system to which he is now tied than he can invest himself in it – and that investment would have to take place, first and foremost, in the field of work and then, more generally, in every aspect of his economic and social behaviour. And above all he cannot lie to himself or delude himself as to the interest he may find in his work. In the absence of that investment – and the material and cultural preconditions for it appear not to have been met – work's only finality is, in the eyes of the immigrant OS, the wage it gives him. That is the only finality he can understand. Provided that the important thing, in other words the wage that is his only reason for working, is guaranteed, any consideration pertaining to work is, for the immigrant worker, equivalent to calling into question, either directly or indirectly, work itself. He therefore tries to avoid work, or more work, even though it is such a rare and precious commodity (so much so that it is worth paying the double price of emigration and immigration). The sole purpose of the demands of the immigrant worker – both those he shares with the workers' world as a whole and his own demands, no matter whether he states them or keeps them secret – is to reduce the constraint to work, the constraints of work and constraints at work. All this has to be understood, in the present context, as though work (in immigration) were a way of escaping immigration, which is of course both the product of work (or the search for work) and a source of work. Immigration and work are states that are so consubstantially bound up with one another that one cannot call one into question without calling the other into question, or without having self-doubts. One cannot negate one without negating the other or negating one's self (as immigrant); one cannot hate one without hating the other, or hating oneself (as immigrant worker).[7] The contradiction is all the harder to overcome in the present state of immigration in that immigration has been 'professionalized' and has, now that it has become continuous, taken on the form of a real career. It therefore invalidates all the subterfuges, simulations and dissimulations that could be invoked when it was intermittent and, in keeping with the old custom, took the form of alternating 'sequences of work' (immigration) and 'sequences of non-work' (non-immigration), the former being the price that had to be paid for the latter.

For the immigrant, work cannot have the meaning that the society of immigration ascribes to it, just as it cannot have the meaning given it, outside immigration, by the economy of his country of origin, that being a degraded and incomplete form of the more accomplished economic system that functions in societies of immigration. It cannot have the first meaning because it has not been acquired and incorporated (in the literal sense of that term), and it cannot have the second because the very context of immigration precludes it. What is more, because immigration is equivalent to a sort of a brutal and total immersion in a fully developed economy, it leaves no room for the multiple intermediary and composite forms that 'underdeveloped' societies, confronted on a world scale with the structures of the modern economy, have been able to adopt in order to contrive a continuum stretching from 'cultural' survivals from the old and more integrated order of society to the more or less complete structures of the capitalist economy. Work is neither a purely profitable activity in the way that the capitalist economy and the ethics associated with it would like it to be, nor a total social function and moral activity in the sense in which the precapitalist tradition understands those terms, or in other words an activity whose productivity – and profitability – can be calculated. What meaning can work possibly have for an immigrant who is a complete stranger to the ethics that the society in which he works associates with the work it orders him to do, especially when he is an immigrant OS at the bottom of the internal social and technical hierarchy of the labour to which he is condemned? Work is meaningful only insofar as it is a profitable activity, but it is profitable only in the sense that it is the source of an immediate profit. Its only other meaning is the feeling of pure constraint induced by the necessary and inevitable opportunity (which is both sought after and detested, both desired and despised) to 'sell his labour power', with only the wage he earns for compensation. In these conditions, it does not matter whether it is this job or that job: the outcome is the same. And if there is a difference that makes one job preferable to another, it always comes down to less work, either directly or indirectly: less work because the wage is relatively better, less work because less time is spent at work or is devoted to work when one adds in the time and energy expended on travel; less work because the job is less tiring, and so on. This relationship with work is no doubt shared by workers of all social conditions. And if we denounce the most external and objectified technical difficulties (assembly-line work, piece-work, repetitive, monotonous work that is devoid of any interest) as the only cause of the discontent, rather than investigating the nature of the immigrant's relationship with work independently of its technical characteristics, we will inevitably provide an explanation that begins with the effects, and then works backwards to the causes of and reasons for this repugnance, and that quite naturally explains them in terms of the content of the tasks performed (see Mothé 1976: 5). The fact that certain jobs – those of the OS, for example – are in themselves a source of discontent and malaise, of a vague discontent which leads to their being avoided completely whenever possible, or which forces the OS to cheat or to abandon them on a more or less episodic basis, is a constituent element of the proletarian condition that explains nothing. It does nothing to explain either the nature of the work involved, the lack of satisfaction that is experienced or the relationship between the two. But in addition to all this there is, in the case of immigrant workers who are 'latecomers' to the proletarian condition or novice proletarians, a supplementary meaning that, because it is inscribed in their politico-juridical status, is specific to them.

Having reluctantly taken an option they cannot reject because their very survival is at stake, immigrant workers discover in the course of their immigration an economic world, a world of work, and a labour organization – which are all elements of the objectified heritage of a society, a culture and a history different to their own – that they cannot apprehend in their totality and that they cannot understand clearly because they cannot reconstruct their coherence and their full intelligibility. Immigrant workers in general, and no doubt OS workers more so than others, have a vision of the world of work that is all the more confused and disorganized because of the position they occupy within the productive apparatus. They are at the very bottom of the technical and social ladder rather as though they were no more than accessories (which is what immigrants are in statutory terms, even if they become permanent and irreplaceable workers).

This does not predispose them to acquire a sufficiently clear aware-ness of the specific logic of the economic system in which they are involved, or even of the contribution they might be making to it. Whilst any OS can say at any given moment what his job, and perhaps even that of the man next to him, consists in, the principles of the system that classifies that job in terms of different professional char-acteristics remain quite opaque to almost all immigrant workers. Because they rely upon their direct experience, in other words, on what they can observe, they see a total disorder. They cannot establish any rational, regular or constant link based upon some observable principle, between the various jobs they see being done by the OS they are acquainted with. A worker who has worked for ten, twelve or fifteen years for the Régie may still be an OS, even though he is actually doing the job of a highly skilled worker [OP: *ouvrier profes-sionnel*]. Many OS find themselves in this situation and are doing jobs they are supposedly incapable of doing – jobs which are in theory beyond their professional competence, as defined by their position in the socio-professional classification. From what little the OS under-stands about it on the basis of the professional careers of familiar workmates, the same apparent 'disorder' governs the way specialisms are divided out: a man with the training and experience of a setter is now working on a machine. A worker who is promoted to a higher category cannot go on doing the job he had before he was promoted, and gains at best only a wage increase (real or potential). This 'appar-ent' disorder is not entirely random and the worker who is scandal-ized by it comes close to discovering its real rationale and meaning. The factory uses its work force to pursue its interests of the moment, and uses it all the more freely and arbitrarily in that it is at the bottom of the hierarchy and is assigned to the most ordinary, most discour-aging, least skilled and least prestigious tasks that simply consist in carrying out orders.

No matter whether it is true or false, in keeping with reality or totally erroneous and contradicted by reality – which, as it happens, is not the problem – the perception that the immigrant – that 'OS for life' – has of the organization of the world of labour, or of his own world, turns it into something obscure, mysterious, incomprehensible, and therefore arbitrary. That perception is presumably not specific to the immigrant worker; it was for a long time and still is, wherever the social conditions that inform it still exist, a perception shared by all workers assigned to the simple task of carrying out orders. This is the worker's banal way of relating to his factory, the mode in which he lives his relationship with work. Although we discover this relation-ship most easily, and in its most tragic form, amongst immigrants, that should not make us forget that it was for a long time and still is the intrinsic characteristic of the position workers, and especially those at the bottom of the ladder and of the chain of command, occupy within the process of production.

'As for me, all I know is that I am an OS and that I will die an OS. It doesn't really matter what job I do. They tell me to do this or that, and I do it.... It isn't even a question of money; I can do the job of a skilled worker, I know how to do it, and I have done it. I can do the job of a setter, and I have done it. In the time I've been in this job, I've seen foremen come and go, I've seen them arrive knowing nothing, we have to teach them everything and, before you know it, they're giving you orders, telling you what to do, and becoming your boss. And they never tell you anything: who they are, why they are there, why they were taken on, what they will become. And you never suspect anything; to start with, they're just youngsters, raw recruits [*des bleus; boujadi*] and you tend to treat them as such, but a few months later they've been promoted over your head. So you no longer know who you are dealing with.

'In any case, the pay is the same, the same money in my pocket no matter what job I have to do, that of an OS or that of an OP; I'm still paid the same, so I may as well do the job of an OS, it's not as bad as when I worked like a plough [like an ox] on someone else's behalf [i.e., when I was being exploited at my own expense]. Those who let themselves be taken in like that are stupid fools: an OS's pay for an OP's job. As far as I'm concerned, they can keep their flattery. If I can do the job of a setter, I want a setter's money, and if I'm only worth an OS wage, then give me a job as an OS; no way I'm doing more than I'm being paid for or being paid for less than what I do. They are the ones who decide everything, who decide what an OS has to do, and what an OP has to do, what an OS should get and what an OP should get, so they should stick to their decisions.

'They don't take you on because of what you can do, but because of what you are; they don't pay you for your work, for the work that you do, but for what you are. Either you are French or you are an immigrant; it's not the same [thing], not the same work and not the same wage; and even when it is the same work, it's never the same wage; for the same work, the wage of a Frenchman is at least one and a half times that of an immigrant. If you are an immigrant, it's not the same if you are an Arab or a black – Arabs and blacks are the same, almost the same – or by contrast, if you are Spanish, Portuguese or Yugoslav, then things begin to get different. They take you on and they pay you on the basis of what you learned at school, of the diplomas you have, CAP [*certificate d'aptitude professionnelle*: vocational training certificate] or whatever it is, and not on the basis of the work you do. If you have a CAP, are trained as a lathe setter, they pay you a setter's wage, a turner's wage, even if you do the job of an OS for as long as they want you to. That's the way it is, they've got you under their thumb: they give the orders, and you have to obey them and keep quiet. You get on with it. They give the orders, and on top of all that they always find a way of not telling you the truth. . . . What is the truth? Saying, for example, that all immigrants, and especially the Arabs, are OS and that no Frenchman is an OS. That, for example, is the truth. Better tell it like it is than pretend that everyone is the same . . .

'. . . There's nothing to understand; the harder you try to understand something, the less you understand about it. So it's best not to try. If you look at everything and try to understand something of what is going on around you, of how things work, you'll soon be sick of it, because everything is topsy-turvy; you'd want to pack it all in, to chuck it all. It's a miracle that any cars come out of the factory and that they work; the technology really must be cutting edge. The bosses can say what they like, say that we are moronic, that we understand nothing, that we do everything wrong, that it's an "Arab's job", immigrant labour, as they used to say before they said "Arab", "botched work", whatever they want . . . but that's the way it is. To hear them, you'd think they did all the work. If it works, it's always thanks to them; we count for nothing. . . . In all this, there's only one thing you can be sure of: it's the immigrants who come off worst.'

9

Illness, Suffering and the Body

Rather than the phenomenon's constancy or the scale on which it now exists, the important thing about immigration today is, precisely because of the specific effects it has had on every domain of social life, the *permanent presence* within France of the same population of immigrants (workers with their families). Because they are permanently present, immigrants are present everywhere and in everything. They are present within all discourses (economic, social, juridical, political, moral and even ethical). We all hear them being talked about, and we all talk about them. But perhaps we should ask ourselves to what extent the object we are talking about, i.e. the *immigrant*, is due to the fact that we do talk about him and, more importantly, to the way we talk about him. We are not exaggerating if we assert that the immigrant, or the man we are talking about, exists, in reality, only insofar as he has been constructed, shaped and defined. Perhaps no social object is more basically shaped by the perception we have of it than the population of immigrants – and that perception itself is determined by the abstract a priori definition that has been given of that object. As the discourse on the object is part of the object of study and must be taken as an object of study, we must break with the usual phenomenology in order to transform into a sociological problem something that was no more than a social problem likely to give rise to indignation or scandal rather than scientific study.

The discourse on the immigrant

Overlooking the *emigrant*, including his living conditions and the social conditions that generate *emigration*, is almost a constant in the discourse on the *immigrant* and immigrant living conditions. And because we choose to ignore everything that flows from immigration, both collectively (in the social history of emigration) and individually (in the particular social trajectory of each emigrant), we are incapable of understanding that the differences we observe amongst immigrants living in immigration stem from the conditions that lie at the origins of emigration, and especially from the transformations that those conditions undergo in the course of time – in other words in the course of the entire history of the migratory phenomenon and in part as a result of emigration itself. Each set of initial conditions generates a different class of emigrants who will, in immigration, produce a different class of immigrants. If we mutilate the migratory phenomenon by ignoring part of it, as we usually do, there is a danger that we will constitute the population of immigrants as a purely abstract category, and the immigrant as a pure *artefact*.

When we associate immigrants with the various institutions that have to deal with them and with which they necessarily come into contact, we think we are diagnosing and formulating a whole series of problems that we call *the social problems of immigrants*. These include immigrants and unemployment (even though being an immigrant and unemployed is in itself a contradiction), immigrants and housing (even though the housing of both single men and families is a projective test that reveals the immigrant condition), immigrants and training (even though being an immigrant and applying for training or merely making use of a qualification one has already acquired is a further objective contradiction of the immigrant condition), immigrants and their chances of social promotion or full insertion into social life (which is tantamount to talking about their chances of no longer being immigrants, where those chances are themselves closely dependent on their immigrant condition), immigrants and education (the supreme paradox being that of children who are by definition not French, but who are subject to the action of *French* schools or agencies whose objective function is the cultural formation of French subjects) and, finally, where we are concerned, immigrants and the medical institution, the immigrant and medicine or the immigrant and his health. Although these are very real problems which arise in practical terms and concrete situations, and which mobilize a great deal of energy, effort, time and competence, one could spend a long time drawing up an inventory of this kind without knowing whether all these 'problems' are really *the immigrant's problems* or, on the contrary, problems that French society and its institutions have with immigrants. Are these really problems that arise for immigrants, and problems that immigrants raise? And even if that is the case, one wonders whether these problems arise for immigrants to the extent, and only to the extent, that we raise them and that they are raised with respect to them, or whether they are not, rather, problems that are actually posed by the permanent presence of immigrants, who are rather like foreign bodies in French society.

The reason why we do not ask ourselves about the genesis of these problems and about how much they owe to the representation we have of immigrants is probably that the proliferation of discourse about these various problems automatically serves two different functions. First, it regulates a phenomenon that threatens to disturb public *order* (the social, political, moral order and so on); second, and paradoxically, it masks the essential *paradox* of immigration, and removes or neutralizes the question of what an immigrant is and what immigration is.

The epistemological virtue of this preliminary investigation, which we cannot do without, is that it reminds us of certain obvious facts or first truths – the truth about the immigrant and the immigrant condition – that we tend to forget, presumably because we are too familiar with the phenomenon of immigration and immigrants. If we begin to unveil these concealed truths and thereby begin to analyse first the paradox of immigration and then both the implications contained within that paradox and the profound effects it has on the social conditions and even the personality of the immigrant, we come back to a primal question that exists prior to any consideration of the life and fate of immigrants (see chapter 3).

The illness of immigration

Whether we view the situation of the emigrant or the immigrant as emigration or as immigration, there is no shortage of contradictions. One of the major contradictions is of course that affecting the immigrant's relationship with his own body – the body as object of representation and presentation of the self, the body as the seat of affect and of the intellect (for the body is inhabited by the entire group that lives inside us), the body as instrument of labour and as site and expression of illness. Like the contradiction of temporal consciousness, the contradiction of corporeal consciousness, which is an *embodied* contradiction, lies at the source of the other contradictions. It is this contradiction which, in a certain manner, makes the body of the immigrant foreign and 'incomprehensible' to others. *Illness* (or accidents) and its aftermath therefore provide us with the best insight into the contradictions that constitute the immigrant condition itself.

Because the immigrant has no meaning, in either his own eyes or those of others, and because, ultimately, he has no existence except through his work, illness, perhaps even more so than the idleness it brings, is inevitably experienced as the negation of the immigrant. Unlike retirement, early retirement or unemployment, which can also lead the immigrant to discover that he is idle, illness seems to have the sad privilege of pronouncing in definitive and final terms the 'negation' of the immigrant, especially when it rules out the very idea of being able to go back to work. Indeed, even though there is a certain analogy between its effects and those of illness, the status of the retired or unemployed immigrant does supply a justification or alibi for the idleness it forces upon him. Retirement can be legitimized on the basis that it is no more than the final stage of the long history of 'the temporary' that has marked the entire life of the immigrant. Unemployment, for its part, can, despite everything, supply a semblance of justification because of its accidental and temporary character, as the search for work is, in this case, regarded by everyone as an act that rehabilitates the immigrant and restores him to his function as immigrant. This, however, is true only on condition that the period of unemployment does not last so long as to destroy all hope of ever going back to work or, which amounts to the same thing, becomes a structural given.

When illness strikes or when an accident happens, the entire previous equilibrium collapses. It was always a precarious equilibrium that was laboriously forged at the cost of an enormous and persistent social 'lie'. So long as emigration and the immigration that prolonged it were no more than 'accidents' or parentheses in the lives of individuals and their groups that could be opened and then closed as quickly as possible, accidents, illness and their effects could still be mastered.[1] But as emigration ceases to be a solution, or even a stop-gap solution, to a critical situation and becomes a permanent retranslation of a crisis that has itself become endemic, the illness, the accident, the unemployment or the ageing that arise in this permanent state of crisis are experienced as paroxysmal circumstances, as extreme situations that lead into a blind alley.

It is as though the difference between this and other difficult situations is that an immigrant worker who falls ill, and who, as a result, is stripped of the status he has in immigration and of the equilibrium that goes with it, tends to expect the medical institution and the cure it can bring about to almost magically restore both his identity as an immigrant and an equilibrium that has vanished and is impossible to recover. He is therefore inclined to cling frantically to the medical agency and to the illness that binds him to that agency.

Now that the system of alibis he has constructed in order to perpetuate his immigration has been upset, the sick immigrant finds himself faced with the task of creating a structure of behavioural and intellectual models that will allow him to adapt to the new situation created by his illness. Families that move suddenly from a shanty town to an apartment equipped with basic modern facilities do not succeed in taking possession of the space allotted them and 'shantify' their homes because they lack the dispositions and resources that would enable them to modernize their way of life (see Bourdieu 1977a: 96–114). Similarly, immigrants who are so ill that they cannot overcome the effects of their illness even once they have been cured are in danger of regressing towards more rudimentary systems of adaptation or equilibria, either because they wallow in a state of permanent morbidity – and, it follows, in permanent disputes with the social security – or because they are too easily satisfied with their invalid condition, and expect from it and the income it brings them no more than a pretext that allows them to perpetuate themselves as 'immigrants dispensed from work'. The immigrant cannot come to terms with the handicap that afflicts him (illness or accident), and especially not with the repercussions it has on his immigrant condition. He therefore cannot come to terms with the sanctions imposed upon him by a medical apparatus whose objective intention is completely oriented towards therapy for disorders (organic or psychical) that have been duly attested and recorded (or that can be recorded) in a nosology that takes into account only the individual carriers of the disease. All that an immigrant who is uncertain of his status can actually do is to take refuge in his illness and 'settle into it', just as he once settled into his immigrant condition or – and this is the final solution – settle into it so as to be able to go on settling into his state of immigration.

What can the immigrant worker really expect from the hospital or from doctors after his accident or illness? He does not simply expect the restoration of his health; he certainly also expects the restoration of the old state of equilibrium in which he has lived until now. The equilibrium of the future is all the more disturbing in that certain of its characteristics contrast it with the old equilibrium that existed before the break brought about the illness. Whereas the old equilibrium, which was to a large extent shared by all immigrants, had a basically collective social dimension, the equilibrium that must replace it is, it seems, an individual phenomenon because it concerns only a restricted number of individual cases and because it is, it seems, bound up with seemingly more individual factors (the trauma that follows an illness). It is an individual phenomenon resulting from a more individualistic experience that is not part of any broad and collectively sustained complicity. What is more, this equilibrium is all the more uncertain in that it has to be elaborated at a time when, because of his previous history, the immigrant has become more fragile and more vulnerable because he is older, more aware of the realities and disillusionments of immigration, and suffering from the effects of an illness or an accident.

The more the perturbed immigrant struggles to recover his equilibrium, the more he tends to expect from medicine. That he obviously expects it to cure him and to indemnify him for the prejudice he has suffered goes without saying But, as though by magic and despite the compensation he is claiming, he also expects it to act as though his accident or illness had interrupted nothing and disturbed nothing. The more the medical institution disappoints him in that respect, the more likely he is to hold it responsible for the state he is in. Completely inverting the entire process, he tends to blame his illness and the doctors, his illness and the hospital. He does so all the more because he is prey to a general feeling of illness, and because he experiences in a more intense way the 'disorder' and the general dissatisfaction that have taken hold of him, and which he cannot relate to his illness or accident. To make matters worse, it is precisely because he is asking [*revendique*] to be cared for until his illness has been cured, that this patient lays claim to [*revendique*] his illness and settles into it. By laying claim to his illness, he is in fact laying claim to his immigrant condition, now that this is bound up with his status as a patient, or even as an incurable patient. No patient and no illness is more incurable than a patient and an illness that is challenged or not recognized by the two agencies that have the power to do so: the medical agency and the social agency. When illness, which is essentially the negation of the immigrant, ends up, because it is challenged, by providing the immigrant with a new alibi (a substitute alibi, now that the primary alibi of work has been destroyed by illness), it becomes, thanks to a strange paradox, indispensable to an immigrant who is afflicted in this way. It will therefore vanish only when he no longer needs it, only when he finds a solution to his feeling of illness and his contradictions, and they are the very things that reveal or exacerbate the illness. Because there is no solution, the illness becomes permanent and is the object of a permanent claim; it becomes the only way out a situation from which there is no way out.[2] Once they have been cured, or are considered by the medical institution to have been cured, these patients (unlike others) become 'ill' with their cure. They become patients who have been cured, but of only one 'illness': that of not accepting that they have been cured. Do they have to be cured of that illness too before they can be cured of the first illness that generated it, of the illness for which they have been treated and of which they have been cured? But on what condition can they be cured, or in other words accept that they have been cured (as their doctors have asserted on the basis of very objectivist criteria)? On condition that patients and doctors *agree* about the illness and its cure, obviously. Both patients who go on being treated until they are cured even though they have already been treated and declared cured (or because they have been declared cured) and doctors who can do nothing but go on treating them find themselves in a strange situation. In the absence of a minimal understanding between patient and doctor, it is not surprising that the therapeutic relationship should degenerate into a litigious relationship, or into one that is perverted in the sense that it is sustained by the deliberately legalistic intentions of both parties.

Conditions of access to medical 'rationality'

The relationship that is established between the immigrant and the medical institution is therefore ambivalent and based upon misunderstandings. The origins of this unhappy relationship lie in the discourse that divorces the collective demands of the medical profession (organicist demands which insist that any disorder should ultimately be attested to by experience) from the demands the patient makes of medicine and the power he ascribes to it. The latter are judged to be 'aberrational', inappropriate or irregular. Because he expects of medical power (the strictly technical power of doctors, but also their social, political and even magical power) something other than what is objectively contained in the logic and finality of that power, and because he does not 'speak' *correctly* the 'language' (both cultural and functional) of the medical institution, the immigrant patient is forced into a dialogue characterized by a mutual misunderstanding. Such a dialogue quickly becomes violent. Against an almost institutionalized background of conflict, the immigrants' distrust of the medical verdict, which in their view is always too hasty, superficial and therefore guilty – not so much in technical as in moral terms (they do not say 'He is not a good doctor' but 'It's unfair') – is rivalled only by the doctors' distrust of patients who (if they are immigrants) go on being ill or, more accurately, claiming to be ill after they have been discharged.

It is not only the immigrant who, in his own way, does violence to the 'language' and practice of the medical institution by rejecting its finality. In its concern to, first, understand and then act more effectively, the medical institution itself in a sense ignores its own demands and breaks its own rules by resorting to therapeutic 'borrowings' that are of a different nature ('barbarisms') because they contradict its every intention. Doctors give sick notes in the secret hope that when the immigrant returns to a healthy environment with which he is familiar he will also be able to benefit, in accordance with the tradition of his 'culture', from the 'wild' treatment offered by some magician-'psychotherapist'. They tolerate the presence on the hospital wards of a few 'monitors' – the patients' compatriots, who are sometimes used as interpreters, and sometimes as sources of information about the immigrants' culture of origin, or at least as mediators between a patient of a particular (cultural) species, and the medical profession and the medical agency. The doctors will accept, or at least tolerate (in extreme cases), the services of a *marabout*, or *tolba*, those strange 'colleagues' who come out of the shadows – the important thing is that the patients 'believe in it'. Then there is the tendency to make the most synthetic reinterpretations of phenomena relating to radically divergent orders. It is, presumably, such reinterpretations that led to the coining of the neologism or new barbarism of '*jinnophobia*' (fear of *jinns* or spirits), a new pathology and a new theory of rites and modes of behaviour (see the special number of *Thérapie psychomotrice* devoted to Maghrebin children: no 45, May 1980).

We cannot evoke all the moments of crisis that punctuate the experience of an immigrant without speaking of 'sinistrosis' – even if, as we have seen, no one ever uses the word itself. We should recall the famous definition that Professor Brissaud gave:

> Sinistrosis is a *pathological* attitude on the part of the patient *who refuses to recognize that he has been cured* because he believes, in all good faith, that he has not obtained the due recompense for the injury he has suffered provided for by the law; he is basically a claimant [*revendicateur*] whose claim [*revendication*] has as its starting point an exaggerated overestimation of his right to compensation. The sinistrotic attitude can be found in isolation, but it is often combined with other *neurotic attitudes* that appear against a background of *revendication, frustration* or *emotional paranoia* whose specific pathological value is difficult to determine, especially when it is presented as the only real symptom from which all the alleged symptoms derive. (emphasis added)

There is something strange about an illness whose only definite symptom is that the patient presents imaginary symptoms. But are we really sure about this 'symptom' on which all the other alleged symptoms depend, and are we sure that the other symptoms are just alleged?

'Sinistrosis' contains the radical '*sinistre*' ['sinister'], and the reason why so many of the accidents (physical or otherwise) that befall immigrants border upon psychopathic states that are described as 'sinistrotic' is that immigration itself is, or has become, *un sinistre* [a disaster].[3] If we fail to take into consideration the immigrant condition as a whole and, more specifically, the immigrant's relationship with the most critical phases in his condition (such as illness, for example), we condemn ourselves to seeing only *phenomena*, or in other words appearances, and we can neither get back to the principles that constitute and explain those appearances nor reconstruct the complete system of their determinations. Making claims (or even protests), being 'neurotic', 'hysterical', 'frustrated', 'paranoiac', 'malingering', 'cheating', etc. are all characteristics and modes of behaviour whose social characteristics are not in doubt. Their genesis and significance are not always a matter of pathology but they are, in these circumstances, interpreted as an index of pathology. They are all characteristics and modes of behaviour which, when removed from the social context that gives them their full meaning, and when it is forgotten that they are social products, lend themselves to being erected into symptoms of some purpose-built *nosographic* entity (and to that extent universalized). And the symptom quite obviously centres on the making of a claim that is deemed to be unjustified. All this is decided without ever first asking about either the implicit philosophy of or the prejudices that govern the system of justifications shared by everyone (the medical institution and those who use that institution). It is the system that decides which claim is legitimate and which is so 'excessive' as to be suspected of being 'pathological'. No questions are asked about the preconditions for the formation of that system of justifications or, in the case of immigrants, about the preconditions for their involvement, other than as victims or bad patients, in a system which, as they now learn to their cost, demands 'rationality', or a system that is abstract and is assumed to be universal (whereas it has, in reality, its economic, social and cultural conditions of possibility).

There is nothing unnatural about the fact that an immigrant who has been handicapped, who has had an accident or who is ill should try to obtain the level of compensation that is to his best advantage, or that he should try to do all he can to exploit the injury he has suffered to his financial advantage. Indeed, institutional, or in other words perfectly legal, provision has been made for that very purpose: there is a whole series of procedures for appealing to tribunals. There are juridico-medico-social agencies to judge such claims, and a whole arsenal of control commissions, consultations and second consultations, opinions and second opinions. What is astonishing and what does create a problem (or even a scandal) – so much so that it is put down to pathology, or *abnormality* – is the way in which a sick immigrant uses his illness (and medical agencies) to settle a dispute which is, or so it is said, of a social nature (and not a medical nature). It is, to be more accurate, within the remit – which is defined arbitrarily because this is how responsibilities are allocated to the various institutions – of a social (and non-medical) agency. It is the 'irrational' way that the immigrant uses medicine for purposes that are not always therapeutic, for purposes that are not always those that medicine assigns itself that is scandalous. The claim is 'excessive' (in the eyes of medicine) because it is 'anarchic' or out of order because it does not surrender to the demands of 'rationality'. It no more obeys the rules governing relations between institutions than it subordinates itself to the specificity of each of those institutions (which would be a token of 'rationality'). It is confused by the 'rational' way different systems of attributions and competence divide things up between themselves, and it therefore confuses two powers which are, in theory, independent of one another: the power of medicine, which has its own field, and the power of social security. It does not (or cannot) distinguish between the specific demands of the two powers and between the functions they fulfil – functions which are specialized and reputedly autonomous, even though they are in fact closely connected, as the social institution expects the medical institution to examine and justify its decisions.

The claim is also 'excessive', and above all 'incomprehensible' from the medical point of view, because it confuses things that a concern for 'rationalization' has separated out, and because it is therefore addressed as a matter of priority to the medical authority (and not to the social services, as the 'rationality' of the institutions concerned requires). It is seen as a reassertion that the patient is ill (a 'refusal to recognize the cure') or as a challenge to the very essence or 'truth' of the medical decision (that the patient has been cured) because it is put forward in the name of principles that have nothing to do with medicine's intentions (which are scientific as well as therapeutic). It might in extreme cases be acceptable to question the judgement of a doctor, of even more than one doctor, because such a challenge is made in the name of medicine and appeals to medicine. But to deny that a cure has been effected when medicine as a whole – in other words, and in the last analysis, science (and the qualities of the scientific mind) – is agreed, on the basis of objective criteria, that a cure *has* been effected can only be the action of an illogical (or 'prelogical') mind, or the result of some 'aberration' or 'madness' (in the view of the scientific rationality that founds medicine and of the social rationality that inspires medical practice).

The imbalance we see here between the medical institution and certain of its patients obliges us to reflect upon the implicit preconditions for the coherent dialogue that is established when all the partners are speaking the same language and acting in accordance with the same models: the language and models of 'rationality'. It is only on condition that we adopt and master the system of objective demands on which the medical agency insists and, in the present circumstances, only if we agree as to the meaning, the opportuneness and the legitimacy of claims put forward after an illness or accident that we can establish the essential dialogue between, on the one hand, the health system (which obviously includes the system that ascertains and checks that the patient's claim is justified) and, on the other hand, the agents' system of dispositions. This is a precondition for any understanding of the *meaning* (which is a class meaning) of a legitimate demand (and it is not legitimate in an absolute sense, but only with reference to one's class condition). In other words, what has to be elucidated is the very genesis of the relationship – which is sometimes harmonious and sometimes in complete disharmony – between objective structures (those of the economy or medicine) and *habitus* that are in part produced by those structures but which are also essential to the workings of those structures. Here as elsewhere (or in other words as in the economy), it is no accident that, in reality, the question should arise almost spontaneously, or that it should take the form of a permanent *conflict* between the agents' dispositions and the world in which those agents have to move and act, or between, for example, economic dispositions on the one hand and the economic world on the other. The objectivist abstraction about which economists so often agree is also to be found amongst doctors. They too seem to overlook the fact that the subject of medical acts is, like the subject of economic acts, a concrete person. He is a real being who has, in practice, been created by the economy (or medicine), and not some abstract man or the hypothetical man of economic (or medical) theory.

The parallel between the economic system and the medical system, between the economy itself and the economy of health, which are two systems and two manifestations of the same social whole, does not end there. Just like inequalities in the face of 'rational' medicine (or medical 'rationality'), inequalities in the face of the 'rational' economy (or economic 'rationality'), or in other words the uneven rhythm (which varies from individual to individual and from group to group) of the transformation of economic attitudes towards both the economy and health, derive from economic and social inequalities. Economics and medicine would prefer to overlook the economic and social conditions that generate the dispositions they demand of economic and ill subjects respectively. They therefore often have to negate those conditions and, correlatively, to universalize a particular class of dispositions in order to be able to produce an entire justificatory and moralizing discourse that can transfigure the objective demands of an economy and a medicine into the universal precepts of an ethics: foresight and saving on the one hand, and courage, the disinterested primacy accorded to physical integrity, etc., on the other.

The differential value of bodies

The emigrant worker's struggle with the social service to obtain better compensation for the prejudice he has suffered as a result of illness or an accident is one he cannot hope to win. In this unequal struggle, all he can do is arm himself with the greatest possible perseverance, or even take refuge in what is seen as extreme stubbornness. For someone who is never sure of what he is owed or of what he can demand, and who therefore no more knows how far he can go with his demands than he knows whether his claims have been dealt with fairly (he always has a vague suspicion that he has been wronged or that anyone but him – i.e. someone in a better social position than him – would have got more than he has), the best strategy here seems to be that of 'no compromise' with the enemy. Because he has nothing to lose by taking the process he has initiated to its extreme limits, and nothing to win by reaching an amicable solution, it is in the interests of the weak man to go on looking like a victim who is very reluctantly being forced to be satisfied with what is on offer.

The origins of this basically distrustful relationship with the social services lie, of course, in the divergent evaluations made, by both sides and on the basis of divergent criteria, of the injury that has been suffered. One side observes the injury from the outside and assesses it objectively; the immigrant who has suffered it experiences it in overall terms, and as a sustained assault on his whole being. These antithetical appraisals will therefore give rise to very different 'assessments of the right to compensation'. On the one hand, we have an objective assessment, which the victim will find inadequate to the extent that it does not do justice to his immediate interests and prejudices his future interests and, on the other, we have a subjective assessment that is judged to be 'excessive' by the apparatus (doctors and the social security) that controls the yardstick by which things are measured because it is not, in its view, based upon any of the officially recognized criteria.

The difference of opinion exists not only because the interests of the parties concerned do not coincide, but also for the more basic reason that their respective conceptions of the body, its economic function and especially its social meaning, and therefore the implications of anything (illness or accidents) that affects it, differ in every respect, as do their assessments of its implications. For the social services and for medicine, the body, especially that of a manual labourer, and even more so that of an immigrant worker, is no more than a tool or, more specifically, a hierarchical set of tools in which every individual tool (that is, every organ or every part of the body) has its function, as well as a place and an (economic) value determined by its involvement and role in the production cycle. The immigrant worker, in contrast, experiences his body as a way of being present in the world. It is a way of being present in the physical world and the social world, and way of being present to the self. When the two parties are faced with a body affected by illness or mutilated in an accident, one of them is preoccupied with determining the extent of the resultant incapacity, but only the physical incapacity. The 'fair' assessment of the compensation that should be awarded is also purely physical. As the worker is 'worth' what his labour is worth, his body is indemnified on the same basis and within the limits of his loss of physical strength, in other words in accordance with the 'value' of the organ that has been mutilated or the limb that has been injured. The mutilation of a nose or the pinna of an ear brings much less compensation than the loss of a hand, no doubt because it does not reduce the ability to work. The other party worries about the repercussions that even a local trauma will have on the person as a whole, in all the circumstances of his existence, and on every aspect of his social identity. In other words, the assessment of the right to compensation is in fact socially determined. If all the parties involved – the social services, medicine and the private individual – are to agree on this assessment, even though they may dispute the amount of compensation, they must share the social categories on which it is based and, in the final analysis, the social conditions that lie at the origin of those same categories. The economics of labour, for example, require the body to be represented as an abstract entity required by the economy of labour. It is this analytic and functional representation of the body that make possible all the measurements and all the calculations of how much each part of the body contributes, as well as the monetary equivalents that compensate for part or all of the labour that cannot be performed and, correlatively, the way in which the injury suffered, or the (partial or total) incapacity for work, is related to the social value of the profession concerned, to the quality of the person exercising that profession and, basically, the social position he occupies and the characteristics he displays. If, that is, the assessment of the injury suffered, as established by the social services and the doctors, and, subsequently, the compensation they offer are all the more readily accepted because they are advantageous on the one hand and relatively high on the other, given the profession involved, it is so not only or not always for economic reasons, but probably for reasons of social order. Indeed, the higher the position of a worker who has been the victim of an accident or an industrial illness in the professional hierarchy, the more likely it is that he will see himself, his own body, his situation as an invalid, the social organization of the world of work, and the world as a whole, in the same terms as the implicit viewpoint or world-view that inspires social security and medicine and which has produced them.

Let us suppose that it is not a manual labourer – and a fortiori an immigrant worker – who has suffered an accident at work, but a senior manager. The 'social cover' he enjoys (complementary pension funds, insurance and contractual guarantees relating to his professional involvement and his professional status, other private insurance etc.) and the high salary he is paid provide, in his case, a much more effective system of protection than that available to a worker who has neither the economic means nor, which is more important, the cultural means to insure himself against future risks. But quite apart from the protection provided by all the resources at his disposal in addition to and independent of his salary, the senior manager has an immense advantage over the worker, and a fortiori the immigrant worker. He has a better understanding of the entire system of relations he can expect to have with social security and the doctors. Sharing the same assumptions that they share – and they are, as it happens, all to his advantage because he is socially 'better disposed' than others to take advantage of them – he knows from experience, and especially because he has a class *habitus* generated by the same social conditions that have established the objective intentions of the medical and social agency, how to conduct properly – i.e. in accordance with their own logic – the abstract relationship involved in dealing with any institution (as a consultant, a claimant, a plaintiff, a defence lawyer, and so on) or in dealings with doctors and judges. Because he also understands the internal logic and the functional mechanisms of both medicine and the social security system, he knows at every moment where to intervene, when to intervene, how and with which arguments to intervene. The appropriateness of this 'knowledge', or the 'rationality' of which he is the bearer, guarantees that his interventions will be effective. And because he has a more accurate, more logical and above all more rational vision of the therapeutic process (the evolution of the treatment, the chronology of the various medical interventions, the sequence of the different phases of the treatment), he is spared the helplessness experienced by immigrant workers. Nothing in his condition provides any basis for the immigrant workers' feeling of being lost in the 'imbroglio' forced upon them by doctors and the social security system, as though out of some desire to do them harm, or the impression of being the plaything of both those forces ('They do what they like', 'They tell us anything to get rid of us' or 'They're laughing at us'). With an interlocutor who conforms to the model assumed by 'rationality', or an ideal partner who is incapable of acting other than 'rationally', the 'dialogue' is easy. Everything is settled in advance. It is, one might say, a 'complicitous dialogue'. It involves, on the one hand, an accident victim who knows how to behave in accordance with the implicit demands of medicine and social security, and who also knows how to anticipate the objective expectations of both agencies, just as he knows how to predict them in practical terms, and on the other hand, institutions which recognize their partner as the man of their demands. They can recognize apparently individual qualities (it is possible, even pleasant, to have a dialogue with him: he has foreseen everything, prepared everything; he has all the information that is needed, all the documents, all the papers, all the proof, he is on time and punctual, his story is consistent, he is even courteous, etc.) that are in reality class attributes or ways of being that are socially determined and therefore unevenly distributed. As relations with the institutions are perfectly harmonious, there is no need to use violence (even if a dispute should arise). Such 'gratuitous' violence is reserved for the most disadvantaged who, because they have no understanding of where they stand in relation to the social services or medicine, because they do not know where they stand or what the cause of their difficulties is, and because they do not know how to approach the people who are at the centre of the decision-making process (the social security's medical advisers, the hospital consultants) in order to explain the situation from their point of view, have no option but to turn on the lower-ranking staff who have to deal with their cases (care-assistants, nurses, social security receptionists and staff, social workers, etc.), and to treat both institutions and their staff incoherently and 'irrationally' because they have a poor understanding of their real functions and authority.[4]

Institutions in conflict

But this is not all. Even though they are effects of the relationship between medicine (or some of the ways in which it functions) and a particular category of users, or 'ill-disposed' patients who lack the dispositions required to use medicine as it demands to be used, many particularly critical states which medicine (be it somatic, psychiatric or psychosomatic) commonly, and perhaps also all too conveniently, sees as sinistrosis or sinistrosic tendencies, are not reducible to mere failures to conform to medical (and economic) 'rationality'. We cannot overlook how much the 'irrational' behaviour of so-called 'sinistrosic' patients owes, both in its genesis and its current manifestations, to the workings of institutions (medical, social and juridical) and to the determinisms they bring to bear, especially on immigrants.

The immigrant worker who is ill or who has had an accident experiences the social security system, with which he is usually in trouble, and then the medical agency – and in his view the two institutions are in it together – as though they were courts of law. His dealings with them are like a trial in which juridical power, the power of the social security and medical power are in league against him. They all collude and are, in his view, intent upon doing all they can to deny him the rights his injury gives him, if not to dispossess him of those rights completely. Indeed, as Rémi Lenoir (1980) quite rightly shows in an excellent study devoted to the notion of 'accidents at work', *reporting* the accident, which is the first act in the long procedure that should end in the award of monetary compensation for the injury suffered, is not reducible to either a simple 'statement of fact' or the purely administrative act of recording something. It is the object of relations of force, first between the victim and his employer, and then between the victim and the social security system. The recognition that an accident at work has happened is at issue in a struggle between partners who have antagonistic interests. Wage-earners are interested in obtaining an income – as high an income as possible – and employers are interested in gaining a reduction, or at the very least a non-increase, in their social insurance contributions (and their contributions are calculated, factory by factory and industry by industry, on the basis of the frequency and seriousness of the risk of accidents or illness that they pose). As the juridical definition of 'accidents at work' is relatively indeterminate, fraud, attempts to defraud and fraudulent intentions are not uncommon on either side. Similarly, even before the decision that has been given is challenged, or even before the immigrant who is ill and at odds with the social services decides to make use of the recourse made available to him by the relevant procedures, he has the feeling that he is always dealing with a juridical agency represented by, depending upon the time and the agency involved, a doctor, a social security administrator and sometimes a man who really is from the juridical authority. And the most surprising of these tribunals, and perhaps the most terrifying, is, paradoxically, the 'medical' tribunal. The consultative opinions the doctor is required to give (normally requested by colleagues – or by their intermediary – they are also given to colleagues) in fact constitute so many sources of rights and so many stages in the process leading to a final decision. This tribunal has its own hierarchy, namely the various commissions made up of general practitioners, specialists of various ranks and expert witnesses who combine medical science with juridical and social science, etc., and whose medical authority is without doubt also a 'judicial' authority. It has its hearings, its procedures, its standards of proof, its practices of examination (or even cross-examination), and of confrontation, and it too can award benefits. All its procedures are broadly analogous with those of a court (pleas from the 'lawyer'-doctors acting for both parties, 'closing speeches', deliberations). In the circumstances, the accusatory nature of the medical agency becomes even more pronounced when the immigrant is faced with doctors from the social services (practitioner-consultants, medical supervisors), when he is 'brought before' the 'medical board' of the social institution, or in other words when he has to respond to a summons, meet strict deadlines and obey strict administrative rules. He has to undergo further medical examinations and consultations, but also – in the event of the social services not being satisfied with the outcome of these examinations and reports, some of which are compulsory for an immigrant who is liable to all these procedures, and some of which are at his own request – second opinions and further consultations. In all these cases, the medicine encountered by an immigrant making a case against the social services, is first and foremost the medicine of that institution. It represents a medical corps that is paid by the social services. 'They are the assurance's doctors, they are paid by the assurance; it's only natural that they should defend the assurance. That's their boss': they say this of these medical advisers or the doctors called in by the social services. Quite independently of the best intentioned attitudes that often motivate the institution's doctors, and quite independently of the history of the workings of this institution and the philosophy on which it is based (this is a system founded on the principle of solidarity and financed by workers' contributions), the immigrant worker's representation of the social security system and the medicine associated with it actually helps to separate out the three partners or, to be more accurate, the four partners (if we include the employers), and to involve them in a complete system of antagonistic relations. When it is autonomized in this way and constantly called as a witness by the social services (and usually only by then) and, as a rule, to testify against the immigrant – or at least that is the way the immigrant sees relations between the doctors and the social services – medicine does often seem in these circumstances to be an objective ally of the social services, or even its complete slave.

Because the immigrant worker has every reason to see medicine as a party to his dispute with the social services, or even as a supplementary force that intervenes on the latter's behalf, he too tends to use it as a procedural device or, at best, as though it were a 'lawyer' he had entrusted with the defence of his interests. In such cases, the best doctor is the best lawyer. As the dispute with the social services can only be resolved as though it were a trial, and as medicine is, almost despite itself, involved in that trial, why not use medicine as a procedural weapon and for procedural purposes – assuming that one has the means required to pursue that strategy? Even when the immigrant can (within certain limitations) make use of medicine, it almost unwittingly lends itself to the type of bargaining required by juridico-social procedures. The 'good' doctor is the one who can make the best contribution to this bargaining, who can give his client the best medical records by supplying him with the best negotiating arguments. He must be able to demonstrate the highest possible rate of invalidity, even though he is well aware that the sole purpose of the appearances before medical boards and of the reports is to discuss that rate in order to reduce it. We know that the doctors are involved in a gamble in which the stakes are all the higher, in that when the 'real' rate of invalidity, as determined by the doctor, approaches 50 per cent, the level of compensation is increased by half, and when it falls below that level it is, in contrast, cut by half (see article L. 453 of the Code de sécurité sociale). This is not simply the subjective, and therefore suspect, perception of the victim of a work-related accident or illness. This view of the role ascribed to the doctor in evaluating the rate of disability, and of the influence that rate should have on the admission of responsibility and the award of compensation for the injury suffered, is quite in keeping with the facts. Indeed, the very peculiar relationship that exists between an immigrant worker who has suffered an accident or illness because of his job and his doctor is one of the mediations that help to determine the rate of disability.[5] Its assessment is, as we know, 'automatically' determined not only by the relations between doctors (who authorize the compensation), the social services (a control agency) and the companies (the agencies that pay the compensation), but also by the intensity of competition within the medical market' (Lenoir 1980: 79); it has, for example, been possible to demonstrate (Jardillier 1965: 290) that the presence of several doctors within the same locality tends to increase the frequency and average duration of absences from work.

Secure in the certainty, which he has gained from experience, that his 'case' will be better pleaded and better defended if he has at his side a doctor who is well disposed towards him, the so-called sinistrosic handicapped worker goes from surgery to surgery to look for the most 'competent' doctor, which means, in these cicumstances, the most accommodating doctor. With his well-organized medical records under his arm, the arguments he developed a long time ago, the history of his illness and his symptoms (and of the judgements passed on his illness), which he has established and learned once and for all, he gets ready for the fray well in advance. Everyone is familiar with these totally illiterate patients, who are usually assumed to be disoriented and snowed under by the 'flood' of papers that results from their dealings with the administration, and who now astonish everyone by the meticulous, almost fetishistic and manic care – and this is in fact one of the symptoms on which the diagnosis of sinistrosis is based – with which they file all the items in their medical records, no matter whether they are important or not (medical certificates, doctors' reports, notifications of decisions, but also mere scraps of paper to remind them of the address or telephone number of a doctor, a lawyer, a date and so on), the speed with which they produce all these documents and refer to them at every opportunity, presumably in order to fill in the gaps and correct the misunderstandings in a dialogue they know to be biased against them because the only language their interlocutors understand is, as they put it, 'the language of arguments and proofs, with papers and written reports to support them'.

> 'You should see how the file is organized: everything is meticulously classified. He knew how many sheets of paper there were in every sub-file, with the precise dates, etc. and then – I'm not even sure he could read – he would pull out a *Code de droit civil* and point to it, saying "I have rights, my rights are in there, so why won't they give me my rights?"' (Social worker at the Centre Médico-Social Bossuet, Paris)

Monsieur X complains of multiple pains down his left side. And, as though to confirm that the pains are real, he takes from his pocket a page torn from a dictionary showing the human body, points to a zone,

to the area where it hurts and names it: 'It's my spleen'...Another
Maghrebin complains of pains in his head. He shows me where it hurts
by pointing to a specific spot and turning his head slightly, and adopts
an analgesic pose; his papers include a photo of a woman making the
same gesture...a publicity shot for a drug company that mentions
Glifanan, which is an analgesic. (Bennani 1980: 31–2)

The doctor becomes a 'witness' (for either the prosecution or the
defence), a 'prosecutor' (whose task is to catch out a patient who is
'pretending' or 'cheating'), and a 'lawyer' (for one party or the other).
In these conditions, there is no longer anything medical about him: he
is the social security tribunal's auxiliary. Medicine's therapeutic function seems to have been forgotten throughout the dispute It is eclipsed
by the secondary role it is forced to play: supplying proofs, certifying
the reasons that have been adduced and justifying the decision that is
handed down – always at his expense, in the opinion of the immigrant. And yet it has to be said that, despite their clumsy attempts to
dominate medicine and, especially, to get it to see that they are still ill,
immigrants do make every effort to 'persuade medicine to take a
fairer view of its role', as they put it, or in other words to dissociate
it from the social services and to get it back on their side to some
extent. From this point of view, the stubborn attempts they make to
have themselves recognized as people who are ill, rather than people
who have been ill (or 'recovered patients', to use medico-social terminology), and who have come for advice and consultations in preparation for their meetings with the social services, and also to ask their
doctors to give the prognosis for the effects and future effect of their
illness that is most in keeping with their interests – all these requests
for treatment and for advice on how to behave in front of the social
security tribunal are so many ways of recalling or saying (in a practical way) that medical practice should conform to its true nature: it
should treat patients and not pass judgement on them. Medicine's
'neutrality', or at least the 'neutrality' that is usually assumed by the
'rationality' of the organization and workings of its institutions and
that is proclaimed by medical ethics, is powerless when it is refuted by
experience. When it is faced with the facts, it shatters into pieces.
Even though a worker who is in dispute with the social services can in
theory appeal to the science of medical judgement on the same basis
as can the social services, or even on equal terms – he can, for
instance, be accompanied or advised by his doctor or 'treating phys-
ician', whose fees may in some cases even be paid by the social
services – he in fact often feels that that his voice is not always
being heard, or that it counts for less (or nothing) compared to the

weight and influence that is being brought to bear by the very 'official' institution of the social security system and its powerful doctors. This is true at every stage in the dispute, and throughout the entire dispute. When it is a matter of establishing a medical history, proving that the illness was caused by work or demonstrating the causes and circumstances of the accident, the enquiry is required to provide this body of proof as quickly as possible. It is therefore common, especially in the case of an accident, for an investigation to be launched. Even if it is not handed over to the police, it looks very much like a police investigation because it is designed to produce a whole set of objective proofs. In the immigrant's view, however, the only valid proof, the only proof that is beyond doubt, the only proof that is worthy of consideration and that does away with the need for any other, is his illness or accident – in other words and in the last analysis, himself insofar as he is or has been ill or has had an accident. In the eyes of the 'judges', it may be essential to hear witnesses, to reconstruct the accident and to discover who was responsible in order to re-establish the truth, but in the eyes of the victim, all this is superfluous, and he suspects it of being no more that a bureaucratic ploy or a procedural device designed to confuse the victim still further and to make it easier to cheat him by successfully denying that the accident was an industrial accident.

When it comes to the 'objective' evaluation of the injury suffered and, even more so, to the assessment of the 'right to compensation' and of the amount of compensation, there is a danger, as is always the case, that the self-proclaimed objectivity of an institution, which has on its side science, experimentation and *objective* quantification, will dismiss any expression of the conflicting point of view or opinion as *subjectivity* (in other words sensibility, the qualitative and anything else that might be influenced by personal interests).

When, finally, it comes to the procedural ritual that decides the degree of incapacity resulting from the illness or accident and the amount of compensation, and that ends with all the verdicts (medical, social and juridical) being brought in, the battle is once again very unequal. During the strictly therapeutic phases the patient and his doctor are still concerned only with, on the one hand, the treatment he is receiving and, on the other, the treatment that has to be given. In other respects, the overall experience that an immigrant worker, who is seeking compensation for his illness or his accident, has of his relations with social security and, in this instance, medicine and the authority (which is mainly social) it embodies, leads him to see the latter first as a party in the dispute that brings him into conflict with the social security, and second, and in the best of cases, as a referee or yet one more piece in the jigsaw or the juridico-socio-medical trap in which the claimant feels he is caught or, in the worst of cases, as a practice and a power that are totally subordinate to the practice and power of social security. Indeed, it is very easy for the immigrant to convince himself that medicine exists only to provide the social security tribunal with the series of proofs and justifications it needs to pass judgement, proofs and judgements that almost never run in the immigrant's favour or to his advantage.

Paradoxically, it is when medicine appears to accede to the demands of this particular class of patients, who are eager to be treated as though they were ill (and not as partners involved in a process whose outcome is essentially decided by the judgement of doctors), that it realizes that its position with regard to the social security system is one of structural opposition. Having completely revised its position, it can now arrive at a deeper and fuller understanding of patients who are usually seen as such insatiable litigants (or 'cheats') that doctors either act as their 'lawyers' (to remain within the logic of the trial) or claim to be able to cure them of the attitude that turns them into sick claimants. Sometimes they do both things at once. In the context of the conflict in which it is involved with both the social security system and the worker who is appealing against it, treating a patient for sinistrosis is a way of reasserting medicine's *right to treat* patients who have been denied treatment because they are seen only as 'cheats', 'malingerers' and 'claimants'.[6] It also allows medicine to discover the *objectively* conflictual position in which it finds itself with respect to social security, even if that 'conflict' never becomes explicit and never actually materializes. Doctors therefore treat 'patients' who demand to be treated only so that they can be recognized as and declared to be still ill. They treat them so as to enable them, they think, to outwit the social services (even though this might in fact be to the latter's relief, as it is not in its interests to go on indefinitely reimbursing the medical expenses of people who are interminably 'ill', or to delay the settlement of an invalidity pension that has usually been won in principle). This is in a way equivalent to objectively siding with their patients. And so, because both sides are obsessed only with external appearances, or in other words with what is described as a 'complaining' attitude and the materiality of that claim, rather than interpreting them as signs of a malaise which, in itself and in all its causes, may exist quite independently of the illness or accident, we arrive at an extreme situation and a question that borders on the absurd: who is responsible for the sinistrosis of a worker who has suffered an accident – medicine or the social services? Is it the social security system, to the extent that it is a system of

compensation and indemnification, that generates the claim that gives
rise to the sinistrosis? Or has medicine invented sinistrosis – an illness
that it would be difficult to indemnify – in order to force the social
security system to take a more conciliatory line in the dispute that
divides it from these claimants?

A distorted temporality

A bad relationship between an individual and the institutions which,
in the circumstances, are responsible for defining much of his status
(work, medicine, social security and, in more general terms, immigration itself), a bad relationship with his condition as a whole and with
his own body: when the immigrant is ill, all these states seem to take a
paroxysmal form. But whilst this situation reaches its extreme point
in the context of immigration, it can also exist in the immigration
whose effects it prolongs, and even outside immigration and quite
independently of immigration.[7] Indeed, it spares neither former immigrants who have returned home nor, increasingly, today's false
peasants or 'depeasantified' peasants. They are 'emigrants at home',
as the social transformations that have taken place at an accelerated
rate have, because they have identical effects, replaced real emigration
with 'domestic emigration'. The former immigrants do not succeed in
regaining possession of their old place because it no longer exists.
Quite apart from the transformations they themselves have undergone as a result of their emigration, the whole field of possible
positions within the social space of their community has been modified during their absence. They cannot win or create for themselves a
new place in the new context. These 'depeasantified' peasants, who
are just as ill at ease with their 'peasant' bodies because they are no
longer peasants as they are with their 'worker' bodies because they are
not really workers finally discover that illness can have its 'good
points'. The illness needs to be fictive or simulated to serve as an
alibi. It occurs at just the right moment to mask and justify what the
capitalist vision of labour sees as the elative (or absolute) inactivity of
both former emigrants and depeasantified peasants. Henceforth, free
time can be defined only in negative terms. Being neither leisure time
(non-labour) nor work time, time that is spent not working – a notion
that is essentially and actually alien to the logic of the precapitalist
economy – is the opposite of both the time (busy, gainfully employed)
that the productivity-oriented economy regards as being fully occupied, and the time characteristic of the traditional economy (which
does not have to be either full or empty, wasted or squandered, saved

or well spent). Experienced in the form of a malaise and a boredom that reflect the 'depeasantification' and disintegration of the group as a whole, this time, whose sole purpose is no longer, as it once was, to allow the group to survive, has to be merely 'filled', if only fictively. The break with the old peasant condition and the temporality that was characteristic of it, has to be compensated for. Whenever possible or, to be more accurate, when it is impossible to do otherwise, it demands compensation from the various trades (labouring, day-labour, owning a café or shop, working as a mason) that are taken up by many fellahs (who may or may not have been emigrants) from regions with a high level of emigration. At other times, and on the slightest pretext, it demands compensation from illness. Once certi-fied (which in this context means being indemnified or in the process of being indemnified), illness helps to confer a status or a new social identity. In these circumstances, and even if it is temporary or merely potential (in the process of being settled or in dispute, and thus sustaining the expectation or illusion of a future status, which is in itself already a status), even the smallest amount of compensation that is awarded as a result of an accident, incapacity for work or retire-ment allows the beneficiary to say that he is a 'pensioner' or 'retired'. Anyone who is in the process of claiming that status can say that he is a 'future pensioner' or 'about to retire'. The fact that 'France (mean-ing immigration) gives you nothing for free' is there to prove that they are indeed ill, worn out, incapable of work and therefore 'old' – and the proof is backed up by the authority of France, its doctors, its experts and its courts. The medical examinations to which they are called and the regular check-ups they have to undergo – and they never go for them discreetly and sometimes even do so with a certain ostentation – periodically supply further proof. But, even when it is not certified in such an obvious way, illness helps to conceal the enforced idleness to which they are condemned from those who do not wish to admit to being inactive and who do not want to admit to themselves that they are aware of their inactivity; but in that case, they must be able to affect every appearance of being ill (and this is of course what, in a different place and time, would be called 'feigning' illness). There is certainly no shortage of external signs that can be used to this end. Living and working conditions in France certainly have worn the immigrants out prematurely. They have exhausted their physical resistance prematurely and resulted in both previously unknown illnesses (tuberculosis, digestive, cardiovascular or venereal disease, psychical troubles, etc.) and multiple handicaps (trauma, mutilations resulting from accidents, and so on), but only a change in the attitude that peasant morality forces them to take towards their bodies could persuade them to use illness as the final admissible justification.[8]

The discovery of the social use of illness and an indulgent attitude towards the body are no more than expressions of the more general change in the overall attitude towards the economy. It is not surprising that these men have 'been broken by France', as they put it, and that many others, whilst they have never emigrated to France, are physically 'broken' because their morale has been 'broken'. They are members of groups that have themselves been morphologically and socially 'broken', and they can define themselves only in terms of the activity they once pursued in France (this is the one activity that can be named) or the effects of that activity. They define themselves as 'former' emigrants, as 'retired', 'pensioned' or 'invalids' who are unfit for work; those who have never emigrated define themselves in terms of the multiple pretexts they invoke to explain their non-activity. Apart from illness, only age – or a combination of illness and age – can be manipulated in so many ways. Rather as though they were anxious to come to terms with the incapacity that has been forced upon them, former emigrants 'age' themselves almost deliberately, and thus hasten a sort of retirement (or, to be more accurate, the state they describe as retirement) which is, in this case, nothing other than an exclusion or marginalization from the world of work. It is as though, not being at all certain that they will be able to grow old enough (in the normal sense of the term) to enjoy their retirement (legally), and having no interest in remaining in some way 'young' until they reach that age, they adapt their modes of behaviour by ageing them (turning them into 'old men's ways'). Being neither really 'young' enough to throw themselves into any work that comes along, nor really 'old' enough to play the role of the old man properly, former emigrants of this type have to acquire a status that gets them out of this ambiguity. As men 'between two ages' and 'between two conditions', all that remains for them to do is to exploit their age and also a whole body language in the same way that others exploit their illness for different purposes.

This image of the old man, which they have constructed themselves and which they try to persuade others to respect, is projected on to every act in their lives. It is reflected in even the most ordinary of their practices, which therefore differentiate them from other men in the group. Their itineraries are restricted to the village, or take them only a little way outside it. Their timetable, which also tends to become more common amongst non-immigrants, contradicts the rhythms that are still shared by the collectivity. Characterized by a profound boredom, the organization of their days, which has more in common with that of the idle than that of old men – who still remain fully socially occupied, even when they have stopped work – now owes almost nothing to the old distribution of agricultural tasks. They dress in the long flowing clothes of 'people who work neither with their hands nor their bodies' (robes, *burnous*, rudimentary turbans worn in such a way as to accentuate the pallor of their faces and the impression of illness, flat shoes, etc.), as opposed to the tight, girded or belted garments suited to active peasants. Everything about their posture and gestures (their slow and cautious gait, their habit of sitting cross-legged, the gravitas of their gestures: all these attitudes are in keeping with the state of men who are ill, old or literate – i.e. idle) is designed to remind everyone of their inactive status. Being ill, they are allowed to get up late, or at least to leave the house late in the morning. Being no longer 'young' but not really 'old', they can allow themselves to spend the whole day in the village, where nothing – and especially not the coming and goings of the women – escapes their notice. Because they are men 'in the house' (or in other words men who occupy a space that is normally reserved for women), they spend most of their time either at home or in the streets of the village, going from one *djemma* to the next, or gathering on the doorstep. Being idle (because they do not work in the fields), they can allow themselves to take all their meals at home, often at inopportune times – in other words in keeping with *grosso modo*, urban habits which, in this context, are similar to the habits of women.

Because it blurs the distinctions that have been established between different age groups and, thus, classifications based upon those distinctions and the roles that are usually associated with each age group, the particular form of new-style 'old age' or 'illness' generated by emigration (either in or after immigration), constitutes a disruptive factor that goes far beyond mere relations between age groups: it represents a real challenge to the entire old *order*, and to all the categories on which that order is based. There is an obvious opposition between a *young* age group, which lacks experience but which is excused and indulged precisely because it lacks experience, and an *old* age group which has a monopoly on wisdom and decision-making. There are also oppositions between age groups, between a male time and space and a female time and space, and between the condition and activity of *labour* (such as that of the peasant) and the condition of status of idleness (such as, for example, that of the traditional scribe).

The individuation of the body

Beneath all these 'ill' attitudes and attitudes towards illness, we find, of course, the relationship with the body and especially the transformations which that relationship undergoes. As a general rule, these transformations correlate to the changes that have occurred in the physical and social environment in which the body is immersed – in other words in the external stimuli that affect the body, and in the socially differentiated uses to which the body is put. The real reason why illness is now blamed for the indefinable feeling of malaise caused by the abandoning of the old routine, to which it is impossible to return, rather as though illness were the sole possible justification for not so much this enforced inactivity as for the resignation from and rejection of the real role of the head of the family, is that every corporeal schema (an incorporation, in the true sense of the word, of the natural world and the social world) deteriorates as the incorporated (or incorporable) world itself deteriorates.

In the communitarian world that was once his and as the communitarian man he once was, the emigrant had a different representation of his own body and, what is more important, put it to a different use. Without going so far as to say that the body was not experienced as a labouring body – how could it be when the emigrant's daily experience of his body was that of a 'working' body?[9] – it was experienced, first and foremost and almost collectively, as a way of being of the group and within the group. Every individual identified with the group and the group was present in each of its members because the body was a *cultivated* object, i.e. the product of an implicit pedagogy or a work of inculcation that did not speak its name. The body is not only something that makes the individual a distinct entity, and the group a sum total of biological individuals who are identifiable, who can be counted and who can be quantified. The body is the group incorporated: the group made flesh.

In immigration, the emigrant experiences his body in a different way. He discovers it to be different both from the body of others and from the way he had represented it until now, the way it was reflected back to him by the group with which he identified. He is plunged into an economic and social world whose cardinal virtue is a generalized individualism; he is subjected to mechanisms (economic, social, juridical, cultural mechanisms, etc.) which, quite apart from the regimentation they impose and the way they also regulate behaviour, all have, each in their own domain, the effect of inculcating the individualist morale with which they are imbued into *foreigners*, and foreigners *of a lowly social condition* (immigrants). The immigrant worker (especially if he is from the Maghreb) serves, often with great reluctance and almost always at his own expense, an apprenticeship that inculcates the *individuation* characteristic of the society of immigration. Thanks to waged labour, the immigrant worker who originates from a third world society (and economy) discovers mathematical time, which can be measured and quantified (quantities of time worked can be converted into money). He discovers an individualized time (involving only him and his work) and, correlatively, the individual dimensions of the work that has been performed (even when he is working as part of a team, both the effort he puts in and the resultant output remain individualized). He discovers the individual dimension of the remuneration he receives (he discovers that it is directly proportional to the duration, the quantity, or even the quality of the work he has done) and, therefore, of the budget he is forced to adopt (a time budget, a space budget, a travel budget, a budget for outgoings and savings, etc.). At the same time, he also discovers the *individuation* of his body insofar as it is an organ or tool for work, and insofar as it is the seat of biological functions, and a 'body' that is socially and *aesthetically* designated as a foreign body.

To the extent that he is an individual whose sole *raison d'être* is work and whose presence is therefore legal, authorized and legitimate only when it is subordinated to work, the immigrant worker experiences an existence that is reduced to the body that materializes his existence, and which is therefore its instrument. His existence is therefore the existence of a body. Both his existence and his body are completely dependent upon work. The immigrant is the only worker whose other functions are all reducible to the first and final function of work (in extreme cases, these other functions are non-existent). He is also the only worker who, not being a citizen or a member of the social and political body (the nation) in which he is living, has no other function but work. Ideally, the immigrant worker should be nothing more than a pure body, a purely corporeal machine, a pure mechanism, a system of levers which requires no more than the minimum input needed to keep its cogs working properly. His entire experience of immigration teaches the immigrant worker about this 'ideal'.

To the extent that he is isolated from his fellows and from the entire group with which he is in communion, the immigrant worker also experiences his body as a biologically individualized unit, not only in the labour he performs with his whole body but also in a more banal or everyday way, thanks to the revelation of the individual nature of a certain number of the body's organic functions. They are normally concealed behind a communitarian façade or the semblance of a collective ceremonial, but, because his isolation, which is a result of emigration, reduces him to being, as he puts it, 'just his head', it obligates him to cater, individually and in isolation, by himself and for himself, for his own needs. He has to prepare, on the basis of his own budget, his own meals and to eat them on his own (even when this takes place, as happens when immigrants are housed in 'hostels' for immigrant workers, in front of witnesses who are themselves occupied in the same way – i.e. carrying out the same act and the same function – or within a group whose members are indifferently watching an act in which they cannot be involved). He begins to discover the purely organic and individualist function of absorbing nutrients, as opposed to the social function of the meal as an act of commensality and communion, in other words as an act of communication through which the community asserts its existence, and as act of integration through which it reconstructs itself. It is not only alimentary practice that gives rise to an individualistic mode of behaviour that brings about a sort of awareness of one's own body or, more specifically a reconversion of the relationship with the body. As a general rule, all the technologies of the body are also involved (table manners, of course, but also sleep, getting dressed, etc.), as is personal hygiene, since an incorporated individualism is the basis for all those modes of behaviour known as hygiene (sanitary hygiene, but also hygiene as a whole, because even moral hygiene is, ultimately, a bodily hygiene). We can thus understand the suspicion with which men who are used to sharing everything view anything that might divide them, all the customs that they inevitably see as individualistic customs, or customs that might divide and separate them. We can also understand their suspicion of individualist practices, such as that of the individual place-setting (each to his own plate, glass, napkin, etc.) – such rules of etiquette and hygiene are mistrusted by individuals who are predisposed by their earlier cultural traditions, which are strongly communitarian, to commune together, even to the extent of sharing the same plate, the same pitcher and the same napkin. These individualist practices are criticized, amongst other things, for being egotistical, too self-seeking or, to be more accurate, cynically self-seeking and therefore shameful to the extent that they obviate the need to mask the interests that inspire them.

Insofar as he is a foreigner or designates himself as such within the social, political, cultural and aesthetic panorama of the society of immigration (he is seen as a different 'type'), the immigrant worker experiences suspicion everywhere and throughout his immigration. He is different from everyone else (i.e. from the nationals) because he is the only person to display every possible distinctive sign (in addition to the usual social distinctions, there are ethnic, political, juridical and linguistic cultural distinctions and so on). The immigrant therefore has the feeling that he is permanently *under surveillance*, in the way that a foreign body is kept under surveillance. He has the feeling that he has become an eternal suspect whose every gesture and every action is the object of an accusation: in the street, in the shops, at home, in the public services (especially social services, social security offices and hospitals) and even at work. The presence of the immigrant is a source of surprise and, whatever intentions he is assumed to have, there is always the suspicion that he is at fault. He comes under suspicion of disturbing the aesthetic order, the political order, the social order and especially the sanitary order (immigrants are the victims of all kinds of clichés: they cost the social security 'dear', lead to overcrowding in hospitals, and carry diseases), also the cultural or moral order (one loses count of the offences immigrants are supposed to have committed against the code of 'behaving properly' or the code of good manners, of their barbarisms and their infractions of the rules of polite society), in a word the national order (they are foreign to our history, our national existence, our national interests), and sometimes, when times are difficult, the economic order, even though they are its very obedient servants (more so than ever, immigrants are now inevitably seen as surplus to requirements). It is this generalized suspicion that the immigrants' experience is so all-encompassing that makes them say that they 'steal their presence in France', even though they in fact pay a very high price in every respect for being present there. As we have seen, the distrust with which they view medicine and social security is not simply the result of a difficult relationship or of some particular conflict with those institutions; it is a particular, and particularly critical instance of a broader and more constant situation, a particular modality of the distrust that influences all relations between the immigrant and the society of immigration. Quite independently of the disputes that may bring the two agencies into conflict, the immigrant worker is all the more likely to suspect and distrust the social security system and medicine because he has learned to suspect and distrust a society that regards him with suspicion and which distrusts him. No sooner has the immigrant worker discovered the *individuation* of his body than he is dispossessed of it. Not having the cultural means (because he does not have the material means on which cultural means depend) required to take possession of the *individuation* of his body, he discovers his *individuation* only to lose possession of his body.

The body of the immigrant

As it becomes the object of multiple investigations, the body of the other known as the immigrant (or, which amounts to the same thing, the immigrant who has been reduced to being just a body) eventually gives rise to a proliferation of discourses, beginning with that of the psychiatrists. Being a language elaborated about the body and the language of the immigrant's body, and a language elaborated and produced in order to interpret body language, which is an immediate language, psychiatric discourse sees the immigrant's body, or at least the language through which that body expresses itself, as a system of signs that has to be deciphered. But because it has no understanding of its own conditions of production – i.e. of the specific reasons that lead it, when it relates to the sick immigrant, to pay particular attention to the body and what it calls the 'language of the body'[10] – psychiatry's medical discourse prevents it, in the case in point, from asking any questions about its own nature, its social function or even the reason for its existence.[11] We therefore find psychiatrists who know all about the 'soul' or, to use more modern language, the 'culture' of the Maghrebin immigrant. They write about circumcision and, more generally, all technologies of the body. These range from swaddling, to weaning (Jalil Bennani (1980: 43–4) describes this as 'the bodily encounter with the mother and even with other women', and the mother as 'an essential environment for the child who behaves towards her like an *absolute master*' – the mother who, for her part, 'never rejects her child, especially if it is a boy, because it provides her with a guarantee of social recognition') to the servile use that is made on building sites and in factories of the body of the immigrant for the entire duration of his immigration. ('Because it deprives the individual of his usual social defences, his transplantation causes him to lose this necessary quasi-phallus' – meaning the 'castrating transplantation', an allusion to and a psychoanalytic evocation of the child's 'circumcision-castration' – and 'we therefore have a *compensatory search for an invalidity pension.* Obtaining a pension *compensates for his professional failure* and prevents the patient from losing face' (Berthellier 1972; emphasis added).) The psychiatrists write learned papers which, combining social anthropology and psychoanalysis, attempt to establish, on the basis of a priori comparisons, purely metaphorical links, or even mere analogies (which are rarely justified and sometimes obviously forced) between, on the one hand, certain cultural features that have been almost deliberately chosen but whose pertinence has yet to be demonstrated (as their specificity is far from having been proven) and, on the other, the

therapeutic practice of psychiatry when it has to deal with 'patients' –
in other words a certain number of statements – most of which are real
clichés – designed to provide an outline sketch of the 'basic Maghrebin
personality'. They assume that they can determine a psychic configuration specific to both Maghrebins (at least as revealed by its observable
pathological manifestations) and what they regard as psychotic behaviour. That is how they view any reaction to the therapeutic relationship
they are trying to promote. To take only one example: because psychiatry sees no need to investigate the real import of the pronounced
discrimination between the sexes, or in other words the sexual division
of space, time, age and activities of all kinds (which are all necessarily
bound up with sexually discriminated spaces, times and ages), starting
with activities that have a differential effect upon male and female
bodies, it tends to overdetermine the place and power attributed to
women and particularly to mothers (to *sexually* overdetermine things
that are already mythically determined).[12] It therefore tends to over-
estimate the significance of the role attributed to women and the
mother to such an extent as to regard that role as the *antecedent* that
can, according to Dr Berthelier, 'explain' 'neurotic depressive reactions'. Immigration and its difficulties provide an opportunity to 'remember' and therefore to experience once more the frustration
occasioned by the disappearance of the 'mothering' provided by both
the 'mother-society', the nurturing land (there is no shortage of metaphors to describe the magical relationship between the two experiences: weaning from the mother during childhood and, later, weaning
from the 'mother-society' as a result of immigration), and the actual
mother, who is complacently described as being omnipotent and omni-
present, first in early childhood and then in the imaginary of the adult.
For psychiatrists who are in a hurry to 'read' in the behaviour and
psyche of their Maghrebin 'patients' the marks of the social, affective
and cultural structures they think they have identified as component
elements of their personality, it is never in doubt that the relationship
they sense between the 'body', the 'father' and the 'mother' is a direct
and immediate relationship. Even Robert Berthelier, who, because he at
least introduces the 'social' dimension ('any subject is caught up in both
these dimensions: that of a personal history and that of a social history':
1973: 42), is the best informed of them, feels justified in establishing a
link, first between the 'body' and 'patriarchy', and then between 'circumcision' (a mark on the body) and 'the mother':

> Let us look for a moment at this circumcision and the relationship with
> the mother. . . . It is the mother who initiates the child into the ceremony
> and who organizes it. . . . The mother therefore marks the child with

this symbolic castration and, by that very fact has power over the child. Over the father too. . . . It is therefore the mother who names the law. It is the mother who introduces the 'name of the father'. It is the mother who teaches the child to pronounce it. It is the mother who signifies the threat of castration and the law of the prohibition of incest. The Maghrebin's relationship with the mother is important. . . . The mother signifies the law of the father but her gaze remains directed towards her child. Her child remains near her, within earshot, and her gaze continues to sustain the imaginary of the child. . . . This relationship with the mother and the body lives on in the adult. (ibid. 42–5)

In the same way, the privileged relationship with the mother explains, according to Berthelier, all the 'compensatory' attitudes he diagnoses in his Maghrebin 'patients':

Because it represents a loss of the object, transplantation [recalls] a mode of raising children and a relationship with the mother that characterizes a fixation on her. Normally compensated for by a protective and reassuring social structure in which society creates a substitute for the maternal object by perpetuating the infantile situation of dependency, this characteristic re-emerges when transportation isolates the individual. Hence the frequency of depressive neurotic reactions and the importance of the affective demands made on the doctor, which allow the patient to recreate the relationship with the mother.

What all these assertions (which are, when taken at face value, neither true nor false) naively forget is that the primal relationship with the father and mother or, if we prefer, the paternal body and the maternal body – in other words the body of the other and therefore one's own body – is necessarily filtered through categories of perception that it would be naive to describe as 'sexual' (or as only sexual). They have much wider implications and a field of application that is infinitely greater than that of the region of affectivity alone. They help to organize the entire cosmos. Insofar as it is, to some extent, a product of those categories, the relationship with the father and mother is also part of (which is not to say derives from) the set of mythical oppositions that structure both the world and the ego. It is possible that the world is structured before the ego, and the world certainly has a more solid structure than the ego. Because it provides the most primitive and also the most dramatic opportunity to experience the mythical structuration of space as a whole (physical space and social space), or in other words the projection of all the basic oppositions that are symbolically embodied in the male/female opposition (or, more accurately, in the opposition, which provides the paradigm for all other opposition, between the penis and the vagina, which are the biologically defined properties of the two sexes), the relationship with the father and mother is basic to the acquisition of the principles that structure the ego and the world (and, more specifically, the homosexual/heterosexual distinction) only on condition – which is often forgotten – that the relationship is established in and with a world of mythologically sexuate objects and not only biologically sexuate persons.[13]

The body as substitute for language

A 'somatic' language is, according to some, like Bennani, a language that remains attached to the body that is its 'source' and to bodily experience as a whole. For others, like Berthelier, it is a language that attempts to make up for the inadequacies of the 'word':

> The body represents a habitual means of expression . . . what we readily describe as hypermnesia is inscribed in the norm. . . . Because it is semantically poor, the patient's original language – dialectal Arabic – has no or few terms capable of translating anything to do with the order of affect. Hence the metaphoric use of the body which, once it is acted upon, *attempts to say what words cannot express*. The problem therefore consists, firstly, in deciphering that language.

Here we have the psychiatrist rediscovering in his turn, and for his own purposes, the old linguistic concept that differentiated between languages and arranged them into a hierarchy based upon the *intrinsic* capacities and virtues it ascribed to them or liked to find in them. The qualities are always the same and are always attributed to the same languages. On the one hand, we have a 'disposition' for abstraction, an intrinsic power ability for reasoning and intellection, and an intrinsic ability to meet the demands of intellectual rationality. These are all characteristic of languages 'made' for thinking and expressing the great ideas of the mind, the languages of culture, civilization and the great intellectual and humanist tradition, or, in a word, the cultivated languages typical of cultivated things, cultivated men and cultivated societies. On the other hand, we have the conceptual poverty, or in this case the 'semantic poverty' of the languages of the concrete (as opposed to the abstract), of the empirical (as opposed to the theoretical) and of direct and immediate experience (as opposed to thought, a withdrawal from action, and from things and the world). As they have no great intellectual ambitions or no great pretensions to think about the world on which they simply act, such languages are only of practical use. The 'poverty' ascribed to what are described as the 'primary' or 'elementary' languages appropriate to societies that have nothing to express but their perception and 'primary' or 'elementary' experience of the world (the physical world, the world of material objects to which they relate immediately) is contrasted – and this is a related criticism – with the disorderly profusion of the lexicon used to designate the objects and concrete things of the world, or even the ego (such as, for example, bodily movements, gestures, postures etc. or anything to do with the vegetative) and the practical experience one has of both. Whilst some languages are habitually criticized for being too 'concrete', for being unsuitable for abstraction – because they are incapable of achieving and expressing it – and therefore, for sinning against the conceptual order, here we have psychiatry criticizing the Arabic language of Maghrebin immigrants for sinning against the affective order. It goes without saying that the distinction is quite arbitrary. It takes, that is, no account of the social conditions that determine the use that is made of these two classes of language (of the social characteristics of those who speak the languages, or of the social situations in which they are spoken). They are retrospectively accorded two sets of characteristic that are thought to be true in themselves (whereas they are in fact socially determined) because they derive in one case from the dignity of intellectual qualities and, in the other, from the imperatives of practice – i.e. the necessities and immediate needs that govern practice.

This categorization overlooks the determinations that weigh upon language and structure it in accordance with the mythical categories that structure the whole universe. It overlooks, that is, the distinction between, for example, masculine language and feminine language (what men and women talk about in different ways, how certain topics of conversation, certain usages and forms of language can be feminine when spoken by men, and other subjects, usages and forms can be masculine when spoken by women), or that between official language and private language. Official language tends to be that of men, of public circumstances and of more highly instituitionalized relations (relations with medicine come into this category, and the language when talking to a doctor or psychiatrist belongs to this category of language: i.e. official language). Private language is the preserve of private or intimate situations. Confessional language (which is precisely the type of language the psychiatrist expects from his Maghrebin patients, but which he cannot, with good reason, get them to speak) is more suited to women, to intimate relations or relations between close friends or lovers, to less formal situations and relations. There is a further distinction between the language of wisdom, moderation, level headedness and experience, which is the attribute of the old, and the language of energy, immediacy or even haste, and determination (often somewhat excessive or too radical), which can be excused because it is the language of the young. All these distinctions have to be overlooked before it can be asserted that it is solely or primarily because the 'patient's original language [is] semantically poor, and has few or no terms capable of translating anything to do with the affective order' that the patient prefers, because of his sense of moderation and his need to 'compensate', to speak 'corporeally (to make his body speak or to speak through his body) rather than to speak 'verbally' because, for him, the body takes the place of the word (which he cannot use).

Another way of describing the opposition between body and language is to replace 'body' with its primal equivalent or 'mother', and to replace 'primacy of the body' with 'primacy of the mother' and the role she plays, first in the early education of the child and then in the 'unconscious' of the adult. The prolific discourse on 'mother' and 'mothering', the relationship with the mother, and the memory of and nostalgia for a lost 'maternal' security (circumcision is characterized as the first date to mark that loss) and on the resultant 'frustration' (castration), and on this relationship's power to explain visibly pathological behaviour, is rivalled only by its counterpart: the discourse on the 'body' and 'body language'. The two discourses – the discourse on the Maghrebin's relationship with the mother and the discourse on the 'body' of the Maghrebin immigrant and on the body language used by that same immigrant – are closely linked. Both represent the opposite of *language* (the 'body', as opposed to the word, and 'body language', as opposed to the language of the word) and to the break that must be made 'between the body and its symbol' (the 'mother' insofar as she opposed the 'cut'). From that point of view, Bennani is not mistaken when he sees the 'mother', and also the body (which is associated with the 'mother'), as the 'source' of language. This, however, is a body language: 'he [the child] remains close to her [the mother]. She continues to listen to the child, and the two of them perpetuate memories of the body. *Access to language or to the symbolic, remains close to its source*' (emphasis added); and, a little further on: 'this body will be spoken like a language.[14] Depressive states are therefore expressed through the body and the symptoms it presents to the listener. *Spoken language remains close to its source*, and the break between the body and its symbol, spoken language, seems to be less pronounced that in "western patients"' (Bennani 1980: 44–5). The 'western patient' therefore uses conceptual language, the language of thought and ideas, or an elaborate language demanding a major 'break between the body and its symbol'. The Maghrebin patient, in contrast, uses somatic language, the language of the organic and the vegetative, or a language that remains 'close to its source', the 'body' and the 'mother'. The western patient can express himself in words, whereas the Maghrebin patient can speak only through the medium of the body. In one case, it is the word that is made flesh; in the other, it is the flesh that is made word.

The immigrant is only a body

When it establishes or suggests an opposition between body and word, is not medical language expressing, in its own way, the general situation of immigrants? And in doing so, is it not, in reality, translating the objective truth of the condition of the immigrant, or of one aspect of that condition? And is not the reason why it is so prolific and so widely shared simply that it too is a product of a set of categories of perception and analysis that habitually presides over the image we have of immigrants and the treatment (practical and theoretical) that we reserve for them? If it is so determined, it may be no more than a variant – a variant that is, of course, more elaborated and has more authority in that it is a product of medicine's scientific and moral authority – on the commonplace discourse on immigrants and the immigrant condition. The immigrant is no more than his body. The importance of what is called the 'language of the body', or, to put it a different way, the organic importance of the body, is, basically, nothing more than the importance of the body as organ, or in other words, first as labour power, and only then as a form of self-presentation: the immigrant is primarily his body, his bodily strength and the presence he acquires because he has a biological body that is different from other bodies. Away from work and other circumstances that concern and address the immigrant only insofar as he is a body, the immigrant remains a *minor*. This explains the great number of exercises in philanthropic 'solicitude' of which the immigrant (especially the Maghrebin immigrant or one originating from a third world country) is the object: they provide him with forms of care (private or public) that are basically similar to the work of pedagogy and inculcation that is undertaken with a child, even though, by acting in this way, they also help to keep the immigrant in the situation that turns him into a permanent recipient of welfare and an eternal 'apprentice'. Throughout his immigration, the immigrant is treated like a 'child' in every respect. He is treated like a child who has to be taught how to behave properly (technically and morally), to conform to norms and demands (moral and technical) – in other words to 'live' by the rules of the society of immigration.

It is not entirely without reason that the immigrant finally comes to be suspicious – he has learned to be suspicious – of everything that is said to him about the origins (and the originality), effects and importance of the 'somatization' that is taking place in his body. Because the 'body' is generally seen as the structural opposite of the 'head', and because, like it or not, the body and the bodily are, either explicitly or implicitly, contrasted and compared with the head and the mental, somatization, or the fact that the immigrant can express himself (express his illness) only through his body – which implies the exclusion of verbal language or the language of the 'head' – eventually becomes a pretext for denying the existence of both the illness of the body and the ill body: if the 'body' speaks and speaks too much, it must be because the 'head', the 'head' that cannot speak the 'body' (the 'head' that does not verbalize), is 'ill'. As somatization is objectively treated as the negation of somatic illness, it is quite understandable that it should arouse the suspicions of the patient who is 'somatizing' in this way; it is quite understandable that he is suspicious of the importance attached to it by medical discourse. In the eyes of such a patient, and objectively too, it inevitably looks like no more than a way of displacing the 'hurt' from the 'body' that is suffering, but whose illness is denied, to the 'head' – the mental – which is not suffering but to which the 'hurt' is ascribed; the illness is displaced away from the somatic field, where the immigrant struggles to locate and maintain it, to the mental field where medicine intends to repress it. The 'illness' of the 'body' therefore tends to become the 'hurt' in the 'head' (madness). The (somatic) problem which the immigrant complains about (wrongly, he is told) is in the process of being converted into a mental problem he does not complain about (or at least not at the moment). From his own point of view and on the basis of his own bodily experience, he has no cause to complain about that problem, but he does, if we are to believe the science of the doctors and specialists, complain even though he has no physical complaints. Rather as though the immigrant could see what is at stake in the body-language opposition into which he is being trapped, he reacts to this opposition, which in his view reproduces the body–mind opposition, by asserting his body. The 'body', and especially the sick body (and only the sick body), is asserted in opposition to the 'mental' as the immigrant struggles against the temptation to replace it with the 'head' and the hurt in the head. The assertion of organic illness is now taken to extremes, and it takes on the meaning of a rejection of madness. Because he believes that he can speak – and wants to speak, when he speaks of his body – the same language as medicine, i.e. an organicist language, the patient complains about that medicine and suspects it of not wanting to take into consideration his body, and only his body. In his view, it has the power to make his body translucid and therefore to look into it in all its transparency (which can be done by a radiological examination or an X-ray – techniques which many patients regard as sovereign). An immigrant who is ill believes that, when it denies that he is ill, medicine is refusing to look closely at the signs of his illness, to 'read' and diagnose his body (and only his body) for the sole purpose of driving him mad. Because he wants at all cost, without ever succeeding in doing so, to convince the doctor who is treating his body of what seems to him to be self-evident, namely that the seat of his illness is in his body, the immigrant whose illness is denied comes to doubt the validity of his own judge-ment and the integrity of his reason. Above all, he doubts the reason and judgement of his doctor, despite the latter's social and scientific authority. 'They want to drive me mad . . . they will end up driving me mad'; 'They say I am mad, they suspect me of being mad . . . they would rather I went mad than pay me what they owe me', 'if you talk to mad-doctors, you go mad . . . and in any case, all these doctors who treat madmen are mad themselves.' It is almost from experience that those immigrants afflicted in this way discover the relationship that medicine establishes between their state of health or their social condition and their psychic state.

Always torn between his permanent present, which he dare not admit to himself, and the 'return' which, whilst it is never resolutely ruled out, is never seriously contemplated, the immigrant is doomed to oscillate constantly between, on the one hand, the preoccupations of the here and now and, on the other, yesterday's retrospective hopes and the eschatological expectation that there will be an end to his immigration. Because this seems to be the condition of the immigrant, and especially the Maghrebin immigrant, the slightest crisis in his itinerary – unemployment, illness, an accident, an infraction of the regulations that concern him specifically, and the more general regu-lations – necessarily has repercussions that affect him very deeply. It affects his very identity as an immigrant. If the effects of each of these crises on his behavioural system and his system of representations border upon the pathological, this is presumably because it is not merely a crisis affecting his external environment, but an internal crisis. It is a crisis that affects the status that defines him, and it is completely imposed upon him from outside.

10

The Weight of Words

Integration is one of those processes that we can talk about only after the event, in order to say whether it has been a success or a failure. It is a process that consists, ideally, in moving from the most radical alterity to the most total *identity* (or what is seen as such). It is a process whose outcome or result can be observed, but which we cannot grasp as it is occurring because it involves the entire social being of the persons concerned, as well as the whole of society's social being. Integration is a continuous process to which we can assign no beginning and no end, and it affects every instant in the lives of those concerned and every act in their existence. Integration is a process which, in the best of cases, can be no more than observed, and it is not certain that it can be oriented, directed or deliberately encouraged. The most important thing is that we have to be wary of imagining that this process is perfectly harmonious or devoid of all conflict. That is an illusion we like to sustain because each partner has an interest in this inverted retrospective fiction which, as it happens, finds in the vocabulary of the social and political world a lexicon that might have been designed for what it has to say. To the extent that integration manufactures identity, or in other words the identical or the same and, in doing so, denies or reduces alterity, it takes on, in the social imaginary, the value of both the principle and the process of accord, concord and consensus.

Semantic sedimentations

The conciliatory connotations (both social and political) of the word 'integration' encourage us not only to idealize the history of past 'integrations' that have already been accomplished and, correlatively, to 'blacken' the history of present conflicts; it also encourages us to imagine that the sociological process of integration can be the product of a political will, that it can be the outcome of an action that is consciously and decisively controlled by means of mechanisms of state. Without wishing to overlook or neglect the effects it can produce, we have to see that the (political) discourse on integration is the expression of a vague political will rather than of any real action on reality.[1] Truth requires us to rid ourselves of all the mythologies (even if they are scientific) that cling to the notion of integration in order to grasp the acuity of the social and political issues, and especially the identitarian issues it conceals.

We know that individuals and groups invest their entire social being in struggles over classification. They invest everything that defines the idea they have of themselves, all the social unthought [*impensé*] they use to constitute themselves as a 'we', as opposed to a 'them' or 'others', and to which they cling in an almost physical sense. This no doubt explains why anything to do with identity has such an exceptional power to mobilize. The discourse on integration, which is necessarily a discourse on identity – one's own or someone else's – and, in the last analysis, on the unequal balance of power in which those identities are involved, is not a discourse of truth, but a discourse designed to produce a *truth-effect*. In this domain, social science still wavers between science and myth. Even though it claims to be scientific or alludes to science, the discourse on integration is a discourse founded upon belief (and prejudice) (see Laacher 1992). It is a discourse that combines two conflicting principles of coherence: on the one hand, the self-proclaimed scientific-looking coherence that is *officially* asserted by multiple external signs of scientificity and by the production of pseudo-technical (or bureaucratic) arguments; on the other, a hidden coherence with a mythical basis.[2]

Like the notion of culture, with which it is closely bound up, the notion of integration is eminently polysemic, but its peculiarity is that none of the meanings that accrue to it in a new context can completely erase its older meanings. What takes place is a kind of sedimentation of meaning, as one semantic stratum recuperates part of the signification deposited by the semantic strata that went before it. What we now understand by the word 'integration' has inherited the meanings of other concomitant notions such as adaptation and assimilation. Each of these notions claims to be novel but they are in reality no more than different expressions, in different moments, in different contexts and for different social purposes, of the same sociological process. That process has its conditions of realization and its own history, and it is the product of a set of well-determined historical circumstances, to which it must be related if we are to understand its genesis and the forms it can take.[3]

It is as though, when it has to give a name to the same process in different social and mental contexts, each epoch needs to invent its own taxonomy. Quite apart from the fact that external variations influence the system of designations, the designations themselves very soon become worn out, go out of fashion and take on parasitic meanings or connotations that are too specifically located. Because they are too directly linked to one particular (socio-political) context, they prove all too quickly to be anachronistic and, so to speak, cease to be socially and politically productive.

So it is with 'adaptation'. The term served its purpose when it was simply a matter of adaptation to industrial labour, machines, the timetables, rhythms and cadences of production, or even to the over-all condition of the working class and, more generally, urban life. The term has obviously become dated, and as it did so its most passive meaning emerged: it was a concept that resulted from a misunder-standing based upon purely ethnocentric reflexes. And so it is with *assimilation*, a term that the avatars of history have treated so harshly as to discredit it, or at least, now that the colonial past appears to have gone, to cast a shadow of retrospective suspicion over it. In order to have an accurate understanding of the semantic halo that sur-rounds all this 'identitarian' vocabulary (which is necessarily na-tional-identitarian too), we have to remember past history, or in other words the history of the past social usage of this vocabulary and, in this instance, the history of the use to which it was put in the colonial context and for purposes of colonization. The antecedents this vocabulary owes to its past, to the political and ideological context specific to the time of colonization, when it was more easily subject than it is today – and in the context of immigration – to multiple interpretations and reinterpretations, still influence its contemporary meaning, and *objectively* determine (that is, unbe-knownst to everyone, and quite independently of anyone's will) the meaning that is given to it today, even though that meaning and that signification are believed to be specifically contemporary and quite *autonomous*.

Illuminating as it may be, a comparison of the two situations – the colonial situation of the past and the situation of contemporary immigration (which is no more than an extension of the former and almost a paradigmatic variation on it) – and also of the two moments, of the two contexts in which it has become obligatory to employ this seemingly identitarian vocabulary (once it was the 'assimilation' of the colonized, and now it is the 'assimilation' of immigrants), cannot mask the essential difference – and it is a difference of nature – that separates the two instances. In the first case – that of colonization – it was the 'assimilating' society and the nationality of that society that went of their own accord to the colonized. They were forced upon the colonized in their country and on their territory. In the second case – that of immigration – it was, in contrast, the population that was in the process of being 'assimilated' and 'naturalized' that came to the society that was 'assimilating' it and to the nationality or the naturality that was 'naturalizing' it in its own country and on its own territory. The anti-assimilationist nationalism which was in the former case almost the only possible way of resolving the contradiction imposed by colonization is therefore quite inconceivable and completely out of the question when it comes to immigration. And the social marginalization which could in this case be imputed to a refusal to assimilate is not, strictly speaking, the opposite of assimilation, as assimilation is not always a guarantee against marginalization.

With the help of the guilty conscience that is linked to reminders of the colonial past, we have begun to laugh at the digestive metaphor contained within the word itself and to deplore a kind of anthropophagy which is seen as a specifically French characteristic and which consists in consuming and assimilating individuals, groups, ethnicities, cultures, languages, nations, etc. Truth to tell, the reaction to France's 'assimilationist' reputation is very ambiguous: just as it is mocked when it is a matter of reconsidering its past history and its forgotten effects, notably in the colonial situation, so it is still celebrated today in the present state and because of its contemporary effects (the assimilation of immigrants), and continues to be praised as a primarily, or even specifically, French virtue. It is a civic virtue that is described as a guarantee or safeguard against essentialist discrimination (which uses nature as a criterion and which is therefore racist). France prides itself on this. In France and in the French tradition, the social and political contract takes priority over ethnic bonds, and France (which is complacently contrasted with Germany) accepts that any man can (in theory) be turned into a Frenchman. This takes little account of the element of chauvinism, or even imperialism (the 'imperialism of the universal' described by Pierre Bourdieu) that may be present in this 'universalism' and in the assumption that it is possible to have a monopoly on that universalism (witness the way France speaks of 'universal human rights').

Rather as though it still bore the weight of the colonial past, assimilation suffers from the negative connotations given it by that past. Besides, and more so than all the other homologous terms, the usual acceptation of the word 'assimilation' is a wonderful illustration of the ethnocentric point of view. This is the dominant point of view (or the point of view of the dominant) on whose basis we define what is being produced, what must be produced and what we should be producing – because, in this case, the descriptive point of view is also a prescriptive point of view – in our dealings with others or with the adaptable and the 'adapted', the assimilable and the 'assimilated'.

The point of view of the outside observer, or of an observer who is confident in himself and in his world-view, attributes a totally passive role to those whose adaptation or non-adaptation, assimilation or non-assimilation he is observing. In this instance, the vocabulary bears witness to this prejudice: it is French society that 'assimilates' and all it asks of those who are the object of the process is that they allow themselves to be assimilated, to accept the assimilation of which they are the object, or at least not to thwart it. We do not hear it being said – we do not hear it because no one thinks it – that Frenchness too can be assimilated or that, as it assimilates others, and for it to be able to assimilate others, it can be assimilated by those others. Those others are remembered only in order to criticize them, to criticize them for their bad assimilation; that is their fault, whereas good assimilation is to the credit and the profit of the assimilating society.

As the term 'assimilation' became worn out, it seemed appropriate to replace it with another term which was new in terms of the use that could be made of it, which was capable of rendering the same services and which promised greater social profitability. For a while, it was thought that the word 'insertion' would serve the purpose. It seemed destined to have a wider audience because it had not been marked at some given moment by any particular usage. It seemed fairly neutral, and appeared to have no great ideological or ethno-ideological reson-ances because it did not make preferential reference to any particular population that was distinguished by its origins. Insertion appeared to concern only the social bond, modes of relating within society, and modes of relating to social agencies as a whole and to individual positions within the social system. The function of insertion was to do everything possible to restore to or give everyone their rightful and coherent position at the centre of the system, and to promote the illusion that it was no more than a quasi-technical operation (and here, technicalization is seen as the opposite of politicization; to technicalize a social problem is to depoliticize it). As a result, inser-tion, which is a social and political rather than an ethnic concept, seems to have a great extension, or a less localized extension, than adaptation, and especially assimilation – which was a process that applied only to a *foreign* body, and only if that body were metabolizable. That was all that was expected or demanded of it. And this appears to be the weakness of its replacement, which has had little success: its cardinal sin is its excessive syncretism and, because it attempts to encompass every situation (social, political, economic, cultural, etc.) in which the process of insertion is involved, it ends up being unable to identify any specific case.

Integration: a loaded notion

The social lexicon and social semantics do, however, have their limits. They are not inexhaustible and are, moreover, always caught up in a process of debasement and depreciation as they wear out and are then restored and rehabilitated after the event. And so it is with the term *integration*. This too is an old term. It has long been used in different contexts to designate relatively diverse situations. It too has had its ups and downs, its moments of prestige and its reversals of fortune. It is a term that has been given its letters of 'intellectual' patent, and it has eminently sociological connotations (one cannot use it without thinking of the sociology of Durkheim and without going back to his writings). Sociology is more familiar with what might be called well (or badly) integrated societies, with individual integration or with integration as individual process. We have a better understanding of what is meant by a highly integrated group with a high degree of internal coherence. Integration is also understood to be a state, a point of arrival, a quality to which several factors contribute, some of them objective and materially objectified, others immaterial or of a symbolic order, and transcending the whole group or society and giving it the makings of its spirit, its own style, and its internal coherence. And integration, as understood in this sense or as a social and therefore collective reality, is no doubt the first precondition for integration in the second sense of the individual integration of the parts into the whole. The greater and more powerful the integration of the whole, the greater and more powerful the group's ability to integrate, and the more necessary and the easier it becomes to integrate into the group each of its constituent parts, old and new.

For want of a better or more appropriate term, the word 'integration' is enjoying a new popularity. We now make a convenient distinction between integration and the word 'assimilation': integration presupposes the integrity of the individual who is absorbed but not dissolved into the group, whereas assimilation is, it is argued, equivalent to the negation and disappearance of that integrity.

Because it is the integration of the whole that is at stake, and not simply the integration into the whole of a few individuals who are foreigners or outsiders, the discourse on integration is of necessity an impassioned one. It is a symbolically loaded discourse which is overburdened with secondary meanings that have to be clarified if we are to arrive at a better understanding of the phenomenon's real nature and true import. It therefore cannot, with some rare exceptions, be a predictive discourse. It is a discourse that always lags behind the social reality it has to explain, that it has to deplore or that, on the contrary, and as seems to be the case, it has to further (whether or nor it is successful is a different question). *Hysterisis* is an inevitable factor here, as it always takes time to complete profound social transformations which involve society's whole being, as is the case with integration. If such transformations are to be completed, there must also be a relative misrecognition, a relative collective blindness.

It might also be said that a discourse on this form of reality almost constitutes an admission. It is a way of stating what we could have foreseen but did not want to see, what we could have known and understood, but what we preferred to misrecognize. One of the reasons why talk of integration creates such unease on all sides, amongst both 'integrators' (assimilationist or not) and the 'integrable' (integrated or not), has a lot to do with this time lag: the discourse on integration is audible and acceptable only to those members of its audience – the public that is the object of integration – who are already the most integrated.

The analysis of integration therefore calls into question the migratory process in its entirety – in other words the immigrant's whole trajectory and not only what happens when it has been completed. And from that point of view, we can say that integration begins when emigration begins,[4] or even before that act, which is no more than a manifestation of the integration into the world market in waged labour of individuals who, willingly or not, had until then lived on the margins and in ignorance of that market and the whole economic system of which it is part. This first integration, which we do not see (because it is not in our interests to see it), determines all the other forms of integration that we never stop talking about; it explains them and we cannot talk about them without thinking about it.

Once he has found his place in immigration, the immigrant's whole condition and his whole existence are the focus of an intense effort to integrate him, a completely anonymous, subterranean and almost invisible effort, rather like a real attempt at inculcation or a second socialization. It consists of minor details, but these are minor details that constantly accumulate day by day until they produce, as though nothing had happened, without us always realizing it and above all with no apparent solution of continuity, profound changes – which are, as it happens, the most lasting changes.

The way we look at immigration must change as a result of several concomitant phenomena, some relating to the phenomenon itself,[5] and others to the world economic climate,[6] as we try to speed up an integration in which we have until now shown little or no interest. Whilst it is not entirely suspect, this desire to speed it up is basically clumsy and may even be an obstacle to its stated goals.

At this point, it should be recalled that immigration and integration (the integration of immigrants) are similar to the many other social objects and especially mental states in which one begins to 'want what cannot be wanted', to use Jon Elster's fine formula. It is like wanting to forget, wanting to be natural or wanting to sleep. Wanting to forget is enough to ensure that we do not forget. Wanting to be natural is enough to make us appear unnatural, and we cannot give the impression that we are not trying to give an impression. Integration is similar: if we promote an integration which does not, strictly speaking, objectively depend on the will of agents, there is a danger that we will fail completely. Like all these other states, one of the characteristics of the integration we are trying to promote is that it can be achieved only as a *side effect* of actions undertaken for different purposes.

Even if we agree that integration should not be understood as merely a form of social promotion,[7] it is the result of actions and efforts that do need to take integration as their objective. Just as sleep can be the side effect of actions one performs in order to go to sleep (counting sheep in order to go to sleep does not necessarily send us to sleep, unless we do not know that we are counting them so as to get to sleep), so integration cannot, even though it is not unaffected by what is said about it and what is done to encourage it, be the direct result of what is done or said to promote it. Invitations to integrate, and the superabundance of discourses on integration, inevitably look to those who are most aware of and most lucid about their position in society and in every domain of existence like criticisms of their lack of integration, their failure to integrate adequately or even condemnations of an impossible integration which is never total and never totally or definitively achieved.

When it comes to immigration, it is difficult to make a distinction between morality and politics. It is by definition more difficult to do so in the case of immigration than in the case of all other social objects, even if they are primarily objects of charity. The non-national and therefore 'a-political' being known as an immigrant is, on the one hand, the perfect illustration of the eminently political nature of immigration (even if this is never admitted). On the other hand, the immigrant is a paradigmatic example of a type of object we would like to deal with in purely ethical terms. The most pernicious way of subverting immigration by ensuring that it is subject to the most total domination possible is to depoliticize it. And the best way to depoliticize a social problem is to technicalize it or absorb it completely into the field of ethics.

Ethics and politics complement one another and collude in converting the rights possessed by this category of subjects (who do not have the right to have rights because they are not nationals) into duties, or into the other party's obligations towards them. Rather than recognizing our partner's rights, we are careful to describe and represent them to him as duties we take upon ourselves, as acts of generosity or unilateral largesse. Even when, in the real world and in purely accounting terms, we pay the same price, this price is transfigured once it can be removed from its purely contractual plinth and then divorced, by juridical guarantee, from rights.

11
Naturalization

A dialectical relationship has been established between immigration (defined both as a process and as a population of immigrants) and the nation – in other words, at base, between immigration and naturalization. Naturalization feeds upon immigration and, once the eventuality of a definitive return has been ruled out, immigration is dissolved into and by means of naturalization. From the point of view of membership of the nation alone or, which comes to the same thing, according to the criteria of nationality alone, immigration realizes a quite particular, specific mode of existence within the nation. Indeed, the demands of the political order ensure that there are only two modes of political existence within the nation. One is the 'natural' mode that is self-evident and specific to the nation's 'naturals' or nationals and, in very extreme cases, the mode of the 'naturalized' citizen. The other is an extraordinary mode that escapes national 'orthodoxy' and which, in itself, is basically illegitimate and therefore requires an intense and continuous process of legitimization.

In theory, and provided that the intrinsic logic of the national order is pushed to its final limits, the only real immigration – especially when, in contradiction to what it would be *in an ideal world*, that immigration proves to be 'permanent' – merges, thanks to naturalization, into French 'nature' or 'naturality' (as nationality used to be known). And conversely, the only true naturalization is one which 'naturalizes' candidates who are judged to be 'naturalizable' – a quality that must be guaranteed before the event by ensuring that they meet the conditions (and first and foremost the condition of residence) required for its acquisition. That, no doubt, is the meaning of the juridico-political operation we call 'naturalization'. It is a real transubstantiation which, when combined with the immigration (the transition from one territory to another, from one nation to another) whose effects it prolongs, ensures the transition from one nationality to another, or even from one 'blood' to another 'blood'.

If we define immigration as the presence within the nation of non-nationals, and naturalization as the absorption of those non-nationals into the nation (or nationality) and as their total identification with nationals (at least in juridical terms), we can understand why immigration and naturalization are, *grosso modo*, subject to the same rules. Entering the nation (i.e. immigrating) and, a fortiori, entering a nationality (being naturalized) are both operations that are subject to the same concern with *order*: public order, in the administrative sense of the term (article 79 of the Code de la nationalité) and also in the sociological sense of 'honest living and good morals' (article 68 of the Code de la nationalité), the moral or political order (in the institutional sense, or for what has been instituted) and the cultural order. And yet if we look at it more closely, the similarity we can observe between the respective functions of immigration and naturalization, and therefore between ways of legislating on both and between ways of regulating them, begins to look less obvious. Immigration and naturalization come within the remit of two relatively autonomous domains. They are within the remit of the economic order, which always has an interest in immigration no matter what the economic situation may be, and of the cultural or political order, which is, rather, concerned with the national integration or homogeneity of the national population in every respect.[1]

Whilst the imperatives of the economic order appear to be more determinant where immigration is concerned, subject to reserving the right to send the immigrants back when necessary (or when they are no longer necessary), the political order is in theory, or ideally, sovereign when it comes to naturalization. It is obvious that the national economy can turn anyone into a worker if it needs to do so, but can it – or must it – make that worker, or that 'anyone', into a citizen of the nation? Do we have to subordinate present immigration to the future (or potential) naturalization that will complete it, and do we actually have the means to implement that policy? Do we have to select in advance the immigrants we need, and what selection criteria are to be used to prevent any damage being done to the cultural homogeneity of the nation or to prevent any harm being done to the nationality they may acquire? Or, should both that and the opposite solution – the total subordination of naturalization to immigration – prove impossible, do we have to tolerate immigration and accept all immigrants? Do we have to make virtue out of necessity, refuse to make any explicit choice (so as not to risk being accused of discrimination) and simply hope that immigration will regulate itself by ensuring that the only immigrants, or the only long-term immigrants, are those who are 'naturalizable' or those who, in other words, are likely to be converted, or let themselves be converted, into good national citizens? We constantly move from one position to the other, as the circumstances demand. And even if we did wish to establish a standard policy in this matter, we would come up against the impossibility of reconciling in advance the criteria that define the immigrant worker with those that distinguish (in the sense of separating out and the sense of qualifying or electing) potential immigrant-citizens. Do we want workers or citizens? But can we admit to having any policy in this area? Can there be a real immigration policy? Or is the policy, or even the only policy, precisely to have no policy?

It is of course inherent in the status of the immigrant that he must be excluded *de jure* from the political to the extent that he is alien to the national order in which he is living. His exclusion appears to be both the explanation for and the result of all the other characteristics that constitute the immigrant condition. Being a foreigner, he is present only on a temporary basis, and his presence is therefore a presence that is subordinated to some other reason (in this case, work) and, to cap it all and to complete the circuit, he is under an obligation to be politically neutral, and therefore ethically neutral.

It is also inherent in the status of the emigrant (and the immigrant is always an emigrant) that he must be excluded *de facto* from the political within the national order of which he is a subject, because he is living abroad. And one can never overstate the dangers inherent in this double exclusion, one of which serves to justify the other. Exclusion and self-exclusion, or *de jure* and *de facto* exclusion from, on the one hand, the political order in which one happens to be living and, on the other hand, the political order to which one still belongs (in theory) despite one's absence, means being deprived of and depriving oneself of the most elementary and basic right: the right to have rights, to be a subject by right. The emigrant does not have the right to belong to a body politic in which he has a place of residence, or the right to be actively involved – in other words the right to give a sense and a meaning to his action, words and existence. His exclusion means that he is not able to have a history – i.e. a past and a future – or, most importantly, to appropriate that past and that future, to control that history.[2]

Although it appears to be an individual act, naturalization, and especially the naturalization of immigrants (particularly if they were once colonized or come from former colonies) is objectively determined by the balance of power established between the two nationalities that replace one another and, basically, between the two nations that come into contact thanks to the act that makes the citizen of one a citizen of the other.

Naturalization is, truth to tell, an act of annexation or of annexing on the one hand, and allowing oneself to be annexed on the other – and few such acts are so far reaching or so total. It requires a great deal of faith (in the sense that bad faith can be faith) for the relationship inscribed in naturalization, which is described as a fair exchange from the point of view of juridical nationality (acquiring, along with a nationality, the rights it confers and, in exchange, the duties that go with those rights), not to be or appear what it basically is, namely a relationship of force or a relationship in the challenge-and-response mode that typifies relations of honour. And it is the language of honour that is used to describe everything to do with naturalization, whether it is requested or desired (even if it is not demanded) or, on the contrary, scorned or even rejected, whether it is granted or refused. Naturalization is thought of as an honour that has to be earned, and that has to be paid for before and after the event. The ceremony has its propitiatory rites and its votive rites. Like a special favour, it *honours* the naturalized subject it is integrating by conferring upon him a *quality* (of being French) and a dignity (of being French).

By becoming naturalized, the citizen in his turn honours the nationality he acquires and, by swearing allegiance to it, he does himself the honour of having acquired it (or having been acquired by it). He honours himself more than he honours it. In fact we do not really know which of the two partners in this mutual exchange of honours is honouring the other or doing the other the greater honour. They probably do not know either or, to be more accurate, do not want to know because it is in both their interests not to know: they have a mutual interest in not knowing. The whole vocabulary of honour (*dignity, privilege, merit, obligation,* etc.) constantly reappears in everything that is said about nationality and naturalization, and this is an ethical rather than a political vocabulary. Even in the most favourable conjuncture, or when the nationalities involved are usually on equal terms, and when the candidate's attitude towards both nationalities (and especially his nationality of origin) is the socially determined attitude of detachment appropriate to those who are able and willing to rise above minor susceptibilities, naturalization is actually a real issue in struggles between two national prides and two antithetical systems of (symbolic) interests. As a result, it takes on two different meanings, depending on where one stands with respect to the nationality that is being sought and to naturalization. When his own naturalization is at stake, each candidate would like to obtain it at the lowest possible (symbolic) cost, or at least to convince himself and others that such is the case. But when the naturalization of others is at stake, everyone in possession of the nationality that is being sought thinks, without feeling that they are being at all contradictory, that it is in their interests to raise the price they charge for the naturalization of the foreigner.

A gentle violence

The naturalization market does not seem to be strictly and exclusively governed by the law of supply and demand. When it comes to acquiring the nationality of others, we would like our own naturalization to be no more than an administrative process that is as banal as any other. We would like it to mean simply the attribution of new identity papers that have been requested and obtained solely for the sake of the practical advantages they give us, without that purely technical change in our individual civil status leading to any change in our personal identity, and still less to a denial of our original identity. But when it is a matter of the naturalization of others, we would like them to come to the nationality that has been granted them as though they were being forced to eat humble pie – a small pie, of course, and one which must not be acknowledged because, in the circumstances, it must be concealed behind a show of grateful homage. We celebrate, fête and 'drink to' our nationalization, as is only right. In the course of this ritual, which is both an initiatory rite and an enthronement ceremony, the applicant is required to make the most obvious and solemn act of allegiance. That is the meaning, in particular, of the 'civic oath', which is a purely formal oath. That is also the meaning of all the struggles over this issue, respect for form being a form of respect, if not the supreme form of respect.

Being a form of symbolic violence and, therefore, a masked violence that cannot be named as such, naturalization is more easily acceptable when it can take on the appearance or use the alibi of being an institutionalized and legally justified violence. As violence goes, it then seems to convert itself into a *gentle violence*. It is as though we were doing ourselves a 'gentle violence' by receiving or even appropriating, without needing to request – which is a supreme advantage in that it gives the illusion that the balance of power has been reversed – a nationality that is indeed useful and convenient ('residential nationality') and to which we became accustomed both collectively and individually. Some became accustomed to it long ago (since the colonial era in the case of certain immigrants, who often add that past to the capital constituted by the many years they have spent as immigrants to France), whilst others – who are, as a general rule, their children – have been used to it since the day they were born, usually in France. We have here, especially in the particular case of France and its colonial empire, all the imbrications that bind together yesterday's colonization and today's immigration, the one being a continuation of the other. We also find all the similarities or, to be more accurate, all the homologies that we can establish between the two situations, both in terms of their genesis, as the former is the cause of the latter, their structure and, most important, between the relations that those situations have with French nationality, or in other words and ultimately, between naturalization in the colonial situation and naturalization in the situation of immigration.

In all these respects, the case of Algeria, or the Algeria of contemporary immigration, appears to be exemplary. Objective determinisms, some belonging to history (such as the political status of certain colonies and the juridical status of certain categories of the inhabitants of those colonies), and others to the present situation (such as the sociological fact of immigration and, especially, the fact that the 'family' form of immigration has been in continuous existence for such a long time), mean that Algerian immigrants have, amongst other characteristics, the peculiar ability to combine both determinisms. Their relationship with French nationality is therefore quite exceptional. The immediate and logical effect of Algerian independence was that it brought about a change in the political status of these 'immigrants', who were at the time described as 'French Muslims originating from Algeria, but working and residing in France' (Algerian immigrants in France). From one day to the next, the same immigrants who, in the past had been made French by a series of collective measures became, in their vast majority, Algerian immigrants, or in other words immigrants like any others (foreigners in the juridical or national sense of that term). One of the first consequences of that political fact is that they had to be apprenticed to their new condition by learning about, on the one hand, the normal rules that apply to immigration and, on the other, the provisions of the bilateral agreements reached by the two countries, especially from 1964 onwards.[3] On the eve of Algerian independence, these immigrants included a number of people working in public services or institutions whose status was assimilated to that of civil servants (rather like those jobs now held by 'immigrants' originating from the Overseas Departments and Territories).

After a transitional period which, in extreme cases, lasted until 1965–66 for privileged categories (for other categories – notably garbage collectors – it ended as early as 1964), all these Algerian personnel, who went overnight from being French to being Algerian, were required to conform to the requirements of the public sector, which included the imperative to be in possession of French nationality. They had to choose as a matter of urgency between two alternatives. They could go on enjoying the privileges awarded them by their jobs or, more accurately, the status associated with those jobs, but in order to so, they had to meet the requirement to opt for French nationality and, more specifically, to readopt (on an individual basis and as the result of an individual act) the French nationality they had previously been granted, and which they had, briefly, rejected in a collective mode. In short, they had to become French by being naturalized once more. The alternative was to retain possession of their recently acquired Algerian nationality, and to agree to give up not the jobs they held (because, given the state of the labour market and especially of the division of labour between the national and immigrant labour forces, they were still needed), but the status that went with those jobs to the extent that it was incompatible with their non-possession of French nationality.

In the context of the day (the first years of Algerian independence), very few of the Algerian workers faced with this choice opted for French nationality. And yet those immigrants who still, thanks to the privileges they had acquired (on a provisional basis), held positions that were no longer theirs by right (or in law) and still enjoyed one of the 'privileges' reserved for nationals (and therefore denied to immigrants) were, as a general rule, amongst the first Algerian immigrants to have settled in France with their families. It was, it seems, precisely those immigrants who had an objective interest in readopting French nationality who refused to do so.

But in the circumstances, just what interests were at stake? They were immediate interests, and they were almost all of a material nature. They existed only from the objective viewpoint of the outside observer and could be constituted as strictly economic interests only by those individuals who were socially and culturally able to objectify them, or in other words make them autonomous. They could do so only on condition that their importance to the economy as such had been demonstrated, which presupposes that the economy had already been constituted as an autonomous domain and, finally, on condition that so-called economic interests – which a particular form of economic consciousness tends to repress – were no longer denied in the name of individual, individualist and individualizing interests. The vast majority of the immigrants of the time preferred to renounce what were assumed to be 'objective' interests (and especially career interests) which, had they existed as openly declared interests, should have persuaded them to take French nationality once more.

Immigrant resistance

It is those immigrants who are lowest in the social hierarchy and on the professional ladder (within the immigrant population as a whole, which is itself clearly a hierarchy of nationalities, as well as within the immigrant population of the same nationality) – in other words, those immigrants who are the most underprivileged in both economic and cultural terms – who are most irreducibly hostile to the idea of naturalization. Such hostility can, as a first approximation and until we find proof to the contrary, be interpreted as indicating a greater attachment to their nationality of origin. In the case of Algerian immigrants, this is an attachment to an Algerian nationality that has been recognized. Before that, it was an attachment to their status as 'French Muslims', as defined by their civil status and local (or personal) law, and as 'citizens of the second college' in electoral terms – all of which constituted a sort of nationality *minimi juris* a substitute nationality, or even a 'pseudo-nationality' or 'chimerical nationality'[4] that exists only in private life, within the domestic realm and the sphere of affectivity. Because they invest nationality with a significance and a symbolism (which can be social, cultural, religious, mythical and therefore political, or even racial) that extend far beyond the merely juridical dimension, they cannot bring themselves to regard naturalization – i.e. a change of nationality – as a mere administrative process.

Conversely, it is those immigrants or, strictly speaking, those foreigners – can we speak in such cases of immigrants (in the social sense of the term) and can we go on describing them as immigrants? – who occupy relatively privileged positions, both within French society and within the space of those professions open to immigrants (the two things are mutually dependent, and here we reach the limits of that space), who are most inclined, or least reluctant, to acquire French nationality. They tend to describe their naturalization not as the substitution of one nationality for another, but as a subjective acquisition of two nationalities – French nationality in France and Algerian nationality in Algeria – and therefore as an objective combination of the advantages associated with both nationalities. In general terms, the further we rise up the social hierarchy and, therefore, the further we move away from the (social) condition of the immigrant and retain only his 'foreigner' status, the closer naturalization comes to its juridical truth. It is described and experienced by everyone – both those who are claiming naturalization and the society that naturalizes them – as tendentially being no more than a mere procedure or a mechanism of a purely administrative nature, regardless of its other meanings, which are always present but which they choose to ignore so as to give the impression of having risen above them.[5] They strive to convince others, and to convince themselves, that they can rise 'above' the parasitic meanings that 'clutter up' the notion of nationality because they are all a matter of affect and subjectivity.

Being the final completion of the rupture that is implicit in emigration, but which began even before emigration, the naturalization of immigrants and, even more so, the naturalization of their children, can shed a retrospective light on the destructive effect emigration has on their communities of origin or of emigration when it persists and when it is repeated and continued by a large number of individuals – men and women – and, before long, by families. To emigrate is, objectively, to desert and to betray. To emigrate is, in a sense, to 'weaken' the community one leaves behind, even when one leaves it behind only to strengthen it and to work for its prosperity. Every departure for emigration and every emigrant mutilates it.

In order to understand why a certain relationship between the emigrant and his emigrant condition prevents him from seeking naturalization, we have to rediscover the original meaning of emigration. Ever since it began, emigration was suspected of posing the threat of an intellectual break and not just a physical break. We can then understand that, if the taboo on naturalization is to function, it is not enough to condemn it and to condemn those who accept their naturalization. The community must be sanctified (in the strong sense of the term), as must unshakeable loyalty (a sort of eternal allegiance) to the community insofar as it is a social group and, beyond the group, to a structure or set of communitarian structures. The community must sanctify the various bonds that unite its various members, especially when they are dispersed, and which bind them to the community, especially when they are away from it, so as to exorcise the demon of the 'subversive' contamination to which emigration exposes them and which naturalization completes.

The modern form of community membership, just like the modern representation that allows the community – now elevated to the rank of the nation – to live on in each of its members (and especially in each of its emigrants), is of course nationality. It has to be added that, for the vast majority of Algerian emigrants, nationality – i.e. their assertion of belonging to the nation – is determined or overdetermined by two complementary facts. We are talking about a nationalism which is still young and which was for a long time denied or smothered. We are also talking about a nationality that was acquired very recently and at an extremely high cost.[6] How, in these conditions, is it possible to sacrifice that nationality and that nationalism, or even to adopt a slightly detached attitude towards them? It is because the relationship between the two nations concerned is still one of domination, especially in the case of immigrants or these new-style *colonisés*. They are dominated in two senses (to the extent that they are nationals of the dominated countries and to the extent that they are resident within the territory, and therefore under the sovereignty, of a nation in which they are foreigners), and their naturalization naturally takes the form of 'allegiance' to the dominant country. They seek and request its protection, and the dominant country gives anyone who adopts its nationality enviable advantages. By the same criterion it cannot but seem to be, symmetrically, an act whereby one dissociates oneself from the weak, the poor and the dominated. In the circumstances, this means dissociation from the country of emigration, its emigrants and its nationality, now that the only real immigrants, so to speak, are those who originate from dominated countries or countries of the Third World, regardless of whether they have or have not been colonized.

In the case of Algerian immigrants, the cumulative effects of a double domination, one old (the colonizing country's dominance over the country that is its colony) and the other contemporary (the dominance of the country of immigration over the country of emigration), confer upon naturalization and the balance of power that explains it an overdetermined meaning that now appears to become paroxysmal. Whilst the same is, in varying degrees, true of all immigrants originating from the former colonies, and especially those that were most intensely colonized (they were colonized very early, and decolonized late), and more generally of all immigrants originating from third world countries, which are reputedly just as 'nationalist', the case of Algeria and of Algerian immigrants is, in this respect, indeed an extreme case, just as the colonization and decolonization of Algeria were extreme cases. Both the violence with which the very existence of the nation was denied, and the violent reaction responsible for the establishment of the Algerian nation and Algerian nationality were extreme. Hence the cult (in the strongest sense of the term) of nationality, and the fanatical loyalty of Algerians, and especially certain Algerian immigrants, to their nationality. It is a form of political or national, and cultural, fundamentalism (and is modelled on 'religious' fundamentalism). Because of the history that preceded its formation, nationality was and is the object of an intense investment that can take many forms: patriotic and political, obviously, but also religious, cultural, linguistic, social, technological (or even 'racial').

A betrayal

It is as though formerly colonized countries had first had to resist the colonizer's attempts at 'assimilation'[7], and then, as one thing confirmed the other, to acquire a national consciousness, or in other words the conditions for the formation of a nationality. In order to assert that nationality, they – and here Algeria is in the forefront because it experienced a quite exceptional form of colonization – were obliged to mobilize all the attributes of nationality or all attributes favourable to nationality, no matter what domain they belonged to. History, geography (i.e. the territory and the frontiers that delineated and sanctified the 'national' territory), politics, language and religion[8] were all invoked, as were all sorts of different emblems. In such a context, national identity can only be – rightly or wrongly, actually or chimerically – an identity that is at once moral, religious, linguistic, social economic and, in broader terms, cultural, before becoming a political and territorial identity, as *la patrie* comes to coincide with the nation and becomes a nation.[9] Conversely, and because of the political attempt to make the political autonomous, these different 'regional' ('partial') identities or different dimensions of the same identity had to be given a unified and coherent form, and therefore a political form. Distinct identities that were once sequentially juxtaposed manifestations had to become different manifestations and expressions of a single identity, which was now a political and a national identity.

Having been acquired and constituted in this way, nationalism is, insofar as it is a political category, still strongly marked by all the features that militated in favour of its formation or which accompanied its formation. It remains limed by, cluttered up with and eaten into by everything that, in rational terms, can be justifiably regarded as non-political. Ultimately, there is therefore nothing surprising about the fact that, in this case, nationality still bears witness to its past and to the conditions of its formation. In the colonial situation of old, becoming naturalized was equivalent to dissociating oneself from the condition of the colonized. As a result of this 'unnatural' act (in social and political terms) or the wrong side of a naturalization which, when seen from the opposite pole, becomes an 'anti-naturalization', people moved from the camp of the colonized, the 'natives' or even the

'French Muslims', as they were called at the time, to that of the colonizers (or the *colonisants*, as General Clauzel put it), the 'Europeans', the 'French', or the 'Roumi', as the colonized called them.

The national and social (class) betrayal or the naturalization that is described in Algeria as a 'reversal' or 'turnabout' (*retournement*: *m'tourni*)[10] did bring its authors some advantages, all of them discriminatory advantages which other non-naturalized *colonisés* were, of course, denied. They escaped, first, 'native' status or the Code de l'indigénat – and the ignominious obligations imposed by that code – and, second, the status of 'citizen of the second college' and the limitations imposed by that status. This inevitably made naturalization more suspect and more blameworthy still because it was obviously – too obviously – self-seeking.[11]

Even today, to extend the parallelism between, roughly speaking, two moments in the same history, two phases within the same process, or even between the meanings of naturalization in Algeria and France, becoming naturalized is, for an immigrant – perhaps to a lesser degree than in the case of colonization – equivalent to dissociating himself from the condition shared by all immigrants because, thanks to his naturalization, he joins the camp of the non-immigrants, of the 'nationals', to which he did not previously belong, and of which he cannot, despite his naturalization, be a full member. He has committed a double betrayal, which is at once social and political (i.e. national). He has betrayed both his immigrant condition and his status as a national (i.e. his nationality).

Socially 'betraying' the (social) condition of the immigrant, or no longer sharing the juridico-political status common to all immigrants (the status that creates immigrants, as distinct from 'nationals' and, in doing so, implicitly recognizes them as 'nationals' of some other nation) also means politically betraying the identificatory 'national' form that always goes hand in hand with the immigrant condition. Naturalization is not enough to put an end to this form of identification because this is precisely the form that the social condition of immigrants takes in the national consciousness of immigrants. It is a 'national pseudo-identity', as opposed to the national identity and nationality of nationals. It has the peculiar characteristic of being forged, in part, on the basis of elements of a social condition (or class condition). So long as communitarian bonds remain strong enough, and the 'group spirit' (or 'group morale') remains alive, the sort of social and communitarian (i.e. national) betrayal constituted by naturalization is reduplicated by another 'betrayal'. As the distinction between immigrants and nationals is founded, in law, on a national or even nationalistic basis, attempting to escape that distinction and trying to denounce it by becoming naturalized is tantamount to a social and political betrayal of one's nationality. Naturalization is tantamount to denouncing and renouncing one's nationality – and to denouncing it by the very fact of renouncing it. Paradoxically, it is when the balance of power between the nationalities concerned is such that the nationality one is repudiating or which one feels one is betraying has the least reality (an official reality, and no more than that) that one feels the greatest need to remain true to it. This was particularly true of those colonized who had only an 'inner' nationality of their own, a nationality that existed deep inside them, in the form of a subjective belief or conviction, or in the form of an aspirational or ideal nationalist struggle. The same is still true today of those immigrants who, because they are living outside their nation and are cut off from their nationality (because they are cut off from its field of application) and, in more general terms, from the day-to-day life of their nation, no longer have the opportunity to actively 'practise' their nationality (in the sense in which one practises a religion) or to experience it in positive terms. They cannot practise or experience it except in the form of a stigma or an excuse for their exclusion or segregation. When their nationality of origin is, in fact, no more than a feeling (which is vague in some cases and intense in others) of belonging to a disembodied nationality that has been stripped of its attributes, they too bear their nationality inside them, but, unlike the colonized, they do so because it is quite external to them, and then experience it at a distance.

Almost all those who have been naturalized have a fairly strong feeling of having excommunicated themselves. In extreme cases, this merges with an intense feeling of guilt, so much so that, believing that they have been banished and have banished themselves from the community to which they once belonged, many of those who have been naturalized will not allow themselves to reappear in their community or to re-establish links with their community. They regard the break introduced by their naturalization as a definitive and irremediable renunciation, and take the view that being rejected in their turn by their fellow countrymen is, as is only fair, the price they have to pay. As a general rule, these naturalized citizens are obviously those who cannot regard their naturalization as just an administrative process and who, for the same reasons, seem less justified in seeking naturalization because it is a product of exceptional circumstances that are beyond their control. But if the exclusion is to be total, the feeling of rejection must be reciprocal. Those who accept naturalization must regard themselves as having rejected their community, and therefore as having acted as renegades, if their community is to feel justified in rejecting them in its turn.

Like the banishment of old, which was the result of some crime, naturalization is a public act that publicly involves its author and subsequently his family. To that extent, and given the current division of roles and status in the majority of immigrant families, it is an eminently masculine act. It is only the man who, because of the excuses he can produce for acting in this way and because of the future uses he will make of his acquired nationality – and they are all in the public domain – feels the need to become naturalized. This also means that it is the man, and only the man, who has to incur the sanctions that befit his act: excommunication, anathema and damnation. The others, and especially his wife and children, are only indirectly affected by his act and by the consequences of that act. The fact that not even all the wives of the *harkis* took French nationality is a demonstration of this differential attitude.[12] Because they remain at home, because they are concerned only with domestic matters and because they do not have to reveal their identity or show their identity papers, women are not directly affected by naturalization. Whereas the immigrant's nationality of origin, or the nationality into which he was born, which he had left behind and rejected, used to be the concern of men, it now concerns women. It is now becoming a female nationality, or the nationality of private and domestic life, of the secrecy internal to the house and the family. In contrast, the nationality acquired by immigrants or the nationality that requires them to take steps, either boldly and triumphantly or hesitatingly and in resignation, is becoming a male nationality.

We can thus understand why women who have become 'masculine' – with masculine preoccupations, tasks and roles (either of necessity, as is the case with widows or women living alone without the support of any family or close male relatives, or as a result of an education that has led them to break with traditional socialization) – tend to be less opposed than men to their own naturalization, that of their children, and especially that of their daughters. Presumably because they were for a long time, and still are, kept on the margins of 'official' morality (that of honour), and a male morality that is infinitely more constraining, they can now adopt a less rigorous or more permissive attitude towards that morality. They can treat it and its imperatives with a (relatively) greater freedom than men. But because it is not really acceptable for them to adopt the male roles that they increasingly have to play, they have more to lose by perpetuating a 'female' nationality that would confirm them in and confine them to their traditional status. Reminders of tradition or, which amounts to the same thing, strict religious observance, which is always praiseworthy where women are concerned, remind them of their status at the very moment when their position, their activities and their new responsibilities are encouraging them to adopt the 'male' nationality they need more imperatively than men.

As an example, let me cite the case of a woman who, after she was widowed, convinced herself that she should request the French nationality that her husband had already obtained immediately after Algeria become independent, which was when he came to France to pursue his career:

'My husband came [to France], alone for a while at first. I don't know if he was working or not. He didn't talk to me about that sort of thing; I knew nothing about all that, his business, anything to do with his work... what I do know is that in Algiers he had an important post in the administration; we were fine. That was "during France" [i.e. during the colonial period]. When the French left, things were not like they used to be. Everything changed. I don't know if he really went on working, or just pretended, waited. Things went on that way for at least two years. He often came to France, presumably to regularize his situation. What is certain is that there was no more money coming into the house.... We all came to France in 1965.... To get his job back in France, to continue his career, to go on working until he retired, he obviously had to take French nationality [literally: take French papers]. It was like it used to be, under the French in Algeria, he'd kept the same papers. It was the same for the children, or at least the ones who were still at home; it's only our eldest girl, who was already married (at the time) who doesn't have French papers. She came to France after us with her husband, but she came like everyone else, with the Algerian papers she still has.... So why change my papers? I didn't need them. Not to work – I don't work – not to go out – I don't go out, I don't leave the house, either here in France or back there in Algeria; that's not the way we do things. So I stayed with my Algerian papers. It's not the same for the children; they were young when they came and either went on with or started their studies here in France; they will have to work in France.... Yes, both the boys and the girls... Besides, they're working now. The situation has changed now. So long as he [her husband] was there, I didn't need French papers. After he had come to France and taken French papers, he never went back to Algeria. He went back there only to be buried there.... It wasn't the same for me. I had no reason not to go back to Algeria – except money. It is very expensive. When it was necessary, when we needed to be in Algeria, I would go with some of the children.... My husband died in 1978, when he had already been retired for three years. Since he died, things have obviously changed. First of all, our income has fallen; now, I have only half his pension... less than half; not all the children work, or don't work all the time. I was losing over 100,000 francs [old francs] a month because I didn't have any French papers; I was losing too much money. My son looked into it, he tried to take care of everything: I had to supply proof that I was already living in France with my husband in 1963; that isn't possible. So, I had to change my papers too . . . I thought about it a lot, I waited for a long time before taking the plunge. I couldn't talk about it with the others; you don't talk about things like that. It has to remain within the family, between ourselves; you don't talk. It's not that you have to hide it, it's something that can't be hidden, but it's best if people find out about it afterwards rather than going and telling them in advance. Even so, you have to tell your closest relatives in Algiers. When? How? It's not easy. So, softly, softly, you have to prepare the ground. I began to complain that I was losing a lot of money, which was true; I asked them to find out, and to tell me why I was losing so much money, why couldn't I have that money? Then they found out that I had to have French papers. I didn't stop phoning Algiers to bring them up to date, to ask them how I should go about getting back the money I was losing. I sent them all the letters I got [about this business]. Besides, they knew why I was doing all this. It was a way of letting them know, without actually telling them I was taking French papers. We understood each other perfectly well, without there being any need to say anything to each other; I know they understood me, and they knew that I knew they understood . . . . The idea got around. I pretended to be asking them for their advice, but really I was letting them know, I had them up against the wall. I persuaded them to take the same path as me; it was really a way of telling them; a way of telling them what my intentions were, but without seeming to do so. It was better that way. That way, I no longer had to fear their hostile judgements, their disapproval. . . . After that, my only worry was that they might not give me my French papers. Everyone knows you're asking for them, and then they tell you: "God, you've lost everything." For your relatives, for you, for all those who are in the know, it's finished, it's as though you had French papers; but when it comes to you, you have nothing, you're back to where you started. When that happens, you've lost everything. What shame! I wouldn't want that to happen. . . . Because, basically, what have they got to do with me? They're nothing to do with me. What can I give them? Nothing. They've nothing to gain. And yet, they might reproach me for having waited so long, for having waited fifteen years before asking to become French. Now that I'm no good for anything. And when they find out that all this is about nothing more than getting 100,000 francs a month. And they are quite capable of refusing to change my papers, just for the sake of saving 100,000 francs. I didn't do it with joy in my heart. What I'm frightened of is that it's blatantly obvious that I am only asking for French papers for the money; no other reason, it's not for the pleasure of being "French" . . . it's not as though I liked them! I know what I am, and I will stay what I am. Everyone should know that, but for them, for them it's 100,000 francs down the drain. Just to save that money, they are quite capable of telling me: "We don't want you, stay as you are ... " And they are quite right ... each to their own religion, each to their own blood. That's the only thing that's true ... yes. Even so, I had to take the plunge; I had to come to a decision. Fortunately, they did not refuse to give me French papers! ... No, I don't tell anyone, not even the people I know. Personally, I don't like to look at those papers. Fortunately I'm not obliged to look at them every day!'

Automatic naturalization

That the attitude of Algerian immigrants towards their possible naturalization is undergoing an extremely profound transformation is undeniable.[13] Two series of factors seem to lie at the origin of this development. They include, first, the fading over time of a number of attitudes that have become anachronistic as well as the conjunctural effects typical of any situation in which there is a jobs crisis. Today's difficulties, for example, pose a threat to the future of immigrants and, basically, to the status hitherto granted them. Not all the threats are purely economic. There are also administrative threats pertaining to the order of regulations and legislation, and therefore political threats. There are restrictive measures, legal and otherwise, designed to limit how long immigrants can stay in the country (especially when they are unemployed) or to bring about their 'expulsion'. And, finally, there is the whole climate of uncertainty that the crisis, and especially the way it is being exploited, has created. Secondly, we also have transformations specific to the immigrant population as a whole, and then the changes they bring about in terms of their relationship with French society and, correlatively, their society of origin. This is especially true of the population of young people born in France and, usually, brought up and educated in France, and that situation is not without its effects on the attitudes of their parents.

More important still, the fact that French nationality is now automatically, mechanically and universally granted to all children born in France after 1 January 1963 has been a prodigious factor in accelerating the transformation of systems of attitudes and opinions towards nationality. This is the case both in France and Algeria, both amongst immigrants and amongst the Algerian population, which cannot remain indifferent to the influence and pressure brought to bear by these 'emigrants'. In the eyes of the French law (article 23 of the Code de la nationalité, as established by the law of 9 January 1973[14]), all children born in France to Algerian families, or in other words to parents both of whom were themselves born in Algeria, which was then a French *département* (and therefore part of France[15]), as of 1 January 1963 are automatically French by birth. And there can be no possible objections on the part of any of the parties concerned. The French government cannot object unless it breaks its own laws by trying to exclude them from French nationality. Nor, a fortiori, can Algeria, which cannot go on pretending for ever to ignore the fact that this fraction of its 'emigrant' nationals enjoys French nationality in France. And nor, ultimately, can the individuals concerned, unless they leave French territory or are freed at their own request from allegiance to French nationality.

And yet all these young people are, in the eyes of Algerian law, also Algerian and necessarily Algerian by descent.[16] Two different laws, one legislating on the basis of *jus soli* and the other on the basis of *jus sanguinis*, mean that the children of immigration, or the grandchildren of colonization (or at least some of them), are children 'divided' between two nations and two nationalities, and will remain so for a long time to come, or until such time as their actual nationality wins out. Indeed, being both the products and the victims of a twofold history – that of colonization and that of emigration – they are, much as they may dislike it, the object of a dispute and the pretext for a difference of opinion that they do not find easy to resolve. Thanks to the definition given of the territorial competence of French sovereignty, and therefore the reminder of the role of the colonial past, both parties prolong and reactivate the old relationship of domination.

Insofar as it is a country of immigration and therefore has to concern itself with its absent nationals, Algeria appears to be more attached to the principle of sovereignty in itself or, if we like, to the statist aspect or even the international dimension of nationality. Given that it is faced with a *fait accompli*, and has no influence at all on the current situation of the emigrant population, it can only fall back on positions of principle, and can do nothing but insist on asserting its rights. In an ideal world, Algeria would be satisfied, in the circumstances, only if some measure – a unilateral measure, insofar as that is possible – were to release, both collectively and automatically, from their allegiance to French nationality all those young Algerians who are French by virtue of having been born in France. For Algeria, such a measure – improbable as it seems – would be a way of seeing that justice had been done, and of seeing that justice had been done to its national (and nationalist) history.

France, on the other hand, seems more inclined to take more interest in individual cases and particular situations, and to want to negotiate on terrain that is in its favour in two senses. The concrete situations and individual cases that are almost deliberately referred to in all discussions (even when they are about principles) give the impression of apparently being closer to reality. France is therefore disposed to make the 'concessions' needed in this domain – and it is always perfectly at liberty to make such concessions because, for France, the real argument has already been won.

In the best of cases, would France be prepared, in order to prevent conflicts over nationality, to release from the allegiance it claims as its due those young people – who are French in France and Algerian in Algeria – who ask to be released from it? Even if that were the case, those young people themselves would have to make the request, which would be a manifest proof of what they wanted, and would have to 'merit' their liberation. They would have to have 'done' enough to make a convincing case for their 'Algerianness' (or their will to 'Algerianity') – and their 'national' attachment to Algeria, military service being, of course, the most obvious criterion because of the symbolic value it is recognized as having in these circumstances.

It is impossible to distinguish between the role played by condescension and that played by contempt or even by the most cynical and racist strategy, well intentioned as it may be, and, finally, by classic blackmail and the protocols of the exchange of 'good offices' between countries bound together by common interests, especially when the relationship between them is one between dominant and dominated. The same language, or roughly the same language, can, however, be used to promote the most radically opposed political positions and the most antithetical professions of faith.

When the circumstances lend themselves to it, or in other words whenever they hope to profit from them in both symbolic and material terms, both 'left' and 'right' can, if not denounce in the same terms the 'violence' that has been done to the children of Algerian immigrants families by the fact of their having been born in France (because they were born 'twice' into French nationality), at least question the desirability (on the left) and the legitimacy (on the right) of this state of affairs. Restoring their Algerian nationality (the nationality of their parents) to these children and restoring them to the nationality from which they have been divorced, can be described as a measure of 'historical' rehabilitation, as a way of making the reparations for some past 'sin' (the colonial sin) that the current situation demands, but it can also be no more than the result of further discrimination. This tends to be the position of the left. Such discrimination affects those who are deemed to be unworthy of continuing a history that immigration continues to revive and perpetuate, and who continue to enjoy all the benefits of a nationality that has reluctantly been granted them. What is more, such discrimination does not infringe the letter of the Code, as it is merely a matter of generously releasing them from their allegiance to their French nationality (a subtle way of nullifying the effect of article 23 without altering the article itself). This tends to be the position of the right.

The fact remains that both positions have their advantages, for both right and left. Although right and left have different intentions, and although their intentions are moral rather than political, their respective positions allow them to profit from the situation in two ways. They 'free' France of certain French citizens (whom France does not want) by liberating them, with extreme generosity, from the allegiance they have contracted. In doing so, they win the support of the country whose nationals are being 'restored' to it, and thus recognize that they were originally and fundamentally 'its' nationals and that it is only as a result of past and present acts of violence that they were 'annexed'. There is no other way of understanding the insistent way in which they denounce the 'automatic' nature of some attributions of nationality. Such attributions are described as so many acts of 'violence' against the will and initiative of the individuals concerned – 'they made Frenchmen out of people who did not want to be French'. Hence their eagerness to 'reform' article 23 of the Code de la nationalité, which would not be an easy goal to achieve, even in juridical terms.

To go beyond this example, which brings *jus soli* into play, it seems that the real issue – if there is a real issue involved – is not the specific influence that one or other of the two laws – *jus soli* and *jus sanguinis* – can have, or the priority that is to be given to one or the other. The real issue lies elsewhere. It concerns something of a different nature and, for the moment, it does come within the remit of institutional law. It concerns neither *jus soli*, which is the royal road to an existence that fully conforms to orthodoxy, nor *jus sanguinis*, which is no more than a stopgap solution, or an access road for those who do not have 'birth' (their national coat of arms) on their side. The real issue is a right to nationality (or citizenship) that is based solely upon the criterion of residence.

How have we arrived at the objective situation of a conflict of nationalities between France and Algeria, when neither of the two parties has any desire to make the conflict explicit (or any interest in doing so), and when, in the circumstances, each prefers to act unilaterally within its sovereign territory? This situation results mainly from the provisions of the French Code de la nationalité. Article 23 seems to be specifically directed at children who are born in France to immigrant Algerian families. Some even believe that it was deliberately drafted with them in mind (until such time as other '*départements*' or 'territories' still covered by French nationality finally achieve their national independence). In reality, the provisions of article 23, as currently formulated, go back to at least the middle of the nineteenth century. The law of February 1851 declared 'any individual born in France to a foreigner (father or mother) who was himself born there' to be French, unless they choose to renounce French citizenship. This actually modified article 9 of the Code civil (which had already been extended by the law of March 1849), which authorized a child born in France to request French nationality only in the year following its age of majority. Since then, the law has been changed on many occasions, usually as a result of diplomatic protests; it was such protests that brought about the variations affecting the option to renounce French nationality. That option was successively restricted (by the law of 16 December 1874), repealed (in 1889), reintroduced, but only in cases where the mother was born in France (by the law of 22 July 1893), and then remained in force until 1973. In the history of the right to nationality, the rule of attributive 'double birth' (with or without the option of renunciation) corresponded to a general tendency typical of the period, as did the juridical and economic structures that were being established at the time (or which had already been established). *Jus soli* was becoming as important as *jus sanguinis* and, to a certain extent, the 'private' aspect was becoming as important as the 'state' aspect of nationality. The privilege granted to this double *jus soli* derived from the general principle according to which the 'birth' rule, which militated in favour of the effective and automatic attribution of nationality, became attributive, provided that there was also some connection: in the present case, the fact that both parents were born in France. That 'double birth' in France – in other words, after two generations of continuous residence – was simply the result of a coincidence was highly improbable, and it therefore seemed quite natural to grant that child French nationality at birth. Since the family of a child who received French nationality at birth had obviously been living in France – though it all depends on what is meant by 'France' – for three generations, the automatic attribution of French nationality seemed to be no more than the *de jure* or *de facto* state: the child's 'quality' of being French was already an established fact (see Lagarde 1997: 62). That is what the legislator must have had in mind. To change that view and to believe the opposite, one would have had to have had serious doubts about the identificatory power of social mechanisms, and above all education, which is still the best agent of 'naturalization' in every sense of the word. One would have to despair of the ability of subjects to identify with the human environment – even in its political dimension – into which they are born, in which they have grown up and have been socialized throughout their lives. And why should something that was possible for decades no longer be possible today?

The link established by the Code de la nationalité is not the only link between naturalization and education.[17] Given the characteristic situation of immigrant families, there is also a link that is objectively established. There is, in this case, a profound homology between the function of education and the function of naturalization and, relatively speaking, between the system of the expectations we have of both institutions. Immigrants' parents expect (not without certain inevitable illusions) both education or, to be more accurate, the 'metamorphosis' education is supposed to bring about in their children, and naturalization to authorize something that they cannot authorize themselves to do and that no agency can authorize them to do. But they expect this to happen only after the event (which, in many cases, does nothing to lessen the anger or pain they experience when they see their children changing nationality). Even a long and continuous period of residence in France, or any other kind of capital they may have accumulated, cannot authorize this. It is authorized by what authorizes their children (education and naturalization) – or what their children are bold enough to authorize of their own accord – to put down roots and to acquire, in their own eyes and the eyes of others, a legitimacy, which is, they hope, less debatable and less revocable, than the legitimacy bestowed by work. By doing so, they can *exist* in the full sense, even if they do so by proxy, by the proxy given to their children and which those children give back in return. It is in that sense that school can be said 'to naturalize', and that it is a preparation for naturalization.

With the rights they have acquired over nationality, nations do not like conflict between nationalities: they all try to prevent these from happening. They would all like membership of one nation to preclude any form of allegiance to any other power, even if it is not, strictly speaking, political. And this is happening at a time when the extraordinary extension and imbrication of different spaces (geographical, economic, linguistic, cultural, ideological and so on), which are also political and national spaces, can result in people having several nationalities, either at the same time or at different times. But can something that is permitted only in exceptional circumstances and in certain situations also be more broadly and ordinarily acceptable, in both the statistical sense of the normal word (more frequently) and in the social sense (by ordinary citizens)? Whichever solution is adopted – liberalizing and popularizing the process of releasing people from their ties of allegiance to a degree that goes beyond what is reasonable, or reducing the effects of the automatic acquisition of nationality through *jus soli* – it seems that the major concern is, in this case, to discourage the type of behaviour the jurist Niboyet calls the 'picking and choosing' of nationalities (1947: vol 1; see also Lagarde 1997: 62), or in other words claiming to have lived in one country, sometimes for generations, whilst retaining a foreign political allegiance.

This representation, which might be said to be authorized because it is promoted by people who are authorities on the subject, concurs with and confirms the widespread opinion of this new population of 'immigrants who enjoy French nationality'. They are a new class of 'parasites' who enjoy all the rights conferred by 'national' status but who avoid the duties that go hand in hand with those rights. They are, for example, suspected of not paying their taxes, of avoiding military service and thus not being sufficiently patriotic, and, in extreme cases, of being potential traitors because their adoption of French national- ity is no more than circumstantial and is motivated only by practical and material interests. Ultimately, it is just a ploy.[18] It is, presumably, in order to provide a symbolic guarantee against that threat and the subversion it implies that they like to submit the 'neo-national' to the ordeal of taking a civic oath and to the solemnity that goes with it – it is of course a purely formal ordeal, as there is no offence of perjury, no judge to give a guilty verdict and no sanction to punish its author, but respect for form is, in the circumstance, the greatest form of respect.

If all those subjects who are described as having 'dual nationality', which is another way of saying that they are no more than 'bi-nationals' or, at best, 'semi-nationals', resolve to become French and only French, or Algerian and only Algerian, this should be more than enough to clarify the situation for both the countries concerned and, at the same time, to satisfy the national order of both parties. However, it does more to satisfy the national order that is annexing the new nationals than the national order that is impoverishing itself by letting some of its nationals leave. If it were pursued to its logical conclusion, this argument would mean asking or even requiring (if that were possible) Algeria to take reciprocal measures in order to balance the relationship by releasing from their ties of allegiance to Algerian nationality all those Algero-French (or Franco-Algerians, if that terms seems preferable) who have demonstrated their attachment to and identification with the French nation and French nationality. And this would have to go on until such time as their actual national- ity, having effaced the rival nationality, became their only possible nationality.

The national loyalty or loyalties of these French-born children – and the resultant compatibilities and incompatibilities – will be a topic for discussion and disputes for a long time to come. For France, they are 'children from elsewhere', but they are French because they have been born 'twice' ('twice' in the space of two generations) on French territory. For Algeria, they are 'Algerian children' but have been born outside Algerian territory. But the fact remains that between 16,000 and 18,000 children are born every year to Algerian families (in which both partners are Algerian) living in France, and that they are therefore granted French nationality at birth. Every year, almost the same number of young people reach the age of majority, or at least the age of sixteen – at which point they must have a resident's permit if they have not been automatically granted French nationality – and discover that they are inevitably of French nationality. These annual cohorts of young people who are French-Algerians (or Algerian-French) simply by virtue of having been born in France provide one example of how naturalization can be 'licitated'. In the eyes of all and everyone, they represent a way of removing the total taboo (social, moral, religious, communitarian, political etc.) on acquiring French nationality in particular. Having a son who is of necessity 'French', but who remains in the eyes of all (and especially if it can be proved) just as 'good' a son or even a better son, 'just as good' an Algerian or even a better Algerian, just as good a Muslim if not a better Muslim (being a good son, a 'good' Algerian and a 'good' Muslim are one and the same thing), can only 'reconcile' his parents to his naturalization. Then how can one object to the eldest brother (born before 1963) of a 'good son even if he is French' acquiring French nationality, if that is what he wants and if he believes that is in his interests to do so? And once Frenchness has entered a family, and once that family has realized that it will not produce any of the upheavals or 'catastrophes' it feared, either within the family itself or in its cherished network of relations in both France and Algeria, a whole cumulative fear of naturalization is dispelled, and a lot of people who cannot benefit from *jus soli* begin to request naturalization. The form of gentle violence that is done to individuals who have received French nationality in this way (and to their families rather than the individuals themselves) is becoming more widespread.

Ambiguities and double consciousness

Those who enjoy the benefits of having a nationality without having had to request naturalization can easily come to terms with it, and their ritual protests (which may of course be perfectly sincere) are no proof to the contrary. Their families, who would have refused to be naturalized in accordance with the normal process, are relieved, after the event, that French nationality ('French papers', as they put it) has been granted them automatically, as though under 'duress' or in the guise of a collectively imposed constraint. Naturalization is their common lot and not the result of an individual and voluntary act whereby some call attention to themselves and divorce themselves from the rest. All in all, the way in which French nationality is acquired is more important than the ongoing actual relationship with their nationality and nation of origin (which is not the same as the personal and purely affective relationship they have with regard to both).

Despite all the conventional protests and despite the feeling of guilt or unease that still haunts those who have been naturalized, so-called 'compulsory' naturalization therefore eventually gives rise to a feeling of satisfaction that must, for a whole series of reasons, remain secret and, sometimes, resigned. The only proof that the required change of attitude has occurred is the wish, which is more and more frequently expressed by every family that is 'divided' in terms of its nationality, to recreate its unity and to rediscover a relative homogeneity by paying, if necessary (and it is necessary), the price of naturalization. This is obviously not the first time an innovation, no matter how bitter, has come to the aid of a demand that might seem anachronistic. In this case, the concern with family cohesion seems to be a way of ensuring the survival of 'traditional' morality, unless, which amounts to the same thing, it is the apparent need to conform to the 'traditional' imperative that serves to justify the innovation.

> 'We cannot be divided, with some on one side and the rest on the other, some Algerian and the rest French. They are brothers and sisters, the children of the same father and mother; there is no difference – between the eldest and the youngest, between the first and the last. They all have to be either French or Algerian, and not just some of them, some Algerian and some French. It isn't fair. . . . But if we can't all be Algerians here in France, then they might as well all be French. Even we parents would be French if they asked us to. Why not? . . . Except that they don't ask us, and that it's a bit late for us. . . . We are not going to ask for it ourselves. All they have to say to us is that anyone who has had their children "taken by" French nationality is, like their children, "taken by" that same nationality. And then the problem would be solved!'

The fact that some parents speak this way does not mean that the naturalization of their children cannot be an object of conflict. On the contrary, this language is itself the product of the type of conflict that is objectively inherent in naturalization to the extent that there is always a danger that, when the occasion arises, it will add a further element of dissension to everything that already divides two generations whose social trajectories are different in every respect. The clash of nationalities, and especially divergent attitudes towards naturalization, merely exacerbates, and perhaps even reveals, the gap that immigration has created between generations of parents and children. Conflicts of this type may erupt openly or may remain beneath the surface. They may remain buried, rather like possibilities that both generations agree to ignore by using avoidance strategies that are both knowingly elaborated and shared. Yet everyone – parents, children and the whole family circle – concurs in deploring not so much the reason for the dispute, as the impossibility of arriving at a reconciliation based solely upon one nationality: French, which is the only possible nationality because it is the only one that can be shared in the situation common to both generations (i.e. the immigrant situation).

Even if they deny it, Algerian immigrants are paving the way for a different form of naturalization and a different category of possible candidates for naturalization, not only within the population of immigrants of other nationalities but, more fundamentally, within the population of Algerians in Algeria itself. They are creating a form of naturalization and candidates for French nationality who, although they share the history that produced immigration, are not themselves part of the immigration and its history. They take from it only what they need in the circumstances, namely the example they can borrow from it and the justification that same example gives them. It allows them to justify themselves, and to justify and authorize their behaviour in this domain.[19] And all these cumulative reasons help to both desanctify, in the true sense of the term, and 'secularize' the notion of nationality and therefore the notion of naturalization.

'Desanctification' should be understood, first of all, in the religious sense of the word, as it is now possible to be a good Muslim (a true believer and a practising Muslim) whilst being of French nationality. Many Muslims who have, for one reason or another, acquired French nationality are making greater and greater efforts to prove this to themselves and others (Muslims or not) by demonstrating more and more, and in the most ostentatious ways, that they remain true to their faith. 'Desancitification' is also essential because it is a way of lifting a taboo: the social and communitarian taboo on naturalization, which is moral rather than political in the strict sense. The new usage, which derives from a new and increasingly widespread conception of nationality and naturalization, means that the term must in future be used in a more strictly political and administrative sense. All this justifies us in our view that the growing number of 'Algerians of French nationality', some of whom have requested naturalization whilst others could not refuse it, will help to vulgarize and popularize[20] naturalization, at least amongst the population of immigrants, who are the first to be concerned.

One might also think that all these recent developments would be enough to overcome resistances, or at least reticence. But that is to overlook the fact that, in this domain, there are no unambiguous attitudes. The 'licitation' of naturalization no longer means simply that one set of 'papers' is replaced by another, or that 'green papers' (the colour of Algerian passports and identity cards) are replaced by 'yellow papers' (the colour of a French identity card), as the nationalities in question are commonly described in terms of their emblems. It coexists with its opposite. Naturalization is disapproved of to the extent that it is a mark and an admission of alienation, as well as an adulteration and denial of one's basic being. The two attitudes coexist in contradictory fashion within the same individual, with one or the other reaction becoming dominant depending on the context and the needs and customs of the moment. And the only way to express this contradictory situation is to use a language that is itself contradictory.

'I am Algerian despite my French papers; I am French despite my Algerian appearance. I am French [this is said in neutral terms], as French as anyone else [like a true Frenchman, of old French stock]. I was born here, brought up here, grew up here, was made here, for here, to live here; I feel at home here, have French habits and French ideas....But, deep inside me, I feel myself to be Algerian despite it all; in my heart of hearts, I feel...something tells me that I am Algerian...uniquely Algerian by birth...born into an Algerian family. You are always something or someone by birth; no one asked to be born here or there, there's no choice. I didn't choose to be Algerian or to be French. That makes no sense. Algerian without having wanted to be and French without having wanted to be, even when you ask to be naturalized...my parents did not choose to immigrate to France; they immigrated, that's all; my parents did not choose to be French in their day, they did not choose to be colonized: they were colonized, they were French, that's all...I can even say that I've made more effort to be French than to be Algerian, since I went to school in France, in the French mentality, and so on. Is that or isn't that what you call a culture?'[21]

Another, and frequently expressed, variant on this ambiguity, or even this antinomy, is to play unwittingly on the two constituent dimensions of nationality, and to say 'France is just my country, Algeria is my homeland', and to add, as though to make the distinction more explicit: 'You live in a country, work in a country and even work for that country, but you are *from* a homeland.' One can therefore have a country or nationality but belong to a different country or nationality, be possessed by a different country or a different nationality.

In some cases it is possible to be '*de facto* French', as when one was born, brought up and educated in France, or grew up in French society and in accordance (even approximately) with French norms, or when one has of necessity to live in France, without necessarily being completely French because one is not French by right. This can, contrary to all expectations, happen, and this too makes it possible to denounce, on the grounds of injustice or arbitrariness, a situation of exclusion that is in accordance with the law, but which is, it seems, seen as a paradigmatic variation that sums up and symbolizes every other form of exclusion. This is particularly true of all 'young' Algerians, some of them born in Algeria (when it was still France, and for a long time afterwards) and who came to France as very young children, others born in France, but too early (before 1 January 1963) to receive French nationality automatically. Both groups have always lived in France, without, one might add, being able to live anywhere but in France.[22] It is also possible to be *de jure* French (or, as is said more and more often and without further ado, to be 'French on paper' or 'French according to one's papers'). This is the position of many of the young people who were born in France – and their numbers will increase – without being completely *de facto* French because of the multiple discriminations and exclusions of which they are the victims (apparently simply because of their origins), or, what is more important, without being subjectively French because they feel that they are the victims of exclusions and discriminations based solely upon their origins.

Such is the paradox that has now been generated by immigration. It does not make the *de jure* position correspond to the *de facto* one. Non-fulfilment of the *de facto* situation has repercussions on the *de jure* one, and thus brings naturalization into further disrepute after the event, or after everyone has experienced it. This means that one cannot be fully French when one is not *de jure* French. In the eyes of the law, this is self-evidently logical. It is a given fact that has all the certainty conferred by the law and belief in the force of law. It is, besides, on that condition and because this legally given fact contains within it the principle for understanding it – here, it is the principle that generates the consolation – that it can be tolerated, or quite 'naturally' accepted even by those who are its victims. Conversely, knowing (theoretically) that one is French *de jure* and in the eyes of the law, and discovering on a daily basis that this is not enough to make one completely or truly French, is something that can turn one against naturalization. One cannot be fully French by right when one is not truly *de facto* French, in other words when one is not normally French in normal life. Symmetrically, one cannot be truly be *de facto* French if one is not legitimately French by right. Someone who has been assigned an identity can be French or can describe himself as French informally ('not for real') even if he is not officially French (i.e. *de jure*). Conversely, someone who has been assigned French nationality *de jure* may be 'not French' – because they subjectively refuse to be French or to accept that they are French – or may be French 'differently', once they have officially (*de jure*) become French.

How, in such conditions, can anyone criticize this entire class of 'naturalized at birth' and 'approximately French' citizens for their lack of enthusiasm, for not showing any great eagerness to possess French nationality? And, above all, how can we criticize them for using naturalization for purely utilitarian ends, for the sake of advantages (they imagine) it might give them, and without any patriotic or even passionate commitment? After all, their entire experience of 'being French' confirms their view that the change in their civil status that they have brought about by acquiring French nationality has done nothing to change their condition as immigrants (and they are still immigrants in social terms), as 'Arabs' and as 'Arab immigrants'. Even if its reality is no more than juridical, their naturalization will, at best, have allowed them, as they themselves say, not without an ironic awareness of their own fate, to be 'vaccinated against deportation'. This is a juridical defence against a threat whose entire basis is juridical – it is based wholly on the national/non-national distinction, as a non-national can in theory be deported, even though that might never actually happen. Naturalization is both everything and nothing. Naturalization is everything to the extent that it involves the individual's whole being and the whole of his existence. The euphemistic periphrasis, 'changing your papers, that's what naturalization means', suggests that 'deep inside, you have not changed and you cannot change just by changing the papers you have in your pocket'. It certainly does not mean that 'you have changed so much that you then have to change your papers', but it does mean that naturalization consists in acquiring the elementary and irreducible means of having a legal existence in the place where one is now living and where one's present and future existence will be played out. Yet despite that, naturalization really is nothing in the sense that it changes nothing. It changes neither the 'nature of things' nor the identity of the individuals concerned.

All these constants are at once subjective and objective. On the one hand, they are inscribed in the very being of subjects, in their *habitus* and their own ways of structuring the social world. On the other, they are part of the outside world in which one has to operate and which also has to be conquered. They constitute an identity and therefore appear to be differences that naturalization alone cannot erase. They give rise to representations (objects and signs) that are both mental and objective, and which have, no matter what sign (positive or negative) they are placed under, an emblematic value and function. The field is therefore open to a whole series of manipulations designed to impose the representation one would like to give of oneself, the representation others should have, first, of the characteristics we agree to regard as distinctive and, then, of those who bear those same differential marks.

As the struggle over the definition of identities – national, regional, ethnic or cultural identities and so on – is a struggle over the manipulation of mental representations, the children of immigrant Algerian families are, irrespective of whether or not they have French nationality, 'Algerian' in France only if they wish to be (when they wish, for themselves and in their heart of hearts, to be Algerian):

'I am French when no one says anything to me, when they tell me I am neither French nor Algerian – I am even more French and in an even stronger sense when they tell me I am not French, either in France or in Algeria; back there, I don't know, but here, yes; yes in the Algeria that is here in France, because there is an Algeria here, and I suspect that it is more terrible than the Algeria that exists in Algeria. In any case, even in Algeria, over there, I wouldn't accept it if I was told I wasn't French...nor if I was told I wasn't Algerian either, come to that...I am not French when they tell me I am French, or in other words when they want me to be compulsorily French, i.e. to be at their feet, to kiss their knees; it's as though they were ordering me to be French, I'm not having that....Same thing with Algeria and Algerian. If anyone tells me I'm not Algerian, here in France, even more so back there in Algeria, I'd be up in arms.'

'Being French or not being French' and, similarly, 'being Algerian or not being Algerian': the same logic governs the definition one gives of oneself. And that definition depends upon the context and the intention we can sense thanks to the context, or in other words through the definition others mobilize in that context:

'I am Algerian when no one says anything to me, when they don't tell me I'm Algerian, like it or not...and even when they tell me I'm not Algerian, it's up to me, only I can say whether I am this or that, as the fancy takes me....And it all depends on who tells me "you are French" or "you are Algerian" – where it is said – with what intention, in what spirit it is said to me. I'm not Algerian, not French, when I see that they want at all cost for me to be Algerian or French. The fact that I'm Algerian, that I'm French pisses them off. None of this is easy, it gets you down, it makes you enemies, leads to misunderstandings, even within the family. But it makes me laugh all the same!'[23]

The sometimes pathetic effort and the almost desperate energy that 'Algerians from France' put, because they are so keen to forget that they are legally French, into constantly contradicting all the identifications that are lent them, or in other words all the representations that are given to them (in both France and Algeria), are not the result of some 'bad instinct' on their part. Representations that appear to be both socially negative and self-destructive – denying what one is as soon as one is named – can be explained if we see them as the effects of systematic stigmatization. Reactions of this type provide an introduction to a whole sociology of the stigma that surrounds them, and allow the stigma to be seen for what it is: a set of relations between socially determined positions (no matter who occupies them) within a field, and not merely a particular relationship between singular agents. That relationship is no more than an effect of the stigmatization.[24] Within French society, these structural relations are a manifestation of hidden relations (of domination and of force, and the history of the social genesis of those relations) that are revealed only by their effects on a completely interpersonal interactive relationship. They therefore exist quite independently of the many conjunctural determinations, some spatial and others temporal, that allow that particular relationship to be materialized at a given place and time.

One of the laws of social physics is that stigmatization will provoke a rebellion against the stigma. The rebellion begins with the public reappropriation of the stigma, which thus becomes an emblem: 'I am Algerian – I am an immigrant and I am proud to be an immigrant.' It should end with the establishment of a group formed on the basis of the stigma, or which is, in other words, to a large extent a product of the economic and social effects of the stigmatization. The rise in the number of so-called 'foreign' associations or immigrant associations obviously testifies, first, to the desire of the immigrants they bring together (and they are almost always young) to distinguish themselves, to establish themselves as a group with a *name* – in other words with the basis for a common identification. It also testifies to how they see themselves and what they call themselves. The names they agree to call themselves by – 'new generation', 'Young Arabs of...', 'cultural association of...', 'Berber association of...' – are no more than so many ways of reappropriating the names they are called by others. They reveal the very founding principle of the common identity they recognize in one another, and in which they all recognize themselves, namely the stigma constituted, in the eyes of their whole social environment and therefore in their own eyes, by the multiple discriminations that affect them: territorial discrimination (neighbourhood associations 'for immigrants'), ethnic discrimination (associations of 'Arabs', 'Berbers', 'Maghrebins', 'French from . . .'), cultural discrimination and so on.

In that sense, we can say that immigrants, whoever they may be and whatever their trajectory in France may be, do not behave any differently from any other dominated group. This is even truer of the young, of the children of immigrant families, whatever their situation is with regard to French nationality. For, appearances to the contrary notwithstanding, the position they occupy in the field of symbolic power relations is even more dominated and more critical than the position occupied by their parents. Unlike the traditional immigrant, who could still delude himself that he was 'not involved' and ignore the very process of stigmatization, they can neither abandon the game in which they are involved, nor even pretend that it does not concern them. All they can do is accept (willingly or with resignation, submissively or angrily) the dominant definition, or that given by the dominant, of their identity. Their only alternative is to try – when, that is, they do not do both at the same time – to assimilate thanks to a subtle game of bluff that is designed to conceal the stigma, or at least to mask its most obvious external signs. They therefore promote a self-image that is as close as possible to a legitimate identity: the dominant identity. As is always the case in struggles against stigmatization and the domination that is one of its major effects, in struggles – which amount to the same thing – for *a self-identity* (a national identity or some other identity), and in struggles to achieve an *autonomous* self-definition – in other words to define the principles that define the social world in terms of one's interests (material and symbolic) – the outcome is usually nothing more than an inverted reproduction of the stigma attached to the representation they are trying to fight. Is inverting, as though thanks to some magical operation, the relationship of heteronomy and the work of hetero-definition from which all the dominated suffer equivalent to creating and imposing the autonomy, self-determination and self-definition they are trying to win? A purely symbolic negation of the one is not enough actually to establish the other. The difficult, if not impossible, choice here is one between different strategies: those of recognition and of subversion. The former involve the recognition of the criteria of judgement that base identity on a legitimate foundation; the latter attempt, by attacking symbolic power relations, to invert the scale of values that authorizes stigmatization, rather than to erase the stigmatized features. As the situation, which is in this regard exemplary, of young (Algerian) people born in France illustrates, everyone invests powerful and passionate interests in anything to do with the legitimate criteria for evaluating individuals.

This struggle, which has the advantage of being able to count upon the exceptionally mobilizing form of anything to do with identity, brings into play interests that are all the more vital in that what is at stake is the very value of individuals who have been reduced to their social identity. These individuals invest their energy into invoking everything that defines them as a distinct group ('we, the...' as opposed to 'them'). Such, no doubt, is the specificity of immigration and of the dominated situation specific to immigrants. They are forced to oscillate between strategies of recognition and strategies of subversion without having the means to implement either. They are, in other words, unable either to impose that recognition or to impose themselves.[25] In the context of immigration, they cannot realize the conditions of possibility for an effective subversive strategy.[26]

As in all situations where one has to reach a compromise with a fundamentally contradictory situation one cannot resolve, and which one cannot even escape, the dream of all 'immigrants' who are faced in this way with the dual (national) identity they have been assigned is to be able to enjoy both the symbolic benefits conferred by the fact of having a perfectly legitimate identity. They dream of being able to assert that identity in public and of having it recognized in public. On the other hand, they also dream of the benefits of being autonomous, in the sense of being able to construct and evaluate their own identity (and it is difficult to reconcile the two). And in the context of integration, the dominated are required to renounce their (impossible) autonomy to the extent that, in order to be recognized, they are doomed to being rejected by their fellows. Their fellow-countrymen do not usually recognize themselves in their attempt at self-assertion and they are therefore forced to deny what they are in front of the very fellows from whom they have objectively distanced themselves. The outcome is that both parties find themselves caught up in a process of mutual rejection, which is also a process of mutual accusations of rejection. Sub-proletarians dream of enjoying, simultaneously, despite the incompatibility that exists between the two systems, the economic advantages associated with 'risk' (advantages that they have discovered thanks to the capitalist economy), moral and material security, and the solidarity guaranteed them by tradition (advantages specific to the precapitalist social and economic system).

In the same way, immigrants, who are 'sub-proletarians' in the order of identity, inevitably attempt to reconcile the twofold benefits of, on the one hand, a heterogeneity that is desired, total and totally original, and, on the other, of no longer being obliged to submit themselves to a perpetual evaluation and to evaluate themselves in a heteronymous way, and therefore to force themselves to undertake the work of correction – which is experienced as shame – needed if they are to obtain and be awarded marks for good behaviour. From that point of view, the situation generated by immigration is like no other. Indeed, whereas a stigma could, in other circumstances, provide the economic and social foundations, the political and symbolic arguments, the unifying principles and a mobilizing base for a rebellion (e.g. nationalist or regionalist), it may not be enough to truly guarantee the cultural identity of immigrants. At risk of contradicting the fictions that inspire politicians who boast of recognizing and promoting their 'cultural identity', are we not entitled to ask whether a cultural identity can be based solely upon a stigma, and whether or not it can be valid and recognized in the absence of any guarantee supplied by a state? Thanks to a sort of ironic revenge on the part of history, it is those who were and still are both the first and the last victims of 'blood and soil' nationalist ideologies who are now being forced, in order to realize their identity, to create from scratch their 'soil', their 'blood', their 'language', their 'ethnicity' (which is no more than a euphemism for 'race'), their 'culture', or all the 'objective' criteria that can serve as 'proofs' of their identity and as reasons for laying claim to that identity. The paradox finally becomes complete when we end up with a sort of 'nationalism without a nation' or 'patriotism without a *patrie*', or a 'territoriality without a territory'. This can lead to the demand for a territory, and for relocation within what is still an impossible territory – and it is impossible because *jus soli* has not been converted, or 'naturalized', into *jus sanguinis*.

Any stigmatization that is, apparently, the product of a territory that has been stigmatized always eventually produces an actual territory that is claimed as a stigmatized territory and a territory for the stigmatized. As a result of spatial discrimination, which is also necessarily a social and cultural discrimination through the intermediary of space, certain estates in the suburbs of the big conglomerations (Paris, Lyons, Grenoble, Marseille, etc.), temporary hostels and council estates inhabited exclusively or mainly by immigrant families, most of them from the Maghreb, have during recent clashes been claimed as 'independent' territories that have to be appropriated in the face of a French population that is nationally and socially different, and especially the police, who are the guardians of the social and spatial order: 'This is our place', 'We are on our own territory', 'The estate belongs to us'. This should be understood as meaning: 'We (the stigmatized) are at home here, in our stigmatized place, which stigmatizes us and which we stigmatize.' In the circumstances, these slogans are so many manifestations of self-assertion. And is it not precisely this 'appropriation', which is 'impossible' not only for reasons of a cultural order, but also for supplementary reasons of a juridical order, that lies at the origin of the violence and the culture of violence, of a pathetic will to appropriate an impossible world?

The body of the naturalized citizen

Until such time as we see the conversion of one set of laws and rights into another set and, in the case of immigrant populations, the simultaneous conversion of 'naturalization' into the realization of a process of naturalization in the mode of 'it goes without saying', all we can do is to act as though becoming a naturalized French citizen were merely a technical operation that had no effect on the profound identity of the individual concerned. We have to act as though it were nothing more and nothing less than 'changing one's papers' or 'taking French papers', even if it means discovering after the event that one is only 'French on paper' and that one cannot be and does not want to be – because one cannot be – anything more than 'French on paper'.

> 'Does becoming a naturalized French citizen change anything about the way I look? Is it written on my forehead so that everyone can read it, because if there is anything written on my face, it's my face itself, the face my parents gave me when they brought me into the world in which they made me; that's what you can read on my face, and not the French nationality I might or might not have. Or do I have to go around proclaiming "Here I am – take a good look at me, I am not the man you think I am, and not even the man you see" – and then take out my French national identity card – but what identity is that? – and say to them: "You may not have realized it yet, but take a good look at me; I do have French nationality (which, between you and me, is not at all the same as saying: I am French) and I'll prove it to you. Look!".'[27]

Because stigma is primarily, as Erving Goffman (1963) reminds us, a matter of *visibility*, it is the most obviously physical features, or a person's physical appearance, that we see first. More so than any other dominated person – as this is, as a general rule, true of all the dominated – the immigrant possesses only his body. He exists only to the extent that he is his body and, ultimately, only to the extent that he is a physical body, a labour-body. Names, speech (accent and pronunciation), the marks imprinted on the body or worn on the body (tattoos, hair, beards, moustaches, etc.), clothes – i.e. the body as a whole, incorporated features as well as everything to do with the body – all serve as supports for the stigma, and become stigmatized features. Stigmatization (social, cultural, ethnic or even political) produces stigmatized features to precisely the same extent that they seem, thanks to the backlash effect, to be its product. These features are, as a general rule, the first to be affected – and those that are most affected – by assimilation, no matter whether it is designed to reduce them or make them disappear as though by magic, or whether it forces them constantly to make an attempt to correct them (which can take the form of hypercorrection), to euphemize them, to knock them into shape or even to magically negate them. The reason why all those who are stigmatized – i.e. all those who occupy stigmatized positions within social space – experience the body as the geometric locus for all the stigmas that can be inflicted upon them, is no doubt that the body, which is both a physical individuality and a social product, is both, on the one hand, the most difficult thing of all to modify and, on the other, the very thing that has been most worked upon, polished and cultivated, and that is most amenable to modification when social pressures demand it. Because the body is the first part of a person we see, it is an object of presentation and self-presentation. We present ourselves and are present through our bodies, and the body is the bearer of social identity: it is that identity. That is why the body is the object of attempts to make it presentable, or in other words to model it in such a way as to make it conform as closely as possible to what is seen as a legitimate configuration.

One's relationship with one's body, and the representation one has or wishes to give of it, are particular ways of experiencing the social position one occupies, and of experiencing it through one's experience of the discrepancy between the ideal body and one's own body, as it is reflected back to us by the reactions of others. Seen and named by others, objectified by the gaze of others, the dominated body is a shameful body, a shy, clumsy body with little self-assurance, a body that is experienced with unease. It is a body that betrays itself.

Being comfortable and uncomfortable with one's body are as different as the two ways of being naturalized that we evoked earlier. Being comfortable and being uncomfortable with one's body are to one another what a naturalization of which one is ashamed is to a naturalization that is fully assumed. Both assume, in their respective domains, classes of agents who, whilst they give the same recognition to, in the one case, physical conformity and legitimate bodily behaviour and, in the other, legitimate nationality, do not have the same ability to do so.[28]

An unhappy relationship with the body (and, correlatively, with nationality) betrays the discomfort experienced by anyone who feels betrayed by their body (and also by their nationality) or by any part of the body that is subject to representation – to being presented to others and to the way others represent it. This is why the body or part of the body can become the object of a stigma. A name, language or an accent can all become a stigma. In more general terms, so can everything we call a 'culture' – that mark, which is at once hidden and displayed, inscribed on the body, on gestures, postures, ways of 'carrying [*porter*] one's body and behaving [*se comporter*] with one's body' (Bourdieu), because the body is that which embodies a culture. The discomfort one feels in one's body and through one's body has its equivalent in the discomfort one experiences in one's nationality or through one's nationality (both old and new) and, therefore, when faced with one's naturalization. It might even be said that there are circumstances in which a body of which we are ashamed simply reproduces and expresses the discomfort and 'shame' that are bound up with the fact of being naturalized. Always uncertain of themselves, always correcting themselves, the naturalized constantly watch themselves, as though they feel themselves to be under constant surveillance, and tirelessly correct their behaviour. They often run the risk of overdoing it, of, as one might say, going too far in the attempt to get it right (which is another way of betraying oneself), rather than through mere clumsiness or inappropriate behaviour.

Seeing themselves through the eyes of others (or what they imagine to be the eyes of others), as though they were looking at themselves from the outside, people who have been naturalized come to see themselves as other than what they are, as strangers to themselves. Depending on whether one is dominant or dominated, one is either to oneself what one is for others and thanks to others, or one is for others what one is for or through oneself. And, to the extent that they are part of the body and name, neither the body nor the names themselves – even the names we bear, or what we call 'proper' names – escape stigmatization and the effects of stigmatization, in other words the characteristic logic of symbolic domination.[29]

'When I introduce myself as Bou– Hammas [Hammas is his forename], everyone sees the immigrant, the Arab immigrant, as they put it, or in other words my appearance: the black hair, which is obviously black and curly – that's how they see people of my type, a bit artistic, and therefore with long hair – the swarthy skin, as they also put it – it's a cliché, the moustache – Arabs always have a moustache, an Arab without a moustache is almost not an Arab; they don't know why Arabs are more likely to have moustaches rather than beards, but they can see perfectly well that they do have them: big moustaches, little moustaches, a wisp, a shadow, a hint of a moustache, but always something on the lips so that it cannot be said that "He's cut his moustache off" – and I actually do look like that: dark, long curly hair, moustache. . . . But if I introduce myself as Bou– Bernard, it's Bernard they see and not Bou–, and it's Bernard they hear and picture. . . . Obviously, they are astonished to find out that this Bernard is really a Muslim, and not a Bernard like any other Bernard. But, unless you come across a self-confessed racist – it happens – an unrepentant racist – because ordinary racists are two a penny, and they deny being racists; "racist" has become an insult and no one wants to be insulted or to insult themselves by being called a racist; their behaviour is racist but they deny being racists – people can put up with that, even find it flattering; in their heart of hearts they're pleased. . . . Pleased to find an immigrant who is not like all the rest, and they obviously take credit for that, their society, the French society that has "civilized" them: "He's an Arab, but he's a good worker"; pleased to prove to themselves that they are not racists: "He's an Arab, but I gave him a job: Arab, Black or Jew, what I see is work that has been well done, that's all, the rest is nothing to do with me." They are also pleased because, intuitively, they feel that they are in a position of strength, that they always have the upper hand and that an Arab will probably cost them less for the same work – which is true, you only have to look, for example, at markets where there are Arabs, Blacks, Asians, when they have a fruit and vegetable stall, they squeeze the profit margins a little bit more and they are cheaper – and they can't lose. And then, if it's an Arab, they can always say: "Arab work"; and it's always "Arab work": if it is well done, it is good work despite the fact that he's an Arab; if it's badly done, it's not surprising: it's "Arab work". And the Arab knows that: he knows that his work, good or bad, is always "Arab's work", and so it has to be better so as to be work, because it is Arab's "work"; and because it is "Arab's work", it is cheaper. That means they win both ways: the quality of the work and its cost. So you can understand why waiters in cafés call themselves Marcel. Can you imagine a customer calling out "Mohamed, a Ricard"? It's "Jeannot", if not "Jean". A nickname is even more acceptable than a forename. Even those concerned find nicknames easier to accept; they are given them, they get given them despite themselves, they don't choose them – like the (French) nationality you are talking about – in the way you chose the nicknames you give yourself . . . Kader, Karim, Mus– [short for Mustapha; the other nicknames are diminutives of Abdelkader, Abdelkrim, etc.], that's beginning to be acceptable, the French are beginning to get used to it. But you don't hear "Mo-amed, get yourself over here". In extreme cases, you might hear that on a building site; that's what "Mohamed" is for; whereas at home, "Si Mohamed" is a respectful way of addressing someone you don't know; we call him "Si Mohamed" in the way that you say "Please, sir". So you understand that in the service industry, especially if you are dealing with clients, you need a nickname and you always get one: the way that you are careful about how you dress (tie, waistcoat, white shirt), about how you move, about how you speak, about how you behave; if you don't give yourself a nickname, your boss, your pals or the customers will do it for you.' (Bou– Hamass, 25, originally from the south of Algeria; graphic designer in an advertising agency; after having 'knocked around', as he puts it, all over the world, and especially in Scandinavia, took courses at an art school in Belgium).

Far from solving the paradox of immigration, as one might expect it to do, and far from guaranteeing or completing the full integration of immigrants into French society and the French nation, naturalization, to the extent that it can no more suppress objective differences and the conflicts that are objectively generated by those differences than it can suppress the will to differentiate or the objective effect of the differentiation, tends, contrary to all expectations, to perpetuate the problems of immigration. What is worse, it seems to exacerbate them because of the way it converts them. Whilst it does little or nothing to change the social condition of immigrants – even if it does change their social status – naturalization does modify the whole nature of the problems that arise for them and the problems they create. To the extent that they are constituted as 'immigrants' problems', or in other words problems for groups that are 'extraordinary' because of the specificity (which is first and foremost juridical) of immigrants (and this way of identifying them by assigning them an origin and a group, constitutes our whole understanding of immigration; it is the alpha and the omega of all that can be thought, known and said about them), even ordinary problems become problems of identity within the nation, or national problems concerning groups of nationals.

Appendix
Three Interviews Concerning Identity

I

'You are always asking yourself questions and they are always asking you questions. Are you French, and in what sense? If you're not French, why not? It's all suspicion. The suspicion has changed its tone. For our parents, the suspicions were about work. Aren't they taking jobs from the French? Do they pay taxes? Aren't they robbing France, family allowances, social security and so on? It's the same thing for us: are they French, do they love France or not? They have to prove it: military service, war; we saw that with the Gulf War. They begin to ask you if you are still in contact with Algeria, with the Algerian you are. How often do you go there, even if you don't go there and have no reason to? You read newspapers from back there, you listen to the radio from back there, even if there's nothing to read and nothing to listen to. Anyone can listen to *raï* in the same way that they listen to rock, but when I listen to *raï*, it's suspicious, it's because I'm not French or because I'm a bad Frenchman, it's atavism, it's in the blood. And I tell you, it's scientists who are doing this work, it's science; I've answered questionnaires like that, and now they are asking kids at school these questions: "couscous or steak?" and of course all the kids say "steak, McDonald's". It's enough to put you off couscous, and it has put them off it – the moment you hear, even at school, intercultural this and intercultural that – multicultural; identity this and identity that....I don't know who designs these questionnaires, who bets on them, who makes something out of it – it must bring something in for someone, I don't know who, or who has an interest in it – but what I can say is that the scientists, sociologists, psychologists, – I don't know – they're no good, they're not bright, they're not clever. They call it the *quid*, in search of the *quid*: who are you? I'll tell them who I am. It's not as though I had problems with myself; I'm not seeing a psychiatrist, or in a hospital. I know very well who I am, and I don't need them to tell me. They know nothing about me. And if they want to know, they just have to look at people. But they are incapable of understanding anything, nothing at all, so they should stop asking questions, asking you questions. Let them ask themselves about what they are, see if they can answer their own questions about themselves, before answering questions about others – questions that the others never even ask themselves. They should ask themselves why they are asking questions, why they enjoy asking questions. Who are you? *Quid*? It's unhealthy. . . . Please, you are part of that world, they're your colleagues, please, tell them that. Tell them they're perverts, sick, voyeurs, interrogators with the souls of cops, they're soul cops. Tell them that, please. That would make me happy. When is all this going to stop? For us, it's questions 24 hours a day, 365 days a year; you hear it, see it and read it everywhere all your life, from the day you are born to the day you die – and especially on everyone's face, in everyone's eyes. And now the identity checks have started again, the look in the cop's eyes, you see that – that moron, and it can't be said that he looks like a genius, asks you: "Your papers [*tes papiers*]." No, sorry, they've taught them now, even Pasqua has learned that lesson, they've taught them to say *vous*: "Your papers, please [*vos papiers, s'il vous plaît*]." You take out your CNI [Carte nationale d'identité]: French, nationality: French. He shakes his head. Deep inside himself, he must be saying to himself: "Another one." He'd have liked to be the only one who was French, the good Frenchman, along with all the other Frenchmen like him. They say he has "French roots". What roots? Roots aren't pretty but they are roots. I suppose other French people just have French branches, French foliage. You can see all that going through the cop's mind, even if his eyes don't shine with intelligence. So he says: "OK, OK. Move along [*circule*]." He gives you back your papers. But I say to myself "*circule, virgule*" [literally: "move along, comma"]. That's what you are: a comma, that's all. Perhaps less than a comma, as commas have their uses; they give sentences a meaning. You learn punctuation at school, and you don't put commas just anywhere. But try telling that to the cop. If he's learned to use commas, that is. For him the *virgule* is your features, he doesn't know that a comma can give France a meaning. A France without commas would be an incomprehensible France. But it's the comma that says so, not France. I'm not fooling myself.

'. . . What does it mean, this integration that is all the rage, that they keep bending our ears with? Either it exists, and there's nothing more to be said about it: that's the way it is, that's all there is to it; it's not worth talking about, it's talking about it that makes it exist. On the contrary. The way things are going, it might well be the best "integrated" who'll shout loudest, who'll rebel against integration. In my view, integration is an accusation. "What, after everything we have done for you, you were born in our country, in our hospitals; we brought you up in our crèches, our nursery schools, we educated you, taught you in our schools, and, after all that, you are still not ''integrated''. You are hopeless. You are Arabs, and you will remain Arabs.'' If that's not racism, what is? And we experience it every day, it's humiliating, shameful. They want to get us on their side, but at the same time they make it clear to us that we can never catch up with them. And they call it integration.'

AÏCHA (a girl in the group): 'We learned about integration at school, in maths. We learned about exponential integrals: it's an asymptotic curve that you can extend to infinity, but it never touches the abscissa. It's the same with integration: you have to chase after it, and the closer you get, the more they tell you've not quite made it.'

SAÏD: 'If we are going to talk maths, I think it's set theory myself, where you have integrated sets defined by the limits that separate what is inside from what is outside. That is why we are ill at ease with all this talk: there are ''good immigrants'' who are integrated or who can be integrated, and ''bad immigrants'' who are hopeless. Our parents are ''bad immigrants''. Being products of French society, we are ''better'' than our parents; society is obliged to recognize that, otherwise it's pointless; what does it think it's doing with its schools? – they place a lot of emphasis on schools – but we don't want to have anything to do with French society, because of our origins, because of our parents. I wonder why all the politicians who talk about that fail to realize how provocative it is, how crude, I would go so far as to say how racist all this well-intentioned talk about integration is. And it will end up by having the opposite result: the best integrated will end up saying: we want nothing to do with your integration; even those who feel the most French will say: we don't want your nationality if we have to go through the Caudine Forks and the humiliations of your new Code de la nationalité.'

AÏCHA: 'It's like the Gulf War we were just talking about – I've been thinking about it – I said to myself: suppose there was a war between France and Brazil, not that it's very likely. I wonder if any journalist would have the nerve, or even think of going around every porter's lodge in the XVI, XVII and XVIII *arrondissements* and asking the Portuguese kids if they supported France or Brazil? The same applies to me: I'm no more Iraqi than a Portuguese kid in a porter's lodge is Brazilian. If that happened, I'm sure there would be a general outcry: there would be talk of journalistic ethics, of freedom of opinion. With Arabs in France – and there's nothing Arab about them – it just goes unnoticed. Not only did no one protest, but some of ''our lot'' (inverted commas) took advantage, manipulated – and it's them I hate most – they and the... – they were saying it everywhere, because they can profit from it, profit from it at our expense, that ''It is thanks to us that the suburbs remained calm''. Did anyone really see them? I don't think so, but everyone pretended they had because it was in everyone's interest. And obviously they were paid accordingly and then came and told us they'd been defending us! They conned us, exploited us for their own ends. And they call themselves "brothers", solidarity.'

II

'A European passport. I wave it. It reconciles me to myself. Ever since I got it, it has never left me, it's always in my pocket, I kiss it [he takes out his passport, pats it and kisses it]. This is a European passport; before, I only had a French passport. Every passport has its colour. We call them by their colours. You have the green, that's what we call it, the "green passport" [*basbour lakhdar* in Arabic] – at home there is a pop song called "The Green Passport": that was at a time when it was very difficult in Morocco to obtain a passport to emigrate, so we sang about the green passport, the passport of freedom; you have the blue, the ordinary French passport; you have the maroon passport, the European passport. It opens every door, crosses every border, even if you are called Mohamed, even if you have a moustache and look like an Arab. That's when you realize how much power a passport has. It transforms you.'

'Transforms you into what? French nationality makes you French by right, French in the eyes of the law, but a European passport does not transform you into, say, a German.'

'Yes it does. It transforms me completely. Freedom is not just the freedom to travel: no visa, no trouble at the border. It's with myself. It gives me the freedom to be me. It means freedom, life.'

'I don't understand. "It's with myself." I thought it was the green passport that gave you the freedom to be yourself. So why doesn't the blue passport give you that freedom and why is it only the maroon passport that reconciles you to yourself, as you put it?'

'It's obvious: because the European passport does not really exist; it's an abstraction. What is Europe? It's geography pure and simple. Nothing else.'

'It's a territory, a set of national territories where you are free from the allegiance that comes from belonging to any particular national territory, or in other words a nation or a nationality.'

'Yes, absolutely. You are free from that allegiance. Because there is an allegiance. How can I put it? The allegiance you were born into, the one you forget, it seems quite natural, it is part of it and you

don't realize it. Then there is the allegiance you experience as something new, the allegiance inscribed in naturalization, that you pay to
the nationality you acquire. That is something everyone has to live
with, something that everyone experiences. And anyone who has
had anything to do with law learns that from the textbooks. And
then there is the situation in which a territory is not yours, is not the
territory you appropriate.'

'*Or that appropriates you –* '

'Yes, it works both ways. You appropriate it and it appropriates you
by appropriating the nationality of that territory for you, and by
being appropriated by that nationality. So, a national territory with
which you have no relationship of allegiance, because that is what
nationality is, opens up to you as though you were in your own
country and at the same time allows you to go on thinking that you
are not in your own country.'

'*Is that what you mean by freedom with yourself, the freedom to be
yourself?*'

'Yes, that's it. It's more than that. I am no longer trapped inside
myself, with me, and the other me, the Moroccan and that other
me (French nationality). Me and myself just stare at each other.
Where is the truth? It is either the Moroccan me or the French me,
each reminds me of the other. You are French, you think of yourself
as French, people take you for French, and that reminds you of the
Moroccan who has been smothered, who is deep down inside you,
silent, absent, discreet, dumb, who hides, keeps quiet and keeps to
himself. And so, deep inside, you are more Moroccan than ever in this
situation. You are Moroccan, you regard yourself as Moroccan, but
with the first move you make, you realize that it's not true, that you
are not as Moroccan as all that. Perhaps you lie to yourself, just for
the pleasure of it. But that doesn't prevent you from living. Let's not
exaggerate.'

'*But how does the European passport free you from all that – from
being trapped inside yourself?*'

'Trapped inside myself. Inside myself, that's all. In that impossible
dialogue with the France where I am living. As we say in Arabic, "I
am in her belly" [in Arabic] and perhaps now "she is in my belly" [in
Arabic]. Am I French, aren't I French? There has to be an answer.
That's between France and me. And, increasingly, the answer is, by
becoming naturalized or, as they say here, through culture, assimilation, integration – that's today's fashion – the more the question
arises, the more crucial it becomes, the more obsessional. You have

to pretend to be deaf, you have to not want to hear for its not to be asked. Some play that game – they cheat, or perhaps they are being sincere, but I still admire them. No, they are cheating, telling themselves lies. And they certainly take their revenge, let off steam somewhere, spit out the lies, play act, act out a part. Otherwise, it's impossible to keep going.'

III

DJ was born in France and, to be more specific, in the Belleville area and, as he likes to say, in 1968. His father, who was in his forties at the time, had already been an immigrant in France for a long time. Originally from the Oranie and, to be more precise, from the region of the Lala Maghnia mountains in the west of Algeria, he originally emigrated in accordance with the mode of emigration common to all men of his generation. Just after the Second World War (in 1947–8), when he was still very young (19–20 years old) and therefore unmarried (he would remain unmarried until relatively late, or until he was over 30), he came to France to join all the other emigrants from his region, who were employed in farms in the north of France and then in the mines of the Valenciennes coal basin. Like the majority of the emigrants who were both his contemporaries and his compatriots, he was constantly coming and going between his *douar* [village] and France, alternating between the state of being a fellah or traditional peasant and the condition of the immigrant worker, except for the period between 1956 and 1962, when he was trapped in Algeria because of the fighting there. Immediately after independence and the restoration of freedom of movement between Algeria and France in the spring of 1963, he again emigrated to France, but this time with his family (his wife and three children). In France, and with the most total discretion as even his wife was not informed, he opted for French nationality, taking care, according to what his children now say, not to be confused with the '*harkis*'.[30] His children (two brothers and their younger sister), who acted as informants, wanted to make it clear that he 'enjoyed none of the benefits provided for the repatriated' (because either he was not repatriated or he did not want to be), that 'he became a naturalized French citizen as soon as he came to France', that he 'held an Algerian passport' (and therefore Algerian nationality), that 'he took French nationality with us, his children in mind, so as to give us an easier life in France'. They themselves only discovered their father's French nationality – and therefore their own – when they, or at least the three eldest who were born in Algeria before 1953, had to apply for the French nationality that was already theirs by right (because their father was naturalized) although they didn't know it.

The fourth child in the family, and the first to be born in immigration in France, DJ has his *baccalauréat*. It was a miracle. And DJ is acutely aware of that miracle: it was a social miracle because he is, as he still says today, the only one of his friends, who are children from the same estate and children who went to the same classes (at the local elementary school and then at middle school) 'to have gone to the *lycée*, to have completed his secondary education and to have got his *bac*'. It was indeed an educational miracle in that his *bac* was obtained in a quite unexpected way, as was the whole school career that led up to it. DJ was taken in hand – completely and not just in educational terms – by a friendly and protective French family which had noticed his talent for football and which, being both generous and sympathetic, wanted to be of some help to the boy's parents and to his whole family at a difficult time in their lives: DJ's father, a truck driver, had just suffered a serious accident from which he never completely recovered, and had to support a family of seven children (three boys and four girls), the eldest of whom, a boy, was mentally handicapped.

DJ: 'I was starting to show off. I was the eldest boy, as my brother, who is older than me, was out of it; he wasn't quite right in the head and was put in a home where he could have occupational therapy. . . . It was that family who got me out of a tight corner, even if it was too hard for me. I couldn't accept leaving the house, the estate, the neighbourhood, all my mates. It was a whole different education at their place. . . . I now greatly regret that I didn't take more advantage of it – Of what? They invited a lot of people home, for example – all good people; so I played the fool, I said that didn't interest me, that it was nothing to do with me, I sulked, didn't show up. Whereas I should have taken advantage of all that. . . . Yes, I was stupid – that's right; deep down inside, I must have thought that their world was nothing to do with me. It's true; for example, they insisted on keeping me with them on Saturdays and Sundays, but I never wanted to; as soon as I got out of school on the Friday, I went home immediately; in reality, I went back to the neighbourhood, the estate, the mates. That was my own world. Freedom! Back there, it was like prison, a cage. . . . Yes, an animal in a cage. . . . Yes, football. They did everything to get me playing football. I signed up with Red Star. A dream! But I went to two training sessions and then gave up. . . . Why? It was the same thing all over again, it wasn't my world. At the training sessions, they had us playing fifteen or seventeen a side, to give everyone a trial. You couldn't choose your position, they made you play in every position. Whereas I just wanted to play. I preferred being a little star in the local team to all the work they made you do in football academy. So I dropped it. There may have been an element of revenge in it too – I dropped football. All the same, it was that family who got me out of a tight spot, even though it was very hard for me. They don't talk to me about it now, but I tell them. What a fool I was – that's what I tell them. It put me off football, but it did get me my *bac*. Just think, of all my mates, out of the whole neighbourhood and perhaps the whole school, I'm the only one to have gone to *lycée*, to have got as far as the *bac* and to have passed my *bac*. All the rest of them: nothing. And it still goes on today . . . it's the same everywhere, the same for everyone, jail, unemployment and, what's worse than all that, drugs, AIDS. I've just lost my friend, an ace guy and a genius in his own way: addiction and AIDS! So you understand, I could have been like all those people, me too; and I did come close to it. So you understand: I can't abandon them now, I can't – be unfaithful to them. That's the way it is. Just because I've got away, because I've got a job and because I'm earning money, doesn't mean that the rest of them are worthless, good for nothings, useless, or that they aren't intelligent.'

NORA (DJ's partner): 'Oh yes, he can talk. That's the way it is when monsieur makes some money, he gives it away to them. Money: he's given away almost 5,000 francs like that. Monsieur is generous. How many times when I come home late at night, I have to step over bodies sprawled on the floor: these are monsieur's pals who have nowhere else to go, who are usually half-pissed and who have come asking for hospitality. It's a never-ending battle between the two of us.'

DJ: 'After my *bac*, I enrolled at university to pass the time, to see what it was like, because I didn't know what I wanted to do. I enrolled in AES (economic and social administration) because, with my *bac G*, I was told that that was what would suit me best. I enrolled, but didn't get very far. I got no further. In the meantime, I discovered photography, found my way, as they say. Now I make my living from photography. . . . I make a good living. On top of that, it gives me the chance to travel, to visit other countries, and not as a tourist in a hurry. I've been to all the Eastern bloc countries: Poland, Hungary, Romania; a lot of other countries in the third world, ideologically or politically close to the communist world. . . . I used to travel on behalf of the mayor's office in the town where I live, it's a communist council. That's how I got to go to Angola, Mozambique, Namibia – Algeria, that's the one and only time I've been there – the Western Sahara. And Asia, China, Vietnam; in America, I've been to Cuba, Costa Rica, and so on.'

And, armed with the eye of his camera and also with the eye of a former child of the suburban estates, he does indeed bring back reportages with a high social content from his travels. DJ is now thinking of starting his own business, his own photo agency, with the help of his partner, who has also taken up photography. Nora, who is also the daughter of an immigrant Algerian family, trained to work in the communications industry; she has also done publicity work for an amateur dramatic company in the suburbs.

DJ often speaks of the social injustices suffered by the young people with whom he feels himself to be in communion and who share, he thinks, a common destiny. His friends have the same background and come from the same origins and the same social condition. They are childhood friends he likes to see again and with whom he has always stayed in contact, and he has shown himself to be very generous to them – generous with everything, with money but also with advice – and he is all the more inclined to understand and excuse them because he is socially divorced from them:

'I am the only one of the whole gang to have got away, the only one to have a *bac*, and now I'm the only one with a job, who is making money; all the others are unemployed, in jail or dealers, either they are shooting up or they've already passed away, like my best friend who died from drugs and AIDS. Or, at the very least they are "on the sidelines", play no part in life and society, just watch and wait for it to throw them something – it's hard, lads of the same age as you, lads you grew up with, they were good-looking and intelligent – they could have done anything, and then a few years later you see them looking like wrecks. It makes you wonder why.... Why the injustice? What's the difference between you and them? Nothing makes any sense: that's the conclusion you reach. And nothing does make sense any more. Why aren't they like you, or why aren't you like them? And when they come knocking on your door – or asking for money, you can't refuse – you can't do that, its not possible. That would be spineless, heartless, brainless, too. Because you do have to think about it a bit. It's a hard world, and they are not always in the wrong.'

He knows from his own experience of the educational system that both academic success (and to some extent his own success) and failure (the failure of all his other friends) are very arbitrary, and may, as he says, 'depend on trivial things, the accidents of life'. DJ's father is a member of that generation of emigrants who discovered nationalism, and therefore politics, thanks to the immigration in France, or in other words by coming into contact with militants involved in political action, by learning from the trade unions, and workers' political struggles of all kinds, as well as from what was to him the novel experience of urban and working-class life. And even if that double experience was at the time inevitably very limited, in both his case and that of many other immigrants who were his compatriots, extremely poor and reduced to a minimum of elementary and indispensable contacts, it did lead to a political awakening and an awakening to the political for a whole generation of emigrants. As DJ's father never fails to remind his children – sons and daughters – they have received this as their heritage.

> 'That is our father's heritage, and perhaps the only heritage he will leave us.... We had a television before we got the fridge, much to my mother's annoyance. When we were kids, the news was the only thing my father made us watch together. He would comment on it – in his own way. When I think about it now, I laugh. It was all so naive. But something of that still stays with us...an awareness of political life; not political parties but the realities of life. All of us, my brothers, my other sisters, belong to local associations, neighbourhood associations, charitable associations. We talk, we think. We listen to the politicians, especially when the election campaigns begin, we don't miss anything, we listen to what they say, read what they say. If only to laugh at them. They can be such bloody fools, they just talk nonsense about things they know nothing about: young people, the suburbs, drugs, and even AIDS and condoms.'

It is therefore not surprising that contemporary debates about young people (or the *beurs* as they are called – it is difficult to find a single *beur*, not to mention a *beurette*, who likes being called that), about the French nationality they already have or that will be granted them one day, and about the relationship (good or bad) they are likely to have with that nationality and the way they come to terms with it, not to mention all that is said at such length about integration, should be followed, talked about, discussed and debated and analysed with care and great interest. Besides, there is no shortage of opportunities, as current affairs demonstrate in several ways. This is especially true whenever some event of a political or social nature that occurs in the life of the nation reveals the truth about their situation – in obviously contradictory ways, because it varies, depending on how different people view immigration, that is to say, French society (one is seen through the intermediary of the other). But there is always an element of suspicion. The French children of this category of immigrants are expected to be loyal to the French nation and a French nationality that do not accept them, and their loyalty therefore has to be put to the test. This is what happened, as DJ and his other friends never stop recalling, when a certain number of events 'hit the headlines' in their lifetimes. What was said on these occasions must have had a major impact on all these young people, who take such a particularly critical and often – it has to be said – extremely lucid view of their position that they can still quote what they see as the most damning comments, complete with dates and the names of their authors: journalists, politicians, community activists and so on.

The Gulf War was, of course, a prime example of these events that 'leave them speechless' and provide them with 'proof of their impotence':

> 'We realize that we can't do anything, that we are totally impotent – we have no means of reacting – we put up with all that without saying a word – a silence that suits everyone, starting with our people, our people more so than all the rest.'

To be more accurate, it was the commentaries it gave rise to that affected them (the commentaries rather than the war itself, because when one hears the reflections and protests of these young people, it is as though the war existed only through what was said about it, what was reported about it, and it was certainly in that way that it existed for them):

> 'We were all lumped together, just to make it more sensational, to shock, to make people more afraid. It wasn't just to set people talking, or even to bring tears to their eyes, but to give them an excuse for carrying a shot gun and opening fire on the first kid that comes along.... The battlefield is not just over there in the sand dunes, it's here in the suburbs too, the enemy is here at home, the enemy is the Arab and all the Arabs are living next door, even if they do have French nationality. Yes, they have the nationality, but they aren't French. So – careful!'

Before the Gulf War, there was a whole series of other events in which they were implicated, according to public opinion – mainly because of the way the papers exploited and interpreted them – states or just groups of Arab or Muslim groups and, here in France, as one thing leads to another, immigrant populations that are supposedly Arab and Muslim (even when they are of French nationality). The most important were the so-called 'Islamic headscarf' affair and, more generally, the whole discourse on Islam (ordinary Islam and 'fundamentalist' Islam) and the issue of whether or not it is compatible with having French nationality. Then there was the question of polygamy (as though only Muslims were polygamous). This mode of behaviour is quite alien to French cultural traditions (and national identity, one might say), and it is criticized because of social cost.

Similarly, excision is seen as a 'barbaric' practice and as an assault on the physical integrity of the individual. Even the more than prolific discourse on integration does not escape serious criticism. Objectively, it has the same secret, and unspoken, meaning as the denunciatory intention that is behind every other form of discourse about the ever more burdensome presence of immigrants. Their presence is, if we recall the stigmatization effect and the stigmatized body, really only that of a body that is both disgraceful and unaesthetic. That, at all events, is what they see as the meaning of constant talk of integration, which they hear everywhere, in connection with anything and everything, and in almost unanimous terms. It means that their integration is never complete and that it will probably never be complete, because it does not depend on them, on 'what we are, what we do, what we think, what we believe, but on what they want us to be, do, think, believe and feel'. This is a discourse whose function is to recall that the integration we are talking about – and which they are talking about – is, in their case, something 'that always has to be begun again, always to be continued, never completed'. It is an achievement that is incomplete and therefore always liable to be revoked.

Being a discourse of suspicion and a discourse that is experienced by those concerned as offensive, or even as hurtful to their pride – and one might almost say their national pride, both to the extent that they are French and to the extent that they could have been other than French – it always alludes to the alternative nationality that continues to haunt everyone's mind, both theirs and that of their observers, who are watching them and never stop asking them questions and asking themselves questions about them. Whatever the content of the discourse, and whether or not it praises their success, even if we do not know what its evaluative criterion is (in reality, it comes down to the power to integrate, as the saying goes, France, its schools, its flag and its military service, its institutions as well as the integrative power of republican philosophy) or if we deem it to be inadequate, and whether or not it strives to ensure their promotion or, worst of all, decrees it impossible, usually on the basis of mere prejudice (because of their ethnic or national origins, because of a certain number of cultural dispositions, because of their confessional loyalties, etc.), it is seen as a stigmatizing discourse. It is an accusatory discourse that is in itself a basically unjust and ungrateful discourse. Despite the undoubtedly good intentions that lie behind it, it can prove to be a discourse of discrimination and exclusion.

What is being said here about DJ, about his relationship with the French nationality he received at birth, and whose possession is seen not so much as a right, as a *de facto* given – like it or not – and not, or no longer, as 'a favour you have to ask and then wait for it to be granted', does not apply to him alone. What DJ himself says of the French nationality he claims as of right, which he has of right just like every other French national who has been naturally naturalized – and this is of course not the same thing as claiming naturalization or demanding its acquisition (which is or should be automatic) – could be said by many other people. The same is true of everything that is being said about immigration. He finds it quite unacceptable: 'When they talk about your father, about your mother, and I don't just mean now, because I assume it's always been that way, you can't say "I'm French, that's nothing to do with me".' It seems that everyone who is, roughly speaking, in the same position, or who has the same position in French society, objectively agrees with him.

'If you are not French, what are you?'

> DJ: 'I don't know what I am, but I do know what I am not: I am not French, even though I am of French nationality, and still less am I Algerian.'

'What does that mean? That you are stateless? That it's a new way of being stateless?'

> 'Perhaps – but worse than that. Because someone who is stateless, who has been banished from his country, or has had to disappear from his country, basically knows what he is, knows that's what he is. Whereas for me, I mean us, there is nothing to stop us being Algerian and nothing to stop us being French. We've not been banished from anywhere. France is always there, and there is always the possibility that we, anyone, can be French, and we are French in France; now that Algeria exists, it is no longer like it used to be when there was no such thing as Algerian nationality. There again, Algeria has not banned us from being Algerian. On the contrary. No one is stopping us from being Algerian. We are not Algerian, and that's all there is to it, that's the way it is. So there is no statelessness. Perhaps there are even too many fatherlands, or rather a surplus of fatherlands, two fatherlands at once is too much. Which one is superfluous? Perhaps neither is a *patrie*. Perhaps, if that is what statelessness means, there are two possible *patries*, but they are both "abroad". How can I put it? They are all around us, like an environment. It's academic. Even France, we are there, we live there, we have to put up with it every day, and with its bloody problems, but also with its joys, and they do exist. But Algeria, that's a complete fiction. It's like the planet Mars. It means that we have no *patrie* at a gut level. But who does all this depend on? It depends on us, depends on me; not just me, or not me alone, but all of us. It depends on my relationship with the French

nationality I have, that I have always had. Even my father, he jokes about it now. But it's not a funny joke. I find his way of putting it truer than anything they say.'

'*How does he put it?*'

'He tells us this: "for 130 years we were French under France, but that did not make us French citizens; as for you – at the age of 10 you were already French citizens like other French citizens." And to cheer him up, I say "Once France was in our country – now, we are in France's country; that changes everything".'

12

Immigration and 'State Thought'

Although it is a universal phenomenon, migration is always discussed within the framework of the local unit and, insofar as we are concerned, within the framework of the nation-state.[1] Despite the extreme diversity of situations in which it occurs and despite the variations it displays in time and space, the phenomenon of emigration-immigration does exhibit *constants*, in other words characteristics (social, economic, juridical and political) that reappear throughout its history. These constants constitute, as it were, a sort of common and irreducible basis, which is both a product and an objectification of 'state thought'. State thought is a form of thought that reflects, through its own structures (mental structures), the structures of the state, which thus acquires a body (see Bourdieu 1993). The categories through which we think about immigration (and, more generally, our whole social and political world), or our social, economic, cultural and ethical categories – and we can never place too much emphasis on the role morality plays in the way we perceive the phenomenon of immigration – and, in a word, our political categories, are definitely and objectively (that is, without our being aware of it and, therefore, independently of our will), national or even nationalist categories. The structures of our most ordinary political understanding, or of the understanding that is spontaneously translated into our world-view, shape our perception of immigration, but they are at the same time shaped by it. They are basically *national* structures and they therefore act as such. They are structured structures in the sense that they are socially and historically determined products, but they are also structuring structures in the sense that they predetermine and organize our whole representation of the world, and therefore the world itself.

It is, without any doubt, because of all this that the migratory phenomenon as a whole – emigration and immigration – can only be described and interpreted through the categories of state thought. That mode of thought is completely inscribed within the line of demarcation that radically divides 'nationals' from 'non-nationals'. The line itself is invisible or scarcely perceptible but it has major implications. On the one hand, we have those who have quite naturally, or, as the lawyers put it, have 'by right', the nationality of the country (*their* country) from which they come – in other words of the state whose nationals they are and of the territory over which that state has sovereignty – and, on the other, we have those who do not have the nationality of the country in which they are resident.

The spirit of the state

It is also for all these reasons that we can say that thinking about immigration means thinking about the state, and that it is 'the state that is thinking about itself when it thinks about immigration'. And this is perhaps one of the last things we discover when we reflect upon the problem of immigration and work on immigration, whereas we should of course have begun with this, or at least should have known this before we started. What we discover in this way is the secret virtue of immigration: it provides an introduction, and perhaps the best introduction of all, to the sociology of the state. Why? Because immigration constitutes the limit of what constitutes the national state. Immigration is the limit that reveals what it is intrinsically, or its basic truth. It is as though it were in the very nature of the state to discriminate and, in order to do so, to acquire in advance all the necessary criteria of pertinence that are required to make the distinction, without which there can be no national state, between the 'nationals' it recognizes as such and in which it therefore recognizes itself, just as they recognize themselves in it (this double mutual recognition-effect is indispensable to the existence and function of the state), and 'others' with whom it deals only in 'material' or instrumental terms. It deals with them only because they are present within the field of its national sovereignty and in the national territory covered by that sovereignty. It has been said that this diacritical function of the state, which, strictly speaking, is one of *definition*, i.e. delineation,[2] is in the very nature of the state, and that it constitutes the state in all its forms and throughout its history. The need to discriminate is, it would seem, more imperative and by that very fact more prescriptive in the case of a republican nation-state. Such a state aspires to total national homogeneity – in other words homogeneity at every level: political, social, economic, cultural (and especially linguistic and religious).

Quite aside from the fact that it disturbs the national order, blurs the divide or the border line between what is and what is not national, and therefore perturbs or disturbs the order based upon that separation, immigration, or in other words the presence within the nation of 'non-nationals' (rather than those who are simply foreign to the nation), infringes upon the integrity of that order. It disturbs the mythical purity or perfection of that order, and it therefore prevents the full realization of that order's implicit logic. We can thus understand why, without taking to extremes the logic implicit in this state of affairs – that is, without perverting it – there is always a great temptation to lapse into a form of fundamentalism that is known all over the world, and that is cultivated and celebrated all over the world (today's religious fundamentalism is no more than a variant, and not even a new variant, as it exists prior to national fundamentalism, having existed before the reality of the nation itself, and because it has always coexisted alongside that fundamentalism). For those who take a 'purist' (or fundamentalist) view of the national order, immigration is supposedly the agent of the perversion of the national social order in its integrity and integrality because it concerns people who should not be there (if the national order were perfect, it would not have this flaw, this inadequacy) but who are there (rather as though they were the objectification or materialization of that flaw, that inadequacy and that inability to complete the nation). Immigration is undeniably a subversive factor to the extent that it reveals in broad daylight the hidden truth and the deepest foundations of the social and political order we describe as national. Thinking about immigration basically means interrogating the state, interrogating its foundation and interrogating the internal mechanisms of its structuration and workings. Using immigration to interrogate the state in this way means, in the final analysis, 'denaturalizing', so to speak, what we take to be natural, and 'rehistoricizing' the state or that element within the state that seems to have been afflicted by historical amnesia. It means, in other words, recalling the social and historical conditions of its genesis. Time helps us forget all these things, but time is not the only factor involved: time can succeed in this repressive operation only because it is both in our interests and in the interests of the state itself to forget its history. The 'naturalization' of the state, or of the state that exists inside our heads, makes it seem as though the state were an immediate given, as though it were an object that existed by itself or that was created by nature. It makes it seem that the state has been in existence from all eternity, that it has been freed of all determinations external to itself. It appears to exist independently of all historical considerations, independently of history and of its own history, from which we prefer to divorce it for ever, even though we never stop elaborating and telling that history. Immigration – and this is of course why it is so disturbing – forces us to unveil the state, to unveil the way we think about the state and the way it thinks about itself. And it is the way it thinks about immigration that gives this away. Being children of the nation-state and of the national categories we bear within us and which the state has implanted in us, we all think about immigration (in other words about those who are 'other' than ourselves, what they are, and through them, what we ourselves are) in the way that the state requires us to think and, ultimately, in the way that the state itself thinks.

'State thought' or 'spirit of the state' as analysed by Pierre Bourdieu is a mode of thought and a distinct way of thinking. The two appear to be inseparable. It is state thought that creates the state's mode of thinking about everything it is and about all the domains to which it is applied. In the same way, state thought may, as a result of its constancy, its repetitions, its own strength, and its ability to impose its way of thinking on others, have generated durable modes of thinking that are typical of state thought. We must therefore subject the postulates of state thought to critical reflection, to a process of 'delegitimizing' what is legitimate, of what goes without saying. We must delegitimize it in the sense of objectifying what is most deeply rooted within us, what is most deeply hidden in our social unconscious. Such an operation makes a desanctifying break with *doxa*. We have here an undertaking that everything within us resists: our entire social being (individual and collective) and everything that we commit to it with such passion – in other words our whole national being. For we exist only in this form and only within this framework: the framework and form of the nation. To take jurists as an example, it took all the audacity of a Hans Kelsen to free himself from state thought and even to rebel against that thought, and ultimately to contest the opposition that is de rigueur amongst jurists and (elsewhere) between 'national' and 'non-national' by demonstrating the arbitrary (or conventional) character of that distinction: the 'national' exists *de jure*, and belongs by nature or by virtue of state (the possession of the state of nationality) to the population that constitutes the state. Anyone who is 'foreign' (non-national) is subject to the competence and authority of a state in which he plays no part, and on whose territory he resides, lives and works only as a result of his presence there and for the duration of that presence. His presence does not have the same status as the presence within that territory of a national. Kelsen regards this difference as *purely conventional* or non-essential, and that leads him to reject the idea that the state is necessarily the juridical expression of a community.

The crimes of immigration; immigration on trial

Why this preamble about state thought? First, because immigration constitutes the privileged terrain on to which this form of thought is projected, as though on to a mirror. Second, because of all the domains of existence and of all the sectors of social life, delinquency is the one that owes, so to speak, most to this way of thinking. In the case of immigration, delinquency implies not only the offences that the police have to deal with or those recorded by the crime statistics but also, as one delinquency can hide another, a delinquency that might be described as situational or statutory (and almost 'onto-logical') because, at the deepest level of our mode of thought (i.e. state thought), it is synonymous with the very existence of the immigrant and with the very fact of immigration.

Unconsciously, or even when we are not fully conscious of it, the fact of being an immigrant is far from being a neutral element within the whole gamut of evaluations and judgements that are passed, should an offence be committed, on the delinquent. Even though those who pass these judgements (both the ones handed down by the juridical apparatus and those of the social apparatus – i.e. social judgements) are unaware of the fact, and even though they almost always do so against their will, the fact of being an immigrant delinquent (or a delinquent immigrant) constitutes, as a general rule, something of an aggravating circumstance. Because we spontaneously endorse expressions of public opinion, which exists inside our heads just as it exists inside the heads of everyone around us (this is *doxa*), we even see such circumstances as a supplementary offence in addition to the offence that has been committed and that has to be judged. Immigration is a latent, camouflaged offence (that of being an immigrant – an offence for which the subject in question bears no responsibility), which is brought to light by the actual offence that has been committed, by the objectified offence that has to be brought before the courts. Any trial involving a delinquent immigrant puts the very process of immigration on trial, first as a form of delinquency in itself and second as a source of delinquency. Before we can even speak of racism or xenophobia, the notion of 'double punishment' is therefore present within any judgement passed on the immigrant (and not only in the judgements handed down by judges sitting in court). It is rooted in state thought, and is the anthropological basis on which all our social judgements rest. 'Double punishment' exists objectively in our way of thinking, even before we make it exist in the objectified form of either the sanction of a legal tribunal or an administrative decision.

'Double punishment' exists inside our 'national' heads, because the very fact of immigration is tainted with the idea of being at *fault*, with the idea of anomaly and anomie. The immigrant presence is always marked by its incompleteness: it is an at-fault presence that is in itself guilty. It is a *displaced* presence in every sense of the term. It is physically and geographically displaced: in other words, it is spatially displaced because migration is primarily a spatial displacement. It is displaced in the moral sense too, in the sense in which we speak, for instance, of 'speaking out of turn' or of 'misplaced' discourse. It is as though our categories of thought, which are in this respect and as can never be said too often national categories, saw immigration itself as a form of delinquency, as an intrinsic delinquency. It is as though, because the immigrant is already in the wrong simply because he is present in a land of immigration, all his other sins are reduplicated and aggravated by the original sin of immigration. That is his first sin in the chronological sense because it necessarily precedes all the other sins that might be committed during the lifetime of an immigrant. It is a generative sin in the sense that it is the cause not of his actual sins themselves, but of the place, time and context (in other words of the social, economic and economic conditions) in which those sins are committed. Because it is an *objective* sin, immigration can never be totally bracketed out or neutralized, even when we try to do so in all objectivity. Immigration, with all the disparagement, disqualification and stigmatization it implies, affects all the most ordinary acts committed by immigrants and, a fortiori, their criminal acts. Conversely, all immigrant behaviour, and especially deviant behaviour, has repercussions on the phenomenon of immigration itself, and leads to greater disapproval, greater disqualification and greater stigmatization.

We therefore have two kinds of sin or guilt: a historically situated sin (that of immigration) and what might be called behavioural sins or crimes, or actual sins that figure in the taxonomy or the usual table of sins that are reprehensible, sanctionable and sanctioned as such (with varying degrees of severity) by the provisions of the Penal Code which, in law (in theory, which means in accordance with a law that has lost all sense of reality), apply to all offenders, whoever they may be. What relationship is there between the two orders of crime? On the one hand, we have a crime that has not been committed intentionally. To that extent, none of those involved, or who become involved despite themselves – immigration and the country of immigration – can admit to it. Even when it is officially authorized, the 'presence' of the immigrant is still, as we have said, basically at fault (it is a presence that cannot be an end in itself and which, no matter whether it is accepted or denounced, requires constant justification). Those who are most concerned, namely the emigrant-immigrants themselves, appear, finally, to be the real victims of the gigantic farce that is being acted out at their expense. On the other hand, we have the crime that has been committed, reported and recorded in canonical fashion. It is viewed and seen in itself for what it is in its materiality and, whenever possible, in the same light as all the crimes of the first kind.

What is relationship between the two? In law, there is none. Historically situated sins or crimes cannot be used as an argument for either the defence or the prosecution of second-order crimes, even when those crimes make the criminal liable to the ever-present sanction of deportation, irrespective of whether or not it is actually implemented. Second-order crimes cannot serve as a pretext for making a more serious and unjust case against immigration. But, in practice, there is a relationship that is always present in everyone's mind. Some strongly deny being influenced in one way or the other by that relationship. Some claim to be totally neutral and to know nothing about the guilty party's previous record or, in this case, his status and quality as an immigrant. Others, in contrast, do not conceal or hide their satisfaction at seeing two different modalities of crime and the two punishments that sanction them overlapping and aggravating one another – in their view, this is only fair and, basically, something that is quite normal and that should be the rule.

The case against immigration is always inseparable from the case made against the immigrant because of some offence, even a minor one, that he has committed. The case against immigration in fact involves the whole system of representation through which we constitute immigration, and the deviancy or delinquency of immigration, through which we define the immigrant and the acts, criminal or otherwise, he is permitted to commit. These representations are of two kinds. First, we have *mental representations* that are translated into acts of perception and evaluation, cognition and recognition. They are translated into a whole series of acts in which agents invest their material and symbolic interests (and the symbolic are perhaps invested with more force and passion than the material), their social prejudices, their presuppositions and, in a word, their whole social being. Second, we have what we might call *object representations*. These consist in all the external signs, all the indices, all the features and all the characteristics that can become the object of the manipulative symbolic strategies we use to determine the (mental) representations that others have of those properties – which are all perceptible from the outside – and their bearers. (In the practical mode, an individual exists mainly in the sense that he is seen and that he allows some part of himself to be seen; and the identity we talk about so much is basically this *being-perceived* that we all share in a social sense, and which basically exists only because it is recognized by others.) That is the way it is in social life, which is an incessant struggle between the perceptions and classifications these representations impose. Everyone would like to impose the definition or (mental) representation that flatters him most and is in his best social interests by using the properties at his disposal and his self-authorized (object) representation. Courts of all kinds are full of these classification struggles, and the greatest condemnation consists, of course, in the a priori denegation and dispossession of all the social attributes – even the most elementary, which are also the most essential – that make it possible to take part, even at the lowest and most dominated level, in the play of these struggles between representations, in the sense of both mental images and manifestations designed to act upon those mental images.

The situation of criminality in immigration – a situation which implies, rather than its objective probability, a guaranteed rise in racism, as it always exists in the presence of and under the gaze of the other – raises the issue of the relationship between *politics* and *politeness*. When an immigrant is involved, breaking the law also means breaking the unwritten law imposing the reserve and neutrality (real and feigned) that befits a foreigner. In such cases, breaking the law means more than the infraction in question: it is an error of a different order, a lack of politeness. This demand for simple politeness, for good manners and nothing more, in reality implies the renunciation of many things. The apparently minor or purely normal concessions known as 'politeness' are valuable only because they are, in reality, or deep inside us, political concessions: enforcing respect for forms comes down to demanding every form of the respect that is owed to order. The political neutrality that the political demands of foreign residents who are confined to the non-political is certainly more acceptable and more easily obtained if we locate it in the register of politeness rather than in the sphere of the political, even though that is its true territory. At an unconscious level, it is politeness that prevents the foreigner from playing a political part in the political affairs (internal and external) of the host country.

Allaying suspicion

A sort of social hyper-correction is required of the immigrant, especially one of lowly social condition. Being socially or even morally
suspect, he must above all reassure everyone as to his morality. There
has never before been so much talk of 'republican values' in France.
That is because it is a way of denouncing what the social and political
morality of French society regards as the deviant behaviour of Muslim
immigrants: wearing veils to school, statutory discrimination against
women, the political use of religion, which is referred to as fundamentalism, and so on. Being conscious of the suspicion that weighs
upon him and which he cannot escape because he is confronted with it
throughout his immigrant life and in every domain of his existence, it
is up to the immigrant to allay it constantly, to foresee it and to ward
it off by repeatedly demonstrating his good faith and his good will. He
finds himself caught up in social struggles despite himself, because
they are of necessity struggles over identity. Because he is involved in
them as an isolated individual and almost without wishing to be
involved – especially in the interindividual interactions of everyday
life – he has no choice but to exaggerate in one way or another.
Making a virtue of necessity, and to a large extent because of the
dominated position he occupies in the structure of symbolic power
relations, the immigrant tends, no doubt rightly, to exaggerate each of
the contradictory options he thinks he has chosen, whereas they have
actually been forced upon him. He is condemned to exaggerate everything; everything he does, everything he experiences and everything
he is. At times, he must, as an immigrant (when he is at the bottom of
the social hierarchy within the world of immigrants), assume the
stigmas which, in the eyes of public opinion, create the immigrant.
He must therefore accept (resignedly or under protest, submissively or
defiantly, or even provocatively) the dominant definition of his identity. We need only recall, in this connection, the fact that the stigma
itself generates a revolt against the stigma, and that one of the first
forms of that revolt consists in reappropriating or laying claim to
the stigma, which is converted into an emblem in accordance with the
classic paradigm of *black is beautiful*. This can even lead to the insti-
tutionalization of the group, which thus turns the stigma – in other
words and roughly speaking the social, economic, political and cultural effects of the stigmatization of which it is the object and in part
the product – into its foundation. At other times, in contrast, the
immigrant devotes himself to the quest for so-called *assimilation*. This
presupposes putting a great deal of effort into his self-presentation

and representation (the representation others have of him, and the representation he wishes to give of himself). The effort is therefore focused essentially on his body, his physical appearance, and those forms of external behaviour that are most loaded with symbolic attributes or meanings. It is intended to remove all the signs that might recall the stigma (physical signs such as complexion, skin colour, hair colour, etc; cultural signs such as accent, manner of speech, clothes, the wearing of a moustache, a whole lifestyle, etc.). The other strategy involves conspicuous mimicry and the adoption of features which, in contrast, seem to be emblematically characteristic of those to whom he wishes to assimilate. Whilst they are not mutually exclusive, the two strategies, or at least parts of them, can be simultaneously juxtaposed, though there is a danger that this will exacerbate the contradictions. In all these examples, no matter how contrasted, the issue appears to centre on the use of strategies of simulation and dissimulation, pretence and bluff, and the acquisition and projection of a self-image that pleases [*qui plaît*] others and in which the immigrant delights [*se complaît*], the image he would like to be in keeping with his material and symbolic interests, or the image that is least removed from the identity he is laying claim to. On the one hand, his original identity is credited with having a greater authenticity – the identity of the 'old man' which he refuses to kill off. He must preserve, or believe he is preserving, his original identity because he thinks he is doing so in order not to have to experience it in shame, timidity and scorn, and to avoid the risk of exoticism, all of which can encourage the racism of which they are a component element. On the other hand is the new identity he wishes to create in order to appropriate, if not all the advantages bound up with the possession of the dominant identity, at least the legitimate identity (i.e. the identity of the dominant) that he will never have and at least the negative advantages he can expect to derive from no longer having to be judged, or having to judge himself, by criteria that he knows will always, and of necessity, work to his disadvantage. There is another point on which the two strategies are basically in agreement: both contain within them, each in its own way, a forced recognition of legitimate identity. The former recognizes it by refusing it, by keeping as great a distance as possible, and by avoiding any superfluous contact or any contact that is not indispensable. The latter, in contrast, recognizes it by taking its inspiration from it, by taking it as a model, by simulating it and by trying to reproduce it as faithfully as possible, but also as slavishly as possible. In both cases – and this is another reason why they converge – what is really at stake in these strategies for social struggles, which are found in any struggle between the dominated and the dominant, or in the face of domination, is not, as is commonly said, the conquest or reconquest of identity. It is the ability to reappropriate for oneself the possibility of constructing one's own identity and of evaluating that identity in complete autonomy. This is the ability that the dominated are obliged to surrender to the dominant, so much so that anyone who finds himself in the dominated position within the field of symbolic power relations has only two possible ways of gaining recognition or, more prosaically, continuing to exist. Either he must be negated, and must therefore consent to his own negation and disqualification, or he must accept the risks involved in any attempt to assimilate. If he adopts the first strategy, he must do what he is being asked to do even though he cannot resign or withdraw completely in the strict sense of the term from a game he knows to be basically stacked against him. He must, that is, simply withdraw from the struggle, as he is being asked to do – in other words, abandon it without necessarily leaving the arena (i.e. immigration) in which such struggles take place. He must agree to do no more than watch the struggle being played out, through him and in front of him, without intervening. He must agree to play the role of the victim designate. This is the fate to which one is almost always condemned when one is involved in a game one is not equipped to play and which one can never master (a game one has not chosen to play, which is always played on the home ground of the dominant, in their way, in accordance with their rules and with their weapons of choice). The alternative is to accept the risks involved in any attempt at assimilation, in other words in any form of behaviour that is explicitly calculated, designed and organized with a view to bringing about a change of identity, or what he believes to be the transition from a dominated identity to a dominant identity. This implies the danger of denying himself and, correlatively, all of his fellows who reject that choice, who cannot or do not want to act in that way, and thus deny themselves. Abandoning an identity, be it social, political (or more specifically national, as in the case of naturalization), cultural, religious or whatever is not without its ambiguity, especially when it is an identity that is dominated from every point of view, an identity that is stigmatized and despised. In the eyes of those who are being abandoned and left behind, this borders upon treachery; in the eyes of the others, or those one dreams of joining, that one aspires to being, it undeniably implies allegiance, but there is still a suspicion of pretension and selfish calculation.

Reassuring others and giving them a sense of security, as well as reassuring oneself, and giving oneself a sense of security, constitute an imperative incumbent upon any foreign presence. This is the constant preoccupation of any foreigner or anyone who has the feeling of being a foreigner where he is living, of any foreigner to the country and the society in which he lives, often continuously, but who does not experience them as his country and society. He is a foreigner to the economy and culture of that country, and a foreigner amongst the population of that country. As a general rule, this is the case with all traditional immigrants, who never stop emigrating from their homeland. Their children may feel the same even though they are not always, or not necessarily, foreigners in the national sense. Anyone who is not in a position of strength, when the balance of power, and especially symbolic power, is not in one's favour (which is collectively the case with immigrants, or, let me repeat, all those who have a feeling of not really being at home in the place where they are), is anxious not to frighten others. He is anxious not to do so even when there is, objectively, no reason for them to be afraid of him (the immigrant himself has no control over the phantasmatic fears he inspires). He is, to be more accurate, always anxious not to disturb them because a foreign presence is (rightly or wrongly, not that it matters) always a cause for concern (foreigners are those of whom we like to say *we don't know* who they are. *We don't know* what they are like; *we don't know* what makes them tick; *we don't know* what they are thinking or how they think; *we don't know* what is going on inside their heads; *we don't know* how they might react; *we cannot* understand them; *you never know* with them).

Reassuring the other is often a precondition for one's own security. There are only two ways of providing reassurance and self-reassurance, only two ways of succeeding in reassuring both oneself and others. They complement one another because they are both ways of dispelling the mutual fears. They dispel both one's own fear (the foreigner's fear of being in a foreign country) and the fear of others (their fear of a foreigner who is in their country). Both fears (which are different in terms of their form and especially their content) are shared – unequally and differently, of course – by both parties, or by both the dominated and the dominant. The two different fears feed on one another; and despite all the differences that may exist between them, they are part of the same attempt to reassure. On the one hand, there is the fear of the dominant – in other words and in this case, the masters of the house – who are all nationals, no matter which social class they belong to. It can be allayed by the strength of those who know they are dominant (because they know that they are *naturally* at home, and know that they are the country's *natural* inhabitants), and who know they are in a position of strength because they possess a legitimacy that merges into domination (a legitimacy which, as such, does not realize that it is dominant). On the other hand, there is the fear of the dominated (i.e. immigrants), of the weak who have, in these circumstances, been deprived of all power and all legitimacy. For the dominant, being reassured means no longer having to reassure themselves in the face of some danger (even though there is nothing for them to be afraid of, and even when the danger is completely imaginary) and, at the same time, reassuring others whose fear is, so to speak, constitutive of their immigrant condition. For the dominated who, despite their structural weakness, or perhaps because of that weakness, are perceived as dangerous (or at least as constituting a collective danger) or, which is worse, are regarded as 'enemies' (and not only as the 'class enemies' of old, with whom we were used to coming into conflict), reassuring the dominant is without doubt the price that has to be paid to ensure their own security (which is purely relative).

As this self-assurance depends upon a security that has to be won from the other or in the face of the other, certain immigrants prefer to withdraw, to take refuge in their hidden fear, and choose (or chose, in an earlier state of immigration) to opt for the greatest possible discretion or, in other words, to become as invisible as they can. They are helped here by the social and spatial relegation of which they are the victims (relegation in space and by space). They also simultaneously turn it into self-relegation: relegation and self-relegation into the same spaces, the space of social relations, the space of housing and, primarily, the space of work. These are all spaces where they find themselves to be in the majority and amongst other immigrants of the same background (originally from the same country, the same region, the same village, the same kinship group). These are the immigrants of whom it is said that they 'hug the walls', which can only please those who tend to see their reserve as a sign of politeness, or even the eminently reassuring subservience they expect and demand from foreigners. For other immigrants who are sufficiently self-confident, or convinced that they can allay suspicion, providing reassurance appears to consist in simulating the greatest resemblance to or similarity with those they are trying to reassure by disguising their own features, or at least by attenuating the distinctive signs that make them stand out and which are normally described as stigmas. In a word, they do all they can to deny and abolish the radical alterity (or the radicality of the alterity) of which they are the bearers. This attitude, which corresponds to a quest for the greatest proximity and which in fact contains within it all the marks of the allegiance shown to the dominant, is inevitably – despite the objective intentions behind it and its self-proclaimed finality – and paradoxically retranslated into potential conflicts. It is always liable to be interpreted in terms of rivalry – of unseemly rivalry, illegitimate rivalry and unfair competition. This is an indication of the relatively narrow limits that are ascribed to assimilation, of the limits within which the dominant inscribe the assimilation they wish to impose upon those they dominate, and which they are also happy to see them succeed in assimilating,[3] by conceding them the form without always recognizing its content.

But the height of both civil and political impoliteness, and the height of rudeness and violence towards *national* understanding, seems to be attained by those 'immigrants' who are not immigrants: the children of immigrants, those 'hybrids' who do not fully share the properties that ideally define the integral immigrant, or the accomplished immigrant who conforms to the representation we have of him. And nor do they really share the objective, and especially not the subjective, characteristics of nationals. They are 'immigrants' who have not emigrated from anywhere. They are immigrants who are not, despite that designation, immigrants like any others, in other words foreigners in the full sense of the term. They are not foreigners in cultural terms, as they are integral products of this society and its mechanisms of reproduction and integration, of a language (a language into which they were born and which, in this country, is not their mother tongue in the literal sense), of education and of all the other social processes. Nor are they foreigners in national terms, as they usually have the nationality of the country in which they are living. In the eyes of some, they are no doubt 'bad' products of French society, but they are still products of that society. Rather like disturbingly ambiguous agents, they blur the borders of the national order, and therefore the symbolic value and pertinence of the criteria that found the hierarchy of groups and their classification. And what it is no doubt most difficult to forgive this category of immigrants for is of course the fact that they disrupt the diacritical function and meaning of the divorce that state thought establishes between nationals and non-nationals. We therefore do not know how to regard or treat these new-style immigrants, and nor do we know what to expect of them. And at this point, ordinary fear, if we can put it that way, or the personal or individual fear inspired by the foreign immigrant, turns into a collective anxiety as the traditional separations are abolished and as we lose the simultaneously physical, moral and mental or intellectual security and comfort afforded by those eminently reassuring separations to the extent that they constitute a protective barrier behind which we can take shelter by asserting that we are 'at home', safe from outside interference.

This form of anxiety, or this new fear of the immigrant, against which the demand for *politeness* is powerless, is even more difficult to dispel. It can be disseminated more widely and projected on to a whole series of related objects: young people, difficult neighbourhoods, bad estates, the suburbs, the unemployed, delinquents and so on. It can be projected on to the same individuals and the same places (the children of immigration or 'second-generation immigrants'). From that point of view, a radical transformation has taken place within immigration, and the suspicion that continues to weigh upon these new-style immigrants is proportional to the changes brought about by the immigration of families and by their reproduction on the spot. And given these new conditions, we have to go back to the *genetic crime* that is consubstantial with this immigration, and all the other crimes that have been committed in practice. Basically, we have to go back to the reactions provoked by these crimes, to the way they are judged, and to the ways in which they are assessed. Crimes and infractions are not just forbidden. When they are committed, they are punished accordingly, in other words for what they undoubtedly are, but they are also, surreptitiously and secretly, punished because of the nature of the offender. Even though the immigrant has changed with regard to the outside world, this type of offender is regarded as being illegitimate, as not being allowed to commit infractions, as being forbidden to offend and as not having the right to offend.

The suspicion always weighs on the same people. It weighs upon people whose every characteristic – their history and their birth (and in this case, their immigration and their having been born in immigration) and, correlatively, their social position, their status, the social and especially the symbolic capital they have acquired – designates them as perpetual suspects. The stigmatization revealed by this form of generalized suspicion derives from a schema of thought and social perception with which we are already familiar. In more general terms, it derives from the suspicious and accusatory relationship we have with the popular classes, which are viewed as dangerous classes. This schema, which is always the same, is as true today as it was yesterday, as every age has its own dangerous classes. If the situation specific to the delinquent foreigner (and even more so the 'immigrant', even if he does have the nationality of the country), who is guilty in two ways, or guilty of being guilty, is not necessarily to work to his disadvantage and is not to act as an aggravating circumstance, judges must display great restraint and a lot of self-control, and make an attempt at self-correction. Even when it is not openly talked about, this implicit combination of crimes and therefore punishments does give rise to another sanction that is often imposed in addition to the other two. It is intrinsically bound up with the foreigner's condition, as a foreigner is by definition liable to be deported, even if, as does happen, it has been agreed not to deport him. Whether the deportation actually takes place or not, the foreigner's liability to deportation is the sign par excellence of one of the essential prerogatives of national sovereignty. This too is a characteristic of state thought, which is not to say that it *is* state thought. It is in fact in the very nature of the sovereignty of the nation to be able to deport those foreign residents (foreign in the nationality sense) it sees fit to deport, and it is in the very nature of the foreigner (speaking nationally) to be liable to deportation, regardless of whether or not he is actually deported. Whilst it is not a juridical sanction in the strict sense, as it is not normally pronounced by a court of law, deportation from the national territory, which is an administrative or politico-administrative measure – taken as a result of the judicial condemnation it extends beyond its effects – clearly demonstrates the risks run by any foreigner who infringes the rules of good conduct. Having supplied proof of his lack of discretion, he is subject to administrative sanctions. The same logic governs, a fortiori, the operation of naturalization: the nation and nationality do not naturalize and nationalize just anyone. Being an act that basically results from a decision, naturalization may be incompatible with certain social and cultural characteristics or with certain customs (in the sense of habits and customs). In the French case, it is incompatible with polygamy, which is regarded as an offence against public order in the particular sense in which international private law understands that term. Naturalization may be incompatible with certain criminal penalties. The nature and hierarchy of some penalties disqualify anyone from claiming the quality of being French, but they also vary according to the context and the moment. Not surprisingly, these crimes reproduce their punishments and bring them into line, roughly speaking, with those that lead to deportation, rather as though the conditions for entering a nationality obeyed, no doubt even more strictly, the same principles as the conditions for entering and residing in the nation, because they precede and prefigure them.

13
Recapitulation

Contemporary migratory movements from the countries of the under-developed world (countries where rural and peasant populations are in the majority) towards the countries of the developed world (countries in which urban and industrial civilization is dominant) are, in a way, similar to the internal migrations of old and to the rural exodus that all the latter countries experienced in their day. Both population movements (of workers and whole families) share the same logic, even though they are very far removed from one another in time and space. Even though they involve, respectively, areas and distances that are incommensurable, they have the same social and economic genesis. As they obey, in different contexts, determinisms of the same nature, today's international displacements (most of which originate from the countries of the Third World) reproduce in their own way and continue the history inaugurated by yesterday's internal migrations. The difference is, however, that the migrations that followed the exodus of the rural populations of industrialized countries took place within the limits of national frontiers, or in other words within the same territory, within a single population, and under the authority of a single state. All these things were defined and characterized in *national* terms. The homology and continuity between the two situations becomes more obvious if we agree to distance ourselves somewhat from state thought. We automatically think in national terms – perhaps more so in this domain than in any other – and state thought therefore introduces the inevitable, and eminently 'statist', distinction, which is as arbitrary as it is pertinent, between the *national* on the one hand and the *non-national* on the other. But in order to distance ourselves from state thought, we must choose provisionally to ignore (or pretend to ignore) the existence of frontiers and the truly political effects of frontiers. And yet, can we really do that? If it is so closely dependent upon our categories of thought, or the categories with which we construct and think the social and political world, can the migratory phenomenon be discussed in inter-national terms or in terms of its twin dimensions of emigration on the one hand and immigration on the other? Can we, in other words, discuss a movement from one territory and to another territory – always defined, respectively, as States – other than in terms of the categories of state thought?

The attempt to reconstitute the genesis of immigrations that are supposedly 'labour immigrations' (nineteenth-century immigrations, where the oldest are concerned; the most recent are still taking place) can discover its truth only when those immigrations concern single workers and no other members of their families, and, more specific-ally, when they still take the alternating form we have described as that of the *noria* (or turn-over). And does it have to be recalled that, with the exception of mass population movements bound up with political conjunctures, all immigrations of an economic kind, even those which are now said to have been settler immigrations from the start – i.e. family immigrations (the immigration of, for instance, Europeans to the United States of America, especially between 1840 and 1920) – began as immigrations of single workers? Conversely, even those immigrations that are supposedly temporary immigrations of men, and only men (for example, the immigration of Algerian workers to France from the beginning of the twentieth century until its last decades), sooner or later end up by being transformed into family immigrations and, ultimately, into settler immigrations. How does this transformation come about?

The case of Algerian immigration to France is an extreme case in this and many other respects. First, because of the conditions of its genesis. Being a direct product of a colonization that was both brutal and total, the immigration that followed was proportional to the extent and gravity of the transformations in all orders (the economic order, but probably the political, social and cultural orders too) that generated it. The 'exemplariness' of colonization in Algeria no doubt also has to do with the fact that it was closely associated with the two aspects or orders that retranslated the two meanings of the colonial phenomenon. This was an intensive and total colonization. It was a settler colonization, but it was not only land, property and wealth, the soil and the subsoil that were colonized. It was also a colonization of men and minds, of 'bodies and souls' as the saying went. Further-more, it occurred at a relatively early date. Under these conditions, its major effects (which, for the most part, outlived the cause that generated them) inevitably included an emigration-immigration that was exceptional or 'exemplary' in terms both of its intensity and of its numerical scale. It was also 'exemplary' in terms of its continuity over time (with the exception of a short period during the Second World War, there were practically no significant interruptions) and in space (the space of the society of immigration and the space of the society of emigration, with the former eventually coming to resemble a small-scale projection of the latter), its overall duration, etc. Its peculiar organizational forms were exemplary too, as was its peculiar mode of *presence* here (in immigration) and *absence* there (thanks to emigration), and, especially, its *precocity*. This was a colonial immigration (even then, there was talk of 'colonial workers'; during the whole of the First World War, some 240,000 Algerian men – over one-third of the male population aged between 20 and 40 – were conscripted, volunteered or requisitioned as workers: Ageron 1962). This was no doubt the first immigration in France, and perhaps even in Europe, not to have been European in origin. Whilst colonization does seem to have been largely responsible for the emigration to France it generated and for the presence in France of colonized Algerian workers, this relates essentially to the fact that, by attacking its land-owning structures, it not only destroyed the foundations of the traditional economy but, by simultaneously attacking the tribes and their tribal organization, also destroyed the basis on which both the social order and the armature of the original society rested.

Recalling the genesis of Algerian immigration to France, which is now no more than one flow amongst others, allows us to understand why the whole of this flow was completely oriented towards France. It is rather as though, for Algerian emigrants and candidates for emigration, immigration to France was the only possible form of immigration. The transformations of all kinds that took place within the land-owning structure, the structures of the distribution of property, modes of exploitation and farming and perhaps also within the market and circuits for the trade in agricultural produce, lay at the origins of the migrations of old, and may still be responsible for the migratory movements that are now taking place almost everywhere. They too are inspired by the search for work. The one thing that these crisis situations have in common is that they break the umbilical links that tie the rural population (and the poorest layers of that population) not only to its land and its territory but, at a more basic level, to the whole art of living, to the ways of being, thinking, acting and perceiving the world that make up the entire peasant *ethos*. The other thing that they have in common is that they contribute to the *individuation* of men who, deep within themselves, remain, or remained for a long time, 'communitarian men' or men who existed (ideally) only as members of a group. This break must do its work and the contagion must gradually spread before the traditional peasant can become aware of his availability. It is only then that he can be transformed into a potential emigrant who is waiting to be transformed into an actual immigrant, or in other words that he can discover that he has been made 'available' or free for the adventure of migration and, by that very fact, for the adventure of proletarianization – in the best of cases, as the sub-proletarian condition is unfortunately widespread.

All these reasons explain why, in a certain way, immigration cannot be conceived, cannot take place and cannot perpetuate itself unless it is based upon a whole series of *illusions* that are collectively sustained and shared by all the parties concerned. The immigrant, and therefore *foreign*, presence is equivalent to a *temporary* presence (in theory), to a presence that is *subordinate* to some other reason external to it and to some end other than itself, namely *work*. It is always subject to the need for constant *legitimation* (thanks to what Pierre Bourdieu calls state thought). Being a non-national presence within the nation, this presence is *excluded from the political*. The reduction of immigration to its economic dimension alone is another of the phenomenon's contradictions. The basic contradiction between the 'temporary that lasts' is transposed from the temporal order to the spatial order: how can one continue to be present in a place from which one is absent? Correlatively, how can one come to terms with being only partly present and therefore, in a way, being (morally) absent from the place in which one is physically present? Then there is the contradiction between the communitarian order of the society of origin on the one hand and, on the other, the more 'individualist' order the immigrant discovers, is subordinated to and apprenticed to in immigration. Confronted with all the difficult contradictions that constitute his social universe, and being unable either to resolve them at home and within their own time, or to leave them behind by putting an end to his immigration, the immigrant is forced to exacerbate them, sometimes to the detriment of his social or psychical equilibrium.

Time must pass and make its effects felt before these dissimulations and simulations, which have been so laboriously and so continuously constructed, can begin to be dispelled. Disillusionment, unmasking, and the revelation of the objective truth of the migratory phenomenon finally complete the process. But the disenchantment simply exacerbates the contradictions and heightens the awareness of them. Being both a cause and an effect of this disillusionment, which is an index of the profound change that has taken place in the meaning of the immigration of Algerian workers, the appearance of family immigration finally completes the break with the earlier state in which there was such a great need to sustain all the illusions that sustained it.

The other great 'exemplariness' of Algerian immigration in fact lies in the way it was, at a very late date, transformed into *family immigration*. We have mentioned the distinction that is habitually made, within the migratory phenomenon, between what can be described as *labour* emigrations and immigrations on the one hand, and what are essentially *settler* emigrations and immigrations on the other. The 'labour function' of the latter is implicitly admitted to come second, and to be secondary compared with the 'settler function'. The forms of immigration that have been so identified are erected into autonomous realities, as though they were different from the outset and as though we could choose one to the exclusion of the other. As the distinction is established a priori, each immigration is condemned to being no more than what we wish to see in it. Each is doomed to be and go on being what one would like it to be and to go on being: on the one hand *labour immigration* from all eternity, and on the other *settler immigration* from the outset. That the two forms that have been separated out in this way might be connected by some relationship of continuity or descent, or that the second might be an extension and derivative of the first, is unthinkable. Yet the Algerian immigration which, for a very long time, was constituted and thought of as the perfect example of labour immigration has unexpectedly become a 'settler immigration'. Neither of the parties concerned – neither the society of immigration nor the society of emigration – nor those individuals concerned (the emigrant-immigrants) dares, for reasons of their own, to admit and fully recognize this, or to contemplate its full implications.

Emigration is self-sustaining. The reason why it is 'contagious' is that it is one of those social processes in which effects become causes that reduplicate and perpetuate the first cause that generated them. Born of the disruptive action of many factors and of the total upheaval to which they give rise, the emigration movement completes, as we have said, the break with the group, with its spatio-temporal rhythms, its activities and, in a word, the system of values and the system of communitarian dispositions that are the group's foundations. As it spreads throughout the territory and to all strata of society, and as it begins to last too long, this break eventually has almost irreversible effects. Emigration then ceases to be the perfectly ordered and orderly form of behaviour that it was in the beginning. And it is when, as a result of emigration, the group has the greatest difficulty in controlling and ordering the emigration of its men that it permits family emigration. For that to happen, the undermining that destructures the group by weakening the ties that bind the members of the group to one another and that bind them to the group has to have reached a prodigiously advanced stage. The initial causes that were responsible for the first form of emigration (the emigration of single men) must have been considerably aggravated, usually as an effect of emigration, for the second phase of emigration, or the emigration of families, to begin. In this final phase, the whole process of migration is beyond the group's moral control and escapes the censure that tries to prevent it: the dissuasive effects of that censure (social disapproval, the feeling of shame and so on) are no longer enough to contain it.

The first signs of migration to France of Algerian families were visible even before the Second World War, at least in those regions where the upheaval had been greatest. These were not necessarily the regions that were the earliest and biggest suppliers of labour immigration (initially, the immigration of men had, rather, helped to stabilize social structures, as that stability was itself the precondition for that form of immigration), but usually marginal regions, both in the physical sense (Piedmontese regions or regions where different reliefs came into contact) and cultural sense (transitional regions between the habitat of the mountain dwellers and the dispersed habitats of the high plains, between Berber-speaking zones and territories inhabited by Arabic-speakers, between rural areas and the peripheries of the cities, and so on). They were regions where the labour force tended to emigrate on a local basis to work on colonial farms rather than to undertake long-distance emigration to France. It was, however, only in the 1950s that family immigration from Algeria became truly established as a real trend. Thanks to both their direct effects (insecurity, especially in rural areas) and indirect ones (such as the effects of the 'regrouping' of the rural population, and especially mountain folk, in centres created for that purpose and under the control of the army), the years of Algeria's war of independence were to women's emigration and, more generally, family emigration, what the years of the First World War had been to male emigration. In both cases, and no doubt more so in the latter than the former, the war and its constraints, or *force majeure*, supplied the indispensable alibi for doing what had to be done. They provided an excuse for admitting what no one dared to admit. For a long time, and even when it became possible for the immigrant and his wife to want (as individuals) to emigrate as a family, they were not unaware that they were in danger of breaking the communitarian rule and undermining the morale of the group. Family emigration was undertaken and experienced as a shameful act, an act they were so careful to conceal that they saw it as their duty to leave their villages by night. Once again, the fragmentation of families had to become widespread and to reach its extreme limits with the conjugal-type family (which we find in immigration), and the rural exodus towards towns in Algeria (for which immigration in France was largely responsible) had to affect whole villages, before families could emigrate to France in broad daylight, without any shame or restraint.

Although family emigration was a sort of obsessive fear or temptation that no doubt went through the minds of all immigrants, and which must have permanently haunted their projects and remained with them throughout their immigration, the immigration of Algerian families occurred, despite all that, almost half a century after the uninterrupted immigration of workers. Without wishing to underestimate the possibility of reluctance and hostility on the part of the society of immigration – from a strictly economic point of view or from the labour market's point of view, an exclusively labour immigration is obviously more 'advantageous' than a family immigration – families take second place when it comes to the resistances and taboos put up by the society of emigration. The latter made the former superfluous or pointless. It is as though the work of censorship (which is also a form of prevention and preservation) had been done, and well done, in the order of emigration, and as though there was therefore no need for it to be done in the order of immigration. The order of immigration did not need to discourage, control or regulate a family immigration that it could not but desire, so long as there was no sign that it would occur and so long as it had yet to happen, either because the demand for it did not exist or did not yet exist, or because it was socially frustrated. Although it was already contained within the first form of immigration – in other words in the behaviour of the first immigrant – family immigration therefore did not, as might have been imagined or expected, simply complete the process begun by the immigration of workers. It did not represent a numerical increase. The number of immigrants did not rise because their wives and children went with them. Family immigration introduced a difference of nature. It was qualitatively different, not just quantitatively: the immigrant who had previously been a worker now became a *progenitor*. He once worked for others, for the prosperity of others and in the prosperity of others, even if it does have to be added, and as he himself added – and there were several reasons for this – that although he was working in another country and for other people, he was also working for himself, for his own (purely relative) prosperity, and for that of his family, his group and his village. The immigrant now became someone who was working for *posterity*. He was now working for his descendants but also, objectively, and whether he liked it or not, for the descendants of others.

For all these and many other reasons, family immigration cannot be of the same order as the immigration of single men. It is not about the order of work alone. It is about something else – i.e. *assimilation*, no matter what word (*adaptation, integration, insertion*), which are all more or less euphemistic variants, is used to describe this social reality. Each of these terms has its social history, depending on whether or not it has ceased to be productive in social and political terms, and on how badly it has been mistreated by history, and especially by the history of colonization and that of immigration, which are not unrelated. No one has any illusions about this: neither those who dread the emigration of families because it represents a threat to the integrity of the social body, a fear that emigrant families will be dissolved or fused into the society that absorbs them, and the danger of their inevitable identification – to a greater or lesser extent and in the long or the short term – with that society; nor those who are loath to accept the immigration of families which, as a result of prejudice [*pré-jugé*] rather than 'post-judgement' [*post-jugé*], are known and said to be 'inassimilable' or 'difficult to assimilate'. And is not the classic distinction between 'labour immigration' and 'family immigration' (in other words settler immigration) a disguised way of using a supposedly technical (and therefore a-political) and would-be objective vocabulary for the a posteriori distinction that is made between immigrants who are almost like 'us', and immigrants who are radically different, or even dissimilar to 'us'? This brings us back to the distinction we discussed earlier. On the one hand, we have an immigration that we judge, retrospectively, to be worthy of quickly becoming a 'settler immigration' – and, if need be, we will help it to become that as soon as possible. On the other, we have an immigration that is condemned to be and remain, even when reality contradicts that assertion, a 'labour immigration' – and if need be we will ensure that it stays that way to some extent. This is an internal contradiction, and it is an intrinsic part of the object. Labour or settlement, settlement or labour: one can exist only if it fails to see that it is the other and that it creates the other, and the other can exist only if it fails to recognize itself for what it is. Whilst immigration policy – and any group involved with immigration must have an immigration policy – has to make a clear distinction between 'labour' and 'settlement', the best or even the only possible policy must be an absence of policy. In this domain, and provided that we do not confuse policy and regulations, and provided also that we do not reduce the former to the latter, the absence of a policy is still a policy.

This indeterminacy, which is consubstantial with the phenomenon of immigration, is an intellectual necessity for state thought, but it is now being put to the test. Unlike Algerian immigration which, because it was in its day a pioneer, for a long time dissociated the two phases of its history and of its final accomplishment, immigrations that should, ideally, have been only 'labour immigrations' (originating from the countries of the third world, and from countries that are, in geographical terms, further and further away) now tend to be family immigrations too.

Notes

INTRODUCTION

1   This subordination is *objective*; it occurs, that is, without the knowledge of any of the participants; and that is why it is so terribly effective and can perpetuate itself. Here, we encounter the socially determined limitations imposed on a science that is still too dependent upon the political, or even public opinion (two factors which interact and influence one another), to be able to constitute its own object in all its autonomy.
2   Because there is nothing about the phenomenon of emigration, or the phenomenon of immigration come to that, that can be stated without automatically leading to its denunciation, much of the data, and even data that might be described as scientific, or produced and used by science, does not escape the logic of the discourse invoked to justify or legitimize the phenomenon or, on the contrary, to condemn it and to denounce its illegitimacy.

CHAPTER 1   THE ORIGINAL SIN AND THE COLLECTIVE LIE

1   The expression 'the son of a widow', which is traditionally used as an insult, is applied to a man who has been brought up by women and whose honour and masculinity are suspect. The inversion of the old values now makes it a quality that can be laid claim to: it means being 'the son of one's works'.
2   This alludes to the practice of watching police checkpoints on the roads linking the village to neighbouring towns and of warning the many 'clandestine transporters' of people (cars and trucks) so that they can drop off their 'customers' before they reach the checkpoints; whilst the lookouts do receive some of the money the 'transporters' would pay in

fines if they were caught *in flagrante*, the look-outs risk heavy repri-
mands and even physical sanctions at the hands of the police, who are
well aware of what they are up to.

3   When applied to jewellery, the terms *nahas* (copper) and *saka* (steel) are
synonymous with 'hypocritical', 'false' and 'deceitful' because the terms
are structural equivalents in mythico-ritual logic and language.

4   The reference is to the amulets written or made either by men of letters
(a *taleb* or a *cheikh*), or by fortune-tellers and other magicians. These
amulets, to which all kinds of magical property are attributed, are
carried either because they have curative powers (they can cure certain
illnesses), prophylactic powers (they offer protection against the evil
eye) or propitiatory powers, as appears to be the case here: they bring
good luck and make the most difficult projects easier.

5   The interview was recorded in 1975, or in other words less than two
years after Algeria banned any further emigration to France, and less
than a year after France, for economic reasons, suspended the further
immigration of workers; to that extent, Mohand A.'s words have, in
retrospect, something prophetic about them.

6   Before he could leave, Mohand A. had to obtain a passport and be
issued with an exit visa.

7   L. is a plot of land belonging to this uncle, from whom Mohand A.
expected a lot. A long way from the village and abandoned many years
ago, it is nothing more than a pasture that all the village flocks can use.
To reach the point of working a field such as this, one really has to have
reached an extreme degree of poverty.

8   This is a room just like the one Mohand A. shares at the moment, with
three other fellow workers in a hotel run by some compatriots at one of
the *portes de Paris*.

9   Mohand A. has had only one job since coming to France; he found work
in a small metal-polishing and engraving factory, thanks to the influence
of a relative who is a foreman there. He works on a buffing wheel, and
complains about breathing in all the dust thrown up by the friction. It
gets into his stomach, as he puts it. What is more, as he is friendly only
with the very few foreign workers in the factory (two Portuguese, one
Malian, one Moroccan, five Algerians, or in other words a total of nine
foreign workers out of fifty or so), he tends to turn in on himself and to
increase his isolation deliberately.

10   Oleander is the symbol of deceitful bitterness, of the bitterness that is
hidden behind a pleasing exterior.

CHAPTER 2   THE THREE AGES OF EMIGRATION

1   These analyses, which have helped to provide a better understanding of
the living conditions of immigrants in France (and especially of their
working condition and housing), have in fact recently been extended to

new domains. They now look at the problems of professional or cultural training, cultural practices, political attitudes (political commitment on the part of immigrants, their attitude towards trade unions, with regard to strikes, different forms of action and specific demands, or even to political regimes in their countries of origin or their diplomatic representatives). A critical account of this literature will be found in Sayad 1984.

2   This tendency has led to the production of many tautologies on the theme of immigrants' adaptation to working and living conditions in France. Thus, the reason why certain immigrants appear to be relatively privileged compared with others (in terms of employment, housing, etc.) is, or so the argument would have it, that they have adapted 'better' to French society, their 'success' being an index of how well they have 'adapted'. Conversely, the reason why they have adapted 'better' to French society – the criteria being, broadly speaking, the adoption of a certain number of modes of behaviour, usually superficial, that are regarded as indicative of the changes that have taken place in the immigrant's system of practices – is that they enjoy better conditions of existence, or in other words better jobs, better housing or, which amounts to the same thing, are able to take greater advantage of the possibilities offered them by the host society.

3   This representation of immigration is implicitly present in the way statistics for immigration are established by measuring the volume of 'inflows' (the number of immigrants who enter France) and 'outflows' (the number of immigrants who leave France) without ever investigating the nature and composition of any surplus that might exist.

4   'The (good) worker is the same in the house as he is outside.' The proverbial certainty established by tradition tends increasingly to be replaced by a formula that is more in keeping with the contemporary experience of emigration: 'It is outside the house that a man is a man; inside the house, every man is naturally a man.'

5   Before leaving his guests, an emigrant (aged 63, he arrived in France for the first time in 1937 and has lived with his family in Pontoise since 1948) explained: 'When we meet up together to talk about things back home, it helps, relieves and encourages us. ... I do it [give a party for all his friends] at least once a month. In the past, when I lived over there [in a more spacious detached house and not in a council flat], it was every Saturday night.'

6   Because of the unusual position he holds both within the community of origin (he is relatively well educated, especially when compared with the emigrants of his generation, and does not quite have the peasant *habitus*), and then in emigration, or within the emigrant community (he has broken with the then obligatory modes of behaviour), S.B, who has a reputation for being *amjah*, i.e. 'marginal', 'deviant' and 'individualist', is in a very good position to give a particularly lucid representation of the emigrant population and the transformations it has experienced over

the last four decades (from 1936, the year in which he emigrated at the age of sixteen, to the present day).

7   On the eve of the Second World War, the average age of Algerian immigrants in France was between 35 and 45: 67 per cent of (North African) immigrant workers in the Paris region were aged between 30 and 45 (see Sanson 1947: 169–70); in 1954, when immigrants aged between 35 and 45 represented not even 20 per cent of the total, younger immigrants, aged between 20 and 35, represented 60 per cent of the total (see 'Les Français musulmans originaires de l'Algérie', *Bulletin de statistiques* 391 and 392, 29 October and 5 November 1955). In the space of only two years, between 1966 and 1968, the proportion of those under 25 who left rose from 40 per cent to 50 per cent (see *Revue algérienne du travail*, July 1967).

8   Whereas emigrating at a young age once tended to mean doing so before marriage – the fall in the average age of emigrants was paralleled by a rise in the proportion of bachelors (28.4 per cent) and of men with more than one child (33.6 per cent) – the bachelor emigrants of the second generation tended to leave before getting married, thereby creating a strong link that would tie them to their families and their group. Their predecessors, on the other hand, emigrated while they were still single (through they were probably older) only in order to be able to 'earn their marriage'.

9   Almost all the emigrants interviewed speak of the broad extension of emigration to all the men in their group or village.

10   In constant progression (both in absolute and relative terms), Algeria's urban population has experienced a very high rate of growth: between 1960 and 1966, it rose from a quarter to 38 per cent of the country's population; Algeria's ten largest cities (departmental capitals) absorbed 75 per cent of internal migration between 1954 and 1966, and, despite the departure of the Europeans, the population of Algiers, for example, doubled in that period, whilst that of Constantine more than doubled (growth index 2.16), and that of Sétif quadrupled. This increase in the rate of urbanization was paralleled by a more pronounced tendency on the part of the urban population to emigrate to France; in 1968, the Algiers *département*, which is the most urbanized in Algeria, recorded a greater number of departures (6,000 emigrants) than Constantine (5,433 departures), which is a more rural *département*.

11   To complete the picture, the proportion of their income that is remitted to their families, the ways in which savings are accumulated and the ways in which remittances are sent home are not the only differences between emigrants of different 'ages'. The entire structure of their budget and system of spending are different.

12   On the eve of the Second World War, J.-J. Rager (the administrator of a *commune mixte* in Algeria) was already describing the Algerian emigrant as 'a worker who goes to settle in France for a long period, interrupted by frequent return visits to the country or origin, where he

will end his days' (Rager 1950: 126). In the absence of correctly col-
lected data (there is no consensus as to either the definition of early
emigration, of which trips home should be taken into consideration, or
the dates of either) and of data applicable to emigrants over relatively
long periods, estimates as to the length of their stays in France vary from
author to author: four years at most according to Rager, between one
and a half and two years according to Robert Montagne (1953: 13),
between three and four years in the case of workers at the Renault
factory according to Andrée Michel (1957: 177). The general trend,
however, is for periods of emigration to become longer: 'In 1954, it
was estimated that an emigrant spent an average of three to four years in
France before returning to his own country; in our day (1962), the
length of the average stay is definitely longer (ten years) ... Our
emigration has a tendency to become emigration for the whole of
one's active life, which means spending between twenty and thirty
years abroad' (Séminaire national sur l'émigration, Algiers, August
1966, p. 40). This tendency is confirmed by the 1968 census which
describes almost 30 per cent of the Algerian population enumerated
(including women) as having been resident in France for at least thirteen
years (emigration prior to 1955), and 13.5 per cent as having been
resident there for at least eighteen years; more recently, another estimate
found that over 32 per cent of Algerians had been resident in France,
without interruption, for at least sixteen years (according to the statistics provided by the Amicale des Algériens en France, *Revue de la
formation permanente*, May 1975).

13   In the Renault factories – and it is true that the company does offer
many relative advantages (general atmosphere, social welfare, the role
of unions, working conditions, remuneration, etc.) – the average length
of service amongst Algerian workers was, as of 1 January 1968, seven or
eight years: 39 per cent of those surveyed had worked there for more
than eleven years.

14   In general terms, the relative professional and geographical 'mobility' of
immigrant workers tends to decrease as emigration becomes a long-
standing phenomenon and as the rhythm of emigrants' comings and
goings between France and their country of origin slows down. Family
emigration, which is not totally independent of this tendency, generally
results in even greater stability: 'When you have children here, it's not
the same, you have to think of them ... you cannot be "light", as
though you were in France by yourself, you can't give up work, you
can't even change jobs. And if you remain unemployed? You can't even
spend a night away from home; you're not going to leave your wife and
children alone in a foreign country. It's not the same for someone who is
here on his own, and for someone who is with *elfamila* [the family].'

15   Although they were illiterate, almost all (93 per cent) of the emigrants
interviewed stated that they 'checked their pay slips', and that they were
especially careful to check that the amount recorded did correspond to

the amount received, and that the number of hours worked was correctly recorded: 30 per cent of them checked their own pay slips, even if it meant getting help or 'consulting' someone when they had difficulties or had doubts; 50 per cent got someone to 'explain' their wage slips.

16 *Ouvrier specialisé* (literally, 'specialized worker') is the French equivalent to 'unskilled worker'. Such a worker is 'specialized' in the Taylorist sense: he 'specializes' in doing one task 'the one best way' [translator's note].

17 Wage slips become 'foodstuff' – or at least are spoken of as though that is what they are – that has to be put aside, to be laid down as provisions to provide a guarantee for the future: 'Those [pays slips] are my retirement, my children. My pension comes first. When I get it, no one will steal it from me, whereas you cannot rely on your children today; if they are "straight" (literally: "licit"), they throw you a scrap of bread and you have to beg for it.'

18 *Bled*, a loan word from the Arabic meaning 'the interior' or 'in the middle of nowhere'; the area around the boulevard Barbès in Paris has long been populated by immigrants from North Africa [translator].

19 Many funny stores are told about all the mistakes emigrants make or pretend to make when they are 'on holiday in their village'. When they attend the village *djemaâ*, they invert the situation, and find themselves swearing by *elghorba* (exile), just as they were in the habit of doing in France, or precisely when they were in *elghorba*: 'By the *elghorba* in which we find ourselves.' Because of the hustle and bustle and the additional day-to-day activities that take place then, they also delight in confusing market day with Sunday.

20 Whereas the emigrant once felt that he was, ultimately, *accountable* for every aspect of his emigration, (time, work, money) – in other words, for that part of himself and his existence that he had diverted from its sole legitimate function (serving both the group and the peasant ideal by remaining within the group) – the contemporary emigrant, who has been freed from all those obligations, submits only to the administrative demands and regulatory constraints (they are more affected by the latter than the former) of the host society (the role of written proof of his status, resident's permit, work permit; and of pay slips to prove his status).

21 In addition to all these reasons, mention must also be made of the latest: the effect of the quotas for emigrants established by bilateral agreements and by the introduction of residents' permits in France. These measures eventually made it impossible for the last families who had several men of an age to emigrate to 'replace' them one at a time, as only the holder of the resident's permit was cast in the emigrant role.

22 At least until Algeria's decision to halt emigration in September 1973 and then France's decision to halt immigration in July 1974.

23 Whereas the bonds of solidarity internal to the community of emigrants were, in the initial state of emigration, established on the model of the

old relations (i.e. the model of kinship and/or geographical proximity), they now tend, in the same way as in the populations transported by the exodus to Algerian towns (but perhaps in a more acute way), to develop on a different basis, namely the common conditions of existence specific to the emigrant condition.

24 The total of 620,000 adults includes 460,000 in employment, of whom fewer than 10,000 are women.

25 Many wives, and especially young wives, experience in France the living conditions of the cloistered woman, of the rural woman who has been transplanted to France, and who is condemned – as a sign of her embourgeoisement, but also for protection against the 'foreign' world of the city – to being sequestered at home.

26 If we take together the two populations – the Algerian population and the population of French Algerian Muslims – the total number of marriages rises to 3,193 for men and 1,690 for women: 1,257 marriages (i.e. 39.4 per cent for men and 74.4 per cent for women) were celebrated within the two communities; the proportion of marriages to French partners rises to 54 per cent and 20 per cent respectively. While twice as many (almost 32 per cent) French Algerian Muslim women as Algerian women marry French men, the discrepancy is much less amongst men: 57.4 per cent of French Muslims and 52.7 per cent of Algerians (INSEE, *Statistiques de l'état civil*).

CHAPTER 3   AN EXEMPLARY IMMIGRATION

1 A very summary attempt to explain the correspondences between these two parallel histories – that of colonization and land seizure and that of emigration – is made in Gillette and Sayad 1984. (See in particular pp. 15–38 and 69–85).

2 Not even the transcontinental migration of Europeans to America (first the United States and then Latin America) in the second half of the nineteenth century and the first two decades of the twentieth escapes this rule. Even though a certain imagery (literature, films, songs and folklore) complacently describes this immigration movement as a massive transfer of 'heroic' families who set out to conquer virgin lands, it actually displays, all other things being equal, the same demographic, social, economic, etc. characteristics as the European immigrations (intra-European or from countries outside Europe) of the post-1945 period (see Sayad 1979c; see also Bastenier and Dasseto 1977; for the statistical data, see in particular, Willcox 1969).

3 We often hear it said, by those who deplore the fact, that France has no coherent policy on immigration, meaning that it cannot decide – as though there were any possible 'choice' – whether to opt for 'settler immigration' (which also brings its capacity for labour), with all the consequences that this implies, especially if one wishes to avoid the

'danger of inassimilable kernels becoming encysted in the country' (Beaujeu-Garnier, 1976: 74), and with all the precautions that have to be taken as to the geographical, social and cultural origin of the immigrants; or whether to opt for a 'labour immigration' that is wanted and treated as such. This was especially true during the inter-war period, when there was a need to compensate for an essentially male demographic deficit of 2.5 million due to wartime mortality rates and the enormous losses suffered during the hostilities (on this point, see Bonnet 1976, and Schor 1980). This was also the case with immigration after 1945, and it still remains the case. To deplore this is to forget the fact that, in such matters, the only possible policy is a 'lack of policy', or a contradictory policy that is as contradictory as the object itself: it is impossible for 'labour immigration', no matter how tightly controlled, especially at a time when it was neither contractual nor based upon an inter-state agreement (and a fortiori when it is recruited from within the colonial Empire), not to contain an element of 'settler immigration'; conversely, 'settler immigration', useful and wanted though it may be, does not provide grounds for making just any settlers French or for making Frenchmen out of just any settlers.

4 See, *inter alia*, Scott 1975; Mirshan 1970; Tapinos 1974; Bourguignon and Gallais-Hamono 1977.

5 In this case, as in the case of the descriptions that are given of 'underdeveloped' economies, we find complacent evocations of, on the one hand, the 'qualitative' effects of certain economic facts (which are defined negatively to the extent that they escape quantitative measurement) and of, on the other hand, the 'many' cultural features of underdeveloped economies (there are in fact 'too many' of them because they get in the way, and they are frequently described as 'obstacles' to economic development or as offending against economic 'rationality').

6 The recent 'statistical quarrel' over the numerical size of the immigrant population does not escape the logic that reconverts political arguments into technical arguments, which are easier to admit to and to proclaim in public: the greater the immigrant population – which implies that it contains many 'illegal immigrants' – the greater its cost to society.

7 Fernand Icart, *député* for the Var, is the author of the report, *Le Coût des travailleurs étrangers en France, note de synthèse*, Paris: Assemblée nationale, 1976.

8 Irrespective of the job situation, the recourse to immigrant labour is often denounced as a 'cost' to the extent that it constitutes an easy solution that may compromise, or at least delay, the technical innovations that would have had to be made in the absence of immigration.

9 Quite apart from data that is not directly economic, economic theory is also capable of overlooking some data that does pertain to its domain. We now find that immigration can generate an entire 'subterranean economy' which is very large. Some of its aspects are highly 'profitable' whilst others are 'prejudicial'. Direct transfers from the savings of

immigrant workers have almost totally dried up and have been replaced by the transfer of consumer goods purchased in France by Algerian 'tourists' using immigrants' money – a true parallel market which is also a 'black' market has thus been established between the Algerian dinar (DA) and the franc – or purchased by immigrants themselves and then sold on in Algeria.

10 One could make an analysis (which would be beyond the scope of this discussion) of the latest Franco-Algerian 'agreements' of 18 September 1980. These take the form of an exchange of letters signed, on behalf of France, by the Secretary of State for Immigrant Workers (a member of the French government) and, on behalf of Algeria, only by the Ministry of Labour's Secretary-General (or in other words by an administrator, even though he does have the highest administrative and political position in the ministry). This exchange was ratified by the Assemblée nationale on 27 November 1980 (*Journal officiel*, 28 November 1980). The agreements provide an excellent illustration of the growing antimony that exists between the real interest of individuals (interests which are, in part, ignored and therefore sacrificed) and the interests that Algeria (with the full agreement of France, which finds this is in its own interest) lends them insofar as they are its 'emigrants', and therefore provides its own definition of their interests – a definition which is basically no more than the definition it gives of its own state interests, which are material but also symbolic.

11 Putting an end to emigration is one thing, but it is not enough. It is not enough to decide that contemporary emigration should revert to being what emigration used to be in the past. The discourse on 'reinsertion' is, independently of its effects, a way of taking 'revenge' on past history (on colonization and on emigration), a magical way of denying that history by 'reintegrating' and denying its effects: insofar as he is a national living abroad, the emigrant's only solution to his immigrant condition is a logical, necessary and inevitable return to his country (even if he returns at the end of his active life, on the eve of his death or simply in order to be buried there).

CHAPTER 4   NATIONALISM AND EMIGRATION

1 Any political act on the part of a colonized man (no matter whether he is or is not an emigrant living in the metropolis), is *objectively* a 'nationalist' act, quite independently of the political intention behind it.

2 There is a relationship of profound similarity between the immigrant and the *colonisé*, even when the immigrant is not a *colonisé* too, and even when the two conditions are not simultaneous and mutually reinforcing. No matter whether he is a new style or recent *colonisé* (colonized in the era of decolonization, or when colonization is over), the immigrant is in a minority position, or in the dominated position in

that he is away from home and living amongst strangers – which may be a consolation – whereas the *colonisé* is, on the contrary, reduced to being in the minority position, in the dominated position, in his own territory, and that position is juxtaposed against the majority-mode position which the others – the conquerors, the dominant or the colonizers – have been able to acquire within his territory.

3 The argument must have been this: 'If the Europeans go on strike (meaning, against their own system and against the system of which they are the prime beneficiaries), I (someone who has been betrayed by that same system, and who is its enemy because he is its victim) am certainly not going to work.' The same reaction led, and to some extent still leads – to this very day – to the involvement in strikes of Algerian immigrant workers (and probably others).

4 Pro-independence party founded in 1926, and the first permanent Maghrebin organization in France. Banned as subversive in 1929, it functioned clandestinely until 1933, then re-emerged as La Gloriense Etoile nord-africaine. [Translator's note]

5 Committee of Action for the Defence of Indigenous North Africans; League of the Defence of North African Muslims; Committee of Action and Solidarity in Favour of Victims of the Repression of Constantine; Committee of Organization of North Africans in Paris; Committee of Action for the Return of the Emir Khaled. [Translator's note]

6 The CGTU was founded in 1922 by militants expelled from the Confédération générale de travail; the two groups merged in 1936. [Translator's note]

7 Association of Algerian Workers in Lyon; Protection Associations of North Africans in Marseille; Committee of the Defence of Rights and Interests of Algerians; Education Circle of Marseille; the Franco-Muslim Association; Provisional Committee of the Mosque at Marseille. [Translator's note]

8 Union démocratique du manifeste algérien: a pro-independence party founded by Ferhat Abbas in 1946. [Translator's note]

9 Curiously enough, *jayah*, in this interpretation, resurrects the old meaning of the French term *épave* (from the Latin *expavefacta*, meaning 'wreck'), which was specifically used to describe frightened animals that had strayed away from the flock and had no known master. *Epaves* was the name that began to be given to foreigners in the *Coutumes* 'or 'customaries' (that is, in the nineteenth century) – the other name, *aubains*, being reserved for a different class of foreigners. The term designated 'men and women born outside the kingdom or in such distant places that no one in the kingdom knew their place of birth' (Demangeat 1844).

CHAPTER 5   THE BACKLASH ON THE SOCIETY OF ORIGIN

1 For an analysis of these mechanisms, see Gillette and Sayad (1984).

2 It is significant that Algerian society calls its emigrants *immigrants*, and thus adopts the term those concerned use to describe themselves in France, and by which they are known there: *limigri, el migri* or *a migri* (*immigri* or *umigra*, 'to immigrate', 'he has immigrated' in, respectively, Kabyle and Arabic); 'immigrant' thus becomes a sort or social and even professional designation – one whose social status and activity are those of an 'immigrant' (who lives amongst others) – a sort of recognition given primarily, or exclusively, to the fact of being an 'immigrant' in France and, more and more often, the fact of simply having been a former 'immigrant' to France.

3 The fall in the sums remitted voluntarily from their savings by emigrant Algerians (the postal orders of the past, the sums transferred when they went home) has been so great that, in order to compensate for this lack of income, the Algerian Ministry of Finance has had to introduce a veritable 'tax on entering the national territory'. It is levied on all Algerians who are not resident in Algeria and who are economically active elsewhere. The obligation to change money has become a de facto way of capping these exchanges, as very few emigrants change anything more than the minimum required at the official rate of exchange.

4 The quarrel over (clandestine) money-changing operations is no more than a paradigmatic variant on a whole series of other and derivative 'accusations' of the same nature. It all starts with arguments with the customs officer (some of them noisy, and others masked and, so to speak, repressed for strategic reasons) . It all begins as soon as one has crossed the frontier and come into contact with that other space, that other society and that other market to which one has come back. The existence of border controls provides an opportunity to objectify the 'hedonistic' system of consumption in which the emigrant is involved and which he imports, partly on a private basis, or even on a collective basis or a 'clandestinely' public basis (there is always the suspicion that imports supply the open market, or in other words the black market). Hence the accusations that are made against the seasonal influx of emigrants who have come back to the country for their holidays, when everything encourages excessive and ostentatious consumption. One of the influx's effects is that the cost of living rises during the summer months, in a market that is already characterized by shortages – emigrants force up the price of commodities. Hence the complaints about how emigrants drive like road hogs when they come home, even though they do not drive like that when they are in France, and about the way they buy cars only for the holidays and only in order to 'impress'. It is the same with all the other economic and non-economic 'costs' that are attributed to emigrants. But perhaps more emphasis should be placed on what is denounced as non-economic, or in other words, cultural 'costs'.

5 The suspicion of treachery, or even of apostasy (in social and cultural, rather then strictly religious, terms) is a constant that haunts emigration both as a practical mode of behaviour and as a category of thought; to

that extent, it is also an 'illegitimate'*absence* which requires an intense and constant effort to legitimize it, as is the basically 'illegitimate' presence of the immigrants, which also requires, according to the same intellectual schema, a different sort of legitimation.

6   Scientific discourse, with all the authority it is recognized as having, itself becomes involved in this generalized accusation: because they live under the effective sovereignty of a foreign country in both a political and a 'cultural' sense, emigrants can be described as 'advertising hoardings for French products' and 'sandwich men for French policies' (see Bourenane 1985: 67).

CHAPTER 6   A RELATIONSHIP OF DOMINATION

1   One could spend a long time identifying in the literature devoted, in all autonomy, or so it is believed, to emigration, the many inversions and substitutions of this kind, some of which give rise to complete misunderstandings and in some cases falsifications that are extremely prejudicial to thinking about and understanding emigration. In, for instance, *L'Emigration maghrébine en Europe, exploitation ou coopération?* (Algiers: SNED, n.d.), which brings together the papers presented at the Algiers colloquium, we can read, amongst other examples taken almost at random from the first pages of the Proceedings: 'Scientific understanding of the crisis and its effects on emigration to Europe' (Benachenou). Which emigration are we talking about? Future emigration? Then the author should have written 'Emigration towards Europe.' Has this emigration already taken place? If it has, we are, strictly speaking, dealing with 'emigration in Europe', as the 'effects of the crisis' are felt by immigration and immigrants, and not by emigration and emigrants. And more blatantly still: 'despite unemployment (in countries of immigration), there has been no noticeable fall in the relative share of all emigrant jobs'. The jobs in question here are, if the phrase is to have any meaning, the jobs available on the market of the country that resorts to immigration and to immigrants. Or again: 'the different attitudes taken by French capitals with regard to the problem of foreign emigrant labour'. These French capitals can only be faced with the 'problem of *immigrant* labour force, and not with any other labour force'. And so on.

2   Public order in the double sense in which the term is understood by administrative law and international private law or the civil law; first, as municipal order, i.e. order in the streets, public safety, tranquillity and security – and some would like to reduce the more general order known as the national order to this municipal order, so as to objectify it as much as possible; secondly, public order in a sense that comes close to what is called 'assimilation to the habits and customs of France' (see article 69 of the Code de nationalité française). The civil law specifically defines

public order in terms of habits and customs – according to this conception, bigamy, for instance, is not one of those habits and customs, and is
therefore an offence against the public order that defines the rights of
individuals (the same public order can be invoked to refuse a bigamous
foreigner naturalization on the grounds that bigamy has to be seen as a
factor that militates against assimilation and as being incompatible with
French customs and habits, and therefore with French nationality).

3   Their respective positions are unequal even when it comes to this aspect
of the negotiations, which appears to be purely *technical*, No account is
taken of the damage or losses (abuses, injustices or economic losses, or
whatever we wish to call them) suffered by the country of emigration
(and sometimes, more directly, by the families of emigrants), because no
accurate estimate of its emigrant population has been made. There are
no accurate statistics about the total population, the number of emigrant
families, the proportion of emigrant workers who have left their families
at home, the structure of the population in terms of age, the socio-
professional structure of the active emigrant population, etc. These
estimates are sometimes explicitly requested, and are almost always
borrowed from the country of immigration, which is the only source
of reliable information; negotiations are based upon the data that the
country of immigration introduces into the debate to support its own
theses. The country of emigration is unable to challenge effectively the
validity and accuracy of this data, because it is unable to produce other
data to replace it.

4   If this is true of a census (especially when it deals with 'the absent), it is
also true of genealogies, which are another way of counting the 'absent'
(the dead, earlier generations). A census is a synchronic recollection, and
a genealogy a diachronic recollection. Both solicit the collective memory
in the same way. When it was a matter of genealogies, it was noticeable
that 'the power of memory' was proportional to the value the group
ascribed to each individual (present or absent) at the time they were
remembered. Genealogies tend to remember men, especially when they
have produced a large number of male descendants (thus proving the
indigenous theory that sees every birth as *a resurrection*). They are better
at recalling close marriages rather than distant ones, and single marriages rather than the complete series of multiple marriages contracted
by the same individual – and therefore all the offspring of those memor-
able marriages, who make their own contribution to their memory. All
this leads one to suppose that whole branches of a genealogical tree can
be ignored if its last representative died childless or, which amounts to
the same thing, it has no male offspring (see Bourdieu and Sayad 1976;
Bourdieu 1972). Similarly, the memory the group retains of its 'absentees' is more faithful to the countryside than to the city, refers to close
rather than to more distant relations, to men who migrated when they
were relatively old rather than to their juniors, of emigrants who are
present in the memory of each and all because they write letters, send

money and return for holidays, rather than those who have forgotten and who are said to have been forgotten, of men rather than women, of men who have emigrated alone rather than of families who have settled in France and so on. An extreme situation is reached when the emigrant family has not even left behind an empty house (as is the case with urban families who have emigrated to France), or in extreme cases, when families are started in France itself or within the immigrant community, as is the case with all the children (some of whom are now adults) born into those families (Sayad 1979b).

5 Cf chapter 3, note 11.

6 Rather as though the primary and sole function of emigration, or the function that gives rise to it, were to provide monetary income (inflows of foreign currency, to use the language of the treasury). Because the value of this essential 'benefit' has fallen in either absolute or relative terms (or both at once) – which is now the case with Algerian emigration – one does not even notice the other 'benefits' that have replaced a benefit that is in decline or that has been lost, such as the goods (consumer goods or capital goods) brought into Algeria by emigrants in place of the money orders they used to send out. Worse still, there is not only a failure to see that one benefit has been replaced by another, but a refusal to accept that one can replace the other. Rather than taking into consideration the savings that would have been made if the equiva-lent to the commodities acquired thanks to emigration had had to be imported – and they would have been if emigration had not supplied them – and, to a lesser extent, the subsequent stimulus to the Algerian economy as a whole, there is a tendency to think that this benefit has become a cost because only the harmful influence it supposedly has on the nation's consumer habits is taken into consideration (whereas those habits, being a cause rather than an effect, are, rather, the source of the demand for the goods that are paid for with foreign currency), thus reinforcing the relations of dependence with the exporter country (the country of immigration). Similarly, there is a tendency to see the reduc-tion in the traditional 'benefits' of emigration (foreign currency) not only as a loss of earnings but as damaging to the balance of payments. This is, no doubt, because we find ourselves at the centre of a 'clandestine' economy: it is not in the interest of any of the contributing partners to objectify it, or in other words to constitute it as such (as something that can be counted, valued or measured). Both the country of emigration and the country of immigration deny that emigration and immigration have acquired a new and 'shameful' function, and prefer to overlook the fact that emigration makes its own contribution to the infrastructure (especially in rural areas) and to meeting the needs of a good proportion of the Algerian population (an improved standard of living, especially for the rural population, more comfortable homes, domestic appliances, clothes, improved hygiene, etc.). Even when this is recalled, emigration is blamed rather than thanked for it. It is in everyone's interest to

overlook the fact that, thanks to the intermediary of Algerian emigration, French industry now has several million 'clandestine' consumers.

7 In the same way that the 'benefits' and 'costs' of immigration are one of the issues at stake in struggles inside the society of immigration (even before they become issues in struggles between the country of emigration and the country of immigration), the 'benefits' and 'costs' attributable to emigration are not (and will not become) the object of a consensus within the society of emigration; they too are issues in the struggle between the different components of the society of emigration, and especially between emigrants and non-emigrants, who both try to impose the most 'advantageous' definition of the 'benefits' and 'costs' of emigration, or in other words the definition that is most in keeping with their interests. Emigration thus becomes an area for a power struggle between emigrants and their society, and the present evolution of the phenomenon does not seem to be in favour of the emigrants, as the balance of power is inverted as emigration becomes less important.

8 When they reach retirement age, many emigrants open a bank or postal account – even though they feel no need to do so during their immigration in France, or in other words during their active lives – solely in order to have their state benefits paid into them, rather than having them remitted to Algeria (as a result, it is the overall volume of social transfers made by French agencies to their Algerian counterparts that is affected, and not only the volume of transfers made by emigrants who use some of their savings to buy postal orders). Their goal is to have, permanently and outside the country, a nest egg of foreign currency (the nest egg is all the more valuable in that is in foreign currency, outside the country, and in a country with a very high level of consumption).

9 Popular rumour, or at least popular humour, attributed the saying to Houari Boumedienne, even during his lifetime.

10 For a more rigorous analysis of the mechanisms that determined the crisis in traditional agriculture when it was confronted with capitalist production techniques and the capitalist habitus (the calculating spirit, an economic consciousness, a consciousness of temporality or particular economic structures and the temporal structures that are specifically bound up with them, notions of productivity and profitability etc.) and the resultant disenchantment with not only peasant labour, but with the entire peasant condition, the peasant art of living and ways of being peasants, see Bourdieu and Sayad 1996.

11 On 18 September 1973 and, it seems, as a result of a campaign of murders and attacks perpetrated on Algerians and Algerian property during the summer of that year, Algeria took the decision to 'suspend' all emigration to France until such time as 'the safety of Algerian nationals could be guaranteed' and until such time as proof that it could be guaranteed had been supplied. These conditions which, quite independently of the measures taken by France (and prior to this measure, as it was not implemented until a year later, or in July 1974) to suspend the

immigration of new workers, meant that Algeria would have had difficulty in reversing the decision even if the economic situation demanded it, were in fact equivalent to putting a definitive halt to emigration. But quite apart from the reasons that were officially invoked, other and objectively more important reasons influenced the decision to put an end to emigration: the political decision to revitalize agriculture so as to re-establish the relationship that once existed between a proletarianized peasantry and emigration; the 'agrarian revolution', which was the socio-economic preoccupation and the great sociological project of the moment, was short of 'volunteers' from amongst even the poorest peasants (and, perhaps, particularly those who had been the most profoundly affected by 'depeasantification'). It could not tolerate direct and indirect 'competition' from emigration, or even the (theoretical) possibility of emigration, or in other words of escaping the condition of the proletarianized fellah.

CHAPTER 7   THE WRONGS OF THE ABSENTEE

1   The theory of the 'sleeping child': conceived at some earlier moment, the baby 'went to sleep' in its mother's womb and waited there for over nine months before 'waking up' on the eve of a delivery that, basically, was just late. This is a brilliant invention on the part of a culture in which, as it puts it, there is 'no situation without a door' (or no impasse without a way out).

2   The language of traditional wisdom, which is a language greatly to the liking of individuals whose social condition leads them to make a virtue out of necessity and to 'renounce' worldly involvement, well captures the series of contradictions into which a situation (immigration) which is itself contradictory traps its agents: the relatively optimistic formula 'there is no situation without a door' contrasts with the different paradigmatic formula according to which 'the living dead' exist as well as the 'dead living.'

3   The Arabic terms used for *planque* (cushy number) and *planqué* (shirker, or someone who has found *une planque*) are often borrowed from the French and forced into the syntactical mould of the Arabic language:- *planeka* (*la planque*), *planka rouhou* (*il s'est planqué*) or *mplanki* (*planqué*), *planki* (*se planquant*); recourse to a truly Arabic vocabulary is rare, and more than suggestive: *m'khabi* (shirker or 'someone waiting in ambush', 'masked', 'hidden' (for *planqué*).

4   *Elbassal* (imbecile), *Labsala* (imbecility) and *yatbassal* (to play the imbecile): the meaning given to the Arabic word, which has been borrowed from the French, is close to fatuous and fatuity, conceited, infatuated (and infatuation) or even inconsistent, lacking in reserve and consideration and, ultimately being without honour or infringing the rules of honour (rather than dishonouring oneself).

5   The "brothers": the allusion is to the nationalist militants of the FLN's Fédération de France during the Algerian war; they called each other "brothers" and used that phrase to one another in order to reassert that they belonged to the same community (that they shared the condition of the colonized and the militant community), as opposed, implicitly here, to the 'community of the colonizers' and, objectively and even if it is never made explicit, to differentiate themselves from the use that was made of the ideologically loaded term 'comrade', even though they were using same paradigm.

6   A cover for political activities: 'I wasn't a full-timer, I was in the "*qasma*" (cell of activists) that's all, I was like the militant in charge of the *qasma* and the *qasma*'s intervention and protection group.'

7   Every precaution was therefore taken not to give anything away that could identify the person being interviewed, without distorting his words, or his personal characteristics, which are essential to any understanding of his discourse and behaviour.

CHAPTER 8   THE IMMIGRANT: 'OS FOR LIFE'

1   *Ouvrier specialisé* (literally, 'specialized worker') is the French equivalent to 'unskilled worker'. Such a worker is 'specialized' in the Taylorist sense: he 'specializes' in doing one task 'the one best way' [translator].

2   This text is a contribution to a collective study describing the findings of research carried out between 1984 and 1986 as a result of a contract signed between the CNRS and the Régie nationale des usines Renault (RNUR). It was meant to be a study of all OS working in the car industry. Extending such a title to include all OS in the car industry is in fact no more than an elegant way of talking about a more restricted social object without naming it as such: only those OS who are also immigrant workers (most but probably not all of whom are OS) working for one car maker (Renault). It is as though there were something discriminatory about a precise definition of the real object of study: the immigrant OS. The generic term has the virtue of being a euphemism, and it does play a euphemistic role. How and why can we describe the function performed by immigrant workers, the position they occupy within the system of production and, more generally, in society, in morally acceptable terms, or in other words in terms that are above any suspicion of 'ethnic' discrimination or even racism? This article also attempts to address that question.

3   In a way, it is the whole of social reality and, more specifically, all the mechanisms that preside over all forms of social selection and hierarchicalization, and they are no more than products of the sort of dialectic between the objective chances that is inscribed in the objective structures of society (in the relations of force or the class positions internal to society), and in the subjective representation that individuals have,

depending on the capital (of all kinds) they have at their disposal and the position they occupy, of their objective chances; they too determine one another: it is both the immigrant who creates the OS that he is (or is not in the strict sense, to use the language of technical qualifications) and the OS who creates the immigrant worker.

4   It is the logic of the recourse to immigration, or in other words the rules that apply to the labour market when it borrows from immigration – i.e. a dominated labour force – which means that immigrant workers are required primarily for the less sought-after jobs and in sectors which are the usual lot of OS in the broadest sense of the term in a generic sense. The logic that thus presides over the division of labour can be seen in its effects and the way it is forced upon immigrant workers, who discover that, as they themselves put it, 'when the workmate at [their] side is not another immigrant, there is a good chance that it will be a French woman and not a French man' – this is one of the labour market's characteristic structural homologies. There are also whole sectors in which, because they introduce other determinations in additions to those that normally give rise to real 'professional ghettos' in some sectors of industrial labour and especially in the public building and works sector, and there are other specific reasons (demographic structures, the structures of companies and employment, a relatively narrow labour marker that is essentially divided, as is the case in Corsica, between agriculture and construction etc.) why almost all manual tasks that do not require a high level of skills (just like the jobs done by OS and their equivalents) should be done by immigrant workers.

5   The relationship of reciprocity between the immigrant and the OS goes beyond manual workers or labourers, as defined in the strict sense: it marks a whole population comprised within the various social categories that constitute the phenomenon of immigration. Being, for example, an 'immigrant' lawyer or an 'immigrant' doctor, or in other words a lawyer or a doctor who shares the same national origin as the many other immigrants who are his 'compatriots' (as they are called, and as they call themselves), almost inevitably means being 'the immigrants' doctor or lawyer' (and being, as they say in a different context, 'the Arabs' lawyer or doctor'). Such people actually are (or become) the Arabs' doctors or lawyers for reasons that are not simply of a moral order (solidarity, political activism, philanthropy, etc.) but which also relate to the needs of or the opportunities offered by the market, which decides that this is how things must be.

6   Learning to read and write also looks like an interminable task, as illiteracy is assumed to be one of the constitutive characteristics of the immigrant, or at least certain immigrants. In the case of immigrants, vocational training has the peculiar effect of making two kinds of impossibility coincide: an objective impossibility which is inscribed in the very structures of immigration and the labour market to the extent that immigration is, broadly speaking, required to respond to a demand

for unskilled labour that the local market cannot supply or has no interest in supplying; and a subjective impossibility inscribed in the system of dispositions specific to the agents concerned because they are bound up with the insecurity intrinsic in the immigrant condition (and in any experience of temporality that shapes a particular relationship with the future). Both are obstacles to the preconditions required to develop the forward-looking and 'planning' attitude required by all training projects.

7 'I hate my life' or 'My life is a bitter life' are the expressions that reoccur most frequently when Algerian OS talk about their working conditions. They complain about the general atmosphere in which they work, labour relations and, when they are at work, their relations with the most immediate hierarchy with even greater vehemence than their actual jobs.

CHAPTER 9 ILLNESS, SUFFERING AND THE BODY

1 Because emigration's sole function at this time was to provide minimal monetary resources, a small income acquired as a result of an accident at work could still be seen as a way of reducing the contradiction of emigration – as an effect that could reduce the cause that produced it (emigration). The monetary income it brought back to the village re-moved the need to emigrate once more; this was a time when emigrants who wanted to return to their country for good would harm themselves almost deliberately (by cutting off a finger or a toe). Because accidents were at this time inserted into a set of modes of behaviour that gave them a meaning because they could be controlled, they did not give rise to interminable disputes with the medical institution or the *institution d'indemnisation* (social services).

2 There is no shortage of witnesses of this attitude, which is regarded as 'pathological' because it too is, or so it is thought, focused on the illness. Any doctor, psychologist, psychotherapist, social worker, lawyer or other expert who has had dealings with these so-called '*sinistrosés*' or 'sinistrosic' patients can give examples of those whose behaviour is 'incomprehensible' to a mind accustomed to thinking that people natur-ally want to be cured and that anyone who is recognized as having been cured naturally regards himself as cured – unless he is a 'malingerer', of 'bad faith' (the 'faith' implicit in a good doctor–patient relationship), or even 'paranoid'.

3 The word 'sinistrosis', which is now reserved almost exclusively for immigrant workers, was coined at the beginning of the twentieth cen-tury – in other words to describe a different state of the job and labour market, a different form of labour organization and above all a different social state (social cover for accidents at work was not what it is now). It was usually used to describe the behaviour of national workers who

were, it is true, similar to today's immigrants: men from the rural world and peasant activity who had been expelled from the countryside and became immigrants in the world of the town or factory.

4 To measure the extent to which the assessment of the rate of compensation to be paid is, just like the accident report, determined by social characteristics of the victim, one has only to recall that it is those categories that enjoy the best protection in both professional (skilled workers and supervisory staff) and union terms – and the two things are often linked – that are most likely to be awarded invalidity pensions for life. Although they are just as likely to have an industrial accident as is a skilled worker or supervisor, OS semi-skilled labourers and apprentices are proportionally less likely to receive a pension as a result of being injured at work.

5 Whilst the relationship between a patient suffering from a work-related illness and the doctor is particularly significant in the case of the immigrant worker, all types of relations between the social categories of victims of accidents at work and work-related illnesses and doctors should be observed and analysed if we wish to identify and understand all the mediations that intervene in the determination of rates of compensation.

6 Because they are unwitting 'malingerers' who put forward their claims in 'good faith', patients who 'feign' symptoms (they are, according to Brissaud's definition, 'alleged symptoms' because they have not been objectively confirmed by any of the means of investigation available to medicine), do not know that they are 'feigning' them. This, as it happens, is a precondition for the existence of 'illness' and possible medical intervention. They 'make claims,' but they do so because they believe in all good faith that they have not obtained, by virtue of the law, fair compensation (see Brissaud's definition).

7 As the same causes produce the same effects, all the critical states that we observe in immigration reappear, when the circumstances lend themselves to it, in other contexts, but only in embryonic form. Then, these states may not present anything that is immediate or that does not provide them with an opportunity to manifest themselves, namely the direct but pointless confrontation with medical and social security institutions. Hence the suspicion that both the symptoms they present and the claims they make are outrageous, as is their (over-)estimation of their right to compensation.

8 For an account of the extent to which illness or, to be more accurate, the sort of indulgent attitude towards oneself and one's own body characteristic of the boredom which affects a peasant society that has lost faith in itself, and of all the forms of behaviour expressing an attitude towards illness, constitutes the clearest index of the break with peasant tradition and the *demoralization* that accompanies that break, see Bourdieu and Sayad 1996: 227, and especially Appendix IV: 'Un aspect de la dépaysannisation: la découverte de la maladie'.

9 Indeed, so long as the peasant knew nothing of other ways of working (that of the waged worker, the artisan, the non-manual worker, etc.), in other words was not aware of being a peasant or, therefore, that his work (state) as peasant (which was all he knew) was only one of many forms of work, it was possible for him to see himself as the only man who really worked, not only with his hands but with his whole body; as the only man who made an effort and wore himself out, as all the rest, and especially the literate ones, (because, unlike the latter, shopkeepers and artisans still remained peasants or labourers who had taken up a secondary activity) were no more than *murthabin* (or *imarthaham*, which is the plural of *murthah* or *amarthah*), in other words 'those who are always resting' or 'those who are always lying down'.

10 '[For Maghrebin patients] the body represents a habitual means of expression. The problem therefore consists, first, in deciphering that language' (Berthelier 1973); 'The traditional Maghrebin family structure *attaches great value to the body of the child* ... It [the child] has complete freedom to be ... physically involved with its mother ... all this *importance of the body*, all this potential, is reflected in the medical agencies' (Bennani 1980: 43–6; emphasis added)

11 For example, 'the Oedipal relationship' which is, according to Bennani (1980: 45) 'reactivated at the moment of marriage', or even circumcision, is 'an unhoped for experience that occurs at just the right moment, as though by the happiest of accidents or as though it were exactly determined and expressly to lend itself to all possible interpretations. Circumcision is a "wound" that is described by some as "primal and narcissistic", and by others as a "castration" whose imperishable memory might explain the acute nature of castration problems in Maghrebin men'. The 'father–mother–castration' relationship seems to have found in circumcision an ideal opportunity to project itself. The Maghrebin immigrant who bears that 'mark' seems to be the perfect subject for its application, especially at the 'Oedipal moment' when the father makes his presence felt, separates the child from its mother and 'asks it to perform adult tasks'. According to Bennani (ibid. 43–4), circumcision is therefore 'equivalent to the threat of castration ... a castration that is lived directly in the body' or as 'a mark placed on the body at the moment of access to language and the symbolic ... the mark of a symbolic castration' presided over by the mother (ibid.)

12 According to Dr. R. Berthelier, for example, while men have only a semblance of the power they do not have in reality, whereas women have the reality of power without its semblance, the society of origin 'attributes to men and valorizes the semblance of a power that is really held by the society of women'.

13 On all the relationships between the body and the structures that act upon the body and within which the body moves, see Bourdieu 1972.

14 'The body will therefore be spoken like a language': it is therefore neither 'the body that talks', 'the body we are talking about', 'body

language' nor 'language about the body'; as though the author were aware of all the ambiguity inherent in metaphors that associate the body and language, he resorts to the stylistic artifice of the pronominal formula which, by identifying the subject (the action) with the complement (that which is acted upon or the result of the action), makes it possible to neutralize the relationship between the two – which, in a way, is tantamount to doing away with that relationship by drowning the subject and the complement in one another – to evade the difficulty, or in other words to go on speaking of the body and language, without ever saying anything about the nature of the relationship between the two and without ever having to remove the ambiguity that weighs upon it.

CHAPTER 10 THE WEIGHT OF WORDS

1　We know the extent to which the discourse on identity is a performative discourse. It is a discourse which, when it is given the means to do so, has the effect of bringing into existence what is being stated and, by that very fact, predicted.

2　In the age of science, 'scientific mythology' takes the form of an unconscious drive to respond to a socially important phenomenon (and all the problems of identity or integration are socially important) in religious or mythological terms, or in other words in total or totalitarian terms, in unified and unitary terms (see Bourdieu 1980b).

3　An analysis should also be made of the notion of 'minorities', which tends now to replace that of 'immigrants', and which no doubt owes the popularity it now enjoys to its extreme ambiguity. When applied to immigrants, the term 'minority' is no more than an extension of the usage that prevails when we have to give a name to other minorities (the Breton or Occitan minority, etc.). Inspired by the desire to promote a cause, this illegitimate extension relies upon the bracketing of the historical specificity of Algerian immigration, which is almost exclusively based upon features that function as stigmata (see Sayad 1985).

4　Or at least a certain form of integration, or integration in the sense of involvement in the economic system that lies at the genesis of both emigration and immigration.

5　Family immigration; the appearance of a generation of immigrants who were born in France and who are 'children of France'; the destruction of all the simulations and dissimulations, or the mythologies that make up the migratory phenomenon, which all our mental categories and our ways of thinking about it – and they are a form of 'state thought' – lead us to perceive as temporary, as subordinate to work, which is the only reason for its existence, and as 'politically neutral', etc.

6　The crisis in employment and its effects on the status of immigration as a whole, and not only the juridical status of immigrants.

7 Integration is at once more than that and something else. One can be poor or even marginal (or even a delinquent) and still be 'integrated' into the society in which one lives.

CHAPTER 11 NATURALIZATION

1 This state of affairs seems not to be new; if the historical evidence is to be relied upon, it can be found in different forms and in varying degrees at different times – it reaches a paroxysm at moments of crisis, and not only when there is a job crisis – throughout the history of the mass immigration of workers into highly centralized or politically centralized societies. An excellent description and analysis of this state of affairs in Germany at the end of the nineteenth century is given by Max Weber, who, good 'nationalist' that he was, studied the effects of the immigration of Polish and Russian rural labourers to East Prussia (Weber 1979; see also Pollak 1986).

2 See Hannah Arendt's (1951) comments on the living conditions of Jews, and the loss of rights that made possible their extermination under Nazism.

3 It was the revision of the special clause in the Evian agreements (article 7) that first guaranteed freedom of movement between the two countries; then the series of agreement reached on 10 October 1964 and 27 December 1968 (which amended the earlier agreement); and finally the series of letters exchanged – this is now a classic protocol, no doubt because it has the advantage of sparing both sides the need to enter into more difficult and more delicate negotiations – between, on the one hand, the Secretary of State for Immigrant Workers and, on the other, Algeria's Ambassador to France, of 26–7 December 1978, 20 December 1979, 10 November 1983 and 3 December 1984; mention should also be made of the amendment (dated 2 December 1985) to the agreement of 27 December 1968. This was the last agreement to be signed by the two countries.

4 The expression is used by Marx in his reply to his master Bruno Bauer: 'The Jew himself can behave only like a Jew towards the state, i.e. treat it as something foreign, for he opposes his chimerical nationality to actual nationality, his illusory law to actual law' (Marx 1843: 213).

5 In all other cases, or in other words whenever the candidate for naturalization originates from the popular classes (the popular classes of both French society and their society of origin), whatever the circumstances that have led them to become naturalized or which have granted them French nationality, naturalization, because it cannot in this case be the object of a rationalization in the sense of constituting the act of being naturalized as a strictly and *absolutely* administrative act (which means ignoring its other aspects) and in the sense of an a posteriori rationalization of that same act, must be accompanied by the obligatory repression of all its other dimensions and meanings which, although always

present, are simply – by making a virtue of a necessity – ignored and overlooked so as not to give rise to remorse or a feeling of guilt.

6 The history of colonization is made up of too many years of political and national alienation, too long a habit of forced 'allegiance' to a foreign nation and nationality, a relationship between colonized and colonizers that was experienced as a relationship between exploiters and exploited and, finally, the cost of the multiple insurrections that succeeded one another and which, from the first war to the final war, which became a war of liberation, became increasingly nationalistic and more testing.

7 This is assimilation as it was understood in the colonial situation, or in other words in a sense that was political and social rather than juridical: political assimilation into French sovereignty and sociological assimilation into French customs.

8 Of all the attributes that can promote the idea of the nation and then the cause of nationalism, we can never say enough about the role played by religion and the role it was made to play, not simply as a force that could preserve the national 'personality', but as an active force that rallied people to the national cause and to nationalism; religion in the service of the political, especially when the political has distanced itself from religious inspiration, religion – *din* – subordinated to the *dounya* (the world, the secular, the here and now, as opposed to the beyond) may, ultimately, be no more than the beginning or a particular form of secularization, just as it can be inverted and lead to a sanctification of the state. The two tendencies are not mutually exclusive.

9 In this case, national identity is synonymous with, respectively, 'being Arab', 'being Muslim', being an Arabic speaker. It is synonymous with being on the side of the colonized (or those who were once colonized) and the dominated, in other words sharing their position in the economic system and, correlatively, in all the systems imposed by the fact of colonization or the fact of domination. It is also synonymous with having the same dispositions (the same *habitus*) with regard to all these systems, and especially economic capital and every other form of capital (rather than being on the side of the colonizers and the dominant, and sharing their system of dispositions with regard to their dominant economy). It is synonymous with being of Arab culture in the double sense of an anthropological culture and academic or learned culture.

10 On the theme of the anathema on *m'tourni*, see Sayad 1979a (especially pp. 130 and 131). The whole popular vocabulary relating to naturalization betrays, often thanks to figurative expressions, the idea of denial implied by naturalization, and revolves around the notions of reversal, transformation, alienation, dressing up, covering up or masking; it is always said that 'he has changed it, 'he has upset it', 'he has abandoned it', 'he has sold it', 'he has burned it', 'he has dyed it, 'he has sold it off cheaply'. These are of course allusions to 'national identity', and more generally, the total identity, the 'being' or even the soul of the person who has been naturalized.

11 It is not as though naturalization should not have been a source of profit or that it would have been more acceptable if it were not self-seeking and did not result in a few privileges. But because that is, ultimately, its only function, it all too obviously betrays, in the absence of other reasons that might have given it a different meaning, the intentions behind it; because they oblige naturalization to reveal the cynical intentions (which are admitted to) behind it, the advantage of the colonial situation and the immigration to which it leads is that it reveals the hidden truth which, in every other case, is surrounded by more symbolic determinations, and determinations that are more gratifying in symbolic terms.

12 [The *harkis* were Algerian auxiliaries who fought on the French side during the war of independence. Translator's note]. This situation is not without its advantages. Whilst some *naturalisés* refuse to go back to Algeria, rather as though they were drawing the logical conclusions (or the conclusions they believe to be logical) from their situation, their wives provide the necessary link with Algeria because, having retained their Algerian nationality, they act as intermediaries between them and Algeria – i.e. all their relatives. In the absence of clear and constant dispositions with respect to this, it is unclear whether those who have been naturalized forbid themselves to go back to Algeria or whether they are forbidden to do so; no doubt one forbids oneself to do what one knows one is forbidden to do and what one is expected to forbid oneself to do, or what one would like to be forbidden to do. Prohibition (even when not formulated) and self-prohibition stem, *grosso modo*, from the same habitus, in other words from the same disposition with regard to naturalization.

13 The effects of this change are definitely at the origin of the proposals to modify, in a more restrictive sense, the modalities of the acquisition of French citizenship, as currently defined by the Code de la nationalité; this no doubt reflect the fear that 'cysts' will be established – that is the term used by geographers and demographers when they speak of the 'pockets' formed by immigrants (before they become 'ghettoes'). See in particular Beaujeu-Garnier 1976.

14 Article 23: 'Any child, legitimate or illegitimate, born in France is French if one of its two parents was born there'; article 24 adds 'If, however, only one of the parents was born in France, a child who is French by virtue of article 23 shall have the option of renouncing that quality in the six months preceding its age of majority.'

15 France is understood in the sense defined by articles 6 and 8 of the Code de la nationalité: 'For the purposes of the present Code, France is understood to mean the metropolitan territory, and the Overseas Departments and Territories.' Why the cut-off date of 1 January 1963? It seems that that date, which is relatively arbitrary, corresponds to the date after which all persons 'originating from Algeria and whose civil status is defined by local law' who, not having signed in France (by 23

March 1967) the declaration provided for by article 152 of the Code de la nationalité, are deemed to have lost their French nationality. See article 1 of the law of 20 December 1966, which modified the edict of 4 July 1962.

16 The Algerian Code de nationalité, both as originally formulated (law of 27 March 1963: Code de la nationalité algérienne, JORA, 2 April 1963, p. 306) and as reformulated (edict of 15 December 1970, JORA, 18 December 1970, p. 1202), stipulates that '1. Any child born to an Algerian father is Algerian by descent' (paragraph 1 of articles 5 and 6 of the first and second codes respectively).

17 Education is, to say the least, a guarantee that the child has a good knowledge of French, and that skill is regarded as both the most object-ive index and the most reliable precondition for assimilation (see article 69 of the Code de la nationalité). What is more, it is specifically men-tioned in the Code and, once the higher level has been achieved, the course is shortened by two years: 'The course mentioned in article 62 is reduced to two years: for a foreigner who has successfully completed two years of higher education with a view to acquiring a diploma awarded by a French university or institute of higher education' (article 63, paragraph 1).

18 This is the only explanation of why proof of civic-mindedness is re-quired in order to acquire a nationality and why tests are set for that purpose, beginning with the most solemn of all: the oath of loyalty to the allegiance implied by the act of naturalization. Similarly, the legisla-tion concerning naturalization has to be related to this context of real suspicion if we are to grasp its real nature and understand its full meaning; unlike legislation that applies only to foreign workers, this legislation can be seen as a means of preventing espionage, as any immigrant can be (and is, in his own way) a 'spy', and as any spy can disguise himself as 'an immigrant worker'; 'nationally' speaking, there is no difference between the worker and the (professional) spy: they look alike and cross the same frontiers in the same way.

19 Border controls provide one example of this normalization process. Borders are places where, as one moves from one territory to another and one sovereignty to another, the nationality of passengers is objecti-fied and where a distinction is made between the country's nationals and foreigners. The fact that, whatever their social characteristics (labour-ers, white-collar workers or shopkeepers, people from the towns or the countryside, men and women, young and not so old), Algerians need, more and more frequently and in ever greater numbers, to show French identity papers in order to enter Algeria or, which amounts to the same thing, to be acknowledged and recognized as Algerian (and/or French), cannot but influence both the behaviour of the agents responsible for the controls and, more generally, public opinion as a whole. As they grow older, an increasing number of these Algerians who describe themselves, or who are in the circumstances (anything to save face) described as

'officially French' or 'French despite themselves', will eventually produce a different representation of national identity and a different conception of naturalization; this is, obviously, because of their growing numbers and also because of the frequency with which they travel in both directions, but it is also because their distinctive social characteristics (their level of education in French, their level of professional skills and other external signs betray their higher social situation: language, clothes, sense of being physically at ease, etc.) distance them, so to speak, from the traditional emigrant, and thus give them a more authoritative persona – which can lead to accusations of apostasy.

20 'Popularize' in both senses of the word, or in both the morphological and the social sense: in the sense of increasing the number of naturalizations and, as a logical corollary, popularizing naturalization amongst the popular classes, which make up the majority of the immigrant population, even though a mode of behaviour that might be described as 'bourgeois' is traditionally alien to them and goes against their ethos or even ethics.

21 Young man of 18, living in Montreuil with his parents; unemployed (has never really worked); holds a CAP in mechanics, wanted to do a BP [*brevet professionnel*: technical certificate] in 'metal processing'; has visited Algeria twice in all, most recently at the age of 13, and shows no enthusiasm for going back there: 'In any case, I've had it now... with military service'; categorically rejects the very idea of doing his military service in Algeria – 'or even in France' – has not even bothered to go and register with the consulate; does not reject French nationality but 'will do nothing to request it'. Had he inverted the terms he himself uses, the same young man could have said: 'I was not born in Algeria, I was not brought up in Algeria, I'm not at home in Algeria (or I don't have Algerian habits), I don't think like an Algerian... but I feel Algerian all the same.'

22 The only result of revising the protocol for granting French nationality, as defined by articles 23 and 24 of the Code de la nationalité, would be a dangerous increase in the number of subjects whose *de facto* identity – they are, sociologically speaking, French – is not corroborated by their *de jure* identity because, not having requested it, they do not have French nationality.

23 Young man of 23 who has, as he himself says, 'two places of birth': his Algerian family in France, and France, 'the country where he was born and where he served his apprenticeship to life'.

24 Interactionism often regards relations of stigmatization as merely interactional relations, or relations between an individual or group of individuals and others (see Goffman 1963).

25 The ultimate expression of the illusory character of this (impossible) recognition is the now famous formula: 'If you are an Arab, you remain an Arab even if you become Colonel Ben Daoud.' Rightly or wrongly – that is not the important point – it has been attributed to a naturalized

French Algerian, who was a graduate of Saint-Cyr and an officer in the French army at the beginning of the twentieth century.

26 The context of immigration differs from the colonial context in that the latter can generate nationalism as a subversive strategy designed not to magically abolish the stigma thanks to a symbolic inversion of the signs of discrimination, but to totally invert the scale of values on which the stigma is based, or in other words to destroy the balance of power which, by establishing the stigma, leads to a quest for rehabilitation, and then to self-assertion and confirmation of the stigma; coming close to home, it also differs from regionalist demands which, ultimately and at bottom, inevitably borrow from nationalist demands (see Bourdieu 1980a).

27 The terms used here are borrowed from Bou– Hammas. Part of the interview he agreed to give – on the social use of names – is reproduced below.

28 For a more detailed analysis of the social representation of the body and the social uses of the body, on the one hand, and of the issues involved in the struggle for an autonomous definition of identity, on the other, see the articles in *Actes de la recherche en sciences sociales*, 4 (April 1977), particularly that by Bourdieu (1977b), as well as Bourdieu 1980a,b.

29 It is significant that, as a general rule, all codes of nationality – or at least all the codes I have consulted: Algerian, Tunisian, Moroccan, Egyptian and Turkish, as well as the codes of almost all other Arab countries – deal with the naturalized citizen's change of name: a name seems to be an alterity that has to be reduced, and therefore a real or potential stigma (a verbal stigma) that has to be abolished. One might add that, the more 'foreign' (or 'barbarian') the original name (or forename) of the naturalized citizen, the greater the social and sometimes even institutional requirement to adopt a new name (or forename).

30 His behaviour appears to have been dictated by a murky affair relating to events during the last years of colonial Algeria. None of the questions asked of his children and his wife – but never directly of him – shed any light on this mysterious business. It appears to have something to do with some plan to take revenge for material wrongs – probably symbolic rather than material – he suffered during the war.

CHAPTER 12 IMMIGRATION AND 'STATE THOUGHT'

1 'The comparative study of foreigners … a subject that can be described as universal in the sense that this social phenomenon is found in all human societies past and present. There have at all times and in all places been foreigners who have, in varying degrees, a status different to those persons who are not regarded as foreigners. … Quite apart from the geographical and historical universality of the subject, the study of the status of foreigners can be extended to every branch of the law and

to human social activities as a whole.' This is how the jurist John Gilissen defines the universality of the migratory phenomenon in his introduction to the work of the Société Jean Bodin (Gilissen 1958: vol. 1, 42–52).

2 This is how Emile Benveniste (1969: 14–15, 41, 150–1 f.) defines the act of division, the act that consists in decreeing the continuity and rupture, the introduction of discontinuity into continuity. It is a matter of 'tracing borders as straight lines', of separating 'inside and outside, the realm of the sacred and the realm of the profane, the national territory and foreign territory'. See also Bourdieu 1980a (frequent reference will be made to this article, from which I have borrowed extensively).

3 In his attempt to found a science of Judaism, which also makes a vital contribution to our understanding of the constitution of Jewish identity, Gershom Scholem (1980), makes a distinction between 'assimilation to the external' and 'assimilation of the external'. The former is a form of alienation, and the latter the precondition for the survival and perpetuation of identity in a dominated situation. Only the latter possibility allows an escape from the alternative between, on the one hand, an alienated identity defined by others and for others, and constituted by the external gaze, and, on the other, a self-affirmation which may be no more than a reprise of the image that the dominant have produced and which is reflected back to them in the form of a challenge. The exemplary case of Jewish identity teaches us that any dominated identity is a focus of struggles, first between dominated and dominant, and then between those who share that identity (between Jews, between immigrants), with internal debates (about naturalization, about the choice between country of immigration and country of origin, about religious affiliation and its modalities, and so on) inevitably being affected by the fact that they always take place beneath the gaze of the dominant and therefore contain the possibility (or probability) of racism.

References

Ageron, Charles-Robert (1962). *Les Algériens musulmans en France (1871–1919)*, Paris: PUF.

Arendt, Hannah (1951). *The Origins of Totalitarianism*, New York: Harcourt, Brace.

Bastenier, A. and Dasseto, F. (1977). *L'Etranger nécessaire, capitalisme et inégalités*, Louvain-la-Neuve: FERES.

Beaujeu-Garnier, J. (1976). *La Population française, après le recensement de 1975*, Paris: Armand Colin.

Bennani, Jalil (1980). *Le Corps suspect*, Paris: Galilée.

Benveniste, Emile (1969). *Le Vocabulaire des institutions indo-européennes* Vol. 2: *Pouvoir, droit, religion*, Paris: Editions de Minuit.

Berque, Jacques (1985). *L'Immigration à l'école de la République: Rapport au Ministre de l'Education Nationale*, Paris: CNDP/La Documentation française.

Berthelier, Robert (1973). *Psychopathologie de la transplantation chez le musulman algérien*, 70è Congrès de psychiatrie et de neurologie de langue française, Tunis, août–septembre 1972, Paris: Masson.

Bonnet, J.-C. (1976). *Les Pouvoirs publics français et l'immigration dans l'entre-deux-guerres*, Lyon: Université de Lyon, Centre d'histoire economique et sociale de la région lyonnaise.

Bourdieu, Pierre (1972). *Esquisse d'une théorie de la pratique*, Geneva: Droz (*Outline of a Theory of Practice*, tr. Richard Nice, Cambridge: Cambridge University Press, 1977).

—— (1977a). *Algérie 60: Structures économiques et structures temporelles*, Paris: Minuit.

—— (1977b). 'Remarques provisoires sur la perception sociale du corps', *Actes de la recherche en sciences sociales*, 4, April: 51–4.

—— (1980a). 'L'Identité et la représentation; elements pour une reflexion critique sur l'idée de région', *Actes de la recherche en sciences sociales*, 35, November: 63–72.

—— (1980b). 'Le Nord et le Midi: contribution à une analyse de l'effet Montesquieu', *Actes de la recherche en sciences sociales*, 35, November: 21–5.

—— (1993). 'Esprits d'état,' *Actes de la recherche en sciences sociales*, 96–97, March: 49–62.

—— and Sayad, Abdermalek (1976). 'Stratégie et rituel dans le mariage kabyle', in J. Peristiany (ed.), *Mediterranean Family Structures*, Cambridge: Cambridge University Press.

—— and Sayad, Abdelmalek (1996). *Le Déracinement: La Crise de l'agriculture traditionnelle en Algérie*, Paris: Minuit (1st edn, 1964).

Bourenane, M. N. (1985). 'Eléments pour une approche critique de la question de l'immigration algérienne en France', in *Les Algériens en France, genèse et devenir d'une immigration*, CNRS, Actes du colloque du GRECO, 13 (Grenoble, 26–27 January 1983), Paris: Publisud.

Bourguignon F. and Gallais-Hamono, G. (1977). *Choix économiques liés aux migrations internationales de main d'oeuvre*, Paris: OCDE.

Demangeat, Charles (1844). *Histoire de la condition civile des étrangers en France dans l'ancien et le nouveau droit*, Paris: Joubet.

Gilissen, J. (1958). 'Le statut des étrangers à la lumière de l'histoire comparative', in *L'Etranger*, Brussels: Editions de la librairie encyclopédique.

Gillette A. and Sayad, A. (1984). *L'Immigration algérienne en France*, Paris: Entente, Collection 'Minorités' (1st edn, 1976).

Goffman, Erving (1963). *Stigma: Notes on the Management of Spoiled Identity*, Englewood Cliffs, NJ: Prentice Hall.

Icart, F. (1976), *Le Coût des travailleurs étrangers en France, note de synthèse*, Paris: Assemblée nationale.

Jardillier, P. (1965). *L'Organisation humaine des enterprises*, Paris: PUF.

Laacher, S. (1992), 'L'Intégration comme objet de croyance', *Confluences*, 1.

Lagarde, P. (1997), *La Nationalité française*, Paris: Dalloz.

Lenoir, Rémi (1980). 'La Notion d'accident du travail: un enjeu de luttes', *Actes de la recherche en sciences sociales*, 32–33, April–June: 77–88.

Le Pors, Anicet (1977). *Immigration et développement économique et sociale*, Paris: La Documentation française; Etudes prioritaires interministérielles.

Marx, Karl (1843). 'On The Jewish Question', in *Early Writings*, tr. Rodney Livingstone and Gregor Benton, Harmondsworth: Penguin, 1975.

Michel, Andrée (1957), *Les Travailleurs algériens en France*, Paris: CNRS.

Mirshan, E.-J. (1970). 'Does Immigration Confer Economic Benefits on the Host Country?', *Economic Issues in Immigration*, London: Institute of Economic Affairs.

Montagne, Robert (1953). *L'Afrique et l'Asie*, 22, Paris.

Mothé, D. (1976). *Autogestion et conditions de travail*, Paris: CERF.

Niboyet, J.-P. (1947), *Traité de droit international privé français*, 7 vols, Paris: Sirey.

Pollack, M. (1986). 'Un texte dans son contexte', *Actes de la recherche en Sciences Sociales*, 65, November: 65–9.

Rager, J.-J. (1950). *Les Musulmans algériens en France et dans les pays islamiques*, Algiers: Université d'Alger.

Sanson, R. (1947). 'Les Travailleurs nord-africains de la région parisienne', *Documents sur l'immigration. Travaux et documents de l'INED, Cahier 2*.

Sayad, Abdelmalek (1979a). 'Les Enfants illégitimes', *Actes de la recherche en sciences sociales*, 26–27, March–April, 117–32.

—— (1979b). 'Immigration et conventions internationales', *Peuples méditerranéens*, 9, October–December: 29–52.

—— (1979c). 'Qu'est-ce qu'un immigré?' *Peuples méditerannéens*, 7, April–June.

—— (1984). 'Tendances et courants des publications en science sociale sur l'immigration en France depuis 1960', *Current Sociology*, 32, 3, Winter: 219–304.

—— (1985). 'De "population d'immigrés" à "minorités", l'enjeu des dénominations', *Educational Policies and Minority Social Groups*, 16–18 January, Paris: OCDE.

Scholem, Gershom (1980). 'L'Identité juive', *Actes de la recherche en sciences sociales*, 35, March: 3–19.

Schor, R. (1980). *L'Opinion française et les étrangers en France, 1919–1939*, 4 vols, Aix and Marseille: Université de Provence.

Scott, N. (1966). *Principes d'une analyse comparative des coûts et avantages des migrations de main d'oeuvre*, OCDE, Séminaire d'Athènes, October.

—— (1975). 'Grandes lignes d'une méthode pour l'analyse des coûts et des avantages des migrations de main-d'oeuvre', *Bulletin de L'Institut des études sociales*, February: 55–72.

Stora, Benjamin (1985). *Dictionnaire des militants nationalistes algériens: ENA, PPA, MTLD, 1926–1954*, Paris: L'Harmattan.

Tapinos, G. (1974). *L'Economie des migrations internationals*, Paris: FNSP.

Weber, Max (1979), 'Developmental Tendencies in the Situation of East Elbian Rural Labourers', *Economy & Society*, 8: 166–205.

Willcox, W. F. (ed.) (1969). *International Migrations*, 2 vols, New York, London and Paris: Gordon and Breach Publications (1st edn, 1929).

Bibliography
The Writings of Abdelmalek Sayad

1960 'Les Libéraux, un pont entre les deux communautés', *Etudes méditerranéennes*, 7, Spring: 43–50.

1964 (and Pierre Bourdieu), 'Paysans déracinés. Bouleversements morphologiques et changements culturels en Algérie', *Etudes rurales*, 12, January–March: 59–94.

— (and Pierre Bourdieu), *Le Déracinement, la crise de l'agriculture traditionnelle en Algérie*, Paris: Minuit (reprinted 1996).

1967 'Bilinguisme et education en Algérie', in Robert Castel and Jean-Claude Passeron, eds, *Education, développement et démocratie*, Paris and The Hague: Mouton; *Cahiers du Centre de sociologie européenne*, 4, pp. 205–16.

1973 'Une Perspective nouvelle à prendre sur le phénomène migratoire: l'immigration dans...est d'abord essentiellement une émigration vers...', *Options méditerranéennes*, 22, December: 52–6.

1975 'El Ghorba: le mécanisme de reproduction de l'émigration', *Actes de la recherche en sciences sociales*, 2, March: 50–66.

1976 (and A. Gillette), *L'Immigration algérienne en France*, Paris: Editions Entente (2nd revised and expanded edn 1984).

— (and Pierre Bourdieu), 'Strategy et rituel dans le mariage kabyle', in J. Peristiany, ed., *Mediterranean Family Structures*, Cambridge: Cambridge University Press.

1977 'Les "Trois Ages" de l'émigration algérienne en France', *Actes de la recherche en sciences sociales*, 15, June: 59–79.

1978 *Les Usages sociaux de la culture des immigrés*, Paris: CIEMM.

1979 'Les Enfants illégitimes', *Actes de la recherche en sciences sociales*, 25, January: 61–81 (Part I), March–April: 117–32 (Part II).

— 'Qu'est-ce qu'un immigré?' *Peuples méditerranéens-Mediterranean Peoples*, 7, April–June: 3–23.

— 'Immigration et conventions internationales', *Peuples méditerranéens-Mediterranean Peoples*, 9, October–December: 29–52.

— 'Etude de l'immigration algérienne en France, étude comparative de cas spécialement choisis en raison de leur pertinence structurale'. Introduction to report commissioned by CORDES (roneoed).

1980 'Le Foyer des sans-famille', *Actes de la recherche en sciences sociales*, 32–3, April–June: 89–103.

— 'Le Concept de classe sociale, ses usages et son application aux sociétés à économie dite "sous-développée"', *Les Classes sociales au Maghreb*, Paris: *Les Cahiers du CRESM*, 2; pp. 40–51.

— 'Le Rapport au logement moderne, les effets du relogement', *Panorama des sciences sociales* (Algiers), October–November: 11–27.

— 'Un logement provisoire pour des travailleurs "provisoires": Habitat et cadre de vie des travailleurs immigrés', *Recherche sociale*, 73, January–March: 3–31.

1981 'Le Phénomène migratoire, une relation de domination', *Annuaire de l'Afrique du Nord*, XX, Paris: CNRS: 365–406. *Maghrébins en France: émigrés ou immigrés?* Paris: CNRS-CRESM, collection 'Etudes de l'Annuaire de l'Afrique du Nord', 1983.

— 'Santé et équilibre social chez les immigrés', XXIIe Colloque de la Société de psychologie médicale de langue française: Psychologie médicale et migrants (Marseille, 30–31 May 1980), *Psychologie médicale*, 13, 11: 1745–75.

— 'La Naturalisation, les conditions sociales et sa signification chez les immigrés algériens' (Part I: 'La Naturalisation comme aboutissement "naturel" de l'immigration'), GRECO 13, *Migrations internationals*, 3: 22–46.

— 'L'Immigration, une réalité nouvelle', *CIMADE-Informations*, 6, April–June.

— 'L'Emigration maghrébine en France: exploitation ou coopération?', *Le Maghreb dans le monde*, Algiers: CREA, 28–30 March: 1091–4.

1982 'La Naturalisation, les conditions sociales et sa signification chez les immigrés algériens' (Part II: 'La Naturalisation comme rapport de force entre nations et entre nationalités'), GRECO 13, *Migrations internationales*, 4–5: 1–55.

— 'Un autre "ordre" pour une autre immigration', *Migrants-Créteil*, (Office des migrants de Creteil), 6, January–February: 21–8.

— (and F. Fassa), *Eléments pour une sociologie de l'immigration*, Luzern: Institut de science politique, Collection travaux de science politique.

1983 'La Délinquance dans l'immigration: l'immigration est en elle-même délinquance', *Le Phénomène de la délinquance chez les jeunes immigrés*, CEFRES, Annales de Vaucresson 20.

— 'Y-a-t-il une sociologie du droit de l'immigration?' in *Le Droit et les immigrés*, Aix-en-Provence: Edisud, pp. 98–104.

— 'Le Marché Velten à Marseille: quelques observations sur les fonctions sociales et commerciales de la vente ambulante dans le quartier de la Porte d'Aix'. Report to the Conseil municipal de la ville, October (roneoed).

— 'Le Logement des immigrés, synthèse des travaux' (Journées d'étude de l'OMINOR, 13–14 May 1982), in *Le Logement des immigrés en France*, Lille, pp. 340–81.

1984 'Etat, nation et immigration: l'ordre national à l'épreuve de l'immigration', *Peuples méditerranéens-Mediterranean Peoples*, 27–28, April–September ('*L'Etat en Méditerranée*'): 187–205.

— 'Les Effets culturels de l'immigration, un enjeu de luttes sociales', *Annuaire de l'Afrique du Nord*, XIII, Paris: CNRS, pp. 383–97.

— *Nouveaux Enjeux culturels au Maghreb*, Paris: CNRS-CRESM, 1986.

— 'Tendances et courants de publications en sciences sociales sur l'immigration en France depuis 1960', *Current Sociology*, ISA, 32, 3 (Sage Publications) Winter: 219–304.

— 'L'Immigration algérienne en France, capitale d'origine et trajectoire sociale', *Méthodes d'approche du monde rural*, Algiers: OPA, pp. 75–89.

1985 'Du Message oral au message sur cassette, la communication avec l'absent', *Actes de la recherche en sciences sociales*, 59, September: 61–72.

— 'L'Immigration algérienne, une migration exemplaire', in J. Costa-Lascoux and E. Temime, eds, *Les Algériens en France, genèse et devenir d'une migration*. Actes du colloque du GRECO 13 (Grenoble 26–27 January 1983), Paris: Publisud, pp. 19–49.

— 'L'Islam au sein du monde moderne non-musulman, les effets de l'immigration sur l'Islam', Pluralismo culturale religioso e coesione sociale, Geneva: Convengo Centri Studi Scalabrine d'Europa (CSERPE), 14–18 June: 35–70.

— (and M. Oriol and P. Vieille), 'Inverser le regard sur l'émigration-immigration', *Peuples méditerranéens-Mediterranean Peoples*, 31–32 ('Migrations et Méditerranée'): 5–21.

— 'Exister, c'est exister politiquement' (Part I: 'Pour une défense des droits civiques des immigrés'), *Presse et immigrés en France*, Paris: CIEMI, 135, November.

— 'Exister, c'est exister politiquement' (Part II: 'Les Droits civiques, pour une plus grande justice), *Presse et immigrés en France*, Paris: CIEMI, 136, December.

— 'Le burnous sous le béret, entretien avec Thomas Ferenczi', *Le Monde aujourd'hui*, 22, 23 December.

— 'Le Miroir trompeur du modèle de l'homogénéisation culturelle de la société', *Economie et humanisme*, January–February: 37–42.

— 'De "Population d'immigrés" à "minorities". L'Enjeu des dénominations', *Educational Policies in Minority Social Groups*, Paris: OCDE (16–18 January), and *L'Education multiculturelle*, Paris: OCDE, 1987, pp. 129–46.

1986 'Coûts et profits de l'immigration. Les présupposés politiques d'un débat économique', *Actes de la recherche en sciences sociales*, 61, March: 79–82.

— 'La "Vacance" comme pathologie de la condition d'immigré. Le cas de la retraite ou de la pré-retraite', *Gérontologie*, 'La Vieillesse des immigrés en France', 60, October: 37–55.

— 'Les Migrations en Méditerranée', *Echanges-Méditerranée*, 'La Méditerranée face à son avenir, de la décolonisation à l'an 2000: développement, migration, coopération', Marseille, June: 47–58.

— 'Une Généalogie d'immigrés algériens', *Réseaux de migration, trajectoires et acculturation*, rapport d'une étude *pour le ministre de la Recherche et de la Technologie, Solidarité, minorités, migration*, March.

— (and E. Temime), 'Trajectoires, réseaux et filières de migration', ibid.

— 'Condition d'immigré et condition d'OS, leurs effets mutuels et leurs effets sur la relation au travail. Les OS dans l'industrie automobile', Paris: rapport CNRS-RNUR.

1987 (and C. Camilleri and I. Taboada-Leonotti, eds), *L'Immigration en France: le choc des cultures*. Actes du colloque, Problèmes de culture posés en France par le phénomène des migrations récentes (May 1984), Dossiers du Centre Thomas More, recherches et documents, 51, L'Arbresle.

— 'La culture en question', ibid., pp. 9–26.

— 'L'Islam "immigré"', ibid., pp. 109–29.

— 'L'Immigration algérienne en France, l'aînée des immigrations maghrébines, un antécédent qui a valeur d'exemple', Actes du colloque, La Migration internationale des travailleurs tunisiens, Tunis, Université de Tunis, *Cahiers du CERES*, 6 (série Démographique), pp. 203–53.

— 'Les Immigrés algériens et la nationalité française', in S. Laacher, ed., *Questions de nationalité. Histoire et enjeux d'un code*, Paris: L'Harmattan, pp. 127–97.

— 'Immigration et naturalisation', *Noroit*, 304, November–December: 2–15.

1988 'Migration et naturalisation', in C. Withol de Wenden, ed., *La Citoyenneté et les changements de structures sociale et nationale de la population française*, Paris: Edilig/Fondation Diderot, pp. 157–85.

— 'La "Faute" de l'absence ou les effets de l'immigration', *Anthropologica medica* (Trieste), 4, July: 50–69.

1989 'Eléments pour une sociologie de l'immigration', *Les Cahiers internationaux de psychologie sociale* (Brussels), 2–3, June–September: 65–109.

1990 'Synthèse et discours de clôture', *La communauté maghrébine immigrée en France et ses perspectives d'insertion dans l'Europe de 1993*, Tunis: Publication du Centre de Documentation Tunisie-Maghreb, pp. 201–20.

— 'Les Maux à mots de l'immigration', interview with Jean Leca, 'Issu(e)s de l'immigration. Identités, mobilisations et représentations des jeunes d'origine maghrébine', *Politix*, 12: 7–24.

1991　*L'Immigration ou les paradoxes de l'altérité*, Brussels: Editions Universitaires and De Boeck-Wesmael.

—　(and E. Temime and J.-J. Jordi), *Migrance. Histoires des migrations à Marseille*. Vol. 4: *Le Choc de la decolonisation (1945–1991)*, Aix-en-Provence: Edisud.

—　'L'Immigration algérienne en France, une lente mais inexorable évolution vers l'immigration de peuplement', Conférence internationale sur les migrations (Rome, 13–15 March), Paris: OCDE.

—　'L'Immigration algérienne à l'heure des ruptures', *Hommes et Migrations*, 1144, June: 54–7.

—　'Uma Pobreza exotica: a imigraçao argelina na França', *Revista Brasileira de Ciências sociais*, 17, October: 84–107.

—　(and G. Balazs), 'La violence de 'l'institution', *Actes de la recherche en sciences sociales*, 90, December: 53–63.

1992　'Religion et politique, l'eschatologie en politique', in G. Ignasse, ed., *Islam et politique*, La Garenne-Colombes: Editions de l'Espace européen, pp. 79–81.

—　'L'Immigration algérienne en France, une lente mais inexorable évolution vers l'immigration de peuplement', *Atti della Conferenza internazionale sulle migrazioni*, Rome: Ufficio del Vice-Presidente del Consiglio dei Ministrie, pp. 197–205 (in Italian).

—　'Minorités et rapport à l'état dans le monde méditerranéen: Etat et "minorités" en Algérie, le "mythe kabyle"', in *Connaissance de l'Islam*, Paris: Syros, pp. 135–81.

1993　'Une Famille déplacée', in Pierre Bourdieu, ed., *La Misère du monde*, Paris: Seuil, pp. 33–48; 'Coûts et profits de l'immigration', ibid., pp. 270–1; 'Le Souffre-douleur', ibid., pp. 399–405; (and G. Balazs), 'La violence de l'institution', ibid., pp. 683–98; 'La Malédiction', ibid., pp. 823–44; 'Emancipation', ibid., pp. 859–69.

—　'Emigration et nationalisme: le cas algérien', *Genèse de l'Etat moderne en Méditerranée. Approches historique et anthropologique des représentations*, Rome: Collection de l'Ecole française de Rome, 163, pp. 407–36.

—　'Naturels et naturalisés', *Actes de la recherche en sciences sociales*, 99, September: pp. 26–35.

—　'Vieillir… dans l'immigration', in *Vieillir et mourir en exil. Immigration maghrébine et vieillissement* (collectif), Lyon: PUL, pp. 43–59.

1994　'Intellectuels à titre posthume', *Liber*, 17, Revue européenne des livres (supplément à *Actes de la recherche en sciences sociales*, 101–2, March: 5).

—　'Le Mode de génération des générations immigrées', Générations et mémoire, *L'Homme et la société*, 111–12 (1–2): 155–74.

—　'Migration, refuge, asile', in *Europe: montrez patte blanche*, Geneva: Centre Europe-Tiers Monde, pp. 276–96.

—　'Aux Origines de l'émigration kabyle ou montagnarde, Les Kabyles, de l'Algérie à la France', *Hommes et migrations*, 1179 September: 6–11.

340 Bibliography

—   'Qu'est-ce que l'intégration? Pour une éthique de l'intégration', *Hommes et migrations*, 1182, December: 8–14.

—   'L'Asile dans "l'espace Schengen"; la définition de l'Autre (immigré ou réfugié) comme enjeu des luttes sociales', in M.-C. Caloz-Tschopp, A. Clevenot and M.-P. Tschopp, eds, *Asile, violence, exclusion en Europe. Histoire, analyse, prospective*, Geneva, pp. 193–238.

1995   (in collaboration with E. Dupuy), *Un Nanterre algérien, terre de bidonvilles*, Paris: Autrement, Collection 'Monde', Français d'ailleurs, peuples d'ici.

—   'OS et double condition', in R. Sainsaulieu and A. Zehraoui, eds, *Ouvriers spécialisés à Billancourt: les derniers témoins*, Paris: L'Harmattan, pp. 295–330.

—   'La Lecture en situation d'urgence', in B. Seibel, ed., *Lire, faire lire: des usages de l'écrit aux politiques de lecture*, Paris: Le Monde Editions, pp. 65–99.

1996   'Entrevista. Colonialismo e migracoès', *Mana. Estudios em antropologica social*, 2, 1, Rio de Janeiro, Relume-Dumara, April: 155–70.

—   'Un Témoignage de fin de colonisation', *Monde arabe et recherche scientifique* (MARS), 6, Paris: Institut du monde arabe, Spring: 7–56.

—   'La Double Peine et l'immigration, réflexion sur la pensée d'Etat', *Aut aut*, 275, September–October: 8–16 (in Italian).

—   'Anthropologie de l'exil', *Le Courrier de l'UNESCO*, November: 10–12.

1997   'Identité: nomination/catégorisation', in B. Bier and B. Rondet, eds, *Citoyenneté, identités. Nouvelles figures de la citoyenneté et formes actuelles de l'engagement des jeunes*, Document de l'INJEP, hors série no. 4, Marly-le-Roi: Institut National de la Jeunesse et de L'Education populaire, January: 34–52.

—   'L'Illettrisme comme sous-produit de la "pensée d'école"' (interview with B. Falaize), in F. Andrieux, J.-M. Besse and B. Falaize (eds), *Illettrismes: quels chemins vers l'écrit?* Actes de l'Université d'été organisée par le ministère du Travail et des Affaires sociales à l'Université Lyon II (8–12 july 1996), Paris: Magnard, pp. 347–57.

—   'L'Immigration et la "pensée d'Etat". Refléxions sur la double peine', in S. Palidda, ed., *Délit d'immigration. La Construction Sociale de la déviance et de la criminalité parmi les immigrés en Europe*. Rapport COST A2, Migrations, Brussels: Communauté européenne, 1996. Reprinted in *Regards sociologiques*, 16, 1999: 5–21.

—   'Lien social, identité et citoyenneté par temps de crise', *Sociétés et représentations*, 5, December: 107–28.

1998   'Le Retour, élément constitutif de la condition de l'immigré', *Migrations société*, X, 57, May–June: 9–45.